The Nature of Adolescence

Completely revised and thoroughly updated, this third edition of *The Nature of Adolescence* provides:

- An eclectic, balanced overview of research on normal adolescent development
- Discussion of the impact of social issues on adolescents
- New chapters on anti-social behaviour, health, coping and adjustment, politics and participation
- An emphasis on issues of gender and race
- **Implications for Practice** in a separate section after each chapter
- **Annotated Further Reading.**

John C. Coleman is Director of The Trust for the Study of Adolescence and editor of the *Journal of Adolescence*. **Leo B. Hendry** is Professor of Education at the University of Aberdeen and Professor of Health Psychology at the Norwegian University of Science and Technology, Trondheim.

Adolescence and Society
Series editor: John C. Coleman
The Trust for the Study of Adolescence

The general aim of the series is to make accessible to a wide readership the growing evidence relating to adolescent development. Much of this material is published in relatively inaccessible professional journals, and the goals of the books in this series will be to summarise, review and place in context current work in the field, so as to interest and engage both an undergraduate and a professional audience.

The intention of the authors is to raise the profile of adolescent studies among professionals and in institutions of higher education. By publishing relatively short, readable books on interesting topics to do with youth and society, the series will make people more aware of the relevance of the subject of adolescence to a wide range of social concerns.

The books will not put forward any one theoretical viewpoint. The authors will outline the most prominent theories in the field and will include a balanced and critical assessment of each of these. While some of the books may have a clinical or applied slant, the majority will concentrate on normal development.

The readership will rest primarily in two major areas: the undergraduate market, particularly in the fields of psychology, sociology and education; and the professional training market, with particular emphasis on social work, clinical and educational psychology, counselling, youth work, nursing and teacher training.

Also available in this series:

Adolescent Health
Patrick C.L. Heaven

Identity in Adolescence
Jane Kroger

Growing Up with Unemployment
Anthony H. Winefield, Marika Tiggermann, Helen R. Winefield and Robert D. Goldney

Young People's Leisure and Lifestyles
Leo B. Hendry, Janet Shucksmith, John G. Love and Anthony Glendinning

Sexuality in Adolescence
Susan Moore and Doreen Rosenthal

Adolescent Gambling
Mark Griffiths

Youth, AIDS, and Sexually Transmitted Diseases
Susan Moore, Doreen Rosenthal and Anne Mitchell

Adolescent Coping
Erica Frydenberg

Fathers and Adolescents
Shmuel Shulman and Inge Seiffge-Krenke

Social Networks and Social Influences in Adolescence
John Cotterell

Smoking in Adolescence
Images and Identities
Barbara Lloyd and Kevin Lucas; and Janet Holland, Sheena McGrellis and Sean Arnold

Health Issues and Adolescents
Growing Up, Speaking Out
Janet Schucksmith and Leo B. Hendry

Illegal Leisure
The Normalization of Adolescent Recreational Drug Use
Howard Parker, Fiona Measham and Judith Aldridge

The Nature of Adolescence

Third Edition

**John Coleman
and Leo B. Hendry**

London and New York

First edition published 1980
by Methuen & Co Ltd

Second edition published 1990
by Routledge
11 New Fetter Lane, London
EC4P 4EE

Reprinted in 1991, 1993, 1995, 1996

Third edition published 1999
by Routledge
11 New Fetter Lane, London
EC4P 4EE

Simultaneously published in the
USA and Canada
by Routledge
29 West 35th Street, New York,
NY 10001

© 1999 John C. Coleman and
Leo B. Hendry

Typeset in Century Old Style by
Graphicraft Limited, Hong Kong

Printed and bound in Great
Britain by TJ International Ltd,
Padstow, Cornwall

*British Library Cataloguing in
Publication Data*
A catalogue record for this book is
available from the British Library

*Library of Congress Cataloging in
Publication Data*
A catalogue record for this book
has been requested

ISBN 0–415–19897–6 (hbk)
ISBN 0–415–19898–4 (pbk)

Contents

CONTENTS

Figures and tables

Figures

Tables

Acknowledgements

The authors would like to express their gratitude to colleagues who have provided support and assistance during the writing of this book. In particular we wish to thank Marion Kloep of NTNU in Trondheim, and Liza Catan, Catherine Dennison, Juliet Lyon, and Debi Roker of the Trust for the Study of Adolescence in Brighton. Debi Roker has played a special role in contributing ideas and materials for Chapter 10, and this chapter has benefited enormously from her wealth of knowledge concerning young people, politics and participation.

The authors also wish to acknowledge the role played by Viv Ward, Senior Editor at Routledge. She has continually encouraged us over the past five years by emphasising the need for a third edition of this book, and we are grateful to her for her interest and enthusiasm for the subject.

The following organizations have kindly given permission to use the following figures: **Chapter 1** – Figures 1.1, 1.2 and 1.3, Trust for the Study of Adolescence; Figure 1.5, J.C. Coleman 1974 *Relationships in Adolescence*. (Routledge & Kegan Paul); Figures 1.6 and 1.7 reprinted with permission from: Simmons, Roberta, G. and Blyth, Dale A. *Moving into Adolescence: The Impact of Pubertal Change and School Context*. (New York: Aldine de Gruyter) Copyright © 1987 Roberta, G. Simmons and Dale, A. Blyth. **Chapter 2** – Figures 2.1 and 2.6 the BMJ Publishing Group; Figures 2.2 and 2.3 *Scientific American*; Figure 2.4, W. Montagna and W.A. Sadler (Eds) 1974 *Reproductive Behaviour*. (New York: Plenum Publishing Corporation); Figure 2.5, J.M. Tanner 1962 *Growth at adolescence*. (Oxford: Blackwell Science Ltd); 2.8, M. Hermann-Giddens *et al.*, 1997 'Secondary sexual characteristics and menses in young girls seen in office practice', *Journal of Paediatrics* 99, 505–512. **Chapter 3** – Figure 3.1, McGraw-Hill; Figure 3.3, M. Shayer and H. Wylam, 'The distribution of Piagetian stages of thinking in British middle and secondary school children' *British Journal of Educational Psychology* (1978), 48, 62–70 © The British Psychological Society; Figures 3.4 and 3.5, in 'The Adolescent as a Philosopher: The Discovery of the Self in a Postconventional World' reprinted by permission of *Dædalus*, Journal of the American Academy of Arts and Sciences, from the issue entitled, "Twelve to Sixteen: Early Adolescence," Fall 1971, Vol. 100, No. 4. **Chapter 4** – Figure 4.1, C. Stoller *et al.*, 1996 in 'Psychiatrist concepts of the adolescent self-image', *Journal of Youth and Adolescence*, Vol. 25, pp. 273–283 (New York: Plenum Publishing Corporation); Figure 4.3, M. Zimmerman *et al.*, 1997 'A longitudinal study of self-esteem: implications for adolescent development',

Journal of Youth and Adolescence, Vol. 25, pp. 117–142 (New York: Plenum Publishing Corporation); Figure 4.4, From IDENTITY: Youth and Crisis by Erik H. Erikson. Copyright © 1968 by W.W. Norton & Company, Inc. Reprinted by permission of W.W. Norton & Company, Inc.; Figure 4.5, from "Variations in bicultural identification among African-American and Mexican-American adolescents," by J. Phinney and M. Devich-Navarro, 1997, *Journal of Research on Adolescence, 7*, p. 6. Copyright 1997 by Lawrence Erlbaum Associates Inc. Reprinted with permission. **Chapter 5** – Figure 5.1, from "Changes in adolescents' daily interactions with their families from ages 10 to 18: disengagement and transformation," by R. Larson *et al.*, 1996, *Developmental Psychology, 32*. Copyright © (1996) by the American Psychological Association. Reprinted with permission; Figure 5.3, Trust for the Study of Adolescence. **Chapter 6** – Figures 6.1, 6.2 and 6.3, Trust for the Study of Adolescence; Figure 6.4, from "Age differences in parent and peer influences on female sexual behaviour," by D. Treboux and N. Busch-Rossnagel, 1995, *Journal of Research on Adolescence, 5*, p. 472. Copyright 1995 by Lawrence Erlbaum Associates Inc. Reprinted with permission. **Chapter 7** – Figure 7.1 and 7.2 Trust for the Study of Adolescence. **Chapter 9** – Figures 9.1, 9.2 and 9.3, Trust for the Study of Adolescence; Figure 9.4, M. Griffiths 1995 *Adolescent gambling*. (Routledge). **Chapter 10** – Figure 10.1, 'Social Focus on Ethnic Minorities' Office for National Statistics © Crown copyright 1999; Figures 10.2 and 10.3, Trust for the Study of Adolescence; Figure 10.4, M. Rutter, M. Giller and A. Hagell 1998, *Antisocial Behaviour by Young People*. (Cambridge: Cambridge University Press); Figure 10.5, from M. Lipsey 1995 'What do we learn from 400 research studies on the effectiveness of treatment with juvenile delinquents?' in J. McGuire (Ed.) *What works: reducing reoffending*. Copyright John Wiley & Sons Limited, reproduced with permission. **Chapter 11** – Figure 11.2, Trust for the Study of Adolescence. **Chapter 12** – Figures 12.2 and 12.5, from B. Compas 1995 'Promoting successful coping during adolescence' in M. Rutter *Psychosocial disturbances in young people*. (Cambridge: Cambridge University Press); Figures 12.3 and 12.4, from *Stress, coping, and relationships in adolescence* (p. 35 and p. 117), by I. Seiffge-Krenke, 1995, Mahwah, NJ: Lawrence Erlbaum. Copyright 1995 by Lawrence Erlbaum Associates Inc. Reprinted with permission.

The following organizations have kindly given permission to use the following tables: **Chapter 5** – Tables 5.1 and 5.2, Reproduced from Fogelman, K. (1976) *Britain's sixteen-year-olds*. With permission from the National Children's Bureau; Table 5.3, Youniss and Smollar 1985, *Adolescent relations with mothers, fathers and friends* (University of Chicago Press); Table 5.4, P. Noller and V. Callan 1991, *The adolescent in the family* (Routledge). **Chapter 7** – Table 7.1, Parker *et al.*, 1998 *Illegal leisure: the normalisation of adolescent recreational drug use* (Routledge); Table 7.2, K. Trew 1997 From 'Time for sport? Activity diaries of young people' in Kremer, J., Trew, K., and Ogles, S. (Eds) *Young people's involvement in sport*. (Routledge). **Chapter 10** – Table 10.1, H. Sattin and D. Magnusson 1996 'Antisocial development: a holistic approach' *Development and Psychopathology* 8, 617–645 (Cambridge: Cambridge University Press).

Every effort has been made to trace copyright holders and obtain permission to reproduce figures and tables. Any omissions brought to our attention will be remedied in future editions.

Introduction

Chapter 1

Adolescent development takes place against a backcloth of changing social and political circumstances. This introductory chapter will review some of the most important recent changes, in order to provide a context within which we can explore the lives of young people today. Adolescence is often conceptualised as a transition between childhood and adulthood, yet the nature of the transition has been significantly affected by the social and political events of the past two decades. In this chapter we will therefore pay some attention to the way in which the adolescent transition has altered during recent years. It will also be necessary to review current theories of adolescence, for these too provide a perspective on the various dimensions of growth and change. As we shall see, one of the most striking theoretical advances during recent years has been an increasing emphasis on the importance of context in making sense of human development. There is today a greater recognition of the key part played by environments, including family, neighbourhood and the wider society, in influencing adolescence, and we shall incorporate such views in our discussions. The chapter will conclude with an outline of the focal model, for we believe that this model is helpful in enabling us to consider the strengths and resources, as well as the potential vulnerability, of young people during this stage of their lives. Throughout the book we will be emphasising the positive elements of adolescent development, and a consideration of the focal model will provide a useful reference point for the final chapter, which will look at coping and adjustment.

Social change

A wide variety of shifts in the social and political landscape have occurred during the years since the first and second editions of this book were written. These shifts have had a profound impact upon the lives of young people, and it is important to outline the nature of such social and political change. It is probable that the greatest degree of change has been experienced in two spheres – those of the family and the labour market – but we will also be noting alterations in attitudes to race and gender, as well as looking at the influence of political developments such as the defeat of Communism and the fall of the Soviet Republic, and the growing influence of Europe on Britain and other countries in the European Union.

First, we will consider the situation with regard to employment, and explore how changes in the labour market have influenced our understanding of adolescence. We will be looking at the situation from a UK perspective, although it should be noted that similar circumstances have obtained in most Western countries during the same historical period. In essence, a dramatic rise in unemployment was experienced in the late 1970s and early 1980s, to the extent that, in Britain, unemployment rates for young men between the ages of 16 and 24 increased from 5 to 25 per cent in the decade 1974–84 (Coleman, 1997a). Similar but less marked increases were also seen for young women. An even more startling trend was the decrease in the number of young people in the labour market as a whole. Over the period 1984–94 the number of individuals between the ages of 16 and 24 in the labour market shrank by more than 25 per cent, as shown in Figure 1.1.

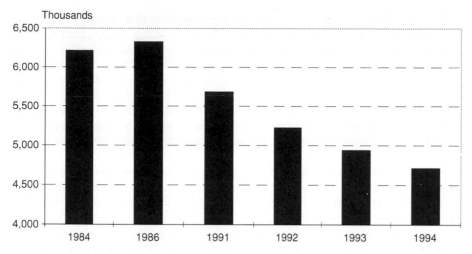

Figure 1.1 Numbers of 16–24 year olds in the UK labour force, 1984–94.
Source: Coleman (1997a).

Changes such as these have had a wide variety of consequences. First, governments have introduced a number of job-training and job-preparation schemes in order to assist young people into employment. These schemes have also had the secondary benefit of ensuring that entry into the labour market is delayed, thus reducing the numbers who might appear in unemployment statistics. A second consequence is that many more young people now go on to higher education after compulsory school-leaving age. In Britain in the 1970s a significant proportion of young people went to work after leaving school at 16. At the end of the century hardly anyone does so, with approximately 70 per cent now continuing in some form of higher or further education, and the remainder in some form of training scheme.

While it is clear that entry into the labour market has become more difficult for this age group, this is not the only change of relevance to adolescence. In addition, the composition of the labour market has altered, as is illustrated in figures quoted in Hickman (1997). Hickman shows that in the second half of the twentieth century manufacturing industry in Britain has decreased from employing 35 per cent of the total labour market to 16 per cent, while service industries have increased from 8 to 23 per cent. These shifts have meant that young men have lost traditional sources of employment, while young women have gained new opportunities for work. In addition, social disadvantage also impacts on employment prospects. One illustration of this is that young people from ethnic minority backgrounds are significantly more likely to be unemployed than white young people. More detail is given on this subject in Chapter 9.

For young people without doubt the most far-reaching implication of the changing labour market is that economic independence – a tangible sign of maturity – is delayed. As a result, the very nature of the adolescent transition is altered. In the years between 16 and 20, when traditionally young people were considered to be entering adulthood, they now continue to depend financially on their parents or the state. Thus, adolescence appears to last longer, relationships with parents and partners have to be renegotiated, independent housing is more difficult to access, and a range of new psychological issues have to be resolved. We will be considering each of these throughout the book, and will return to the nature of the transition shortly.

Before doing so, let us consider briefly some other aspects of social change which have impacted on young people. Alterations in the structure of the family have also had a major influence on the way young adolescents grow up today. As is well known, the divorce rate increased steadily during the 1970s and 1980s, not just in Britain but also in North America and in many European countries. In the 1990s the divorce rate has levelled out, but other changes have become apparent, in particular the fact that more and more children are being born outside marriage. It is especially among young adults that this trend is most marked, and recent evidence shows that in Britain more that three-quarters of children born to parents under 20 are born outside marriage (Coleman, 1997a). Thus, the increase in families with dependent children headed by a lone parent is not only as a result of divorce, but stems also from changes in attitudes to marriage and partnership in relation to child-bearing. The increase in lone-parent families in Britain over the last decades is illustrated in Figure 1.2.

Today, in some European countries nearly 25 per cent of young people experience the divorce of their parents by the time they are 16. In the United States the figure is closer to 33 per cent. Such changes in family structure have repercussions in a range of areas. In the first place, a significant proportion of children and teenagers have to cope with family breakdown, and with the loss of one parent. This will almost certainly lead to an increase in stress levels, and the need for greater support from outside the family.

In addition, a range of new family arrangements are being experienced, with stepfamilies, live-in partners, remarriage, and so on. Of course, it is not just those young people whose parents divorce who are affected by this. In practice, everyone is affected, because everyone will have a friend, a neighbour, or a relative in whose family there is a divorce or some form of rearrangement of living circumstances. Our attitudes to marriage are changing, and our experiences now encompass a much wider range of family types than was the case in previous decades.

Apart from the stress caused by family reconstitution, changing family structures have two other possible implications for young people. In the first place, it is probable that values and beliefs about marriage, family, and parenting are shifting as adolescents grow up in family circumstances which are, relatively speaking, less stable than was the case for their own mothers and fathers. We are still not sure quite how adolescents are being affected by this, but no doubt research will address this issue in the years to come. At present it appears that marriage is still as highly valued, but that there is more caution about this state. There is also a gradually increasing separation between marriage and parenthood, so that getting married is no longer a prerequisite for having children. The second implication of changing family structures is that the parenting of teenagers is more problematic. The parenting roles of lone parents, stepparents, and new partners are hard to define, as is the role of the divorced or separated parent living apart from the

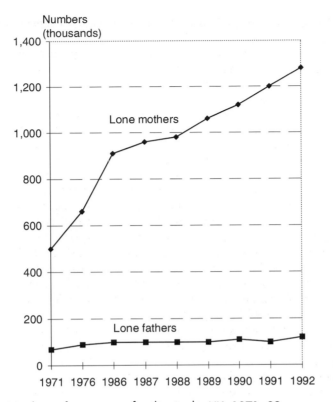

Numbers
(thousands)

Figure 1.2 Numbers of one-parent families in the UK, 1971–92.
Source: Coleman (1997a).

children. Uncertainty about parenting practices is not good for teenagers or parents, especially since adolescence is the time, more than any other in the life of a family, when parenting confidence is at a premium. We shall have more to say about this issue in Chapter 5.

While alterations in employment and the family may be considered to be the most striking examples of social change, there are others to which we should also draw attention. There have, for example, been important shifts in attitude in relation to gender and race in the recent past, which are significant for our understanding of young people. In respect of gender it might be argued that, if the 1980s was a time of concern over young women and inequality, the 1990s have been a decade when the disadvantages experienced by young men have come to the fore. This is not to say that women do not continue to suffer disadvantage in some spheres, especially in employment, and there is a continuing need for attention to be paid to this issue. Nonetheless, a number of factors have contributed to a greater awareness of the needs of young men, especially those who are less able, and those who grow up in disadvantaged circumstances. We have already mentioned the changes in the composition of the labour market, and the loss of jobs in the manufacturing sector. This has meant that employment opportunities

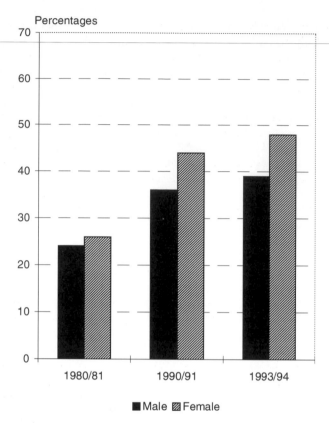

Figure 1.3 Five or more GCSEs, grades A–C, by gender in England, 1980–94.
Source: Coleman (1997a).

for young men have diminished, with worrying consequences. In addition, the marked increase in suicide rates among young men has focused attention on their mental-health needs in an unprecedented fashion. This issue will be discussed further in Chapter 7. Interestingly, young women have been seen to outperform young men in a variety of spheres, the most obvious example being examination results, as illustrated in Figure 1.3. Such findings are important, in that they reflect growing confidence among women, as well as increased motivation because of the opening of new employment opportunities. However, both young men and young women continue to suffer disadvantage in different spheres, and it is essential to pay attention to the needs of both groups.

We have already noted the importance of race in considering the unemployment figures for those from minority backgrounds in the UK. There is little doubt that race has become a more prominent issue in European countries during the 1990s. This is partly to do with increased immigration from North Africa and the Middle East, but even in Britain, where immigration has been minimal over the last two decades, there is a growing recognition of the realities of a multicultural society. We know more about the effects of racism and racial harassment on young people, and there is a greater awareness of the particular disadvantages suffered by black teenagers. Thus, for example, among those excluded from school in the UK there is a higher proportion of African and Afro-Caribbean young people than would be expected in terms of the population. In a valuable article on this issue, Bhattacharyya and Gabriel (1997) outline the impact of equal opportunities policies in the UK. They argue that while prejudice and discrimination remain widespread, there are examples of resistance to racism, especially among black people themselves. They point out that success in such things as sport, cinema and other arts media offers role models to young people, and they call for greater support for such activities. Linked with this has been a growing interest in issues to do with ethnic identity, as will become apparent in our review in Chapter 4. This is an important development, not only for those from minority cultures, but for all who wish to understand how context and human development interact (see Rattansi and Phoenix, 1997).

Lastly, in this section we should note the impact of political change on the lives of young people. As we shall be indicating in Chapter 11, adolescents are not as disconnected from the political world as is often assumed. The Thatcher years in Britain (1979–90), and the long-term effects of Conservative policies, will continue to impact on the attitudes and aspirations of young people for years to come. In addition to national politics, the past decade has seen profound changes in the way Britain and other countries relate to Europe as a whole. Thus, there are closer connections among countries, there are increasing educational and employment opportunities throughout the European Union, and each country is more affected by what happens in others.

Furthermore, particular political events have provided an opportunity for researchers to gain a clearer understanding of the impact of political change on young people. Thus, the reunification of Germany provided a real-life situation in which it has been possible to study how adolescents adapt to political upheaval, and we will be referring to the results of this research in a later chapter. Increased cooperation between social scientists across Europe has also resulted in opportunities for new comparisons between cultures on topics such as parenting, attitudes to sex and sex education, entry into employment, leaving home, and other key issues for young people (see e.g. Alsaker and Flammer, 1998). Throughout this book we will be drawing on these comparisons, enabling those who wish to understand the adolescent experience to gain a broader picture of this stage in the life cycle.

The nature of the transition

In much of the writing about adolescence, beginning with G. Stanley Hall's (see Muuss, 1996) major work published in the first years of the twentieth century, it has been customary to describe this stage as a transition. In many ways this has seemed the closest it is possible to get to describing the nature of the adolescent experience, and, as we shall see, there are undoubtedly many characteristics of transitions which can be ascribed to this stage of development. However, there have always been concerns over the fact that adolescence, however defined, covers a number of years. Is it realistic to describe seven or eight years of some-one's life as a transition? This has led to writers talking of sub-stages, such as early, middle and late adolescence. To many, however, this remains unsatisfact-ory, primarily because there is no agreement about the definitions or ages which apply to each sub-stage.

The situation today is even more complex, because the stage of adolescence has lengthened, both at the beginning and at the end. We have already noted that entry into the labour market takes longer, and occurs at a later age than was the case ten or twenty years ago. This also means that young people remain in the parental home for a longer period, frequently continuing to be economically dependent until they are in their twenties. In addition, it appears that puberty may be starting earlier, although there is considerable debate around this subject. We shall be exploring this further in Chapter 2. Nonetheless, there is little doubt that young people mature socially at an earlier age today. There is an earlier aware-ness of sexuality, dating and other adolescent behaviours commence at a younger age, and interest in clothes, music and other teenage concerns can be seen to preoccupy those who might in previous decades have been described as pre-pubertal. Thus the adolescent stage now begins for some as early as 9 or 10, and continues for many until well after their twenty-first birthday. How then can we make sense of this stage? Indeed, can it possibly be one stage, and is it reasonable to describe it as one transition? There are two ways of dealing with this dilemma. For some social scientists adolescence consists of a number of different trans-itions, each of which has to be researched and understood as a separate event. Thus it may be that puberty should be considered in this category. It can be argued that the two years or so of biological change and maturation at the beginning of adolescence represent a major life transition, deserving attention in its own right. Many of those who have studied puberty would subscribe to this view, including Silbereisen and Kracke (1993) and Alsaker (1996). Apart from puberty one could also look at other transitions, such as the transition from one school to another (e.g. Simmons and Blyth, 1987; Kalakoski and Nurmi, 1998). However, perhaps the most popular focus for writers looking at a discrete aspect of the adolescent period is to consider the transition out of adolescence and into adulthood.

Numerous studies have looked at this question within the European con-text. Thus, for example, some studies have compared transitions in two different countries. Malmberg and Trempala (1997) looked at a country in which there was economic depression (Finland), and compared this with a country changing from socialism to a market economy (Poland). Interestingly, there were fewer differ-ences between countries than between young men and young women or between those at different educational levels. Both Bynner et al. (1997) and Chisholm and Hurrelmann (1995) have taken an even broader perspective, looking across all European countries and drawing conclusions about some general characteristics of transition in the late twentieth century. Both these publications make the point that the stage of youth has been extended in all countries, and that the process of transition to adulthood has become increasingly pluralised and fragmented. In Figure 1.4 Chisholm and Hurrelmann illustrate the historical change by compar-ing the years 1890 and 1990 in diagrammatic form.

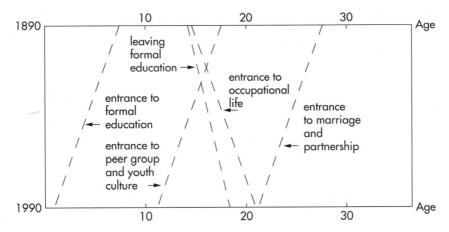

Figure 1.4 Timing of points of status transition to adulthood in historical comparison. *Source*: Chisholm and Hurrelmann (1995).

The point that these writers make – namely that the transition to adulthood is being increasingly delayed – has concerned a wide variety of commentators in the recent past. Indeed, Arnett and Taber (1994) entitled an article 'Adolescence terminable and interminable: when does adolescence end?' to underline the fact that we have gradually entered an era in which there is no longer any clear or defined moment when an individual reaches adulthood. This has a wide range of implications for young people themselves, as well as for society as a whole. It has also led many writers to consider markers of the transition out of adolescence, and to see how these operate for those from different backgrounds.

In Britain both Jones (1995) and Coles (1995) have explored this question. They see entry into adulthood as involving three main status transitions:

1   the school to work transition, where an individual leaves full-time education and enters the labour market;
2   the domestic transition, in which the young person attains (relative) independence from their family of origin;
3   the housing transition, involving a permanent move away from the parental home.

By concentrating on these three transitions, Jones, Coles and others in the same tradition have identified those who suffer particular disadvantage in the move to adult status. Groups such as those who leave care, the disabled and those from ethnic minorities are of especial concern here. Indeed, Williamson (1997) has written about 'Status ZerO', a phrase used to highlight the difficulties facing those who have little stake in society, and thus limited hopes of housing, employment and a settled life. Concerns of this sort have been linked with a growing focus on the process of social exclusion, and the possibility that some very disadvantaged young people might become permanently marginalised as they grow up without any hope (Coles, 1997; MacDonald, 1997).

A second, alternative, approach to the study of transitions is described in a seminal paper by Graber and Brooks-Gunn (1996). In this paper the authors argue for retaining the term 'transition' to describe the adolescent period, but using the notion of turning points to refer to the key moments, such as a move from one school to another. This is helpful, although, as they indicate, there remains the problem of deciding which turning points are important, and which to study:

> The premise underlying integrating notions of transitions and turning points is that transitional periods are characterized by developmental challenges that are relatively universal; that is, most individuals navigate transitional periods, and these periods require new modes of adaptation to biological, psychological, or social change. By definition, then, turning points occurring in the context of transitional periods may be particularly salient to individuals or subsets of individuals. These turning points may be more likely to result in behavioural change, or in larger or more long-lasting changes than turning points that do not occur in the context of a transitional period.
>
> (Graber and Brooks-Gunn, 1996, p. 769)

These authors then go on to identify circumstances in which turning points within transitional periods may be more problematic for particular individuals. They see these situations as being:

(a) when the timing of turning points within transitional periods creates additional stress, as, for example, with early puberty;
(b) when cumulative or simultaneous events occur, so that an individual has too many things to deal with all at one time;
(c) when mental-health issues arise at the same time as turning points are required to be negotiated;
(d) when there is a lack of 'goodness of fit' between context and behaviour during transitions, as, for example, a poor school environment for an academic teenager.

Such ideas will be especially helpful when we consider theories of adolescence towards the end of this chapter. The emphasis on the context of development, as well as recognition of the timing of events as a key determinant of adjustment, are particularly important.

There are many ways of looking at the concept of transition. For Graber and Brooks-Gunn (1996) the very fact that adolescence is a universal experience leads to the position that it may reasonably be called a transition, and the present authors have some sympathy with this position. Transitions could be said to have a number of characteristics. They involve:

1   an eager anticipation of the future;
2   a sense of regret for the stage that has been lost;
3   a feeling of anxiety in relation to the future;
4   a major psychological readjustment;
5   a degree of ambiguity of status during the transition.

As will be apparent, all these characteristics are strikingly true of adolescence. Adulthood beckons and with it freedom and opportunity, which appear very attractive. Yet there is also sadness for what has gone before – it is often said that inside every adolescent is a child struggling to get out. Young people do worry about what is to come, more so perhaps now than ever before. When jobs, housing and relationships seem uncertain it is hardly surprising that adolescents have anxieties about the future. As we shall see during the course of the book, a substantial psychological readjustment is required during the course of the adolescent years, and this is true in all spheres – in the family, with friends, with adults outside the family, and, of course, in relation to one's own sense of identity. Lastly, a number of themes run throughout the adolescent period, including an intensified concern with status and a realignment of roles. Thus, we believe it makes sense to consider adolescence as a transition, while at the same time acknowledging that within this stage there are many turning points which have key significance for later adaptation.

Developmental contextualism

In attempting to understand adolescence as a transition it is obvious that theory has an important part to play, and we will now outline two theoretical approaches which interrelate with each other. We do not have space in this volume to outline the range of theories of adolescence, but a useful review is provided by Muuss (1996). It is important to note that here we will not be discussing early or 'classical' theories. We will not be considering psychoanalytic theory, or others which lay emphasis on turmoil or trauma, apart from a brief discussion of 'storm and stress' in Chapter 12. In our view, these approaches are long outdated (except in a clinical context), and it is our intention in this book to concentrate on theories which pay attention to individual differences. We are particularly interested in approaches which give due recognition both to the adolescent's resources and potential for resilience, as well as to the possible circumstances in which an individual may become vulnerable. It is appropriate, therefore, that we should commence by looking at developmental contextualism.

In the previous edition of this volume we wrote about lifespan developmental psychology, and outlined a number of principles which governed this theoretical position, as well as providing an organising framework for some key research endeavours in the 1980s. Today, almost all of those principles have been incorporated into the approach which has come to be known as developmental contextualism. The key figures in the history of this theoretical position are John Hill, Urie Bronfenbrenner, Paul Baltes and Richard Lerner. Each has made his own personal contribution and, while today there is still no standard outline of this theoretical position, it is possible to draw together the strands of the approach, based primarily on the the volume by Adams *et al.* (1996), entitled *Psychosocial development during adolescence: progress in developmental contextualism*, on summaries of the positions of Bronfenbrenner and Lerner in Muuss (1996), and on Magnusson and Stattin's (1998) review of person–context interaction theories. As will be apparent, many of the principles are similar to those which would have been found in a discussion of lifespan developmental psychology.

There is a human ecology, or context of human development

This first principle originates from the work of a number of people, but the name most closely associated with it is Urie Bronfenbrenner. The intention here is to underline the importance of the environment in the widest sense. It is also to emphasise the fact that, for children and young people, the context of development is not just the family, but the geographical, historical, social and political setting in which the family is living. In the review of theories of adolescence by Muuss (1996), a whole chapter is devoted to Bronfenbrenner's ecological perspective.

There is a continuity to human development

This principle originates from the lifespan developmental model, and is important in two respects. In the first place, it draws attention to similarities and differences between stages, so that consideration of the transition of adolescence can be compared with other transitions, as, for example, the transition from employment to retirement. The principle is significant also in that it points up the fact that the adolescent stage does not suddenly arrive out of the blue, but is a continuation of development in childhood. Too often writers treat adolescence as a stage unconnected to other life experiences. This principle highlights the interrelationship between childhood and adolescence.

Individuals and their families reciprocally influence each other

This principle is one with which Richard Lerner (see Muuss, 1996) is closely associated. It makes reference to the fact that neither a child nor a family is a static entity. Each grows, develops and changes and, most important, influences the other at all times. The young person's maturation produces changes in the family, but at the same time alterations in parental behaviour and family functioning have effects on the adolescent's development.

A multi-disciplinary approach must be taken to studying human development

This may seem like a statement of the obvious, but the fact that lifespan developmental theorists and developmental contextualists have laid particular stress on this principle has had surprising results, and has brought together biologists, paediatricians, sociologists, ecologists, educationalists and psychiatrists in cooperative projects on human development which have undoubtedly paid substantial dividends.

Individuals are producers of their own development

This is one of the key principles of developmental contextualism. Attention is being drawn here to the part that all individuals, of whatever age, play in shaping their own development. This innovative principle has wide implications for social-science research. While it may be generally accepted that child and adolescent development results from an interplay of a variety of causes, the idea that the individual young person is an 'active agent' in shaping or determining his or her own development has generally not been part of the thinking of researchers in this field. The principle is now, however, having a profound effect on the thinking and writing of those studying human development, and has particular significance for the focal model, which we will consider in the next section of this chapter.

When studying person–context interaction we should consider the notion of goodness of fit

The goodness of fit concept takes into account the relationship between the individual and the environment in its widest sense, and asks to what extent the needs and goals of the person are congruent with the context. Thus whether a developmental outcome is adaptive or not does not just depend on the characteristics of the individual, or on the nature of the physical or social environment. Rather, the outcome depends on whether these two systems fit together, and so the emphasis in research must be to look at both elements and to consider the extent to which they are congruent.

Numerous examples can be given of research programmes which have been conceptualised using the framework of developmental contextualism. Work on puberty by Brooks-Gunn *et al.* (1985), by Paikoff *et al.* (1991) and by Silbereisen and Kracke (1993) have all considered context as a factor in determining pubertal development. Many of these studies have been interdisciplinary, and have looked at the ways in which the individual and the environment reciprocally influence each other. The work of Stattin and Magnusson (1996) on leaving home provides another excellent model of the application of the principles of developmental contextualism to the field of adolescent development. These authors were able to show that the age of leaving home is related to events much earlier in the life of the young person, and in particular to conflict and discordant relationships in childhood and early adolescence. As they say, 'the timing of leaving home is embedded in developmental processes that extend far back in the life of the young person and the parents' (p. 67). Thus, one event, however important, cannot be understood unless concepts of reciprocity, continuity and goodness of fit are all taken into the equation.

Developmental contextualism draws together many strands of thought. As Bronfenbrenner himself acknowledged, his theoretical notions were themselves based on earlier thinkers in psychology, such as Lewin and Vygotsky. Today, however, those interested in designing high-quality studies to explore various aspects of adolescent development need to take into account the principles outlined above. No longer can we consider only one side of the picture; the person and the context are inseparable. What is also important is that developmental contextualism allows us to look at the role of the individual in shaping his or her own world, and it is this principle which links most closely to the focal model, to which we now turn.

The focal model

The focal model grew out of the results of a study of normal adolescent development (Coleman, 1974). Briefly, large groups of boys and girls at the ages of 11, 13, 15 and 17 were given sets of identical tests which elicited from them attitudes and opinions about a wide range of relationships. Material was included on self-image, being alone, heterosexual relationships, parental relationships, friendships and large group situations. This material was analysed in terms of the positive and negative elements present in these relationship situations and in terms of the common themes expressed by the young people involved in the study. Findings showed that attitudes to all relationships changed as a function of age, but more importantly the results also indicated that concerns about different issues reached a peak at different stages in the adolescent process.

It was this finding that led to the formulation of the focal model. The model suggests that at different ages, particular sorts of relationship patterns come into focus, in the sense of being most prominent, but that no pattern is specific to one age only. Thus, the patterns overlap, different issues come into focus at different times, but simply because an issue is not the most prominent feature of a specific age, does not mean that it may not be critical for some individuals of that age. A symbolic representation of the model is illustrated in Figure 1.5.

In many ways, such a notion is not dissimilar from any traditional stage theory. However, it carries with it a much more flexible view of development, and therefore differs from stage theory in three important respects. First, the resolution of one issue is not seen as essential for tackling the next. In fact, it is clearly envisaged that a minority of individuals will find themselves facing more than one issue at the same time. Second, the model does not assume the existence of fixed boundaries between stages and, therefore, issues are not necessarily linked with a

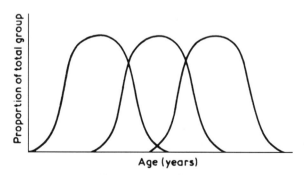

Figure 1.5 Focal theory. Each curve represents a different issue or relationship.
Source: Coleman (1974).

particular age of developmental level. Finally, there is nothing immutable about the sequence involved. In the culture in which the research was first carried out, it appeared that individuals were more likely to face certain issues in the early stages of adolescence and different issues at other stages, but the focal model is not centred on a fixed sequence. It will be of interest to consider recent research by Kloep (1999) and Goossens and Marcoen (1999a), which looks at the sequence of issues in different cultures. A discussion of these studies follows below.

In a previous paper, one of the present writers (Coleman, 1978) considered how it is possible for young people to face a wide range of transitions during the adolescent period and yet appear to cope without undue trauma or stress. One possible explanation for the successful adaptation of so many young people to the developmental demands of the adolescent transition is provided by the focal model. The answer suggested by this model is that they cope by dealing with one issue at a time. They spread the process of adaptation over a span of years, attempting to resolve first one issue and then the next. Different problems, different relationship issues, come into focus and are tackled at different stages, so that the various stresses resulting from the need to adapt to new modes of behaviour are rarely concentrated at one time.

It follows from this that it is precisely among those who, for whatever reason, do have more than one issue to cope with at a time that problems are most likely to occur. Thus, for example, where puberty and the growth spurt occur at the normal time individuals are able to adjust to these changes before other pressures, such as those from teachers and peers, are brought to bear. For the late maturers, however, pressures are more likely to occur simultaneously, inevitably requiring adjustments over a wider area. Feldman and Elliott expressed their view as follows (1990, p. 485):

> More generally, adolescents face changes in essentially all aspects of their lives; their ability to cope with those changes depends not only on intrinsic strength and external support, but also on the timing of the stresses. If disruptions are too numerous or require too much change in too little time, they may be hazardous. Concurrent major changes – for instance, going through puberty while entering a new school and losing an established circle of peer relationships – may be more than many adolescents can handle. Some of the problems associated with poverty may arise from the degree to which it promulgates changes over which neither adolescents nor their family can exert control.

The focal model is only one of a number of ways of conceptualising adolescent development, but it has two particular advantages. First, it is based directly on empirical evidence, and, second, it goes at least some way towards reconciling the apparent contradiction between the amount of adaptation required during the transitional process and the ability of most young people to cope successfully with the pressures inherent in this process. While there is still a long way to go before the focal model can be said to have been validated empirically, there have been some encouraging studies which bear on the model. Thus, Kroger (1985) and Goossens and Marcoen (1999a) have studied the sequence of relationship

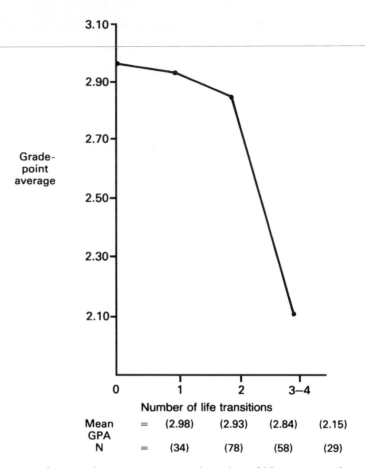

Figure 1.6 Grade 7 grade-point average and number of life transitions for girls.
Source: Simmons and Blyth (1987).

concerns in different cultures. Kroger compared young people in New Zealand and the USA, whereas Goossens and Marcoen carried out their research in Belgium. Results from these studies support the notion of different issues coming to the fore at different times. As Goossens and Marcoen state: 'The general pattern of peak ages for adolescents' interpersonal concerns provided support for the focal model. Negative feelings about being alone, relationships with parents, heterosexual relationships, small groups, and rejection from large groups do not all emerge all at once, but seem to deal with one issue at a time' (1999a, pp. 65–80).

In another study carried out in Norway, Kloep (1999) showed similar results. She illustrated that different issues – such as global concerns – might be salient for some young people, but her research provided strong support for the notion that, where possible, issues be dealt with one at a time, rather than all at once. Other writers have applied the focal model to somewhat different issues.

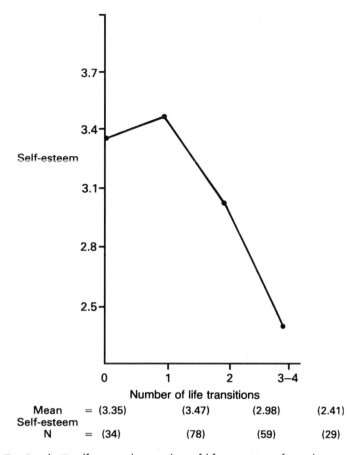

Figure 1.7 Grade 7 self-esteem by number of life transitions for girls.
Source: Simmons and Blyth (1987).

Thus, Hendry *et al.* (1993) looked at leisure activities, and used the focal model to provide a perspective on the way young people move from one activity and relationship to another as they progress through adolescence. In his work on young people leaving care, Stein (1997) applied the notion of the focal model to illustrate the highly stressful nature of this event for vulnerable young people. Finally, in a key study in the USA, Simmons and Blyth (1987) showed how those who faced more than one transition in their lives were likely to have performed less well in school and to have lower self-esteem. Simmons and Blyth's results are illustrated in Figures 1.6 and 1.7.

One criticism of the focal model is that it is nothing more than a theory of life events (Dohrenwend and Dohrenwend, 1974) applied to adolescence. At one level this is correct. The focal model does argue that the more 'issues' the young person has to cope with, the more indications of stress there are likely to be. The findings of Simmons and Blyth (1987) illustrate this well. However, the focal model goes further – for it is in one significant respect different from life-events theory. While life-events theory implies simply that the more events that occur in the individual's life, the more stress there will be, the focal model suggests that the young person is an agent in his or her own development, managing the adolescent transition – where possible – by dealing with one issue at a time.

This is, of course, one of the principles outlined above in our discussion of developmental contextualism. It is highlighted by Jackson and Bosma (1992) in their review of new approaches to adolescence, and discussed in detail in Lerner's publications (Lerner, 1985; Damon and Lerner, 1998). While at first sight this idea may be difficult to grasp, a little thought will indicate that the concept is not so extraordinary after all. Consider for a moment the range of choices available to an individual in their current relationships. In any one day an adolescent may choose to confront a parent over the breakfast table, to argue with a sibling, to accept the suggestion of a best friend, to stand up to an authoritarian teacher, to conform to peer-group pressures, to resist the persuasion of a boyfriend or girlfriend, and so on. Every one of these situations offers the young person a choice and all may well have a bearing on the interpersonal issues with which the focal model is concerned. It is quite realistic to suggest that most young people pace themselves through the adolescent transition. Most of them hold back on one issue, while they are grappling with another. Most sense what they can and cannot cope with and will, in the real sense of the term, be an active agent in their own development.

The notion of agency has become part of the thinking of many commentators in this field. Considering the fragmentation of transitions to adulthood, Roberts (1997) underlines the importance of personal agency for young people who have to adapt to poverty and disadvantage. Furthermore, Grob (1998) talks of the concept of perceived control, arguing the need for more research which will look at the relation between this concept and adolescent adjustment. His plea is almost identical to that contained in Feldman and Elliott (1990). In outlining their agenda for future research endeavours these authors have no doubt that the active role played by the young person in his or her own development should be central to our concerns:

> Future research will need to examine in detail the role of the individual in shaping particular contexts. Lack of homogeneity within contexts gives individuals considerable latitude in shaping their own situations, at least within certain constraints. Too often adolescents are portrayed as passive recipients of circumstances and resources that others make available to them. In reality they play an active role in choosing and shaping the context in which they operate – their friends, their activities and their lifestyles. The desires of parents and society to provide environments that promote healthy development might be simplified if researchers could gain a clearer understanding of why and how teenagers either resist or cooperate with such efforts.
> (1990, p. 495)

To conclude, both developmental contextualism and the focal model have contributions to make to a more realistic conceptual structure within which to understand adolescence. Both approaches also help us to move away from a view which has turmoil or difficulty at its heart. A central question that faces researchers in this field has to do, not with how many young people have difficulty in adjustment, but with the process of successful and adaptive coping. Both theoretical approaches encourage an exploration of the factors that assist adolescents in the transitional process, and this is very much to be welcomed. Throughout this book we will be considering how context impacts on development, and looking at the various dimensions of adolescent development. Once these dimensions have been reviewed, we will turn in the final chapter to a more thorough consideration of the topic of coping and adjustment.

Further reading

Adams, G, Montemayor, R and Gullotta, T (Eds) (1996) *Psychosocial development during adolescence: progress in developmental contextualism*. Sage. London.
This edited book contains a series of essays in honour of John Hill, and shows how developmental contextualism applies to adolescence.

Feldman, S and Elliott, G (Eds) (1990) *At the threshold: the developing adolescent*. Harvard University Press. Cambridge, MA.
This is a key text, with contributions on almost all topics to do with adolescent development. The writing was funded by the Carnegie Corporation, and the authors were able to write some superb essays. The book represents a landmark in the history of literature on adolescence, and cannot be too highly recommended.

Heaven, P (1994) *Contemporary adolescence*. Macmillan. London.
Heaven has written a textbook on adolescence that is eclectic and very readable. Because the author is based in Australia there is an international feel about the book, and this is a good choice for readers who want an introduction to the subject.

Muuss, R (1996) *Theories of adolescence: 6th Edition*. McGraw-Hill. New York.
This is the sixth edition of one of the classics in the literature. It covers a wide range of theories, and provides interesting information about those who have been responsible for conceptual thinking in this field of human development.

Roche, J and Tucker, S (Eds) (1997) *Youth in society*. Sage. London.
This is an edited collection of short articles by mainly British authors. The book was produced as part of an Open University course on working with adolescents, and has an emphasis on applied topics.

Steinberg, L (1996) *Adolescence: 4th Edition*. McGraw-Hill. New York.
Steinberg's textbook was produced for the North American market, but it is undoubtedly the best available work of its kind. It is very accessible, and covers a wide range of topics. Excellent as an introduction for those who want a US perspective.

Physical development

Puberty

Of the many changes experienced by young people during adolescence the first to be described in this book is physical development, or 'puberty' as it is usually described. The word derives from the Latin *pubertas*, meaning age of manhood, and is normally considered to date from the onset of menstruation in girls and the emergence of pubic hair in boys. However, as we shall see, these two easily observable changes are each only a small part of the total picture, since puberty is in reality a complex process involving many bodily functions. It is common knowledge that puberty is associated with sexual maturation. However, this stage is accompanied by changes not only in the reproductive system and in the secondary sexual characteristics of the individual, but in the functioning of the heart, and thus of the cardio-vascular system, in the lungs, which in turn affect the respiratory system, in the size and strength of many of the muscles of the body, and so on. Puberty must be seen, therefore, as an event in the physical life of the body with wide-ranging implications, the most important of which will be considered in this chapter.

One of the many changes associated with puberty is the 'growth spurt'. This term is usually taken to refer to the accelerated rate of increase in height and weight that occurs during early adolescence. Typical curves for individual rates of growth are illustrated in Figure 2.1. It is essential to bear in mind, however, that there are large individual differences in the age of onset and duration of the

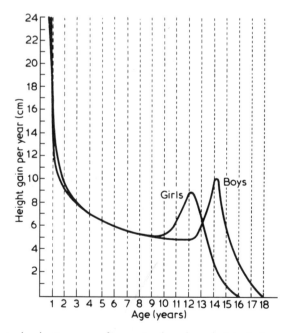

Figure 2.1 Typical velocity curves for supine length or height in boys or girls. These curves represent the velocity of the typical boy or girl at any given moment.

Source: Tanner *et al.* (1966).

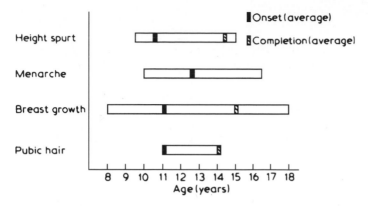

Figure 2.2 Normal range and average age of development of sexual characteristics in females.

Source: Tanner (1973).

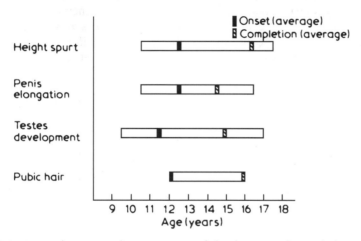

Figure 2.3 Normal range and average age of development of sexual characteristics in males.

Source: Tanner (1973).

growth spurt, even among perfectly normal children, as illustrated in Figures 2.2 and 2.3. Parents and adolescents themselves frequently fail to appreciate this fact, thus causing a great deal of unnecessary anxiety.

In boys the growth spurt may begin as early as 9 years of age, or as late as 15, while in girls the same process can begin at 7 or 8, or not until 12, 13 or even 14. For the average boy, though, rapid growth is likely to begin around 12, and to reach a peak somewhere in the 13th year. Comparable ages for girls are 10 for the onset of the growth spurt, and 11 for the peak age of increase in height and weight. Having said this, we should note that, over the past few years, there has

23

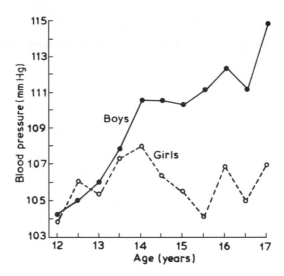

Figure 2.4 Differences in systolic blood pressure between boys and girls at puberty.
Source: Montagna and Sadler (Eds) (1974).

been some debate in the scientific literature over the question of the age of puberty. While some argue that there has been little change in the age of commencement of puberty during the past two or three decades (Leffert and Petersen, 1995), others believe that at least some aspects of the pubertal process are occurring significantly earlier than ten or twenty years ago (Hermann-Giddens *et al.*, 1997). This is a debate to which we will return later in this chapter.

As already noted, other phenomena apart from changes in height and weight are also associated with the growth spurt. Thus, the weight of the heart nearly doubles at this time, there is an accelerated growth of the lungs, and a decline in basal metabolism. Noticeable to children themselves, especially to boys, is a marked increase in physical strength and endurance. Gender differential is also reflected in less obvious external changes, as Bancroft and Reinisch (1990) point out. For example, changes such as the increase in the number of red blood cells, and the increase in systolic blood pressure are far greater in boys than in girls. The extent of such differences, which seem likely to be evolutionary and to be associated with the male's greater capacity to undertake physical exertion, are illustrated in Figure 2.4.

Tanner (1978) has drawn attention to an important difference between boys and girls in the relative positions of the height spurt in the whole sequence of events at puberty. It was only realised as a result of detailed longitudinal studies (Eveleth and Tanner, 1977) that girls experience their height spurts considerably earlier than boys. The difference between the genders in the age of peak velocity is about two years, while the difference in the appearance of pubic hair is about nine months.

The first appearance of breasts in girls precedes the increase in the size of the testes in boys by even less of a time gap. Thus, the growth spurt is placed earlier in the sequence in girls than it is in boys. The practical effects of this are

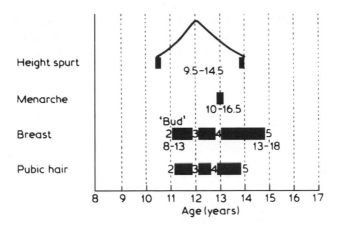

Figure 2.5 Diagram of sequence of events at adolescence in girls. An average girl is represented; the range of ages within which some of the events may occur (and stages in their development) is given by the figures directly below them.

Source: Tanner (1962).

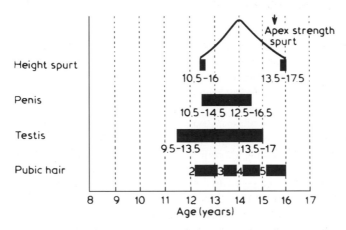

Figure 2.6 Diagram of sequence of events at adolescence in boys. An average boy is represented; the range of ages within which each event charted may begin and end (and stages in their development) is given directly below its start and finish.

Source: Marshall and Tanner (1970).

that in girls the first event of puberty is often an increase in height, which frequently goes unnoticed. In boys, on the other hand, peak height velocity usually occurs late in the sequence, after pubic hair has appeared and genitalia have started to grow. Thus, as Tanner (1978) points out, boys who are shorter than their peers and are late maturers can be reassured that their height spurt is still to come if, at the same time, genital development is not far advanced. On the other hand, girls who are worried about being too tall can be informed that their height spurt is nearly over if menarche has already occurred.

Silbereisen and Kracke (1993, 1997) were able to substantiate this effect in their longitudinal studies. In looking at the younger adolescents, they reported that fast-maturing girls were considerably taller than late or on-time maturers, while slow-maturing boys were very much smaller than those who were on-time or were early maturers. Thus, a fast-maturing girl stands out from her class-mates in terms of her height, while a boy who is slow in maturing is distinguished by being shorter than the rest of the group. These effects may well have an impact on social development, a subject we will examine further shortly.

Psychological effects of puberty

The changes discussed above inevitably exercise a profound effect on the individual. The body alters radically in size and shape, and it is not surprising that many young adolescents experience a period of clumsiness and self-consciousness as they attempt to adapt to these changes. The body also alters in function, and new and sometimes worrying physical experiences, such as the girl's first period or the boy's first wet dream, have to be understood. Because these things are diffi-cult to talk about, there is perhaps too little recognition of the anxieties that are common at this stage. Here are two girls talking about their first period.

'I mean I can remember the day I first learned about periods from my friend. I was saying oh no, you know, I was terrified. I couldn't believe it, and I went home and asked my mum and she told me it was true. And I expected my mum to say no, no it's not true, and I was terrified.'

(Coleman, 1995, p. 8)

'I remember my first fear and hating it so much. I thought I really don't want to go through like this, for so many years. And I hated that, I really did. I sat there and screamed and did just not want it. It wasn't that I hadn't been prepared for it, I mean, I knew it was going to happen and everything. But I hadn't really prepared for what I was going to feel, the sort of feeling that I've got to go through this every month, bla, bla, bla, bla, and my mum just sort of said yes, look on it as a gift rather than you know, sort of like, torture. But I mean to some extent you sort of think I hate going through this every month.'

(Coleman, 1995, p. 7)

The results of a study of 11-year-old Australian girls (Moore, 1995) illustrate a remarkable degree of embarrassment, discomfort and concern about menstrua-tion, indicating that the feelings expressed in the interviews quoted above are perhaps more widespread than is generally appreciated. Moore's research high-lighted a considerable degree of ignorance about menstruation, despite the fact that the group of girls studied lived in a community where sex education at all levels was well integrated into the school curriculum. A similar study by Stein and Reiser (1994) looked at boys, and their attitudes to and knowledge of the first ejaculation. These authors too note that in spite of sex education many boys felt unprepared for their first ejaculation, which on the whole had occurred earlier than expected. Those who felt that they had been prepared had more positive attitudes, yet almost everyone reported that they did not tell anyone, and felt embarrassed and confused by the experience. What is clear from both these studies is that even where sex education is in place in school it is not dealing with these topics in a way that usefully informs and prepares young people, and there are clearly important lessons to be learnt from these findings.

A further consideration is the effect that puberty has on identity. As many writers have pointed out, the development of the individual's identity requires not only the notion of being separate and different from others, but also a sense of self-consistency, and a firm knowledge of how one appears to the rest of the world. Needless to say, marked bodily changes affect these aspects of identity, and represent a challenge in adaptation for most young people. It is unfortunate that many adults – even those in teaching and similar professions – retain only a vague awareness of the psychological impact of the physical changes associated with puberty.

Much recent research has illustrated the degree of sensitivity associated in early adolescence with the changing body (for reviews see Alsaker, 1995, 1996). In particular, teenagers are likely to have idealised norms for physical attractiveness, and to feel inadequate if they do not match these unrealistic criteria. No doubt the media play a significant role here in promoting images of beauty and success which depend on physical attributes unattainable for the majority of human beings. There is compelling evidence to show that during early adolescence physical appearance is a more salient element of the self-concept for girls than for boys (see e.g. Harter, 1990), and, in addition, it appears that girls are more dissatisfied with their bodies than are boys. To be more specific, it seems that boys are more likely to be dissatisfied with their height, whereas for girls weight is the attribute which causes them most difficulty (Stattin and Magnusson, 1990). A large body of research (see Harter, 1990; Bulcroft, 1991; Abell and Richards, 1996) on the development of the self-concept has indicated that during the early years of adolescence both boys and girls rely heavily on physical characteristics to describe themselves. As they progress through the adolescent stage, however, young people are able to make greater use of intellectual or social aspects of personality to describe themselves, and as a result depend less on body image and other physical attributes. It is also of note that teenagers are inclined to dislike their physical characteristics and to like their intellectual and social characteristics. It is, therefore, just at the time of most rapid physical change that appearance is of critical importance for the individual, both in relation to identity and self-esteem and for popularity among friends and peers.

One further area that has received attention in the literature is the effect of puberty on parent–adolescent relationships, as, for example, in research by Papini and colleagues. These studies have reported the onset of puberty as being a time of strain in family interactions (Papini and Sebby, 1987), as well as creating more conflict within families with respect to personal habits (Papini and Clark, 1989). However, other researchers have queried these results, arguing that more accuracy was needed concerning the measurement of pubertal status. In fact, examples can be found of studies which show diminished conflict at this time (e.g. Paikoff *et al.*, 1991), studies which show no effect of pubertal status (e.g. Simmons and

Blyth, 1987), and studies which show increased conflict or more dissatisfaction with the parental relationship (e.g. Stattin and Magnusson, 1990).

Such confusing results illustrate one of the major problems in this area, that of measurement. The fact is that to measure pubertal status is a complex undertaking, especially since pubertal development takes place in a range of areas. Thus, to enquire simply about the timing of menarche is inadequate, but to assess status accurately using the guide provided by Tanner (1962) is costly in terms of both time and the training necessary for the researcher. Conflicting research findings may well be the result of different methodologies, and it is essential to keep this in mind. One of the best studies is that of L. Steinberg (1987), in which he not only used a full assessment of pubertal status, but also took into account the key variables of age, pubertal status and the timing of maturation. From this research it was concluded that pubertal maturation does increase emotional distance between parents and teenagers, independent of age, and in both genders. However, greater intensity of conflict was more likely between mothers and daughters than between other diads in the family. These findings were replicated in a later longitudinal study (Steinberg, 1988).

Early and late developers

Since individuals mature at very different rates, one girl at the age of 13 may be small, with no breast development, and look much as she did during childhood, whereas another at the same age may look like a fully developed adult woman. The question arises as to whether such marked physical differences have particular consequences for psychological adjustment. By and large, studies have shown that, for boys, early maturation carries with it social advantages, whereas late maturation can be more of a problem. Early-maturing boys feel more positive about themselves and their bodies, and more satisfied with their development (Tobin-Richards et al., 1983; Simmons and Blyth, 1987). Other studies have shown that such boys are likely to be popular, and to do well in their school work (Silbereisen and Kracke, 1993, 1997). By contrast, late-maturing boys have been found to be less popular, less successful in school work, less relaxed, and less attractive to both adults and peers (Petersen and Crockett, 1985).

For females the situation is more complex, since early maturation may have both costs and benefits. A number of writers have shown that girls who mature significantly earlier than their peers are less popular (among girls at least), more likely to show signs of inner turbulence (Buchanan, 1991; Alsaker, 1992), and to be less satisfied with their bodies (Silbereisen and Kracke, 1997). In the early literature (e.g. Clausen, 1975) there were indications that early maturation in girls was not all bad, and that in certain circumstances girls who reached puberty earlier than their peers had enhanced self-confidence and social prestige. More recently, however, the emphasis has been on the disadvantages, such as having more psychosomatic symptoms (Stattin and Magnusson, 1990), being more likely to have eating problems (Brooks-Gunn et al., 1989), having higher levels of depression (Alsaker, 1992), and showing a greater likelihood of contact with deviant peers (Silbereisen and Kracke, 1993).

The theme of the onset of puberty has attracted considerable interest in the research community, but there is no doubt that the work of Brooks-Gunn and Petersen has been pivotal in raising questions and in developing new methodologies in this particular area. Key studies may be found in two special issues of the *Journal of Youth and Adolescence* (Brooks-Gunn *et al.*, 1985). Two particular topics addressed in these issues include, first, the meaning of puberty for the individual and for those in his or her immediate environment, and, second, the factors which affect the timing of puberty. It is important to note that the lifespan developmental approach has been the inspiration for a great many of these studies. Of significance here is the 'deviance' hypothesis (Petersen and Crockett, 1985; Alsaker, 1996). This states that early and late maturers differ from on-time maturers because of their status, being socially deviant compared with others in the peer group. Early-maturing girls and late-maturing boys would be most at risk for adjustment problems, since they constitute the two most deviant groups in terms of maturation. In addition, the paper by Lerner *et al.* (1989), in which the centrality of the reciprocal relation between the person and the environment is stressed, offers a valuable example of the application of a conceptual model to the topic of pubertal maturation.

Two classic studies may be mentioned here as examples of this type of approach. Brooks-Gunn and Warren (1985) utilised the on-time model to explain their findings concerning adolescent dancers. Girls in dance and non-dance schools were compared for pubertal status. Because the dance student must maintain a relatively low body weight, it was expected that being a late maturer would be more advantageous to the dancer. Results showed that more dance (55 per cent) than non-dance (29 per cent) girls were late maturers. In addition, the on-time dancers (i.e. those who had already reached puberty) showed more personality and eating problems. Brooks-Gunn and Warren suggest that a goodness of fit exists between the requirements of a particular social context and a person's physical and behavioural characteristics. For the dancers, who must maintain a low body weight to perform, being on-time (and heavier) is a disadvantage. For girls for whom weight is not an issue being on-time may be a positive advantage – at least, it is unlikely to be perceived in a negative manner.

The work of Simmons, Blyth and others, which remains pertinent today, may be quoted as a further example of research which looks at puberty as one element of the individual's social and physical development. Blyth *et al.* (1985) report a longitudinal study exploring the effects of pubertal timing on satisfaction with body image and self-esteem in adolescent girls. Results show a more favourable body image and/or self-esteem if the young person approximates the cultural ideal of thinness, *and* if they are not experiencing simultaneous environmental (school transition) and physical (early puberty) changes. Simmons and Blyth (1987) expand these findings by comparing boys and girls, and showing that being off-time, i.e. out of step with your peers, has more negative effects for boys than girls, especially at the two extreme ends of the developmental spectrum.

A key element of research such as this is the inclusion of a multitude of variables, and the placing of the findings in a lifespan developmental perspective. The work of these social scientists has had a major impact on our understanding of the place of puberty in the lives of young people. Regrettably, during the 1990s there has been considerably less evidence of similar sophisticated research. It may be that the lack of funding has played a part. Nonetheless, urgent questions still need to be asked about the meaning of puberty for adolescents today, especially in view of the substantial social changes which have occurred since the 1980s. It is to this subject that we now turn.

The secular trend

The term 'secular trend' has been used to describe the biological fact that over the past hundred years the rate of physical growth of children and adolescents has accelerated, leading to faster and earlier maturation. This trend has been particularly noticeable in the growth rates of 2 to 5 year olds, but it has also had many implications for adolescent development. Full adult height is now achieved at a much earlier age (i.e. between 16 and 18), final adult stature and weight have increased, and many investigators have reported that height and weight during adolescence are greater today than they have ever been (Eveleth and Tanner, 1990).

In addition to changes in height and weight, the maturation of the reproductive system is also affected by the secular trend. Tanner (1978) estimated that in average populations in western Europe there has been a downward trend in the age of menarche of about four months per decade since 1850. This trend is illustrated in Figure 2.7, from which it will be seen that broadly similar reductions in the age of menarche have taken place in a variety of countries. While there has been much debate over the reason for these trends, it is generally agreed today that better health care and improved nutrition are the primary reasons underlying the secular trend.

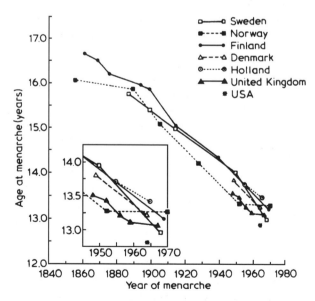

Figure 2.7 Secular trend in age at menarche, 1860–1970.

Source: Tanner (1978).

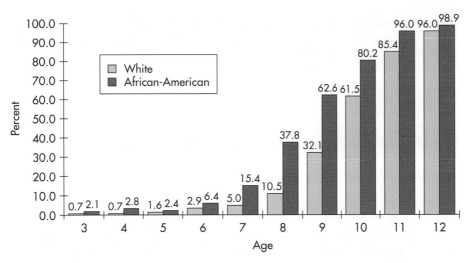

Figure 2.8 Prevalence of breast development at Tanner stage 2 or greater by age and race (Cochran-Mantel-Haenszel X^2 = 168.6, df = 1, P < .001; Breslow-Day X^2 = 10.7, df = 9, P = .300).

Source: Hermann-Giddens *et al.* (1997).

Since the ground-breaking work of Tanner and his colleagues, there have been few substantive studies on this topic. It is of interest to note that it has been argued (see e.g. Wyshak and Frisch, 1982; Leffert and Petersen, 1995) that the age of menarche, in Europe and North America at least, has remained steady over the past few decades. This is in marked contrast to anecdotal evidence from teachers and others, who have little doubt that young people are maturing earlier today than ever before.

In an attempt to resolve this question Hermann-Giddens *et al.* (1997) studied 17,000 girls between the ages of 3 and 12 years of age who presented at paediatric clinics across the USA. The results of this study pose as many questions as they answer. First, the authors report that the age of menarche has remained much the same for white girls in North America over the last fifty years. Thus the mean age of menarche in 1948 was 12.9, whereas in 1992 it was 12.8. Girls of African-American background had a mean age of menarche of 12.2 in 1992, but little comparative data is available to provide any historical perspective for this group. However, if breast-bud development is taken as a criterion, it appears that this is certainly occurring at an earlier age today than in the past. Prevalence of breast development is illustrated in Figure 2.8, from which it will be seen that 60 per cent of white girls and 80 per cent of African-American girls have reached what is known as Tanner Stage 2 by the age of 10. If these figures are compared with existing paediatric data (Harlan *et al.*, 1980) it can be seen that the early stages of pubertal development are still subject to the secular trend.

There is much concern today over precocious sexuality, and the effects of more open attitudes towards sex on children and young people. We will be exploring these issues further in Chapter 6. However, if, as many people believe, sexually mature behaviour is occurring earlier, then it is critical to establish whether this is a biological or a social phenomenon. Those who believe that the secular trend has slowed down or ceased altogether in respect of menarche might argue that social factors are central here. However, the Hermann-Giddens *et al.* (1997) study indicates that puberty is a complex phenomenon. One explanation for these results is that, although the age of menarche may have remained constant for some years, the whole process of puberty is lengthening. Thus, early signs of puberty may be occurring at a younger age, giving the impression, both to adults and to young people, that boys and girls are maturing earlier than in previous decades.

Implications for practice

1. Puberty is poorly understood, not only by teenagers themselves, but also by significant adults. It would help greatly if more information was available for parents and carers. Research has shown that young people who are properly prepared for the arrival of puberty adjust better than those who have had little preparation.
2. This point relates also to the need for more effective health education in junior school. While there may be debate over the rate of biological maturation, there is little doubt that a significant proportion of those below the age of 11 are in need of appropriate knowledge about puberty that will assist them to cope with the physical changes they will be experiencing before they reach secondary school.
3. A greater awareness of the needs and potential difficulties of early and late maturers would be useful for parents, teachers and others who work with young people. As we have seen, both these groups may be vulnerable in their social and emotional development, and support at the right time from a concerned adult may make a considerable difference to the adjustment of the young person.
4. Finally, it is apparent from this review that more research is needed in this area. We know virtually nothing about differences between ethnic groups in respect of pubertal development, we are lacking good methodologies for use in the European context, and we need to have a clearer picture of the impact of the secular trend on pubertal development. We also need to know more about the meaning of puberty to young people in present-day circumstances. If we are to provide appropriate and supportive information and advice, greater knowledge of a young person's own understanding of this aspect of development would pay considerable dividends.

Further reading

Adams, G, Montemayor, R and Gullotta, T (Eds) (1989) *Biology of adolescent behaviour and development.* Sage. London.

This is an edited collection of articles by North American authors. Its primary focus is on the biology of puberty and sexual development.

Alsaker, F (1996) The impact of puberty. *Journal of Child Psychology and Psychiatry.* 37. 249–258.

An excellent review article, which considers a variety of topics on puberty. It includes many references to European work.

Bancroft, J and Reinisch, J (Eds) (1990) *Adolescence and puberty.* Oxford University Press. Oxford.

Another edited collection of papers originating from a conference which took place in Oxford in 1988. This book has a strongly biological focus.

Brooks-Gunn, J, Petersen, A and Eichorn, D (Eds) (1985) The time of maturation and psychosocial functioning in adolescence: Parts 1 and 2. *Journal of Youth and Adolescence.* 14(3) and 14(4).

These two special issues contain some classic papers in the field. Strongly recommended.

Silbereisen, R and Kracke, B (1993) Variation in maturational timing and adjustment in adolescence. In Jackson, S and Rodriguez-Tome, H (Eds) *The social worlds of adolescence.* Erlbaum. Hove.

This chapter reports results from one of the most important European studies of puberty. It is a model of its kind, and worth hunting down in a library.

Thinking and reasoning

Cognitive development in adolescence is one of the areas of maturation which is least apparent to observers. There are no external or visible signs to show what is happening, as is the case with physical development, yet changes in this sphere are occurring all the time. Furthermore, alterations in intellectual function have implications for a wide range of behaviours and attitudes. Such changes render possible the move towards independence of thought and action, they enable the young person to develop a time perspective which includes the future, they facilitate progress towards maturity in relationships, they contribute to the development of communication skills, and, finally, they underlie the individual's ability to take on adult roles in society. This chapter will begin by considering the contribution of Piaget to this field, for it was he who first drew attention to the importance of the intellectual development which follows puberty. Some attention will also be paid to the topic of social cognition, to Elkind's notion of egocentrism, and to the development of moral thought.

Formal operations

The work of Jean Piaget, the Swiss psychologist, is the most obvious starting place for a consideration of cognitive development during the teenage years. It was he who first pointed out that a qualitative change in the nature of mental ability, rather than any simple increase in cognitive skill, is to be expected at or around puberty, and he argued that it is at this point in development that formal operational thought finally becomes possible (Inhelder and Piaget, 1958).

A full description of Piaget's stages of cognitive growth is beyond the scope of this book, but may be found in any standard textbook on child development. For our purposes, the crucial distinction is that which Piaget draws between concrete and formal operations. During the stage of concrete operations (approximately between the ages of 7 and 11) the child's thought may be termed 'relational'. Gradually, he or she begins to master notions of classes, relations and quantities. Conservation and seriation become possible, and the development of these skills enables the individual to formulate hypotheses and explanations about concrete events. These cognitive operations are seen by the child simply as mental tools, the products of which are on a par with perceptual phenomena. In other words, the child at this stage seems unable to differentiate clearly between what is perceptually given and what is mentally constructed. When the child formulates a hypothesis it originates from the data, not from within the person, and if new contradictory data are presented he or she does not change the hypothesis, but rather prefers to alter the data or to rationalise these in one way or another.

With the appearance of formal operations a number of important capabilities become available to the young person. Perhaps the most important of these is the ability to construct 'contrary-to-fact' propositions. This change has been described as a shift in emphasis in adolescent thought from the 'real' to the 'possible', and it facilitates a hypothetico-deductive approach to problem-solving and to the understanding of propositional logic. It also enables the individual to think about mental constructs as objects which can be manipulated, and to come to terms with notions of probability and belief.

Figure 3.1 Piaget's dolls-and-sticks problem. Can the child establish a correspondence between the size of the dolls and the size of the sticks?

Source: Muuss (1996).

The fundamental difference in approach between the young child and the adolescent was neatly demonstrated in a classic study carried out by Elkind (1966). Two groups of individuals, children of 8 and 9, and teenagers of 13 and 14, were presented with a concept-formation task, involving a choice between two pictures. Pictures were presented in pairs, with each pair including both a wheeled object (e.g. a car) and a non-wheeled object (e.g. a spaceship). Choosing a wheeled object made a light go on, while choosing a non-wheeled object did not. The problem for the young people was to determine what it was that made the light go on. Only half of the younger group were able to arrive at the correct solution, and those who did succeed took almost all of the allotted 72 trials to do so. On the other hand all of the older group solved the problem, and most did so in ten or fewer trials. The tendency of adolescents to raise alternative hypotheses successively, test each against the facts, and discard those that proved wrong was apparent in their spontaneous speech during the trials (e.g. 'maybe it's transportation, . . . no, it must be something else, I'll try . . .').

The younger group, however, appeared to become fixated on an initial hypothesis that was strongly suggested by the data (e.g. tool or non-tool, vehicle or non-vehicle). They then clung to this hypothesis even though they continued to fail on most tests.

Another, slightly different, example of this situation is illustrated by the dolls-and-sticks problem (see Figure 3.1). Nine-year-olds can arrange these dolls according to size with little difficulty. Furthermore they can match sticks to dolls according to height, no matter how the dolls and sticks are first presented. However, when the same problem is formulated in an abstract fashion, then this age group is unable to manage the task. Thus the problem 'If B is not as tall as C, and A is not as short as C, then who is the tallest?' cannot be tackled until formal operations have been developed.

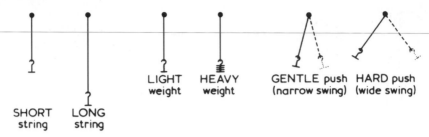

Figure 3.2 The Pendulum Problem. The task is to determine which factor or combination of factors determines the rate of swing of the pendulum.

Source: Original research for M. Shayer (1979).

Indeed, Inhelder and Piaget (1958) developed a whole range of ingenious problems for the investigation of many different aspects of logical thinking, and some of these have been widely used by other researchers. One such test is the pendulum problem. Here the task involves discovering which factor or combination of factors determines the rate of swing of the pendulum. The task is illustrated in Figure 3.2, and depends for its solution once again on the ability of the individual to test alternative hypotheses successively.

In an important chapter, Murray (1990) summarised five criteria for formal operational reasoning:

1   Duration. Operational thought will continue over time, so that the same result will be obtained no matter how long has elapsed since the problem was first presented.
2   Resistance to counter-suggestion. Young people who are operational thinkers will not be influenced by persuasion or arguments which offer alternative explanations.
3   Specific transfer. The original problem-solving ability will remain unaffected, even where different materials or different situations are presented.
4   Non-specific transfer. Young people will show an understanding of the principles behind problem-solving, and will be able to apply learning obtained in one domain to any other domain.
5   Necessity. This notion refers to the idea of continuity in physical objects and materials. Thus, no matter in what form something is presented, of necessity, it remains the same despite its appearance. Those who think in operational terms understand this principle.

Over recent decades there have been a range of criticisms of Piagetian theory. Many have questioned whether discrete stages of cognitive development actually exist at all. It seems unlikely that there is the distinction between stages that Piaget first envisaged (Sutherland, 1992). Furthermore, there have been suggestions that the formal operational stage is not like previous stages, in that it is less clearly defined, and more difficult to identify. In particular, Piaget's theory has been tested and defined during adolescence, primarily with materials derived from science and mathematics. There has been much less attention paid

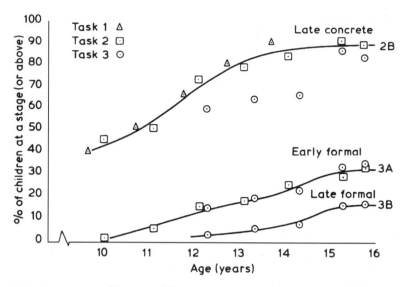

Figure 3.3 Proportion of boys at different Piagetian stages as assessed by three tasks.
Source: Shayer and Wylam (1978).

to formal reasoning in the fields of art and literature, yet these subjects also require advanced reasoning skills.

One of the major problems with the concept of formal operational thought is that, in all probability, Piaget was too optimistic in believing that all young people reach this stage of cognitive development. While studies do not entirely agree on the exact proportions reaching various stages at different age levels, there is a consensus that up to the age of 16 only a minority reach the most advanced level of formal thought.

In Britain studies by Shayer *et al.* (1976) and Shayer and Wylam (1978), using a number of scientifically oriented tasks (including the pendulum problem) in a standardised procedure on over 1,000 young people, have shown that slightly less than 30 per cent of 16 year olds reach the stage of early formal thought, and only 10 per cent reach the level of advanced formal thinking. These results are illustrated in Figure 3.3. Numerous other studies have supported these results, summarised in Keating (1990) and Muuss (1996).

Findings such as these have shifted the emphasis from the theories of Piaget to those which take a more contextual approach, or those which focus on the components of information processing in adolescence. Thus, for example, Keating (1990) suggests that content related to social or interpersonal relationships might allow some individuals to demonstrate formal reasoning where that has not been possible in scientific tasks. Others, such as Ward and Overton (1990), have distinguished between competence and performance, arguing that many may be competent in formal reasoning, but may not perform at this level of competence if materials are of no interest. They demonstrated this distinction by using two types of material – one set had to do with punishments for breaking rules at school, whereas the other set concerned problems for people facing retirement. Results were striking. At the age of 17 over 70 per cent demonstrated formal reasoning on tasks to do with school rules, while only 30 per cent demonstrated such reasoning on material to do with retirement.

A number of writers have argued that to consider only logical reasoning implies a rather narrow perspective, and many prefer an approach such as that of Sternberg (1988), who takes what he calls a 'componential' approach to intellectual development. Steinberg (1996) outlines five components implicit in Sternberg's approach. The first has to do with attention. Young people show improvements in both selective attention (knowing which cues to attend to), as well as in divided attention (being able to attend to more than one set of cues at a time). Second, during the teenage years there is improvement in both short- and long-term memory, a major aid in studying for examinations and for other school-based work (Keating, 1990).

Next, there has been an interest in the speed of information-processing seen in adolescence (Hale, 1990; Kail, 1991). Regardless of the type of cognitive task, researchers find that older adolescents are able to process information at a faster rate than younger adolescents. Improvements can also be seen in young people's organisational strategies (Siegler, 1988). Teenagers are more likely to plan tasks involving memory or learning, and they are more able to stand back and ask themselves which strategy might be most effective in any particular situation. Finally, as they mature, young people are more able to think about their own thinking processes. In many respects this is of considerable value in the realm of reasoning, but it may also lead to increased self-consciousness, and it is to this theme that we now turn.

Social cognition

In spite of the fact that Piagetian theory is today seen as being relatively marginal to an understanding of adolescence, it cannot be denied that almost all those interested in the development of thinking during the teenage years have used the ideas of Piaget as a starting point. Elkind is one writer who leads us into the field of social cognition, and at the same time provides a good example of the way in which it is possible to elaborate on the work of Piaget. In his development of the notion of egocentrism in adolescence, Elkind (1967) has extended our ideas about the reasoning of young people in an important way. He argues that while the attainment of formal reasoning powers frees the individual in many respects from childhood egocentrism, paradoxically, at the same time he or she becomes entangled in a new version of the same thing. This is because the attainment of formal reasoning allows the individual to think not only about his or her own thought (as we have indicated above), but also about the thought of other people.

Elkind believes that it is this capacity to take account of other people's thinking which is the basis of adolescent egocentrism. Essentially, the individual finds it extremely difficult to differentiate between what others are thinking about, and his or her own preoccupations. The assumption is made by the young person that if he or she is obsessed with a thought or a problem then others must also have that preoccupation. The example given by Elkind is the adolescent's appearance.

To a large extent, teenagers are extremely concerned with the way they look to others, and they make the assumption that others must be as involved as they are with the same subject. Elkind ties this in with the concept of the 'imaginary audience'. Because of egocentrism, the adolescent is, either in actual or in fantasised social situations, anticipating the reactions of others. However, these reactions are based on a premise that others are as critical or admiring of them as they are of themselves. Thus, the teenager is continually constructing and reacting to an imaginary audience, which, according to Elkind, explains a lot of adolescent behaviour. Thus, such things as the self-consciousness of young people, the wish for privacy, the preoccupation with clothes, and the long hours spent in front of the mirror may all be related to the notion of an imaginary audience.

One other significant aspect of adolescent egocentrism, seen as an example of over-differentiation of feelings, is that which Elkind calls the 'personal fable'. Possibly because the adolescent believes that he or she is of importance to so many people, their concerns and feelings come to be seen as very special, even unique. A belief in the unique nature of the individual's misery and suffering is, of course, a familiar theme in literature, and Elkind (1967) suggests that it underlies the young person's construction of a personal fable. In essence, this is the individual's story about himself or herself, the myth that is created, which may well include fantasies of omnipotence and immortality. It is not a true story, but it serves a valuable purpose, and is exemplified in some of the most famous adolescent diaries. In this sort of material one can get closest to a belief in the universal significance of the adolescent experience, and it is out of this belief that the personal fable is constructed. Elkind argues that these two foundations of adolescent egocentrism – the imaginary audience and the personal fable – are useful explanations for some aspects of cognitive behaviour at this stage of development, and may be helpful in the treatment of disturbed teenagers. One example he gives is that of adolescent offenders. Here it is often of central importance to help the individual differentiate between the real and imagined audience, which, as Elkind points out, often boils down to a distinction between real and imaginary parents.

A number of studies have explored the nature of egocentrism from an empirical point of view. Both Elkind and Bowen (1979) and Enright et al. (1980) have developed scales for the measurement of various aspects of egocentrism. In broad terms, these investigations support the view that egocentrism declines from early to late adolescence. However, findings are not clear-cut, and more recent studies have been more critical. Some researchers have found it difficult to confirm the developmental trend (e.g. Riley et al., 1984), while others have argued that certain aspects of egocentrism, such as the personal fable, may remain present throughout adolescence, and indeed may be present during adulthood as well (Goossens et al., 1992; Quadrel et al., 1993). One of the most substantive criticisms has been that studies of egocentrism have been based on questionnaires, and have not taken into account the context of situations that young people face in their social lives. Thus, for example, a study by Jahnke and Blanchard-Fields (1993) showed that egocentrism was more closely linked to young people's interpersonal understanding than to their cognitive ability. In conclusion, while Elkind may be correct in arguing that egocentrism is a feature of early adolescence, the explanation for this may be more to do with social and emotional development than with cognitive ability.

In addition to Elkind, a number of other writers have explored the topic of social cognition in adolescence. Barenboim (1981) has looked at impression formation, Turiel (1978) has explored the young person's understanding of social conventions, and Selman (1980) has created a framework for the exploration of social perspective-taking and mutual role-taking in teenagers. The work of Selman is well developed, and has considerable implications for interventions with young people. For this reason, we will outline his theoretical position in some detail. In Selman's view, social cognition is concerned with the processes by which children and young people conceptualise and learn to understand others: their thoughts, their wishes, their feelings, their attitudes to others, and, of course, their social behaviour. Social cognition involves role-taking, perspective-taking, empathy, moral reasoning, interpersonal problem-solving and self-knowledge. Selman makes an important distinction between role-taking and social perspective-taking when he argues that the former involves the question of what social or psychological information may look like from the position of the other person. Social perspective-taking more generally involves an 'understanding of how human points of view are related and coordinated with each other' (Selman, 1980, p. 22). Selman's most important contribution is his proposal concerning a stage theory of social cognition. In the most general terms, he identifies four developmental levels of social perspective-taking (Selman, 1977, 1980):

Stage 1: The differential or subjective perspective-taking stage (ages 5–9).
Here children are beginning to realise that other people can have a social perspective different from their own.

Stage 2: Self-reflective thinking or reciprocal perspective-taking (ages 7–12).
At this stage the child realises not only that other people have their own perspective, but that they may actually be giving thought to the child's own perspective. Thus, the crucial cognitive advance here is the ability to take into account the perspective of another individual.

Stage 3: Third-person or mutual perspective-taking (ages 10–15).
The perspective-taking skills of early adolescence lead on to a capacity for a more complex type of social cognition. The young person moves beyond simply taking the other person's perspective (in a back and forth manner) and is able to see all parties from a more generalised third-person perspective.

Stage 4: In-depth societal perspective-taking (age 15+).
During this stage the individual may move to a still higher and more abstract level of interpersonal perspective-taking, which involves coordinating the perspectives of society with those of the individual and the group.

These stages constitute the developmental structure of Selman's theory, and the assumption is that moves by the young person from one stage to another are accompanied by qualitatively different ways of perceiving the relationship between the self and others. Selman's own research demonstrates that there is an age-related progression with respect to social perspective-taking (Selman *et al.*, 1986). It is important to note also that Selman sees these stages as having application in four different domains – namely, the individual domain, the friendship domain, the peer-group domain and the parent–child domain. The domain-specific framework makes it possible to outline the progression for any individual in these different areas, and to identify the interpersonal issues to which the stage structure will apply.

One of the great strengths of Selman's approach is its potential application to the world of social development, and to the treatment of those who have poor social skills, who are isolated or friendless, or who are vulnerable in social situations. To illustrate the way in which Selman has identified practical issues where perspective-taking and role-taking are pertinent, we will outline the six topics which he sees as central to the friendship domain.

1   The formation of friendships. How and why are friendships formed, and what would make an ideal friend?
2   The closeness of friendships. What are the different types of friendship? What is intimacy in friendship?
3   The role of trust in friendship. Under which circumstances does one do something for a friend, and what is the role of reciprocity in friendship?
4   Jealousy in friendship. How does the person feel about the intrusion of others into an established friendship relationship?
5   Conflict resolution. How do friends resolve their conflicts when there is a disagreement?
6   Termination of friendships. How and why are friendships ended?

As Selman developed his ideas further he became more interested in applications to clinical problems. He was particularly concerned to see how he could facilitate the growth of friendship-making skills, and how he could assist those for whom friendship was problematic. He developed a model which he called pair-therapy, in which the goal was to enhance social perspective-taking, and reach a position where each young person had the skills to regulate the friendship relationship without breakdown and without the support of an adult. This work is described in Selman and Schultz (1990) and in Nakkula and Selman (1991). The authors identify four necessary steps to deal with a social problem: (1) defining the social problem as perceived by the young person; (2) generating different problem-solving strategies; (3) choosing the strategy which appears most appropriate from the perspective of the adolescent; (4) evaluating the result, so that, if the outcome is unsatisfactory, a new problem-solving strategy can be generated.

The important point to note here is that Selman's theoretical structure has enabled a clinical intervention to be developed, with wide-ranging implications for the way in which therapists and others work with young people in difficulty. The examples of theory having direct application in this manner in the field of developmental psychology are few, so the work of Selman provides an encouraging model for future theorists.

Moral thought

Moral thought is, of course, one aspect of social cognition, yet it does have an identity which is in some respects distinct from the concerns we have been discussing; for this reason, it is considered in a separate section here. As with Elkind,

Selman and others, once again Piaget's notions have formed the springboard for later thinking where moral development is concerned. Although there have been a number of different theories put forward to explain the development of concepts of morality in young people, there is little doubt that the 'cognitive-developmental' approach of Piaget and Kohlberg has more relevance to adolescence than any other. In his work on the moral judgement of the child, Piaget (1932) described two major stages of moral thinking. The first, which he called 'moral realism', refers to a period during which young children make judgements on an objective basis, for example, by estimating the amount of damage which has been caused. Thus a child who breaks twelve cups is considered more blameworthy than one who only breaks one cup, regardless of the circumstances. The second stage, applying usually to those between the ages of 8 and 12, has been described as that of the morality of cooperation, or the morality of reciprocity. During this stage, Piaget believed, decisions concerning morality were usually made on a subjective basis, and often depended on an estimate of intention rather than consequence.

Kohlberg (1981, 1984) has elaborated Piaget's scheme into one which has six different stages. The method has been to present hypothetical situations containing moral dilemmas to young people of different ages, and to classify their responses according to a stage theory of moral development. A typical situation, now well known as a result of extensive use by research workers, is the following:

> In Europe a woman was very near to death from a very bad disease, a special kind of cancer. There was one drug that doctors thought might save her. It was a form of radium that a druggist in the same town had recently discovered. The drug was expensive to make, but the druggist was charging ten times what the drug cost him to make. He paid 200 dollars for the radium, and charged 2,000 dollars for a small dose of the drug. The sick woman's husband, Heinz, went to everyone he knew to borrow the money, but he could only get together 1,000 dollars, which is half of what it cost. He told the druggist that his wife was dying, and asked him to sell it cheaper, or let him pay later. But the druggist said: 'No, I discovered the drug, and I'm going to make money from it.' So Heinz got desperate and broke into the man's store to steal the drug for his wife.

> Question: Should the man have done that?
>
> (Kohlberg, 1981)

Based on responses to questions of this sort, Kohlberg (1981) has described the following stages of moral development.

Pre-conventional
Stage 1   Punishment–obedience orientation. Behaviours that are punished are perceived as bad.
Stage 2   Instrumental hedonism. Here the child conforms in order to obtain rewards, have favours returned, etc.
Conventional
Stage 3   Orientation to interpersonal relationships. Good behaviour is that which pleases or helps others and is approved by them.

Stage 4   Maintenance of social order. Good behaviour consists of doing one's duty, having respect for authority, and maintaining the social order for its own sake.

Post-conventional

Stage 5   Social contract and/or conscience orientation. At the beginning of this stage moral behaviour tends to be thought of in terms of general rights and standards agreed upon by society as a whole, but at later moments there is an increasing orientation towards internal decisions of conscience.

Stage 6   The universal ethical principle. At this stage there is an attempt to formulate and be guided by abstract ethical principles (for example, the Golden Rule, Kant's Categorical Imperative).

(Kohlberg, 1981)

Kohlberg's theory of moral development has raised contentious issues, and there has been extensive criticism of his work (for review, see Muuss, 1996). In particular, the methodological problems associated with the testing and scoring of the moral dilemmas have worried some critics, and as a result a number of alternative forms of assessment have been devised. One of the best known of these is the Defining Issues Test (Rest, 1973), which uses a multiple-choice format, and can be scored objectively. Another concern has been to do with the invariant sequence of stages that is seen by Kohlberg to be central to his theory. While considerable research has provided supportive evidence (e.g. Kohlberg and Nisan, 1984; Walker, 1989), other writers have found evidence of regression to less mature moral stages among their subjects (Murphy and Gilligan, 1980). Some of the most interesting work on this topic has involved the study of moral development in different cultures. As may be seen in Figures 3.4 and 3.5, an almost identical sequence appears to occur in three widely differing cultures, the variation among the cultures being found in the rate of development, and the fact that in the less developed societies post-conventional stages of thinking are very rarely used.

The most sustained criticism of Kohlberg's theory has come from Gilligan (1982). In brief, she argues that the essence of morality for women is not the same as that for men, and that Kohlberg's stages are fundamentally flawed, because they are based on a male concept of morality. Gilligan takes the view that the very traits that have traditionally defined 'goodness' for women, such as their care for and sensitivity to others, and the responsibility they take for others, are traits not especially valued by men. Indeed, morality is defined in interpersonal terms at stage 3 in Kohlberg's scheme, while at stage 4 relationships are subordinated to rules, and at stages 5 and 6 rules are subordinated to universal principles of justice.

Gilligan argues that many of the dilemmas used by Kohlberg are unrelated to the moral dilemmas faced by young men and women in their normal lives. Thus, for example, the situation of Heinz, set out above, is an abstract one which has little direct relation to a personal, existential, every-day moral dilemma. Gilligan and others have developed alternative situations by which they believe it is possible to get closer to the moral reasoning of young people. One example is the following:

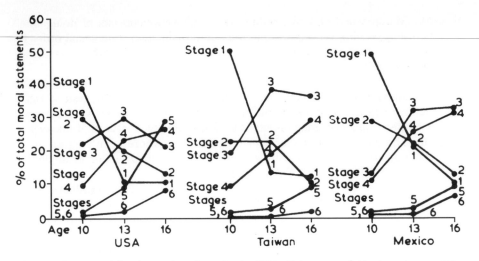

Figure 3.4 Middle-class urban boys in the USA, Taiwan, and Mexico. At age 10 the stages are used according to difficulty. At age 13, stage 3 is most used by all three groups. At age 16, US boys have reversed the order of age 10 stages (with the exception of 6). In Taiwan and Mexico, conventional (3–4) stages prevail at age 16, with stage 5 little used.

Source: Kohlberg and Gilligan (1971).

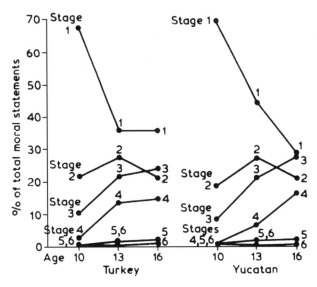

Figure 3.5 Two isolated villages, one in Turkey, the other in Yucatan, show similar patterns in moral thinking. There is no reversal of order, and pre-conventional (1–2) does not gain a clear ascendancy over conventional stages at age 16.

Source: Kohlberg and Gilligan (1971).

A high school girl's parents are away for the weekend and she's alone in the house. Unexpectedly, on a Friday evening, her boyfriend comes over. They spend the evening together in the house, and after a while they start necking and petting.

Questions: Is this right or wrong? What if they went on to have sex? Is that right or wrong? Suppose the girl is less willing than the boy? What reasons would she have for thinking like that? Do you think issues about sex have anything to do with morality?

(Gilligan *et al.*, 1990)

Gilligan and others (Gilligan *et al.*, 1990) developed three such dilemmas, and administered them to different groups of young men and young women. Results showed, as Kohlberg's critics suggested, that moral reasoning is significantly higher when abstract dilemmas are being considered. When sexual-relationship dilemmas are presented, adolescents of both genders showed lower levels of reasoning, although this effect appeared stronger for boys than girls. Gilligan and Belenky (1980) have done similar work, focusing on the issue of abortion, clearly a central concern for women, and one which emphasises the conflict between self-interest and concern for others. Here the largest group of women involved in the study showed much the same result as in other research, namely, that when personal issues are being considered moral reasoning tends to be at a lower level. From these studies it appears that when faced with dilemmas that have direct personal relevance, individuals are less able to apply their moral-reasoning ability.

It will be apparent that the original Kohlberg theory has not emerged unscathed from subsequent research. His failure to recognise that caring for others can be as morally principled as following a universal imperative is certainly one serious flaw, as is his reliance on abstract moral dilemmas to measure moral reasoning. More recent work has also highlighted the notion of justice, and has emphasised that this concept, integral to any theory of morality, is critically different in different cultures. Nonetheless, as Lapsley (1992) points out, Kohlberg's thinking is still used as the basis for the great majority of research on moral development. His work represents one of the most important advances in our understanding of this subject, and, while it will continue to be modified, it stands as a major contribution to theories of morality.

Implications for practice

1. First, the very notion of a major shift in the early teenage years towards more abstract thought is something that needs to be taken into account by any adult who comes into contact with this age group. A growing capacity for logical and scientific reasoning will affect the young person's skills in communication, decision-making and negotiation.
2. In addition, there is a broader concern about the school curriculum, and its impact on the type of thinking exhibited by adolescents today. Does

the curriculum encourage formal operational thinking, or does it inhibit its development? For some writers (e.g. Keating and Sasse, 1996) there is a real anxiety about the way in which current educational practice inhibits what they call 'critical habits of mind' in young people. For these writers schools are places in which too much emphasis is placed on examination performance as opposed to the fostering of imaginative and creative thought.

3. In terms of concepts of egocentrism and other aspects of social cognition examples have already been given of ways in which such notions can be applied to everyday interactions with young people. We have noted how Elkind, Selman and others have used their theories to develop new clinical interventions, but it is not only in this way that such theories are important. If we consider egocentrism, we can see that an understanding of the way young adolescents think about themselves might be helpful to parents, social workers and others. Young people can appear to those who live and work with them to be extremely self-centred. An awareness of the fact that egocentrism is a normal element of the cognitive development of adolescents could assist adults to put this behaviour into perspective.

4. An understanding of moral thought has a variety of implications for practice. Kohlberg himself (1970) designed a training course which attempted to accelerate adolescent moral development, although many people have had serious doubts about the validity of such an exercise. However, there have been a number of attempts to use Kohlberg's framework in programmes with young people. Some of these have been within the broad field of values education, as exemplified by the work of Nucci and Webber (1991). Here a distinction is drawn between morality and social convention, and the student is encouraged to learn how societies may vary in social conventions yet have similar systems of morality.

5. Another field for the application of Kohlberg's theory is that of work with young offenders. Here the belief is that those whose behaviour reflects a deficit in moral reasoning could benefit from training in this area. Such ideas have been explored both in North America (e.g. Ross et al., 1988) and in the UK (Thornton and Reid, 1982). However, the notion that criminal behaviour could be modified by cognitive skills training has not been universally accepted. Some studies have reported that such programmes appear to have no effects at all on young criminals (Robinson, 1995), while others have argued that it all depends on the type of offence (Nelson et al., 1990).

6. To conclude, it will be clear that there are many ways in which an understanding of thinking and reasoning during the adolescent years may have applications in practice. All too often professionals become preoccupied with the behaviour of young people, ignoring some of the less obvious manifestations of development. Changes in thinking and reasoning are a good example of this. It is important both to take account of some of the limitations in the thinking skills of the younger adolescent and to recognise how such skills can grow with age, allowing older adolescents to develop a range of new capabilities.

Further reading

Keating, D (1990) Adolescent thinking. In Feldman, S and Elliott, G (Eds) *At the threshold: the developing adolescent.* Harvard University Press. Cambridge, MA.
This chapter in Feldman and Elliott's book offers a fine summary of research on the topic of adolescent thought, and its development through the teenage years.

Keating, D and Sasse, D (1996) Cognitive socialization in adolescence: critical period for a critical habit of mind. In Adams, G, Montemayor, R and Gullotta, T (Eds) *Psychosocial development during adolescence: progress in developmental contextualism.* Sage. London.
This chapter explores how thinking is socialised during adolescence, and addresses itself particularly to the role of the school in either inhibiting or facilitating creative thought during this stage.

Muuss, R (1996) *Theories of adolescence: 6th edition.* McGraw-Hill. New York.
We have already referred to this book, at the end of Chapter 1. It contains good summaries of the theories of Piaget, Kohlberg, Selman and others concerned with thinking during adolescence.

The self and identity

As far as the self-concept is concerned, adolescence is usually thought of as a time of both change and consolidation. There are a number of reasons for this. First, the major physical changes, which we considered in Chapter 2, carry with them an alteration in body image, and thus in the sense of self. Second, intellectual growth during adolescence, reviewed in the previous chapter, makes possible a more complex and sophisticated self-concept. Third, some development of the self-concept seems likely as a result of increasing emotional independence, and the approach of fundamental decisions relating to occupation, values, sexual behaviour, friendship choices and so on. Finally, the transitional nature of the adolescent period, and in particular the role changes experienced at this time, would seem likely to be associated with some modifications of self-concept.

The ways in which young people understand and perceive themselves, their own agency and personality, have a powerful effect on their subsequent reactions to various life events. The essential dilemma for an individual young person who wishes to be fully integrated in society is that between 'playing appropriate roles' and 'selfhood'. On the one hand, it is important to be able to play the right roles in a variety of social settings, and to follow the prescribed rules for these situations. On the other, it is equally important to be able to maintain elements of individuality or selfhood. Adolescence is a time when an individual struggles to determine the exact nature of his or her self, and to consolidate a series of choices into a coherent whole which makes up the essence of the person, clearly separate from parents and other formative influences. Without this process towards individuality the young person can experience depersonalisation. The relative freedom for the adolescent to escape from behaviour which is regulated by rules can be achieved through stylistic variations of role and role structure, and through the selection of alternative social and environmental contexts in which to develop outside the home.

In the process of socialisation the various adults (parents, teachers, youth leaders) with whom the young person interacts are important as role models and social agents, but so too are the functions of selfhood, perceived competence and coherent identity. The young person is engaged in a process in which making sense of the social world, and finding a comfortable place in it, is the key to psychological maturation.

In this chapter we will, therefore, briefly review the evidence available on the adolescent self-concept. In particular, we will look at four major themes:

(a)   factors associated with self-concept development;
(b)   self-esteem in adolescence;
(c)   theoretical approaches to identity development;
(d)   a review of research on ethnic identity.

Before commencing a discussion of these topics, we must say a word about terminology. Unfortunately, in this area a number of terms tend to be used interchangeably by writers and researchers, so that, for example, 'self-concept', 'self-worth' and 'self-esteem' may all be used to refer to the same notion, while there is also often confusion between 'identity' and the 'self' or the 'self-concept'. For the present we will use the term 'self-concept' to refer to the overall idea of a sense of self, which includes body image, self-esteem and other dimensions of the self. The term 'self-esteem' will be used as far as possible to refer to the individual's self-evaluation or sense of self-worth, and, finally, the term 'identity' will be used when discussing the work of Erikson and those who have built on his original ideas, writers such as Marcia, Waterman, Adams, Cote, Phinney and others.

Factors associated with self-concept development

There are many different ways of conceptualising the self-concept. Indeed, this is a topic with a long history in psychology, and a wide range of theoretical positions can be identified within the literature. For the purposes of this chapter we will remain within the field of adolescence, and look primarily at concepts which have been applied to this life stage. The most common way of delineating the self-concept has been to describe a number of dimensions which may be said to constitute the totality of the self. One good example may be found in the work of Offer and colleagues. Offer is well known for the development of the Offer Self-Image Questionnaire (Offer, 1969; Offer *et al.*, 1992). In this questionnaire, the adolescent self-image is broken down into five global areas of psychosocial functioning, and then further divided into ten scales, as illustrated in Figure 4.1. An alternative multi-dimensional view may be found in the work of Harter (1990). Harter developed a self-perception profile, which she based upon a factor-analytic procedure, and as a result of this procedure identified eight specific domains

---

Adolescent self-image

Psychological self
Impulse Control Scale (4 items)
Emotional Health Scale (4 items)
Body Image Scale (5 items)

Sexual self
Sexuality Scale (5 items)

Social self
Social Functioning Scale (6 items)
Vocational Attitudes Scale (5 items)

Familial self
Family Functioning Scale (10 items)

Coping self
Self-Reliance Scale (5 items)
Self-Confidence Scale (4 items)
Mental Health Scale (5 items)

Figure 4.1 Adolescent self-image broken down into the five global areas of adolescent psychosocial functioning and further divided into ten scales of the OSIQ-53 and the number of items that compose each scale.
Source: Stoller *et al.* (1996).

of the self-concept: scholastic competence, job competence, athletic competence, physical appearance, social acceptance, close friendship, romantic appeal and conduct.

A more complex model has been proposed by Shavelson, who supports a hierarchical view of the self-concept in adolescence, as illustrated in Figure 4.2. Shavelson *et al.* (1976) and Marsh *et al.* (1988) believe that at the top of the model is a fairly stable general self-concept, which is based on two main dimensions – the academic and non-academic self-concept. Within the non-academic self-concept a distinction is made among social, emotional and physical self-concept, each of which is built upon other more detailed facets of the self. These are placed lower in the hierarchy, since it is believed that they are less stable and more situation specific in nature.

It is important to note that these are not the only examples in the literature of approaches to the adolescent self-concept, but they do give an idea of the way in which social scientists view this topic. Such approaches are also helpful when we come to consider the ways in which the self-concept changes and develops during adolescence. First, it can be said that a greater degree of differentiation occurs. On the one hand, aspects of the self-concept are more likely to be linked with specific situations. Thus, a child will describe himself or herself simply as friendly, sad, lazy or sporty. A teenager is more likely to say that he or she is friendly in such and such a situation, or sad under certain circumstances. On the other hand, the adolescent is also more likely than a younger child to be able to include a notion of who is doing the describing. Thus, a teenager might say: 'My parents see me as quiet and shy, but my friends know that I can be quite the opposite.' This ability to see the self from different points of view is a key feature of the changing world view of the young person in the early years of adolescence, and is dependent on the dimensions of cognitive development described in the preceding chapter.

In addition to greater differentiation, better organisation and integration of different aspects of the self also develops (Harter, 1990; Marsh, 1989). When asked to describe themselves children may simply list attributes in no specific order or relationship to each other. As they get older young people show evidence of a greater need to organise traits so that they become linked together and form a coherent whole. Interestingly, this increased awareness of the importance of having a coherent personality may create some problems for those in the middle years of adolescence, since with this awareness comes also a recognition that within one's personality there may be conflicting attributes. In an important study Harter and Monsour (1992) asked young people to characterise their personalities by placing various traits on a series of concentric circles, from most important in the centre to least important on the outside. It was apparent from this study that most young people saw themselves as having conflicting attributes, and being different sorts of people in different situations. Presumably, the resolution or acceptance of these conflicts is part of the developmental process that contributes to the move towards maturity. In this respect it is of interest to bear in mind the view of Harter (1988) and others, who believe that the self-concept is most usefully understood as a theory one constructs about the self. The gradually increasing differentiation and organisation which occurs during adolescence is evidence of precisely this construction that Harter talks about.

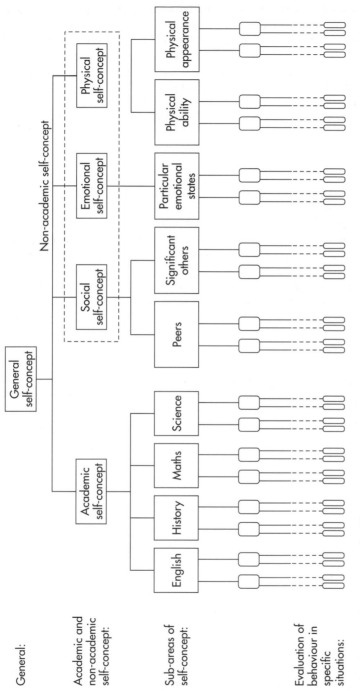

General:

Academic and
non-academic
self-concept:

Sub-areas of
self-concept:

Evaluation of
behaviour in
specific
situations:

Figure 4.2 The structure of self-concept.

Source: Shavelson *et al.* (1976).

Harter and others have also been interested in two other aspects of the global self-concept. One is the preoccupation with the self which is characteristic of this stage, and the other is the question of how much the self-concept fluctuates during this period. In terms of the first of these, there is little doubt that adolescence brings with it a marked increase in introspection. This has been well described by Erikson (1968) and by Rosenberg (1979). This shift towards an often painful awareness of the self and how one appears to others is likely to result from a variety of factors. Increased cognitive ability plays its part, together with the physical growth associated with puberty. A changing body may easily lead to a feeling that the self is altering, and this in turn can cause intense self-consciousness as the young person becomes increasingly aware of other people and how he or she appears to them. We have already noted the idea of adolescent egocentrism, and how new intellectual skills make possible new modes of thinking. Egocentrism and introspection are closely linked, for as the adolescent begins a new phase of attempting to understand the emerging self, so for a while this aspect of the inner world becomes a major preoccupation.

Turning now to the issue of stability in the self-concept, we find that in fact more empirical research has been carried out on the stability of self-esteem than on the global self-concept. We will be considering this research in the next section of the chapter. Nonetheless, we can be sure that some aspects of the self will change more than others. Indeed, Shavelson's model, described above, specifically implies that the higher in the hierarchy the element of the self, the more stable it will be. In addition to this there will also be a growing awareness on the part of the young person that some aspects of the self will be subject to day-to-day fluctuation. Such awareness, however, will not necessarily prevent anxiety about the lack of stability. As Harter notes, a young person may very well ask: 'I really do not understand how I can switch so fast. I mean, how can I be cheerful one minute, anxious the next, and then be sarcastic?' (1990, p. 363). Of course, this is a question that parents too may well be asking, as they struggle to cope with a teenager who appears to be so many different people all rolled into one.

Self-esteem

Self-esteem has received more attention than almost any other concept as a barometer of coping and adaptation. Since the early days of research in this field it has been apparent that low self-esteem was likely to be predictive of adjustment difficulties, and that those with high esteem were likely to do relatively well in a variety of domains. To take one example, the classic study of Rosenberg (1965) illustrates this general conclusion. He was able to show that low self-esteem, characteristic of approximately 20–30 per cent of the sample he studied, was associated with a range of factors. The research focused on older adolescents, the sample including approximately 5,000 17 and 18 year olds in randomly selected schools in New York. Self-esteem was measured with a ten-item self-report scale (i.e. the degree to which the respondents agreed or disagreed with statements such as 'I feel I am a person of worth, at least on an equal level with others').

Low self-esteem was shown to be related to depression, anxiety and poor school performance. Both high- and low-self-esteem adolescents were similar in wishing for success on leaving school, but the low-self-esteem group were more likely to feel that they would never attain such success. In addition, they were more likely to prefer a job which they knew was beyond their grasp, and to feel that they did not have the resources necessary for success. The adolescents who were high in self-esteem were significantly more likely than those with low self-esteem to consider the following qualities as personal assets: self-confidence, hard-working, leadership potential and the ability to make a good impression. Low-self-esteem adolescents were characterised by a sense of incompetence in social relationships, social isolation and the belief that people neither understood nor respected them. Finally, the belief that their parents took an interest in them was significantly more apparent in those with high self-esteem.

Since the appearance of Rosenberg's study (1965) there has been a substantial body of research on various aspects of self-esteem. Most of it has come to acknowledge that it is not only the self-concept which is multi-dimensional, but that self-esteem itself is also likely to be multi-dimensional. Thus, a young man may have high self-esteem when it comes to performance on the football field, but a low sense of self-worth when he has to deal with classwork or think about asking a girl for a date. Work in this area has become more sophisticated since the early work of Rosenberg and others, but nonetheless researchers have continued to look at similar issues, such as the correlates of high self-esteem. Thus, for example, Hoge *et al.* (1995) review studies which explore the relationship between academic achievement and self-esteem. As these authors and many others point out (e.g. Marsh, 1987), the problem is to try and sort out which variable influences which. Is it high self-esteem which leads to better school performance, or is it the other way around? It may well be that success in class enhances self-worth. Hoge *et al.* (1995) came to the conclusion that, for the moment, there can be no firm decision taken about the causal direction of the relationship. Furthermore, results from their research, using structural-equation modelling, showed only weak correlations between the key variables. Lastly, they believe that the Shavelson hierarchical model is critical in interpreting the findings, since the highest correlations were found between achievement in specific subject areas and self-esteem directly related to those domains.

Apart from work of this nature, two areas of self-esteem research have attracted most interest over the past couple of decades. The first has to do with understanding the attributes which contribute most to self-esteem, and the second relates to the longitudinal course of self-esteem stability during adolescence. There have, in addition, been some studies of self-esteem among different ethnic groups, an issue which will be considered in the section on ethnic identity. For the moment, we shall look first at the attributes which contribute to self-esteem. On this subject there appears to be remarkable consensus among researchers – most agree that it is satisfaction with one's physical appearance that contributes most to overall self-esteem. Harter (1990, p. 367) quotes one adolescent who says: 'What's really important to me is how I look. If I like the way I look, then I really like the kind of person I am.' Among young people, especially those in early adolescence, body-image satisfaction correlates most highly with global self-esteem, followed by social acceptance by peers. Academic achievement and sporting success also contribute, although to a lesser degree. There is a clear gender difference in respect of the salience of physical attractiveness, with this being a more important factor for young women than for young men. A number of studies report generally lower levels of self-esteem among girls in the early stages of adolescence (e.g. Simmons and Rosenberg, 1975; Simmons and Blyth, 1987). It seems probable that these findings can be explained by the high degree of variance attributable to body-image satisfaction in global self-esteem, and the fact that girls are particularly sensitive to, and dissatisfied with their body image during the pubertal years.

Another important contributor to self-esteem is the opinion of important others; but which others make most difference in adolescence? The work of Harter (1989, 1990) has been important here. Her research shows that there appears to be a developmental shift, with parents becoming less important as a function of age. Thus, for children, the perceptions of parents play a larger part than any other variable in determining self-esteem. However, with the onset of adolescence peers become increasingly salient. Interestingly, classmates appear to be of more importance than close friends in influencing self-esteem. As Harter says:

> Acknowledgement from peers in the public domain seems more critical than the personal regard of close friends, since close friends, by definition, provide support, and their positive feedback may not be perceived as necessarily self-enhancing. . . . Thus it would appear that the adolescent must turn to somewhat more objective sources of support – to the social mirror, as it were – in order to validate the self.
>
> (1990, p. 368)

In spite of this important conclusion there is no evidence that parents cease to be influential in respect of adolescent self-esteem. Parents continue to have an impact on self-esteem, but not to the overarching degree that is apparent during childhood. As noted, Rosenberg (1965) reported that those whose parents showed an interest in their academic performance had higher self-esteem; indeed, research, which will be reviewed in Chapter 5, shows that self-esteem is one of the variables most obviously influenced by parenting styles in adolescence. Parents and peers both play a part in this important arena, but the balance of influence between the two shifts during adolescence in line with the increasing significance of social relationships outside the home.

The second theme of continuing research is the stability or otherwise of self-esteem during this stage. Early studies reported contradictory results, yet with hindsight this is not surprising, since, on the one hand, many different measures were used, and, on the other, researchers attempted to find an answer which would apply to all young people. More recent research has shown that different groups of young people show different trajectories of self-esteem during the adolescent period. The first people to note this possibility were Hirsch and DuBois (1991), who identified four very different paths taken by groups of adolescents in respect of self-esteem development. The sample they looked at were between the ages of 12 and 14, and their findings indicated that approximately one-third of the group could be classified as being consistently high in self-esteem and a further

15 per cent consistently low in self-esteem during this period. However, roughly half the sample showed marked change during the two-year period. Twenty per cent showed a steep decline, while nearly one-third showed a small but significant increase in self-esteem during the course of the study. This is clearly of considerable importance in contributing to a clearer understanding of self-esteem in adolescence, and underlines the point that to focus on general tendencies may mask key individual differences.

Since the publication of the Hirsch and DuBois (1991) study, others have looked more closely at this issue. In the European context Alsaker and Olweus (1992) showed stability in self-esteem over short periods of time (e.g. one year) but greater change over longer periods (three years). Block and Robins (1993) found that boys are likely to be over-represented in the group whose self-esteem increases, while girls may be over-represented in the group showing a decline in self-esteem. Zimmerman *et al.* (1997) looked at a wider age range than that studied by Hirsch and DuBois (1991). They included young people between the ages of 12 and 16, and, remarkably, were able to replicate in broad fashion the four trajectories first outlined by Hirsch and DuBois; their results are illustrated in Figure 4.3.

These authors note that the groups with either consistently high self-esteem and those with rising self-esteem were more likely to resist peer pressure, and less likely to misuse alcohol and to become involved in deviant behaviour. Of even greater importance is their conclusion that the most striking effects of self-esteem change may be found by comparing the groups which show improving and declining self-esteem. These two groups often start at much the same point, at age 12, but gradually diverge in respect of scores on every dependent variable studied. As Zimmerman and colleagues (1997) point out, these results have profound implications for intervention programmes, and indicate that one programme design cannot be expected to fit all young people. As they say, 'one strategy might reach youth with steadily decreasing self-esteem, while a different approach might be more effective for youth with rising self-esteem' (p. 137). Finally, they note that the use of a single model to describe adolescent development may inhibit the discovery of meaningful individual differences among young people. There seems little doubt that this research, while being of obvious importance for the study of self-esteem, has much wider significance as well. Future studies will need to take into account the fact that different groups appear to progress through adolescence in different ways, and methods will have to be used that reflect this finding.

Theoretical approaches to identity development

A key figure in any discussion of identity development is Erikson (1968). For those who wish to read of his work in detail an excellent review may be found in Kroger (1996). Erikson viewed life as a series of stages, each having a particular developmental task of a psychological nature associated with it. In infancy, for example, the task is to establish a sense of basic trust, and to combat mistrust. The maternal relationship is here considered to be crucial in creating a foundation upon which the infant may build later trusting relationships. As far as adolescence

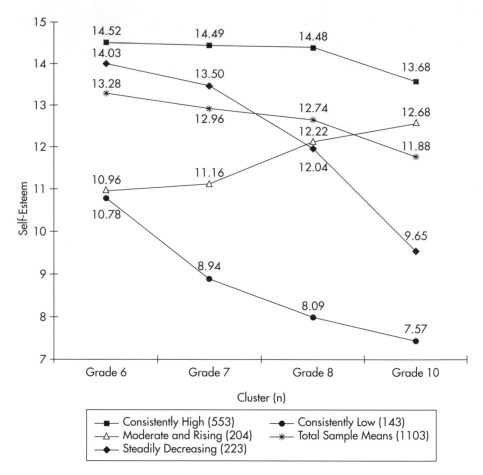

Figure 4.3   Trajectories of self-esteem for total sample (*N* = 1103).

Source: Zimmerman *et al.* (1997).

is concerned, the task involves the establishment of a coherent identity, and the defeat of a sense of identity diffusion. Erikson believed that the search for identity becomes especially acute at this stage as a result of a number of factors. Thus, Erikson laid stress on the phenomenon of rapid biological and social change during adolescence, and pointed especially to the importance for the individual of having to take major decisions at this time in almost all areas of life. In many of his writings Erikson either stated or implied that some form of crisis is necessary for the young person to resolve the identity issue and to defeat identity diffusion. A diagrammatic representation of Erikson's stages is illustrated in Figure 4.4.

According to Erikson (1968), identity diffusion has four major components. First, there is the challenge of intimacy. Here, the individual may fear commitment or involvement in close interpersonal relationships because of the possible loss of his or her own identity. This fear can lead to stereotyped, formalised relationships, to isolation, or the young person may, as Erikson puts it: 'in repeated hectic attempts

Figure 4.4 Erikson's diagram.

Source: Erikson (1968) Reproduced by permission.

	1	2	3	4	5	6	7	8
VIII								INTEGRITY vs. DESPAIR
VII							GENERATIVITY vs. STAGNATION	
VI						INTIMACY vs. ISOLATION		
V	Temporal Perspective vs. Time Confusion	Self-Certainty vs. Self-Consciousness	Role Experimentation vs. Role Fixation	Apprenticeship vs. Work Paralysis	IDENTITY vs. IDENTITY CONFUSION	Sexual Polarization vs. Bisexual Confusion	Leader- and Followership vs. Authority Confusion	Ideological Commitment vs. Confusion of Values
IV				INDUSTRY vs. INFERIORITY	Task Identification vs. Sense of Futility			
III			INITIATIVE vs. GUILT		Anticipation of Roles vs. Role Inhibition			
II		AUTONOMY vs. SHAME, DOUBT			Will to Be Oneself vs. Self-Doubt			
I	TRUST vs. MISTRUST				Mutual Recognition vs. Autistic Isolation			

and dismal failures, seek intimacy with the most improbable partners' (Erikson, 1968, p. 167). Second, there is the possibility of a diffusion of time perspective. Here, the adolescent finds it impossible to plan for the future, or to retain any sense of time. This problem is thought to be associated with anxieties about change and becoming adult, and often 'consists of a decided disbelief in the possibility that time may bring change, and yet also of a violent fear that it might' (p. 169).

Next, there is a diffusion of industry, in which the young person finds it difficult to harness his or her resources in a realistic way in work or study. Both of these activities represent commitment, and as a defence against this the individual may find it impossible to concentrate, or may frenetically engage in one single task to the exclusion of all others. Finally, Erikson outlines the concept of a negative identity. By this is meant the young person's selection of an identity exactly the opposite to that preferred by parents or other important adults.

> The loss of a sense of identity is often expressed in a scornful and snobbish hostility towards the role offered as proper and desirable in one's family or immediate community. Any aspect of the required role or all of it – be it masculinity or femininity, nationality or class membership – can become the main focus of the young person's acid disdain.
>
> (Erikson, 1968, p. 172)

These four elements, therefore, constitute the main features of identity diffusion, although clearly not all will be present in any one individual who experiences an identity crisis. In addition to such concepts, one other notion needs to be mentioned as an important feature of Erikson's theory, that of psychosocial moratorium. This means a period during which decisions are left in abeyance. It is argued that society allows, even encourages, a time of life when the young person may delay major identity choices and experiment with roles in order to discover the sort of person he or she wishes to be. While such a stage may lead to disorientation or disturbance, it has, according to Erikson, a healthy function: 'Much of this apparent confusion thus must be considered social play – the true genetic successor to childhood play' (1968, p. 164).

Inherent in Erikson's conceptualisation of the identity formation process is the integration of biological endowment, significant identifications and ego defences, with roles offered by one's society: it is through their interaction and mutual regulation that a sense of inner identity can evolve. The means by which the adolescent comes into relationship with society are primarily through occupational, ideological and sexual roles, and it is largely via these avenues that the process of identity formation has been explored.

The real problem with Erikson's theory lies in the fact that he is never specific about the extent of the adolescent identity crisis. His use of terms such as 'normative crisis' and 'the psychopathology of everyday adolescence' implies that all young people may be expected to deal with such crises, yet nowhere does he acknowledge the broad range of adolescent experience. He prefers instead to deal in the qualitative aspects of identity development, and while there is a wealth of clinical insight evident in his thinking, it has been left to others to translate his ideas into a form that can be tested empirically.

The work of Marcia (1966, 1980, 1993) is seminal in this respect. Marcia has used Erikson's conceptual dimensions of crisis and commitment to define four identity statuses. The four stages, or identity statuses, as they are called, are as follows:

1   Identity diffusion. Here the individual has not yet experienced an identity crisis, nor has he or she made any committment to a vocation or set of beliefs. There is also no indication that he or she is actively trying to make a committment.
2   Identity foreclosure. In this status the individual has not experienced a crisis but nevertheless is committed in his or her goals and beliefs, largely as a result of choices made by others.
3   Moratorium. An individual in this category has not yet resolved the struggle over identity, but is actively searching among alternatives in an attempt to arrive at a choice of identity.
4   Identity achievement. At this stage the individual is considered to have experienced a crisis, but to have resolved it on his or her own terms, and now to be firmly committed to an occupation, an ideology and to social roles.

The identity achievement, moratorium, foreclosure and diffusion statuses characterise those attempting to resolve or avoid the identity work of adolescence in greater detail. Identity achievement and foreclosure individuals share a commitment to adult roles; however, the former have synthesised important childhood identification figures into an original and personal configuration, whereas the latter have bypassed such development work by adopting identities created for them by others. By contrast, moratorium and diffusion youth share a lack of commitment. However, for the moratorium group that lack is instrumental in acting as a stimulus towards identity synthesis, while for those in foreclosure it represents an inability to make a commitment to some form of adult identity.

In Marcia's view, these four identity statuses may be seen as a developmental sequence, but not necessarily in the sense that one is the prerequisite of the others. Only moratorium appears to be essential for identity achievement, since the searching and exploring which characterises it must precede a resolution of the identity problem. In Marcia's (1966) original research, he found that as students moved through the four years of college the proportion of those in the identity-diffusion category declined, while the number of identity-achievement subjects steadily increased.

Marcia's conceptualisation of identity development has spawned a huge amount of research activity. Two key questions were addressed during the 1970s and 1980s. First, researchers wished to find out if Erikson's theory of identity development was supported by the methodology put forward by Marcia. Broadly speaking, this proved to be the case. For example, identity achievers appear to be psychologically healthier than other individuals on a variety of measures. They score highest on achievement motivation, moral reasoning, career maturity and social skills with peers. Individuals in the moratorium group score highest on measures of anxiety, and show the highest levels of conflict with authority. Those in the foreclosure category have been shown to be the most authoritarian, to have the highest need for social approval and the lowest level of autonomy. Finally, those in a state of identity diffusion are found to have the highest levels of psychological and interpersonal problems. They are also the most socially withdrawn and have the poorest social skills with peers. Reviews and summaries of this research may be found in Adams *et al.* (1992), in Kroger (1993, 1996), and in Phinney and Goossens (1996).

The second important question addressed by those who have followed Marcia has been to do with the developmental process of the four identity statuses. It has been shown by a number of researchers that identity achievement is unlikely to occur much before the age of 18. Those who have looked at teenagers in the middle-adolescent years find few consistent differences (see Archer, 1982; Adams and Jones, 1983). It appears that, although self-examination may take place during this period, the actual formation of an adult identity does not occur until late adolescence at the earliest. In key studies by Waterman and colleagues the identity development of college students was followed during a number of years (Waterman and Waterman, 1971; Waterman *et al.*, 1974; Waterman and Goldman, 1976). The results of this research illustrate that, even by the end of college, identity achievement is primarily in the sphere of occupational identity. Commitment in the area of political and ideological identity is still not in evidence for a considerable proportion of young adults (see also Waterman, 1982).

There has also been considerable interest in whether individuals shift from one identity status to another over time. How stable are the statuses, and is it to be expected that there will be more variation among some individuals than others? A study by Adams and Fitch (1982) showed that over 60 per cent of students who were classified as being in the identity diffusion category had moved to a different status within a period of one year. The research of Waterman and his colleagues, mentioned above, illustrates a similar conclusion. In one study (Waterman and Waterman, 1971) it was reported that 50 per cent had moved away from diffusion over twelve months, while in another (Waterman and Goldman, 1976) approximately 90 per cent who were in the moratorium group had shifted to another category by the end of the study. It is clear, therefore, that the challenge of identity is not necessarily resolved at one point in time, but continues to re-emerge again and again as the individual moves through late adolescence and early adulthood.

As Kroger (1996) makes clear, the vitality of the research endeavour which originated with the work of Erikson and Marcia is still very much in evidence. Studies in the past decade have looked at identity styles and defensive strategies (Berzonsky, 1992), the role of relationships in the identity-formation process (Archer, 1993), the role of optimal experience in facilitating identity development (Waterman, 1992), the events that are associated with identity-status change (Kroger and Green, 1996), and a dynamic systems perspective on the process of adopting commitments (Bosma, 1992). In addition, different types of foreclosures and diffusions have been proposed (Archer and Waterman, 1990), and an important development in thinking may be seen in Cote's work on identity capital (Cote, 1996, 1997). In essence, Cote is arguing that, with the dislocation of late modern society, psychological and social resources have become limited, and that we need to look more closely at both the tangible and the intangible assets available to young people if we are to understand the process of identity formation today.

In concluding this section on theoretical approaches to identity development it remains for us to note one more important trend which has become apparent in recent years. This is of particular significance, since it links closely with the interest currently being shown in developmental contextualism, the theoretical approach outlined in Chapter 1. It is essentially this – that identity theorists are increasingly turning their attention to the context of identity formation. A reflection of this trend may be seen in the titles of recent publications, as, for example, Phinney and Goossens' (1996) special issue of the *Journal of Adolescence*, entitled 'Identity development in context'. Although the Editors of this volume believe that relatively little attention has been paid to contextual factors in identity research, the breadth and scope of the papers in this special issue illustrate a changing focus among researchers in the field. Papers explore the interplay between identity development and historical, geographical and ethnic contexts, and it seems likely that this trend will gather pace in the coming years. Possibly the most important feature of this movement, and one in which Phinney herself has played a key role, is the growing concern with ethnicity. Research on this subject provides a prime example of the way in which contextual and developmental issues come together, and it is to this topic that we now turn.

A review of research on ethnic identity

While this topic has been of interest for decades, it is only recently that theories and methods have developed sufficiently for some important conclusions to be drawn. It will be noted that much of the theory in this area has come from North America, although we will be outlining European writing on this subject later in this section. In terms of a historical perspective, we should first consider theories which are essentially of a linear nature. So, for example, early work by Phinney (Phinney, 1992, 1993; Phinney and Rosenthal, 1992) presented a model which envisaged three stages in the development of ethnic identity. First, young people who had not explored or thought about their ethnic identity were referred to as 'unexamined'. Young people in the next stage were known as 'searchers'. For these individuals some event or incident, such as witnessing or experiencing racial harassment, marked a turning point in their views of themselves, and led to a process of enquiry concerning the roots of their ethnicity. Finally, some managed to come to a resolution of their identity, accepting a position vis-à-vis both their own culture and the majority culture. These young people were known as the 'achieved' group. Such a schema is similar to that of Marcia and others in that there are a number of identity statuses, and an implication that individuals may move from one to another in a developmental process. Considerable research has been carried out using Phinney's model (e.g. Martinez and Dukes, 1997), but at the same time others (e.g. Berry, 1990) have been arguing that acculturation may be a more complex and multi-dimensional concept, so that a simple three-stage model will hardly do justice to the process whereby an individual comes to terms with his or her ethnic identity. It has been suggested that the position of those from minority ethnic groups may best be described in terms of two independent dimensions: the retention of one's cultural traditions, and the establishment and maintenance of relationships with the larger society. Phinney herself accepts this argument, as she makes clear in Phinney and Devich-Navarro (1997). The model proposed by Berry (1990) leads to the possibility of there being four positions for any one individual if the two dimensions – retention of cultural traditions and relationships with the wider society – are dichotomised as high and low. These positions are:

1   Integration. Such individuals would be high on retention of cultural traditions but would also develop and maintain relationships with the mainstream culture.
2   Assimilation. Here young people would have a high maintenance of relationships with the majority culture, while having a low level of retention of their own cultural traditions.
3   Separation. Those in this group would have high cultural retention, and low identification with the mainstream culture.
4   Marginalisation. Individuals in this group would be low on both dimensions.

As Phinney and Devich-Navarro (1997) note, this model is more useful than a linear one, but it still requires further elaboration to accommodate the variation in ethnic and mainstream involvement among minority groups. This has led these two authors to propose an even more elaborate model, which is illustrated in Figure 4.5. As will be apparent, there are three panels in the figure. The top panel represents the pattern of assimilation and fusion with the mainstream culture, where the individual either rejects their own culture entirely, or manages to fuse the two cultures so that they become one. In the second panel, more complex bicultural possibilities are envisaged. Here, the two cultures are perceived as overlapping, with the individual occupying the middle ground in blended biculturalism, and moving from one culture to the other in alternating biculturalism. The third panel represents those for whom the two cultures cannot come together. An individual can either identify solely with one culture and reject the other, or be forced to find a position outside both cultures.

In the study described by Phinney and Devich-Navarro (1997) concerning African-American and Mexican-American young people, a number of interesting examples are given of responses to questions to do with biculturalism. Some who fitted into the category of blended biculturalism appeared reluctant to choose between the two cultures, describing themselves as equally American and ethnic. Thus an African-American young woman described herself as 'like half and half, . . . to me it is the same thing'; and a Mexican-American young man said he was 'both cultures, I am both'. Another said 'I am more American I guess, but that does not mean I am not very Black'. On the other hand, those who fitted the category of alternating biculturalism described themselves as more ethnic than American. Thus an African-American student responded by saying: 'I am mostly Black. I am both, but I am more Black.' A Mexican-American young man said: 'I am American and Hispanic, but I consider myself more Hispanic.' Phinney and Devich-Navarro compared the two groups in terms of their bicultural identity, and revealed interesting differences between the two ethnic groups. Essentially, they showed that African-American young people are more likely to be in the blended

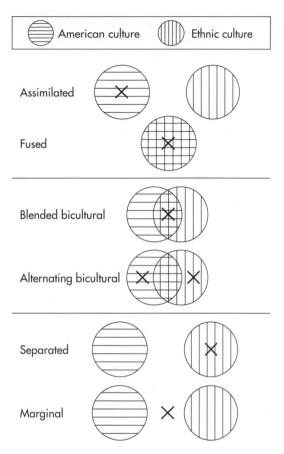

Figure 4.5 Identification patterns based on the individual's perception of American and ethnic cultures (represented by circles) as separated, combined, or overlapping, and his or her position relative to each culture (represented by 'X').

Source: Phinney and Devich-Navarro (1997).

bicultural or separated groups, whereas Mexican-American adolescents were significantly more likely to be in the alternating bicultural group.

Comparisons between different cultures are rare in the European context, although the work of Verkuyten (1993, 1995) is an exception. In the 1995 study young people from four cultures living in Holland were compared for self-esteem and ethnic identity. The groups were from mainstream Dutch culture, from Turkey, Surinam and Morocco. Results showed that there were no differences in global self-esteem between the four groups, but that ethnic identity was of more salience for those from the minority cultures. Similar findings are reported by Martinez and Dukes (1997) in their comparison of four cultural groups in the USA.

A number of studies have looked at family influences on ethnic identity, and the evidence is consistent in showing that family environment shapes development in minority cultures just as it does in those from mainstream cultures (for review see Spencer and Dornbusch, 1990). The attitudes of parents to their own culture will have a profound impact on children and young people, and will inevitably affect the process of ethnic identity formation. Research in the USA with African-American families suggests that many parents socialise their children to be proud of their race, and to have positive feelings about being Black (Thornton *et al.*, 1990). In a study by Marshall (1995) parents from minority cultures were asked which aspects of race they saw as important to discuss with their children. Responses included racial pride, racial barriers, equality and the physical attributes of the particular culture. Interestingly, findings showed that the more discussion there is in the home about racial issues, the further developed is the ethnic identity of the young person.

One important issue is the possibility of conflict between parents and teenagers about the degree of identification that is expected in relation to mainstream and minority cultures. Thus, in Asian cultures in Britain it is likely that parents expect a greater degree of commitment to ethnic values, whether they are to do with religious beliefs or attitudes about family life, than is comfortable for many young people (Gilani, 1995). Phinney and Rosenthal (1992) quote a Mexican-American young woman outlining this problem: 'My parents are sort of old-fashioned, so they tell me that I have to do things . . . like I am a girl, so I am always sent to the kitchen to cook. I am more Americanized than them, and I don't believe in that girl thing. We end up in an argument and it does not get solved' (p. 153).

A number of writers have also looked specifically at gender issues in relation to race. Thus, Shorter-Gooden and Washington (1996) explore the difficulties for young women in North America of what they call 'weaving an identity'. Results showed that, for the women studied here – a sample of late-adolescent-educated African-American women – ethnic identity was of much greater salience than gender identity. This is not to say that gender was not of importance, but it was clear that, for most, race was the defining feature of their identity. A study carried out in Britain by Mirzah (1992) explored the same theme, underlining the talents of young Black women, and the barriers they face as they seek to obtain an education equal to that obtained by their White peers. As the author puts it:

> Young black women bear all the hallmarks of a fundamentally inegalitarian society. They do well at school, do well in society, are good efficient workers, and yet as a group they consistently fail to secure the economic status and occupational prestige that they deserve. This study asked why it is that black women suffer these injustices, and attempted to reveal the processes of inequality that, despite the ideology of a meritocracy, persist in this society.
> (1992, p. 189)

Back (1997) also considers gender and race, but from the point of view of young men. He explores what he calls the 'couplet of fear and desire', in which young Black men are admired for certain characteristics, such as their athleticism, or their musical ability, but feared for what is perceived as their potential for violence and trouble-making. He argues that, in such a context, the formation of a Black masculine identity is problematic, and creates enormous difficulties for young men who wish to be successful in the mainstream culture but also to retain links with their own ethnic background.

Finally, we turn to a different aspect of ethnic identity, that experienced by young people of mixed race. While we have been concentrating on the issues faced by individuals from minority cultures, at least these individuals have a clearly identifiable culture to which they belong. For those of mixed race the situation must be considerably more difficult, and yet there is remarkably little research in this area. In one notable study, however, Tizard and Phoenix (1993) explored the development of identity in young people in Britain who had mixed parentage. They found that, while roughly 60 per cent of the sample had a positive ethnic identity, 20 per cent had what the authors described as a 'problematic' identity, and a further 20 per cent were mixed in their attitudes to their race. Examples of a positive identity are as follows (1993, pp. 58–60):

> I'm lucky. I'm proud of my colour. (What makes you proud?) I'm an individual class. I don't know the word, like we are only a few, sort of thing.

> It's a lot more interesting. If people ask me what nationality I am, I can spend half-an-hour telling them.

Examples of a problematic identity are:

> When I started to mix with boys I just felt different, because in my class I am the only coloured person . . . I felt actually at a disadvantage because everyone is like weighing up what they look like, and I'm different.

> Recently I've wanted to be white. I haven't come across a lot of racial hatred and stuff, but it still hurts, you know. I know that if I was white, I wouldn't be at all worried about my colour.

The adolescents in the study were given eleven topics which might contribute to their overall sense of identity, and were asked to rank these according to how important they were for their sense of identity. Interestingly, one-third of the sample put their colour at or near the top of the list, while 39 per cent did not mention it at all. This finding reflects the general impression given by the research that, while some see their mixed race as a central feature of themselves, others hardly think about it. Those with a positive identity tended to be most likely to attend multi-racial schools, while those with a problematic identity were most likely to be affiliated to adults from the mainstream White culture. There seems little doubt that the context in which young people grow up has a major impact on the way ethnic identity is shaped. We will conclude with the words of two young people who make this point:

> I suppose it is on my mind most of the time. (Why is that?) I worry that people will discriminate against me, because of my colour, and being aware that I am the only coloured person in my class.

In the country, or in cities where there are not a lot of black people, if you go there, it's nudge, wink, look, over there's a black person, as if they'd never seen one before, but when you come back to London, it's like nobody cares whether you are black or white.

(1993, p. 62)

Implications for practice

1. It is clear from the research reviewed here that the self-concept develops rapidly during the adolescent period. This development is linked to concomitant physical, cognitive and emotional growth. In particular, the self-concept becomes more differentiated, while at the same time the young person shows an increasing ability to perceive themselves from the point of view of others. For any adult working with teenagers it is essential to take into account these changes, and to recognise the impact they may have on interpersonal relationships.

2. In terms of self-esteem, there is general agreement that this variable has a powerful influence on adjustment across a wide range of domains. Educational achievement, social relationships, mental health, the ability to deal with stress – all these are affected by self-esteem. Much thought has gone towards establishing the factors which determine the individual's self-esteem level, and in this chapter we have noted the changing balance between parents and peers in terms of influence on self-esteem. We have also noted research showing differences in self-esteem trajectories during the adolescent period, and the importance of shaping interventions so that they are appropriate to the individual's own developmental pathway (Zimmerman *et al.*, 1997).

3. It is important for practitioners to note that the fabled 'adolescent identity crisis', as originally described by Erikson, does not appear to be true of the majority of young people. Recent research indicates that, although identity development is central during this developmental stage, it does not necessarily take the form of a crisis. Rather, an individual is likely to pass through various stages, with considerable fluctuation from one stage to another, only coming to a resolution of the identity question during the later years of adolescence.

4. One of the striking changes in focus in the literature over the past decade has been the increased attention paid to ethnic identity, and it has become clear that those working with young people from minority cultures need to recognise the importance of this dimension of adolescent development. Of course, there are wide individual differences, and culture, context and social background will all have their effect on the salience or otherwise of this feature of identity. Nonetheless, practitioners have much to learn from the research findings, and it is to be hoped that these will become increasingly available to those in the field.

Further reading

Adams, G, Montemayor, R and Gullotta, T (Eds) (1992) *Adolescent identity forma-tion.* Sage. London.
A collection of chapters on the topic, looking at identity primarily from an empirical perspective.

Harter, S (1990) Self and identity development. In Feldman, S and Elliott, G (Eds) *At the threshold: the developing adolescent.* Harvard University Press. Cambridge, MA.
This is a review chapter, within the framework of the Feldman and Elliott text. An excellent starting point for readers wanting an introduction to the topic.

Kroger, J (1996) *Identity in adolescence: the balance between self and other. 2nd edn.* Routledge. London.
Kroger's book is now in its second edition. It includes a critical analysis of five of the major thinkers on this subject, and manages to convey the essence of each theory in a sympathetic and lively manner, and is a delight to read.

Mirzah, H (1992) *Young, female and black.* Routledge. London.
This book charts the experiences of a group of young Black women as they leave school and enter the world of work. It explores inequality, discrimination and racism in Britain, and is an important contribution to the literature on ethnicity and identity.

Skoe, E and von der Lippe, A (Eds) (1998) *Personality development in adolescence: a cross-national and life-span perspective.* Routledge. London.
The authors in this book are from a variety of European countries, as well as from North America. Morality, gender, family contexts, identity and social change are all explored in cross-cultural studies, and the editors contrast findings from different countries in order to highlight cross-national similarities and differences.

Families

The adolescent stage involves a major change in the way parents and young people interact. Such change is gradual and, contrary to popular belief, does not lead to the complete breakdown of relationships. As we shall see, research in the past decade or so has emphasised continuity as much as change, and has highlighted the central role that parents play throughout this life stage. In addition, recent research has indicated that conflict within the family is less prevalent than people assume. Many adolescents get on well with their parents, and look to them for guidance and support as they confront critical issues in the transition to adulthood. Indeed, as noted in Chapter 1, this transition has altered in fundamental ways during the latter half of the twentieth century. As a result of social change, young people leave home later, thus forcing a re-evaluation of their relationships with parents in late adolescence and early adulthood. In the course of this chapter we will examine the way in which autonomy is negotiated in a context in which young people appear to mature earlier, and yet remain dependent on their families for longer. We will look at the issue of conflict and the so-called 'generation gap', and at the different roles of mothers and fathers. We will consider the effects of changing family structures, including the impact of divorce and of living with step-parents. Finally, consideration will be given to the topic of the parenting of teenagers, and the importance of providing support and information about adolescence to this group of adults who appear to receive less support than parents of younger children.

The development of autonomy

It could be argued that the development of independence, or autonomy, in respect of family relationships is one of the key tasks for the adolescent. To be free from parental restraint, and to achieve control over one's own life, is the goal of every young person. Yet the passage towards this goal is never straightforward. To some extent, this will depend on the circumstances of the family, on ethnic background, and on the cultural, social and economic opportunities available in the environment. Gender too will play a part, since autonomy for young women will be interpreted differently from autonomy for young men. In addition, the personality of the young person will be important, as will the parents' own situation and attitudes to their son or daughter. It is also likely that other factors in the family, such as the number and age of siblings, the role of grandparents and so on, will all have an impact on the path taken by the adolescent towards full adult autonomy.

In terms of our understanding of this feature of adolescence, there have been some major shifts in perspective over the last few decades. For many years the psychoanalytic view was considered to provide important insights into the development of autonomy. From this orientation it was believed that emotional disengagement from parents was a fundamental element of the move towards independence, and that unless separation and detachment occurred it was not possible to become a mature adult. However, early empirical research in the USA, such as that of Douvan and Adelson (1966), indicated that relationships between parents and teenagers appeared to be much more positive than would have been

Table 5.1 Disagreement between parents and study child (parents' report) (N = 11,531).

	Often %	Sometimes %	Never or hardly ever %
Choice of friends of the same sex	3	16	81
Choice of friends of opposite sex	2	9	89
Dress or hairstyle	11	35	54
Time of coming in at night or going to bed	8	26	66
Places gone to in own time	2	9	89
Doing homework	6	18	76
Smoking	6	9	85
Drinking	1	5	94

Source: Fogelman (1976).

Table 5.2 Family relationships (children's report) (N = 11,045).

	Very true %	True %	Uncertain %	Untrue %	Very untrue %
I get on well with my mother	41	45	8	4	1
I get on well with my father	35	45	13	5	2
I often quarrel with a brother or sister	23	43	10	19	5
My parents have strong views about my appearance (e.g. dress, hairstyle, etc.)	15	33	19	27	6
My parents want to know where I go in the evening	27	51	8	11	3
My parents disapprove of some of my male friends	9	19	18	37	16
My parents disapprove of some of my female friends	5	15	18	40	22

Source: Fogelman (1976).

expected if these theories were correct. In the UK there were a variety of studies that reported similar results. One example of such work is that carried out by Fogelman (1976), the results of which are illustrated in Tables 5.1 and 5.2.

As a result of empirical work of this sort a new theoretical perspective began to emerge. A number of writers believed that it was possible to develop autonomy without the disengagement that had been envisaged in early theoretical viewpoints. Thus, Greenberger (1984) argued that social responsibility (which involved feelings of community and closeness to others) went hand in hand with the development of autonomy. Youniss and Smollar (1985) talked of interdependence, a stage during which both parent and adolescent worked together to redefine their relationship. In this stage, close ties are maintained, without the young person's growing individuality being threatened. One of the most frequently quoted papers of this period is that of Grotevant and Cooper (1986), in which they put forward the notion of connectedness. Thus, in their view, the young person could move towards a state of individuation while remaining connected to the family. It is of interest to note that notions of connectedness were at first seen to be especially true of young women, but in more recent writing this has become a theoretical perspective that does not depend on gender. An excellent summary of this approach may be found in Grotevant and Cooper (1998).

Grotevant and Cooper (1986) developed a four-part system for coding family communication patterns. In their system individuality is reflected in expressions of separateness and self-assertion, whereas connectedness is expressed through mutuality and permeability. The results from their studies (Grotevant and Cooper, 1985) support the view that an effective combination of cohesion and separateness is associated with adolescent identity exploration and the development of perspective-taking skills. The authors note that those scoring highest on these measures had had the experience of an 'individuated' relationship with at least one parent, 'examining their differences but within the context of connectedness' (Grotevant and Cooper, 1986, p. 92). Nonetheless the actual results are complex, and the authors emphasise the need to look at all dyads in the family. In her more recent work, Cooper (1994) has examined connectedness in families from different ethnic backgrounds, showing that many non-European American families have different expectations of parent–adolescent closeness and support.

A theoretical perspective which encompasses both autonomy and the continuation of close relationships with parents has, as will be obvious, a number of possible inherent contradictions. Perhaps as a result of this a new wave of empirical studies began in the 1980s, which attempted to develop ways of measuring autonomy, and of distinguishing various elements of what is inevitably a complex concept. As an example, Steinberg and Silverberg (1986) developed the Emotional Autonomy Scale (EAS), which measures four aspects of emotional autonomy:

1   'de-idealization', i.e. the extent to which the young person sees the parent as fallible and human;
2   'parents as people', i.e. the realisation that parents are ordinary people who have separate lives;
3   'non-dependency', i.e. whether young people can work things out for themselves;
4   'individuation', i.e. the degree to which the adolescent feels an individual person in their relationship with the parent.

Results from this study showed a steady increase in all aspects of autonomy between ages 10 and 14, except for the second item (parents as people), which showed little change. Interestingly, after age 14 there appeared to be very little increase in autonomy, indicating that the major shift had occurred in the early years of adolescence. Other studies have reported similar results. Thus, for example, Feiring and Lewis (1993) found that, as adolescents get older, their parents know fewer and fewer of their friends.

In the 1990s the debate has shifted somewhat, and more attention has been paid to the significance of autonomy for the teenager's adjustment. On the one hand, researchers such as Lamborn and Steinberg (1993) have argued that young people who score highly on measures of autonomy but also see their parents as unsupportive would be more at risk than autonomous adolescents who have supportive parents. Fuhrman and Holmbeck (1995) take the opposite position. They believe that it is only under conditions of family stress, when parents are not providing support, that emotional autonomy will be adaptive. In their view autonomy under these circumstances gives the young person a distance from family difficulties which will assist him or her to cope and to find support outside the family. For these authors it is only under conditions of positive parental relationships that high autonomy would be maladaptive. As can be seen, the two positions are contradictory, and the debate raises issues about coping and adjustment, to which we will return in Chapter 12. For the present, it is worth noting that work on autonomy has become more sophisticated in recent years, as well as linking with other key areas in adolescent development.

Before leaving this topic, we should make some mention of two other studies in which approaches to the subject of autonomy are rather different. First, the work of Kracke and Noack (1998), carried out in Germany, distinguishes between three stages of adolescence. This enables the authors to show that it is in middle adolescence that the most intense negotiations take place regarding autonomy. As they say, it is at this stage that young people are most in need of establishing their right to freedom, while at the same time it is the stage for parents when they least wish to lose control. Kracke and Noack also note that changes in family members' behaviour indicate a move towards a much more verbal type of negotiation at this stage, and that, in spite of the intensification of such negotiation mentioned above, overall levels of conflict and aggression were low at all stages.

It is also important to mention the work of Larson and colleagues in this context, and in particular their methodological approach. In Larson *et al.* (1996), for example, a study is described which looks at the subject of autonomy from the perspective of young people's daily interactions with their families. The authors use a method known as the Experience Sampling Method (ESM), in which teenagers are given pagers, and sent signals at random moments during the day. Following the signal, the young people are asked to complete a report indicating what they are doing, and the emotions associated with the activity or activities. Using such a method has enabled Larson and others to track daily activities, and to gain an invaluable picture of the lives of adolescents. In the Larson *et al.* (1996) study it emerged that, while the overall time spent with the family decreased throughout the teenage years, time spent with mothers and fathers on a one-to-one basis hardly changed at all between the ages of 10 and 18. Their results, which are illustrated in Figure 5.1, underline the fact that close relationships with parents continue to serve an essential function. Autonomy may be important, but so is connectedness.

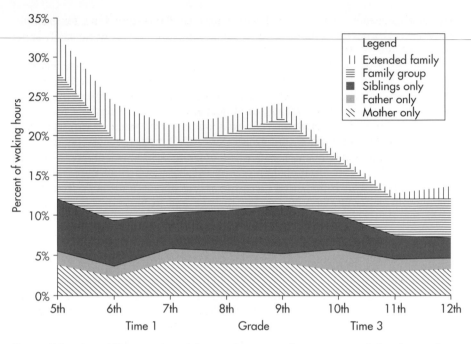

Figure 5.1 Age differences in adolescents' amount of time spent with family members. *Source:* Larson *et al.* (1996).

Conflict and the generation gap

One of the areas which has been the subject of more research than most is that concerned with parent–adolescent conflict. In popular discourse this is known as the 'generation gap'. What is especially interesting about this topic is that there appears to be a clear divergence of opinion between researchers and the general public. It is commonly believed by parents and the general public that the adolescent years bring with them conflict and disagreement in the home, as well as widely divergent views on such topics as sex, drugs and morality. Researchers, on the other hand, report good relationships between parents and teenagers, with relatively little evidence of a generation gap in attitudes to careers, education and morality. Let us look more closely at the evidence relating to this subject.

We have already quoted the Fogelman (1976) research, which looked at 11,000 young people and their parents in the UK, and showed that the very great majority of parents reported good relationships with teenagers, while the young people themselves endorsed this view, making it clear that they respected their parents' opinions, and sought their advice on the major issues that they faced. Study after study has come up with similar findings (for summaries see Steinberg, 1990; Noller and Callan, 1991; Hill, 1993). Of course, there are families in which there are problematic relationships between parents and teenagers, but so too are there families in which there are problematic relationships between parents and younger children. Studies show that where there are serious difficulties in parent–adolescent relationships, there are very likely to have been serious difficulties during childhood (Haggerty *et al.*, 1994).

Research which looks at values and attitudes also finds more similarities than differences between the generations. Gecas and Seff (1990), for example, showed that parents and teenagers shared beliefs about work, religious and moral values, and about personal attributes that are important to them. In fact, this study argues that there are greater differences among young people themselves from different backgrounds than there are between one generation and another. One interesting issue here is the fact that people see the differences as being greater than they are. This is something explored by Noller and Callan (1991), who point out that young people see their parents as more conservative in their attitudes than parents believe themselves to be, while adults view young people as extremely radical, a view which does not stand up to close examination.

Of course, it would be unrealistic to ignore the fact that there are differences between the generations, both in terms of personal taste (e.g. in clothes, music and so on) and in relation to daily living arrangements. Tidiness of bedrooms, eating habits, television watching and bedtimes are obvious examples of areas where disagreements are likely, yet it is possible to differ in these areas without relationship breakdown. In interesting work by Smetana and others (Smetana, 1988; Smetana, 1989; Smetana and Asquith, 1994) it is argued that one of the reasons for disagreements is because the generations define the problem differently. Thus, parents are more likely to believe that behaviour is a matter of convention, i.e. the choice of clothes is dictated by what would be expected by others, or what is normal in those circumstances. Young people, on the other hand, see something like choice of clothes as a matter of personal freedom. If they can choose what they want with no reference to convention, then that is a reflection of their autonomy and maturity.

Smetana and others believe that parents and teenagers are more likely to clash over the definition of an issue rather than over the specific details. In other words, it is more a matter of 'who has the authority' than 'who is right'. If young people and their parents define daily issues differently, then it may be that the resolution of conflicts will prove difficult. However, it is at this point that the idea of communication between the generations becomes critical. In a number of studies it has been shown that the better the communication between parents and teenagers, the more likely it is that conflicts will be resolved. Furthermore, on topics where communication is poor, such as drugs, attitudes between the generations are most likely to diverge. One interesting study (Brody *et al.*, 1994) showed that the more young people were involved in decision-making in the family, the more likely they were to have similar attitudes to their parents in late adolescence and early adulthood.

Quality of communication between parents and young people will vary depending on a range of variables. Noller and Callan (1991) suggest that social background, age of the young person and religious beliefs all affect communication within the home. Drury *et al.* (1998) reported on the attributions used by young people to explain communication breakdown in the family, and showed that the most common reason given was failure to understand the other's point of view. These authors also highlighted the differences, as perceived by young

Table 5.3 Comparisons between parents and friends across selected topics of discussion.

Topics[a]	Females		Males		Total	
	Parents	Friends	Parents	Friends	Parents	Friends
How well I am doing in school	.72	.24	.68	.25	.70	.25
Problems at school	.44	.55	.54	.39	.49	.55
Schoolwork and grades	.86	.83	.89	.80	.88	.82
Career goals	.63	.30	.70	.24	.67	.27
Hopes/plans for the future	.40	.54	.54	.38	.47	.46
Future plans	.87	.81	.88	.76	.88	.78
Feelings about the opposite sex	.07	.92	.14	.78	.11	.85
Problems with the opposite sex	.16	.82	.15	.78	.16	.80
Attitudes towards marriage	.32	.64	.35	.55	.33	.60
Views on sex	.21	.79	.17	.82	.19	.80
Dating behaviours	.45	.73	.43	.73	.44	.73

[a] Forced choices do not necessarily sum to 100% because some subjects gave no response or responded to both choices.
Source: Youniss and Smollar (1985).

people, between communication with fathers and mothers. Communication with the mother was generally seen to be of higher quality and to be more supportive. We will look more closely at differences between mothers and fathers later in this chapter. In an important study, Youniss and Smollar (1985) showed clear differences between topics communicated to parents and those communicated to peers. Findings from this study are illustrated in Table 5.3. As can be seen, young people are likely to discuss issues to do with school and career with parents, but topics relating to sex and social relationships are far more likely to be discussed with peers.

To conclude this section, it can be seen that there is little evidence to support the notion of wide-ranging conflict between the generations. However, it is also essential to recognise that in some families there will be high levels of conflict, either as a result of battles over issues to do with autonomy, or because of a complex variety of relationship problems within the home. Some of the factors which underlie chronic conflict, such as divorce and family separation, or styles of parenting, will be examined in later sections of this chapter. Lastly, we are still faced with the problem of finding an explanation for the public's belief in a 'generation gap' during the adolescent stage. Some might say that the notion is fed by the media, while others believe that too much attention is paid to the small number of young people who step out of line. Possibly, a negative stereotype of adolescence serves an important function for a society which sees teenagers as challengers of the status quo. Whatever the truth of these views, we should not lose sight of the fact that findings from research are unequivocal. Serious conflict between parents and adolescents is true of only a small minority of families, which should bring some comfort to those parents who contemplate the onset of adolescence with trepidation.

Family environment and adolescent development

In thinking about family environment and its effects on young people and their development we need to look at the role of parents, and in particular their style of parenting. For any consideration of parenting style it is essential to first outline the work of Baumrind and of Maccoby. Indeed, it can be argued that these two writers have had a profound effect on our understanding of parenting behaviour, and there are few studies of parenting which do not take their work as a starting point. In the early 1970s Baumrind (1971) first put forward her view that there are two dimensions of parenting behaviour which need to be distinguished: parental responsiveness and parental demandingness. Baumrind believed that parents vary on both these dimensions, and also that the dimensions are more or less independent of each other. This made it possible to look at various combinations of the characteristics of parents, and numerous studies have indicated how significant this classification scheme is for an understanding of family functioning.

As can be seen in the scheme developed by Maccoby and Martin (1983), and illustrated in Figure 5.2, parents can vary both in demandingness and in responsiveness to give four types of parenting behaviour. Parents can be classified as indulgent, indifferent, authoritative and authoritarian. Authoritarian parents place a high value on obedience and conformity. They are more likely to punish for misbehaviour, and tend not to encourage autonomy. Authoritative parents are warm but firm. They set standards and hold to boundaries, but are more likely to give explanations and to reason with the young person than to be punitive. Indulgent (or permissive) parents behave in a benign, accepting, but essentially passive manner. They are unlikely to set standards, or to have high expectations for their children, and do not see punishment as important. Finally, indifferent parents are often also called neglectful. This group knows little of what their children are doing, and tries to minimise the time they spend on childcare activities.

As has been indicated, there have been numerous studies of parenting using this classification, and results are consistent. They show that in almost all cases children and young people reared in families with authoritative parents do better

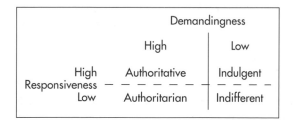

Figure 5.2 A scheme for classifying parenting types.
Source: Maccoby and Martin (1983).

on a range of measures, including self-esteem, perspective-taking, and likelihood of avoiding risk behaviour such as drug-taking, precocious sexual activity, and so on (see Dornbusch *et al.*, 1987; Steinberg *et al.*, 1991). Adolescents brought up in indulgent households are often less mature, more irresponsible and more conforming to their peers. Those who grow up in neglectful or indifferent families are those most at risk, as might be expected. They are likely to be more impulsive and to get involved in high-risk behaviour at an early age (Fuligni and Eccles, 1993; Kurdek and Fine, 1994).

There have been a number of attempts to look more closely at authoritative parenting, and to seek to understand its characteristics. Steinberg (1996) believes that this type of parenting has three core components. Such parents show warmth, in that they love and nurture their children; they provide structure, so that the young person has expectations and rules for his or her behaviour; and, lastly, they give autonomy support, in that they accept and encourage the young person's individuality. All these things are critical in providing a family environment in which autonomy is facilitated while parents also set limits, provide support and acceptance, and encourage achievement.

In one of the few European studies on this topic Shucksmith *et al.* (1995) studied families in Scotland, examining both parenting styles and a range of other variables, including age, social background and family type. Results were informative, since they showed that parenting styles were distributed across families, with permissive parenting being the most common. However, both authoritative and authoritarian parenting were more frequent when young people were at the beginning of adolescence, while permissive parenting was higher in families with older teenagers. In this sample neither psychological well-being nor school disaffection was related to parenting style. In discussion the authors point out that if permissive parenting predominates in this sample, then perhaps the time has come for a reassessment of our views of permissiveness, and an examination of why this style is more prevalent than others in Scotland. Juang and Silbereisen (1998) also carried out a study of parenting styles in two European countries – the former East and West Germany – and were able to show the positive impact of authoritative parenting independent of historical or geographic context.

To conclude this section, some mention needs to be made of the topic of monitoring and supervision. This is a feature of parenting behaviour which has received considerable attention, with studies consistently showing that poor monitoring by parents is linked to a variety of risk behaviours among young people, including offending, drug use, poor school performance and unsafe sex (see Patterson and Stouthamer-Loeber, 1984; Fletcher *et al.*, 1995). However, in a recent paper Stattin and Kerr (1999) have argued that these findings need to be treated with caution. Based on their own empirical work, they suggest that, rather than parental monitoring, it is the young person's disclosure or non-disclosure which is the key variable having links with problematic behaviour. Thus, what has been reported previously as parental monitoring has been measured by whether the parent knew where the young person was at any particular time. However, Stattin and Kerr have shown that parents know the whereabouts of their teenagers only if the teenagers disclose what they are doing. Monitoring and supervision is more a function of communication flowing from young person to parent, rather than of the parent being proactive in seeking information about the adolescent's activities. Clearly, this is a finding of some significance for research as well as for parenting practice, and further work in this area is imperative.

Culture and ethnicity

We have already noted Cooper's (1994) research on the development of autonomy in families from different ethnic backgrounds. While this is clearly a major variable, having an effect on virtually every aspect of family functioning, there is relatively little research to draw upon, particularly outside the context of North America. In this section we will review a few of the studies which have investigated the role of ethnicity in this area. A comparison often drawn is between the differences in time spent in the family setting and the emotional closeness of parents and adolescents in different cultures. Thus, Cooper (1994) showed greater expectations of family closeness in Chinese, Mexican and Vietnamese families in the USA than in European-American families. In a study by Facio and Batistuta (1998), a comparison was drawn between the family relationships described in Hendry *et al.* (1993) in a Scottish sample and those found in a small city in Argentina. The comparison was illuminating. In Argentina nearly 80 per cent of young people in the 15–16-year age-range reported having meals with their parents, while only 35 per cent of the Scottish sample did so. A general picture emerges of warm and positive relationships with both parents in Argentina, similar to studies of life in countries such as Spain and Italy, where relationships are close and where adolescents remain in the family home until well into adulthood.

Japanese culture provides an important comparison point, since, as Gjerde and Shimizu (1995) point out, the role of the father differs significantly from that to which we are accustomed in the West. In Japan the mother is the central parental figure, with the father being 'absent' for most of the time. In addition, any open expression of discord in the family is discouraged, so that conflict is difficult to manage. As Gjerde and others have made clear, little thought has yet been given to the ways in which Japanese cultural values impact on adolescent development, but in the Gjerde and Shimizu (1995) study they were able to show something of the complexity of family relationships. They examined parental agreement or disagreement on how the adolescent should be socialised, and linked this to mother–teenager cohesion and the adjustment of the young person. In brief, results showed that close relationships between teenager and mother (high cohesion) was adaptive so long as the parents were in agreement on matters to do with adolescent socialisation. However, where mother and father disagreed, then mother–teenager cohesion was related to poor adjustment. As the authors note, these results illustrate the fact that the father's role is highly significant, even if he is away from home and participates relatively rarely in family life.

Young people would have a very different experience of family life in Israel. There has been considerable interest in adolescent development in Israel, since, for those brought up on a kibbutz, peers and non-family adults have historically been more influential than parents. However, in recent years there has been a clear move towards what Kaffman (1993) calls the 'familistic revolution'. Partly as a result of the difficulties experienced by kibbutz-reared young people in the 1970s and 1980s, the family has grown in importance in recent years, to the point now that relationships with parents are as central to the young person as they are in European countries. The changes in family functioning are documented in Mazor (1993), providing a fascinating account of a shift in values concerning the role of the parent in adolescent life. In particular, it is argued that as a result of fears concerning a pervasive drug culture, and also the involvement of a number of young Israelis in cults and other destructive group experiences, this society began to believe that it needed to place more emphasis on the family, and reduce the power and influence of the peer group.

In the United States there have been a number of studies comparing styles of parenting in different ethnic groups. Results show that, by and large, there is less evidence of authoritative parenting (as defined in the previous section) in African-American, Asian-American or Hispanic-American families than in European-American families (Dornbusch et al., 1987; Steinberg et al., 1992). However, young people in ethnic minority families whose parents do use this style of parenting still appear to benefit as much as do those in European cultures. Two further findings are of interest here. First, authoritarian parenting is more common in ethnic minority communities, and, second, young people from White backgrounds are more adversely affected by authoritarian parenting than are minority young people (Steinberg et al., 1994). This may be because higher levels of parental control are more adaptive in communities where violence and risk are prevalent, or it may be, as Chao (1994) has suggested, that these dimensions of parenting style have less meaning in non-European cultures.

In conclusion, a distinction should be made between 'individualistic' and 'collectivist' cultures. This is a distinction well known to commentators on culture and values (e.g. Hofstede, 1983), but has particular relevance for any consideration of family life for adolescents. Essentially, in a 'collectivist' culture it is believed that the young person's behaviour and aspirations should centre around the reputation and success of the family and the community, rather than the wishes of the individual. In an 'individualistic' culture the opposite value system obtains, for here it is expected that the young person will seek to identify his or her own personal goals, and will be encouraged to find ways of reaching those goals without undue regard for the needs or wishes of the family or community as a whole. This distinction has been used frequently in studies of different cultures, but rarely in work with adolescents, which makes Gilani's (1995) study of mother–daughter relationships in Asian and White British familes a particularly useful one. Here, she traced the differences in the way the two cultures treated young women, and mothers' expectations in relation to the behaviour of their daughters. Overt conflict was significantly higher in White families, but at the same time young women felt that they had freedom to make decisions, to spend time with their friends, and to choose their life-style. Young women in Asian families had quite different experiences. For them the wishes of their parents came first. They were expected to spend most of their time in the family setting, to conform to family norms, and not to argue or disagree with their parents. Gilani explained these differences in terms of the two cultural types referred to above, an explanation which is helpful not only in the particular context of White and Asian families in Britain, but one which may have a wider relevance in families across the world.

Mothers and fathers

Differences between mothers and fathers in their relationships with their teen-agers has been a topic of enduring interest to researchers. Nonetheless, the picture which has emerged has been somewhat one-sided, since almost all studies have reported mothers as being more supportive, more interested in their sons and daughters, and more engaged in the parenting task. Youniss and Smollar (1985) may be taken as one example of this tendency. In their view, the role of fathers changes little from childhood to adolescence. Fathers, they believe, are important in setting long-term goals, in determining rules and providing discipline, and in acting as role-models. However, they do not get to know their teenagers as indi-vidual personalities or support them in their emotional progress through adoles-cence. Mothers are different:

> First, mothers maintain regular contact with their sons and daughters. Sec-ond, their contact is not focussed primarily on the children's future. Third, mothers engage themselves in adolescents' interests – whatever they might be. Fourth, mothers closely monitor their sons and daughters by acting both as disciplinarians and advisors. Fifth, mothers serve as confidants who share experiences – with the end result being empathy. To this end mutual-ity enters the relationship and the two parties come to be more like persons who see each other as they are, rather than as either is supposed to be.
>
> (1985, pp. 90–1)

While this may be a rather idealised picture, no one will have difficulty recognis-ing it as a representation of motherhood. Indeed, these authors are not alone in finding that mothers appear to play a different and more intimate role with both sons and daughters during this life stage. Research by Noller and colleagues on parent–adolescent communication supports the picture painted by Youniss and Smollar. In looking at communication between parents and teenagers, Noller and Callan (1991) report a situation in which mothers are more closely in touch with their adolescents than fathers on all topics except for one – politics! These findings are illustrated in Table 5.4.

One cannot help feeling that the positive picture painted by so many studies has as much to do with society's values as with the reality of mothering teenagers. It is also possible that the striking dearth of work on fathers may also have some-thing to do with the way we perceive men and parenthood. While, on the one hand, there is no dispute that the role of the father is critical in facilitating optimal develop-ment, on the other, failure to look closely at the needs and behaviour of men in the context of parenting is indicative of something more than difficulty in finding a time to interview them. However, there has of late been a growing number of writers focusing on this topic, as well as the publication of the first book dealing specifically with fathers and adolescents (Shulman and Seiffge-Krenke, 1997).

Table 5.4 Adolescents' perceptions of communication with mothers and fathers.

Topic	Mother	Father
Frequency		
Social issues	3.19	2.33
Interests	4.32	2.79
Sex-roles	3.03	2.01
Family sex-roles	2.59	1.98
Relationships	3.15	2.12
Sex attitudes	2.78	1.75
Politics	2.75	3.41
Sex information	1.93	1.36
Sex problems	1.54	1.21
General problems	4.15	3.24
Self-disclosure		
Interests	4.80	4.10
Sex-roles	4.10	3.50
Relationships	3.92	3.27
Sex information	3.42	2.45
Sex problems	3.32	2.32

Note: Ratings were on a 6-point scale from 1 = rarely discuss this to 6 = frequent long discussions; and 1 = have not disclosed any feelings to 6 = have disclosed all aspects of my views and feelings.
Source: Noller and Callan (1991).

It is clear from reviews of research in this book that involvement with fathering has positive benefits both for men as they progress through mid-life and for adolescents in their daily interactions within the family. In relation to the first point, Montemayor *et al.* (1993) assessed the degree of mid-life stress and the quality of fathers' interactions with their adolescents. Fathers were asked to report on their levels of stress in relation to such issues as work, marriage and health. Findings showed that mid-life stress was negatively correlated with the quality of interaction between these men and their adolescent children. Other studies have reported similar results, so that Greenberger and O'Neill (1990) have evidence relating stress at work to poor family relationships, and Silverberg and Steinberg (1990) were able to link both mothers' and fathers' mid-life concerns to the quality of contact with their teenagers.

As Shulman and Seiffge-Krenke (1997) point out, most discussions of fatherhood in adolescence have as a starting point a 'deficiency' model. Because the mother is seen as being the more involved parent, the father is in some way 'deficient'. Interestingly, not all studies report teenagers as being dissatisfied with their fathers. In both Hanson (1988) and Montemayor and Brownlee (1987) young people indicated that they felt satisfied with the role their fathers were playing in their lives. This can be explained if we look more closely at the differing roles played by mothers and fathers. In Power and Shanks (1988) interviews were carried out with parents regarding the behaviours they encouraged and discouraged. Results showed that fathers saw themselves as being more involved in encouraging instrumental behaviours such as independence and assertiveness, while mothers were more likely to encourage interpersonal skills and commitment to the family. Hauser *et al.* (1987) also looked at this question by analysing verbal interactions while parents and young people worked on a shared task. They found that fathers expressed more interest and support for adolescents' suggestions and ideas, whereas mothers expressed more constraining speech, which was less supportive of the young person. Thus, it is clear that mothers and fathers contribute alternative styles and interests to the parenting task. Without an acknowledgement of both contributions we will not achieve a realistic picture of family functioning during adolescence.

Divorce and the changing nature of families

Our understanding of the family has undergone a profound change during the latter part of this century. Today, a significant proportion of children and young people grow up in families either headed by a lone parent or in which some change has occurred in the parenting relationship. This was noted in Chapter 1. However, this is only partly as a result of divorce and separation. Figures illustrated in Figure 5.3 show also that single-parent families are on the increase, underlining the fact that it is not only increasing divorce rates which are at the heart of changing family structures. Attitudes and values about the family are also changing, especially in younger age groups. In Britain, more and more children born to those under 20 are born outside marriage (Babb and Bethune, 1995), indicating that conventional notions of marriage are being replaced by more fluid relationship structures. International comparisons show the USA having the highest rates of divorce, with Australia, New Zealand and the UK having rates which are lower but similar to each other (Rodgers and Pryor, 1998).

The last decade has seen a significant increase in studies looking at the effects of divorce and family reorganisation on children and young people. Buchanan *et al.* (1996) have reported on a major research project in the USA looking at different custody arrangements and their impact on young people, while in the UK Cockett and Tripp's (1994) Exeter study has provoked heated debate. In addition, analysis of the longitudinal National Child Development Study (Kiernan, 1997) has produced findings which emphasise poorer educational and economic outcomes for individuals who grow up in families affected by divorce. Rodgers and Pryor (1998) have carried out an invaluable review of British research in this field, providing a much-needed summary of findings to date. They point out that, based on current data, 28 per cent of young people in Britain will have experienced the divorce of their parents by the time they reach the age of 16. Such statistics underline how important it is to have a full understanding of the impact of divorce, and we will address some of the major themes which stem from research in the rest of this section.

The first question to consider is whether the developmental stage at which the divorce occurs has any significance for adjustment. While it is difficult to be sure about this, because so many studies confuse the timing of divorce with the

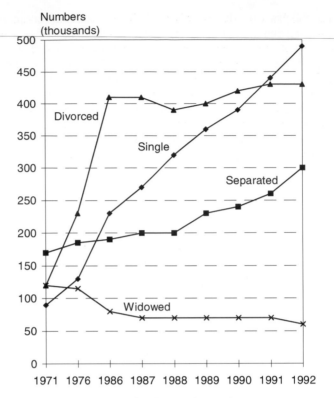

Figure 5.3 Numbers of lone-mother families in the UK by type, 1971–92.

Source: Coleman (1997a).

time which has elapsed since the divorce took place, we can say that it is probable that younger children are affected differently than adolescents. This is not only because of the cognitive capacity of the older individual, and his or her increasing ability to make intellectual sense of the experience, but also because of emotional maturation. As egocentricity diminishes the young person is able to see the situation from more than one viewpoint, which makes it easier to understand what is happening, and to cope with the feelings aroused. A number of studies have indicated that age is a factor to be taken into account, especially because of the young person's increasing emotional autonomy and opportunities for social support outside the family network. Hetherington (1993) reports that those experiencing divorce during the pre-adolescent period continue to demonstrate adjustment difficulties into adolescence, and Wallerstein and Blakeslee (1989) show that those who were very young at the time of the divorce experience difficulties in adolescence which were not apparent during childhood.

One important conclusion from all the research in this field is that divorce is a process rather than an event. This is demonstrated clearly in the research carried out in California by Buchanan *et al.* (1996). They looked at 1,500 children and young people over a six-year period, and were able to show the impact of events occurring both before and after the divorce itself. In particular, they emphasised the significance of continuing conflict between parents after divorce as being a key variable determining adjustment. Those young people who felt 'caught in the middle' and whose parents continued to fight after separation were much more affected by divorce than those whose parents managed their relationship in a more constructive manner. Buchanan and her colleagues also looked at how often custody arrangements altered in the years following divorce. Those young people who had experienced many changes and continuing upheaval in their lives coped less well, regardless of the nature of the custody arrangement. One young woman explains her feelings about her parents in this way:

> 'The worst thing has been the hate between the two of them. Knowing how much they hated each other and being in the middle of that. They were really so horrible to each other all the time, and all they'd do was slag each other off to me. And I hated it, I really did. I felt really in the middle and like I couldn't do anything about it. I think at first I felt like part of it was my fault and I should have stopped it but, I mean, I just couldn't. But I always carry it around, that I should have been able to stop it'.
>
> (16-year-old girl, quoted in Coleman, 1990, p. 18)

One of the key questions for researchers in this field has to do with the long-term consequences of divorce. As Rodgers and Pryor (1998) point out, numerous studies highlight the negative effects of divorce. Thus, there are reports of higher rates of delinquency (e.g. Wadsworth, 1979), poorer educational attainment (e.g. Kiernan, 1997), higher levels of drug and alcohol use (e.g. Hope *et al.*, 1998) and increased risk of mental-health problems (Garnefski and Diekstra, 1997; Rodgers *et al.*, 1997). Nonetheless, there are undoubtedly problems with the methodologies used in many of these studies, and, in particular, it is essential to take into account the effects of poverty and disadvantage which follow divorce for families headed by a lone parent.

Interestingly, not all writers believe that divorce is a negative experience. Some have argued that, for adolescents who have been exposed to chronic family conflict, parental separation can come as a relief (McLoughlin and Whitfield, 1984; Mitchell, 1985). In addition, others have pointed out that divorce may bring with it opportunities for greater autonomy and responsibility in the family, which can foster mature behaviour and enhance development among adolescents (McLoughlin and Whitfield, 1984; Barber and Eccles, 1992). In a meta-analysis of studies on this subject Amato and Keith (1991) were able to show that, while there are undoubtedly differences between children and young people from divorced and intact families in respect of their emotional well-being, the effects are relatively small. Similar findings are reported by Barber and Eccles (1992). Both sets of authors point out that the great majority of studies look at short-term consequences of divorce, which are likely to reflect distress. There is a need for more well-designed longitudinal studies, such as that of Buchanan *et al.* (1996), which may provide a different picture.

Two key variables also need to be taken into account in any attempt to look at divorce and its impact: the gender of the individual young person, and the family arrangements that follow separation and divorce. Numerous studies have attempted to look at these factors, but the results are far from consistent. One example of disagreement between researchers is highlighted by Buchanan *et al.* (1996). These authors report finding that in their study one predictor of good adjustment in young people was living with a remarried parent. By contrast, when the residential parent was living with a new partner, to whom he or she was not married, adjustment was worse in a number of ways, especially for boys. This finding is in contradiction to other research, which suggests that young people are worse off in stepfamilies than in families where a remarriage has not occurred (Ferri, 1984; Hetherington and Clingempeel, 1992). There is also some confusion concerning the differential adjustment of boys and girls. Most studies report that boys suffer more following divorce, especially those who live with their mothers (Hetherington, 1993). As we have seen, boys also did worse in the study by Buchanan and colleagues (1996). In this study there was a particularly marked effect for boys in situations where there was ongoing interparental conflict, whereas girls' adjustment appeared less influenced by this factor. However, not all studies report such clear gender differences. Thus, for example, Allison and Furstenberg (1989) report more similarities than differences between the genders in their reaction to parental divorce, as does Zaslow (1989). As Rodgers and Pryor (1998) point out, it may be that males and females manifest distress in different ways, so that in some studies the acting-out behaviour of the boys will simply get more attention than the less overt emotional manifestations of trauma exhibited by girls.

As remarriage and family reorganisation become more common it is crucial that research looks more closely at the experiences of young people in new families. A number of writers have underlined the difficulties for step-parents in entering families with teenagers, and psychologists such as Hetherington and Steinberg have made suggestions as to how such situations may best be managed. It is clearly of great importance that the new step-parent takes things slowly, and does not attempt to replace the non-residential parent. Several studies indicate that the adjustment of young people declines each time a new family change is experienced (Capaldi and Patterson, 1991; Kurdek and Fine, 1994). Thus, it is important for parents who have adolescents living with them following divorce to recognise the impact of change, and make every attempt to provide the young person with as much stability as possible. Of particular importance here is the need for teenagers to be able to remain in the same school, so that they do not have to make new friends at the same time as they have to adjust to new family arrangements. Here we can see a good example of the potential impact of multiple stressors, as discussed in Chapter 1 when considering the focal model. We will return to this issue in the final chapter of the book. Finally, it is worth mentioning the likelihood that relationships with step-parents will be affected by relationships with the non-residential parent. Young people living in stepfamilies were found by Buchanan *et al.* (1996) to do better if there is consistency in discipline between residential and non-residential families, and if the teenager is able to maintain good contact with the 'absent' parent.

As will be apparent, research in this field does not always come up with consistent results. This is partly because there are a variety of difficulties in carrying out such research. Many families will feel unable or unwilling to share their experiences with researchers because of their own distress or because of fears that young people will be negatively affected by discussing the family history. Thus, there may be a bias in the sample before the study commences. In addition, there are things like sample attrition in long-term studies, as well as the problems of finding control groups which are sufficiently similar so that realistic comparisons can be drawn. Apart from the research difficulties it may actually be the case that there are a wide range of experiences and responses to divorce and family reorganisation. Perhaps the remarriage of parents is more beneficial for some young people in some circumstances, and in some contexts, while in others the opposite is the case. There may not be any simple answers to the complex reality of family change.

In spite of this, however, it is important to be clear that some general conclusions can be drawn, as Richards (1996, 1997) indicates. Conflict both within a marriage and after divorce is damaging for children and young people. Following divorce, the economic impact is possibly of equal significance to any psychological effects, with relative poverty often having a devastating consequence on the family. Divorce brings with it a changed relationship to the non-residential parent – usually the father (Simpson *et al.*, 1995). It seems probable that the quality of relationship between the adolescent and both parents, as well as parenting style, influences adjustment more than actual living arrangements (McFarlane *et al.*, 1995). Finally, communication between the young person and the parents is critical for managing the family readjustment, yet research shows that at this time parents tell their children little about what is happening (Mitchell, 1985). These conclusions have important implications for practice, yet there remain many unanswered questions and contradictory findings. Future research will be of value only if there is an acknowledgement of the multitude of possible experiences for young people in separating and reorganising families.

Parenting teenagers

The topic of parenting appears to be receiving greater attention today than in previous decades. In the USA there has for some time been a recognition that parenting practices may hold the key to the problematic or anti-social behaviour of young people, but in Europe this recognition has dawned rather more slowly. Nonetheless, the situation is changing, and there is undoubtedly a growing interest in this subject in Britain. This is partly the result of work by Pugh *et al.* (1994) and Smith (1996), but it is also a consequence of political concerns over a perceived increase in youth crime and other socially unacceptable behaviour.

One important difference between parents of teenagers and parents of younger children has to do with uncertainty about the parenting role. For parents of young children there is little difficulty in defining roles and responsibilities, yet this is not the case for parents of adolescents. Part of this has to do with the changing nature of power and authority in the family. Today, parents of teenagers are not clear what is expected of them in relation to monitoring and supervision, or in setting boundaries and limits for a 14 year old, or in regulating homework or the amount of television watching that is allowable. Then there are things like confidentiality in relation to medical treatment and the appropriate age for somone to start having sex. Most parents feel at a loss over such matters, which leads to lowered self-confidence, heightened anxiety and less effective parenting (Coleman, 1997b).

In fact, there is much in the literature that can be used to guide and assist parents of teenagers. We have already mentioned the work of Baumrind (1971) and Maccoby and Martin (1983) in establishing dimensions of parenting style. We have also noted the importance of monitoring and supervision. Small and Eastman (1991) established a model of parental functions with four dimensions. These authors argue that parents of adolescents should be involved in meeting the basic needs of young people, in guiding and supporting development, in providing protection for young people, and in acting as advocates for their sons and daughters. Clearly, each of these functions is complex, and can be interpreted in different ways by different people. Nonetheless, Small and Eastman provide useful evidence to suggest that, if the functions are interpreted in an appropriate fashion, they contribute to optimal development. For example, under the rubric of guiding and supporting development they include positive role-modelling, setting boundaries, offering examples of conflict-resolution, providing warmth and concern, and so on. All these are tied to specific research findings.

There are other examples of research which have implications for parenting teenagers. The term 'induction' refers to the process whereby parents legitimise their authority by providing explanations for rules, and by helping young people see things from alternative perspectives. This style is associated with positive outcomes in childhood, and becomes even more significant in adolescence (Holmbeck et al., 1995). This is because, as Hill (1988) points out, the growing intellectual sophistication of the young person leads to an inevitable unwillingness to accept rules 'just because they are there'. Similar findings have been outlined regarding what are known as 'democratic' styles of conflict resolution. Baumrind (1991) showed that this approach to family decision-making was likely to be associated with greater self-esteem, more pro-social behaviour and higher levels of moral reasoning.

One final example may be given of the way in which research can be used to assist parents in developing effective strategies with this age group. The notion of perceived control was first explored by Bugenthal and colleagues in their work with abusive families (Bugenthal et al., 1989), and further developed in Goodnow and Collins (1990), a classic text on parenting. The idea of perceived control goes to the heart of the parenting dilemma. Essentially, it is argued, the more parents perceive that they are in control, the more effective they will be in managing the childcare environment and in providing authoritative rather than authoritarian discipline. The younger the child, the easier it will be for parents to feel that they are in control. With adolescence comes an increasing sense of loss of control, although clearly there will be much individual variation. The notion of perceived control hclps us understand how it feels for parents who believe that they have less and less influence over their teenagers.

Where parents see themselves as losing control over the young person's behaviour they are likely to do one of two things. They may become more anxious, and resort to an increasing use of coercive discipline. It is this group of parents who are more likely to use physical methods of punishment, and all the evidence shows that outcomes for families where such strategies are used are not good. Alternatively, adults who have low perceived control may become depressed and develop a sense of helplessness about their role as parents. In such situations mothers and fathers tend to give up, and let their teenagers go their own way, exhibiting permissive or indulgent parenting styles.

As will be apparent, there is much in the literature which could be of assistance to parents of teenagers, yet few are aware of this. Even those who do have access to such information might question how much it could help in the daily round of grumbling disputes over homework, untidy bedrooms, eating habits, too much television and so on. Why should this be so? First, it has to be acknowledged that the research community has not done a very good job of making the empirical evidence easily available to the public at large. Of course, this is not a problem restricted to adolescence, but the failure to take seriously the need to translate research evidence into useful and usable information is a real obstacle preventing a proper understanding of adolescence. Second, society has placed a low priority on the provision of information for parents of teenagers. While there is a wide range of materials available for parents of babies and younger children, the same cannot be said for the older age range. Parents whose children are reaching puberty or entering secondary school are not seen as a group who need support, and are, by and large, left to struggle with the task on their own.

To conclude this section, we will consider what can be done to improve matters, and briefly review some current initiatives. In terms of what can be done it is clearly essential that more information is made easily available to a broad range of parents. While, as we shall see, there is a growth of activity in this field, there is still a long way to go before the majority of parents receive appropriate support. More research is also needed, so that a clearer picture can emerge of the experiences of parents, and of their needs. Third, where parenting programmes and courses are being developed, the importance of evaluation is not always recognised. Systematic evaluation provides essential feedback, as well as encouragement to others as they see and hear about successful programmes.

In spite of what has been said, there is some good news. As Roker and Coleman (1998) show in their review of parenting programmes in the UK, there has been a significant increase in such programmes during the late 1990s. More programmes are becoming available, and there is greater interest among parents and professionals in this type of support. Results of evaluations also show that there are substantial benefits from involvement in programmes, in terms of both parental confidence and improved communication between parent and teenager. In addition to parenting programmes, there are other initiatives which may lead to new thinking in the field. Bogenschneider and Stone (1997) report on the use of newsletters sent to every parent regularly throughout the school year. These newsletters focus on issues to do with adolescent development, and have been shown to have an impact on attitudes and behaviour. Roker and Coleman (1999) are developing a whole-school approach to parent support, offering materials, advice and opportunities for discussion to all those who wish to make use of such services.

While such approaches are aimed at all parents, it should be noted that there are a range of projects directed at specific problem behaviours. Thus, Van

Acker (1997) has a worthwhile scheme for parents of conduct-disordered young people, and many readers will know of the initiatives coming out of the Oregon Social Learning Centre aimed at young offenders and those involved in substance abuse (Patterson *et al.*, 1993). We will give more attention to such programmes in Chapter 10, when we consider anti-social behaviour.

There are many obstacles to the provision of universal support for parents of teenagers. Spoth *et al.* (1996) looked at the explanations given by parents for non-attendance at school-based programmes in the USA, and found that limitations of time and difficulties of scheduling were the most commonly cited reasons. In addition, it is apparent that concerns about privacy are important to many parents of adolescents. It may well be that there is more shame associated with perceived parenting failure at this age than there is about problems with younger children (Goodnow and Collins, 1990). If this is the case, some parents may well avoid situations where open discussion of problems at home would be expected. Nonetheless, the evidence is encouraging. More interest is being taken in the subject of parenting during adolescence, and there is no doubt that work in this field will pay substantial dividends in terms of heightened parental self-esteem and better communication within the family.

Implications for practice

1. The first point to make is that recent studies of the development of autonomy indicate that young people do not separate entirely from their parents during the adolescent stage. By and large, it would be true to say that a continuing connectedness with parents, for both young men and young women, is helpful for a transition to adulthood.

2. In spite of a general public belief that adolescence is characterised by high levels of conflict in the home, research does not support this conclusion. While there are many issues about which parents and young people disagree, in general, relationships appear to be more positive than negative, and in the majority of families there is no evidence of substantial intergenerational conflict. Many factors will have an impact on the level of conflict, and, in particular, good communication between parents and young people has the effect of reducing conflict. As might be expected, conflict is highest where parents themselves have poor relationships, where the family is experiencing stress or difficulty because of environmental factors, or where there is a long-standing impairment of parental function.

3. In recent years there has been a growing interest in parenting styles. Research has shown consistently that authoritative parenting has the most beneficial effect on adolescent development, since this includes warmth, structure and support for autonomy. By contrast, authoritarian, indifferent or indulgent parenting styles have effects which, while differing to some extent, all encourage less adaptive adolescent development.

4. A small trickle of studies has begun to address the issue of race and ethnicity, and its impact on parental relationships with adolescents. While

more research in this area is urgently needed, we can conclude that ethnicity plays a key role in the way parents behave towards teenagers in different cultures. For practitioners it is essential, therefore, to recognise that there will be variation among cultures, and that what is expected in one setting will not necessarily be expected in another. Where racial background is associated with disadvantage or overt prejudice, parents may respond to these circumstances with parenting styles which they see as adaptive and/or protective of their teenage children. Such styles may differ from those seen as adaptive in majority cultures, where there is less likelihood of prejudice or harassment.

5. Relatively little attention has been directed towards the role of the father in relation to adolescent development, but recent studies have underlined the importance of this role. The necessity of avoiding a 'deficit' model of fathering has been stressed, and it is clear that more effort is needed to support fathers during the stage when children become teenagers.

6. Research findings on the impact of divorce are not always consistent, partly because the subject itself is difficult to study. Nonetheless, it is clear that conflict between parents, whether they are living together or apart, has damaging consequences for children and young people. It is clear also that the economic effects of divorce are almost as significant as the psychological ones, with relative poverty having a major influence on adolescent adjustment. While living arrangements post-divorce are important, they appear to have less of an impact on long-term adjustment than relationships with both parents, parenting style and communication. The most significant practical conclusion is that divorce is part of a process, and that adjustment will be influenced by a range of experiences, rather than by the divorce itself. By and large, the fewer life changes the young person has to cope with, the better he or she will cope with parental separation.

7. The parenting of adolescents has received increased attention in the last few years. Studies have considered different types of education and support for this group of parents, and it is clear that interventions can have a positive effect on parental confidence and esteem. There are, however, numerous barriers to the provision of support for all parents of teenagers, and more work is needed to identify the means whereby effective support can be delivered to as many parents as possible.

Further reading

Furstenberg, F (1990) Coming of age in a changing family system. In Feldman, S and Elliott, G (Eds) *At the threshold: the developing adolescent.* Harvard University Press. Cambridge, MA.
This is another review chapter in the Feldman and Elliott text. The author is, arguably, one of the best-known researchers in the field of family studies in the USA, and in this chapter he shows his breadth of knowledge and perspective on social change and its impact on the families of young people over the past fifty years.

Hess, L (1995) Changing family patterns in Western Europe: opportunity and risk factors for adolescent development. In Rutter, M and Smith, D (Eds) *Psychosocial disorders in young people*. John Wiley. Chichester.

This is another key contribution to the subject of social change and its effects on adolescents, but this time from a European viewpoint. As with other chapters in this book by Rutter and Smith it is of a very high standard, posing a range of interesting and challenging questions.

Noller, P and Callan, V (1991) *The adolescent in the family*. Routledge. London.

A useful book by two Australian authors summarising research on all aspects of family functioning which concern young people. The authors have done a number of studies themselves in this field, and the findings are admirably summarised at various points in the book.

Rodgers, B and Pryor, J (1998) *Divorce and separation: the outcomes for children*. Joseph Rowntree Foundation. York.

An up-to-date review of research on divorce and its impact on children and young people. Short and readable.

Shulman, S and Seiffge-Krenke, I (1997) *Fathers and adolescents: developmental and clinical perspectives*. Routledge. London.

One of the only books on the role of fathers with adolescents. It covers clinical as well as research topics, and provides a valuable discussion of important questions concerning fathers and the difficulties they face as their children grow up.

Steinberg, L (1990) Autonomy, conflict and harmony in the family relationship. In Feldman, S and Elliott, G (Eds) *At the threshold: the developing adolescent*. Harvard University Press. Cambridge, MA.

This chapter by Steinberg in the Feldman and Elliott text is of exceptional quality. The author contributes one of the best reviews of this subject that we have yet seen. Well worth reading.

Adolescent sexuality

Sexual development is a central strand of all adolescent experience. Underlying this is the biological maturation which starts at the outset of puberty and continues for at least three or four years. However, sexual development involves not only biological change, but also growth and maturation in the social and emotional worlds of the young person. In this chapter we will document some of these changes, and consider how the experiences of adolescents interact with and are affected by the context in which they grow up. Adolescent sexuality is influenced by a range of factors; these may be internal, as for example the rate of pubertal maturation, or they may be external, such as the type of family and neighbourhood, and the political climate of the time. The developing sexuality of the young person may be a source of considerable anxiety, both to teenagers themselves and to the adults responsible for their care or education. This is especially so where young people appear to be at risk of unwanted pregnancy or infection from sexually transmitted diseases. In this chapter we will consider the question of safer sexual behaviour, as well as sex education, pregnancy prevention and early parenthood.

Changing patterns of sexual behaviour

There is a general belief that sexual permissiveness reached its height in the 1960s, and that more recently young people have shown greater restraint and a more conservative attitude to sexual behaviour. Before this question is addressed, we have to note that the available evidence concerning the sexual behaviour of adolescents is limited. Thus, for example, there have been very few studies of the sexual behaviour of those under the age of 16, in spite of the fact that, as pointed out in Chapter 2, there is a real possibility of earlier maturation today than was the case in previous decades. In addition, it is apparent that methods for the study of adolescent sexual behaviour have serious limitations. For example, results from one piece of research which interviewed adolescents on more than one occasion show that the timing of first sexual intercourse was reported inconsistently by 67 per cent of the young people in the study (Alexander et al., 1993).

Nonetheless, we do have some evidence to draw upon, and from this it is difficult not to conclude that today more young people are becoming sexually active at a younger age than in the 1960s or the 1970s. To consider this issue, let us begin by looking at the age of first sexual intercourse. In the most extensive study ever carried out in Britain, which is also the most recent, Wellings et al. (1994) interviewed 18,000 adults and young people over the age of 16. If we look at the numbers of individuals who report having had intercourse before the age of 16, we can see great differences between the age groups. Figures in Table 6.1 show that the younger the individual the more likely he or she is to have had sex before the age of 16.

Another way of looking at the same question is to compare the results of three studies carried out in Britain over the past thirty years. Schofield (1965), Farrell (1978) and Wellings et al. (1994) all have data on the number of 16 to 19 year olds reporting having had intercourse before the age of 16. As can be seen from Figure 6.1, the numbers falling into this category have risen steadily over

Table 6.1 First sexual intercourse before the age of 16 by current age.

Age at interview	Males		Females	
	%	Base	%	Base
16–19	27.6	827	18.7	971
20–24	23.8	1137	14.7	1251
25–29	23.8	1126	10.0	1519
30–34	23.2	1012	8.6	1349
35–39	18.4	982	5.8	1261
40–44	14.5	1042	4.3	1277
45–49	13.9	827	3.4	1071
50–54	8.9	684	1.4	933
55–59	5.8	603	0.8	716

Source: Wellings *et al.* (1994).

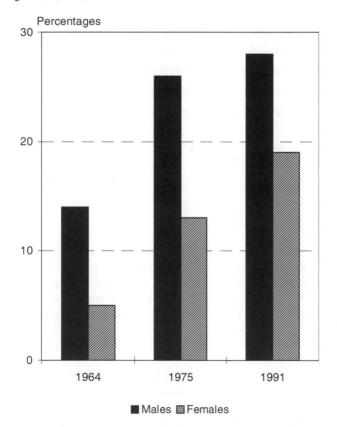

Figure 6.1 First sexual intercourse before the age of 16 by gender: data from three different studies.

Source: Schofield (1965); Farrell (1978) and Wellings *et al.* (1994).

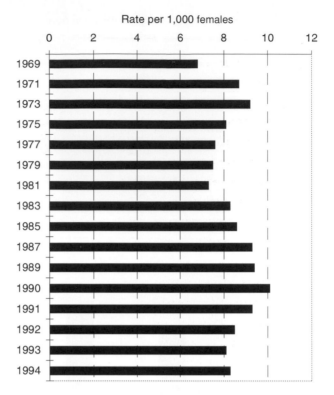

Rate per 1,000 females

Figure 6.2 Teenage conceptions in England and Wales, 1969 to 1994: rates per 1,000 women aged 13–15.

Source: Coleman (1997a).

this period, although it may be that the change has been slower for young women than it has been for young men.

Evidence from other countries indicates similar trends. Thus, for example, in Australia Goldman and Goldman (1988) report that, while in 1980 40 per cent of 17 year olds were sexually active, this figure had risen to 60 per cent by the end of the 1980s. As far as the USA is concerned, evidence summarised in Steinberg (1996) indicates that in the 1990s approximately 33 per cent of boys and 25 per cent of girls have had sex by the age of 15. However, as Steinberg points out, these figures mask very large regional and ethnic variations. It is clear that African-Americans, for example, are likely to become sexually active at an earlier age than European-Americans.

Another change noted by some commentators is the possibility that young people today are likely to engage in a wider range of sexual behaviours than was the case in previous decades. Thus, for example, the practice of oral sex appears to be widespread among adolescents, and there has been a shift in formerly negative attitudes to less conventional sexual behaviour. In Ford and Morgan's (1989) study the authors reported that among 18 year olds 46 per cent of young men and 28 per cent of young women had engaged in oral sex with casual partners. Corres-

Rate per 1,000 females

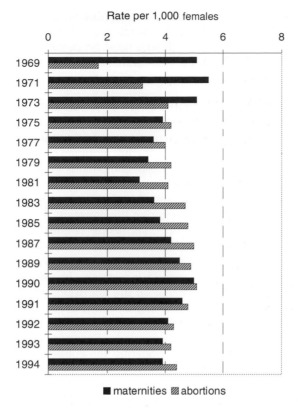

Figure 6.3 Rates of maternities and abortions in England and Wales among 13–15 year olds, 1969–94.

Source: Coleman (1997a).

ponding figures for regular or steady partners were 56 per cent and 58 per cent. In another British study Breakwell and Fife-Shaw (1992) found that 9 per cent of their sample, who were between the ages of 16 and 20, had engaged in anal sex. Studies in Australia show that among vulnerable groups, such as the homeless, rates for sexual practices such as these are much higher (Moore and Rosenthal, 1998).

Another perspective on changes in sexual behaviour may be obtained from statistics on teenage-pregnancy rates. However, these rates do not really tell us about the level of sexual activity, since clearly contraceptive use, or non-use, is the determining factor here. Evidence illustrated in Figure 6.2 indicates that rates of conception in the 13 to 15 age group in England and Wales have not increased markedly since 1970, although, as might be expected, there have been annual fluctuations. It can be seen that the rate in 1971 was 8.7 per 1,000 women, while in 1996 it was 9.4 per 1,000 women.

Where change has occurred, however, has been in the numbers of abortions carried out with young women in this age group. The number of terminations has gradually increased over the years, so that today only 50 per cent of conceptions to young women under 16 lead to maternity. The data shown in Figure 6.3

illustrate a substantial change in attitude among professional adults, assisted by a change in the law in Britain in 1969. Nonetheless, there are still a significant number of young women giving birth who must be considered very young parents, a topic to which we will return later in this chapter.

The context and timing of adolescent sexual behaviour

It may appear self-evident, but it is important to state that the sexual behaviour of young people takes place in the context of adult attitudes and behaviour. In much public debate on this subject commentators and pundits give the impression that they think teenagers are somehow cut off or detached from what is going on in the rest of society. Adolescents are blamed for having permissive attitudes, or for indulging in casual sex without considering the consequences. The fact is, however, that the sexual development of young people is affected in a fundamental sense by what is taking place around them. Today we live in a society which is remarkably open about sexuality. Many of the taboos which operated thirty years ago have disappeared, and as a result sex is pervasive in our lives.

Young people see sexual material on the television, on film and video, on advertising hoardings and in teenage magazines. More importantly, they know about adults around them, whether in the family or in the neighbourhood, who are having sexual relationships outside marriage. They can see that adults pursue sexual gratification without always considering the consequences, they can see that adults place sexual satisfaction high on their list of personal goals, and not, surprisingly, young people are influenced by such experience. To believe that adolescents somehow live in a world of their own is both unrealistic and unhelpful. We will not be able to understand adolescent sexuality unless we recognise the context in which it occurs and acknowledge the major influences of adult society.

Of the range of social factors impacting on the sexuality of the young it is perhaps the family which should be considered first. Writers such as Katchadourian (1990), Moore and Rosenthal (1995), and Taris and Semin (1997) have outlined the ways in which parents and other family members influence young people in this sphere. First, parents have attitudes about sexuality. These may be to do with the body and its functions, about privacy, about pleasure, about shame and guilt, and of course about the nature of intimate relationships. Parents will also have attitudes about gender, including things such as sex-roles, power distribution, and communication between men and women. All these parental attitudes will be influential in the way in which the boy or girl develops sexually. In addition to attitudes, parents also represent role-models for young people. Thus, the way the mother and father relate to each other, the way they deal with decision-making, the way they treat each other, and the way they behave sexually will offer powerful models which will undoubtedly influence their children.

One obvious example of this is the substantial body of research showing that young people in families where parents have divorced or separated are likely to become sexually active at an earlier age than those living in intact families (Newcomer and Udry, 1985; Miller and Bingham, 1989). In a recent study Crockett *et al.* (1996) compared the effects of living with a single parent to other variables such as socio-economic status, pubertal timing, school performance, sibling behaviour and so on. These authors showed that of all the variables, parental circumstance was the most significant factor influencing sexual debut, for both boys and girls. A variety of explanations have been put forward for this finding, including exposure to permissive sexual norms, as well as reduced parental monitoring and supervision. As one young woman explained:

> 'If your parents are divorced or separated, and your mum or dad brings home different people on weekends and each night of the week and stuff, then you sort of think that (having sex) is no big deal. It is not special or anything like that. But if your parents are married and stuff like that, you sort of see it as a big deal, and should only share it if you love the person'.
> (16-year-old woman, quoted in Moore and Rosenthal, 1995, p. 65)

Taris and Semin (1997) remind us that there are other ways too in which parents may be influential. In some circumstances, and with regard to some issues, parents may be the most effective sex educators, especially if they are open without being intrusive, and willing to deal with the young person's agenda, rather than their own. As we have noted above, parents can offer monitoring and supervision, assisting teenagers to delay involvement in sexual activity. Alternatively, they may leave young people to set their own boundaries, and make their own decisions about the pace of their sexual development. In a good study by Meschke and Silbereisen (1997) it was shown that the greater the degree of parental monitoring, the later the sexual debut of young people in former East and West Germany. In this context it is also important to mention religion. There is good evidence to show that religious faith impacts on sexual behaviour during adolescence (Thornton and Camburn, 1987). Those who have religious beliefs are likely to delay sexual activity, and may also be more prone to guilt and anxiety about this area of their lives. Religious attitudes in young people are also strongly linked to parental beliefs.

A number of studies have considered the differential impact of parent and peer influence on sexual behaviour. An example of such work is that reported by Treboux and Busch-Rossnagel (1995). In this study, discussion of sexual topics with parents and friends, perceived approval of sexual behaviour, sexual attitudes and actual sexual behaviour were assessed in a large sample of young women aged between 15 and 19. Results showed that the influence of parents and friends varied as a function of age. The effect of discussion with the mother was strongest in those between 15 and 17, while the effect of friends' approval was most marked in the 19-year-old group. A model developed by these authors is illustrated in Figure 6.4.

A different approach to this issue is exemplified by the important work of Udry and his colleagues (Udry and Billy, 1987; Udry, 1990). Udry has been concerned to distinguish between social and biological influences on sexual behaviour. By measuring the levels of different hormones during adolescence, as well as sexual behaviour and the attitudes of friends and parents, Udry has constructed a model of social and biological interaction. Using this model, he is able to show

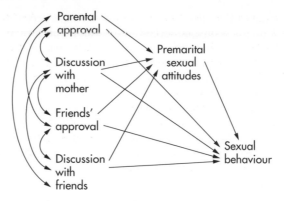

Figure 6.4 Hypothesised model of the relationships among parent and peer variables, sexual attitudes, and sexual behaviour.

Source: Treboux and Busch-Rossnagel (1995).

that social factors are far more important in influencing girls' involvement in sexual intercourse than boys' involvement. Although increases in the hormone androgen lead to an increased interest in sex among girls, whether this interest is translated into behaviour depends on the social environment. Girls who have high levels of androgens will only become sexually active if they have friends who are similarly inclined, or parents who are permissive. If such girls are in a less encouraging environment then they are unlikely to be sexually active. These social controls do not appear to act in the same way for boys, in whom high levels of androgens are likely to lead to sexual activity, regardless of the social context. To explain these gender differences, Udry argues that boys develop in an environment which is generally more tolerant and encouraging of male sexuality than of female sexuality. As a result, the stimulus given to boys by the changes in their hormone levels is quite sufficient to instigate sexual behaviour. For girls the situation is more complex, where social controls may be more influential in determining behaviour.

Finally, in looking at the question of influences on sexual behaviour it is important to consider the role of communication. As we all know, the topic of sex can be acutely embarrassing, especially for young people. Many will sympathise with this young woman, who recalls her mother's attempt to talk seriously with her about the matter.

'It must have been when we were having stuff at school on it, and one day I remember I was walking along the track, and Mum says to me: "So you know how to do it now then?" So I said well I knew it already, you know, because I did. Then she said: "You know properly now, and all this lot". And I was getting really embarrassed, and I was saying yeh, like this, and I was trying to get on to a different subject. And she was saying: "So you know how to make a baby, and how to look after a baby" and all this rubbish. So I goes "yes Mum", and I was trying to get off the subject all the time.'

(Coleman, 1995, p. 3)

Communication on the subject of sexuality has been the focus of a number of studies. A study which compared communication with parents and peers was carried out by Moore and Rosenthal (1991) in Australia. In this research it was found that 69 per cent of sexually active young people felt that they could discuss any concerns they had with their friends, while only 33 per cent felt this way about discussing sexual problems with their mother, and even fewer (15 per cent) felt able to discuss such things with their father. Similar percentages were reported for discussions about contraception. However, the authors note that when it came to the offer of practical help, such as visiting a sexual-health clinic, friends were less of a resource. Only 22 per cent reported having had a friend accompany them to a doctor or assisting them in a practical manner.

As Moore and Rosenthal (1991) indicate, peers clearly have a significant role to play in the sex education of young people. However, there is a question about the nature of this influence. Many have reported that information purveyed by peers is less likely to be accurate than information which originates from adults (e.g. Kraft, 1993). In addition, peers may be less supportive than important adults when young people are in difficulty and need concrete help or direction. One of the challenges for adults is to find ways of maximising the positive influences of peers, and ensuring that more accessible information is available to young people. This would reduce the chance of inaccurate facts being communicated in the playground.

Romance and intimacy

One of the criticisms that is sometimes levelled at academic researchers engaged in studying sexuality in young people is that there is far too much emphasis on behaviour (on who has done what at which age), and too little interest in the meaning of sexual relationships. It is important, therefore, to pay some attention to ideas of love, romance and intimacy. This is especially so, since we know that an experience of passionate love, or an all-consuming involvement in an intimate relationship, can become the most important thing in a young person's life.

As commentators have frequently noted, falling in love is an integral part of the adolescent experience. Both Zani (1993) and Moore and Rosenthal (1998) draw on the ideas of Erikson, and suggest that falling in love is part of the search for identity or self-definition. As they point out, for Erikson the resolution of the identity crisis depends partly on the ability to experience intimacy. For Erikson, intimacy involves openness, sharing, trust and commitment. Thus, an experience of intimacy contributes to the development of identity, and maturity, through opportunities for self-exploration. The intimate relationship enables the young person to hold up a mirror to himself/herself, even if it is a distorted one, as well as to experience a sense of extraordinary closeness with another, which must in some way echo the contact between mother and child in infancy. It is perhaps for this reason that falling in love during the adolescent years has an intensity different from that experienced in adulthood.

Up to this point, research has contributed relatively little to our understanding of love and romance during the teenage years. There have, however, been a

Table 6.2 Positive aspects of romantic relationships.

Qualities	Girls %	Boys %	Total %
Likes about dating partner			
Positive personality traits	85	88	86
Physical attraction[a]	46	68	57
Intimacy[b]	42	26	34
Support[c]	44	14	29
Companionship	27	24	26
Common interests	6	10	8
Advantages of having a dating partner			
Companionship	71	60	66
Intimacy[d]	54	32	43
Support	36	23	30
Friendship	18	16	17
Social status[e]	18	7	12
Learn about opposite sex	9	16	12

[a] $x^2 = 4.11$, $p = .04$. [b] $x^2 = 3.01$, $p = .08$. [c] $x^2 = 9.51$, $p = .001$. [d] $x^2 = 4.73$, $p = .03$. [e] $x^2 = 3.05$, $p = .08$.
Source: Feiring (1996).

few attempts to construct scales or measurement devices relevant to the experience of falling in love. Hatfield and Sprecher (1986) devised a Passionate Love Scale, while Levesque (1993) constructed a Love Experience Index. Both of these were used to explore the components of love in adolescence, and both came up with similar ideas. So, for example, both include measures of elation, sexual arousal, and the need for closeness and acceptance by the loved one, as well as a dimension of pain and distress when difficulties occur. Taking a somewhat different approach, Feiring (1996) looked at experiences of romance in a sample of 15 year olds. This study reported some interesting findings. First, it was shown that at this age dating relationships were of shorter duration than stable same-sex friendships. The mean length of romantic relationships in this group was only three to four months, compared with a year or more for same-sex friendships. However, the contact involved in romantic relationships was much more intense. Young people reported spending hours talking each day either face-to-face or on the telephone. Feiring also noted gender differences, very similar to those found in studies of peer-group functioning. Thus, girls stress the importance of disclosure and support, while boys emphasise the place of shared activities in romantic relationships. In addition, boys are more likely than girls to mention physical attractiveness as a factor in relationship satisfaction. We will have more to say about gendered constructions of sexuality in the next section. Some of Feiring's findings are illustrated in Table 6.2.

    Close relationships of a sexual nature during this stage of development have a high degree of impact on the young person's adjustment. As we have noted, such relationships have a major role to play in the gradual, sometimes painful, construction of a coherent identity. While they may be short-lived, these experiences shape future choices as well as perceptions of self-worth. If the young person manages the break-up of the relationship without too much trauma, and emerges in some sense richer and wiser, then the next step may be developmentally that much more mature. On the other hand, if the loss is too painful, and the experience not fully integrated into other aspects of growth, then it may take some time before new learning can take place. In any event, we should not underestimate the significance of intimate relationships for adolescents. It is true that the research community has, by and large, paid little attention to this aspect of sexuality. One hopes that the focus will change in the years to come.

Young people and safer sex

There is no doubt that the advent of the AIDS/HIV phenomenon in the 1980s had a profound effect on attitudes to sex, as well as on sexual behaviour itself. First, it became apparent to everyone that unprotected sex could have terrible consequences. Of course, unprotected sex had always had consequences, both from sexually transmitted diseases and as a result of pregnancy. Yet, somehow, the concept that an individual could die because of a casual sexual encounter made an impact quite different in scale from anything that had gone before. Enormous sums of money were made available for new approaches to sex education, as well as for research initiatives to investigate the sexual behaviour and life-styles of many groups, including young people. The impact of the AIDS/HIV scare on adolescents has been documented by many writers, including Aggleton *et al.* (1991), Williams and Ponton (1992), and Moore *et al.* (1996).

Looking back on this period, we can see that the anxiety generated by governments and the media in Europe was exaggerated. Today we know that, in the European context, HIV infection is a serious health risk for groups such as intravenous drug users and those involved in casual homosexual acts. For the great majority of young people, however, it poses a relatively minor risk, and this has led to changed public attitudes to HIV/AIDS. Indeed, it may be said that the pendulum has swung too far in the opposite direction, to the extent that young people no longer consider AIDS to be something they need to worry about. Nonetheless, the appearance of this sexually transmitted disease has had a profound effect on virtually everything to do with sexuality, and we will now consider some of the changes that have occurred.

First, the spotlight has been thrown on the topic of sexual knowledge. In the early stages of awareness there was an understandable concern over public ignorance of the disease, and numerous schemes were initiated to improve levels of understanding. Studies such as those of Kraft (1993) in Scandanavia, Dunne *et al.* (1993) in Australia, and Winn *et al.* (1995) in the UK all documented the sexual knowledge of young people. Interestingly, the results of many of these studies highlighted the fact that, although there were some gaps in adolescents' knowledge of HIV/AIDS, on the whole, young people knew more about this topic than they knew about fertility, contraception or other sexually transmitted diseases. This is no doubt explained by the high level of publicity given to AIDS in the media at the time these studies were taking place, but it is nevertheless a worrying finding, and has led to calls for a new look at the sex-education curriculum. We will return to this subject later in the chapter. Of course, it rapidly became clear that knowledge would not necessarily change behaviour, and the focus shifted to other factors which might influence 'safer-sex' practices.

Data from the Wellcome study of sexual behaviour in the UK (Wellings *et al.*, 1994) indicate that there has been a steady increase in the numbers of teenagers using a contraceptive at first intercourse. Condoms are used more often than any other method, with half of all young people reporting this method for their first sexual experience: 20 per cent report the use of the pill, while 24 per cent report using no method at all. In the Wellcome study an attempt was made to define 'unsafe sex', this being identified as having two or more partners in the previous year, but never using a condom in that time. According to the results, approximately 10 per cent of the sample in the age range 16–24 fell into this category, although this may be an underestimate, because various groups were excluded from the analysis.

A number of studies have tried to identify the risk factors of having unprotected sex. Although lack of knowledge may be one factor, it is likely to play a relatively minor part in the overall picture (Moore *et al.*, 1996). More important is the age of the individual concerned. Wellings *et al.* (1994) report that the younger the person at first intercourse, the more likely they are to have unprotected sex. Thus, in the Wellcome study results showed that nearly half of all young women, and over half of all young men who had sex under the age of 16 were likely to use no contraceptive on the first occasion. Other factors include lack of access to contraceptive advice and lack of confidence in being able to purchase or obtain condoms. Groups who are particularly vulnerable include those who have behavioural problems, those who are homeless or in care, or those who are already prone to risk-taking behaviour (Feldman *et al.*, 1995; Crockett *et al.*, 1996; Breakwell and Millward, 1997). Perhaps most important of all, however, is the social and psychological context of early sexual activity, and it is to this that we now turn.

The easiest way to understand how unprotected sex can occur is to consider the requirements for the use of a condom. First, they have to be purchased, and to be available at the right moment. Next, it has to be acceptable to both partners to admit that one of you has planned to have sex. It is also probably necessary to be able to discuss the use of a contraceptive, and to feel confident enough with each other to risk interrupting sexual arousal. In addition, of course, all this assumes that at least one partner is sober and rational at the beginning of the encounter. When you are young, at the beginning of a relationship, and not at all sure of the other person, it is hardly surprising that in some situations not all these conditions are met.

Apart from lack of confidence, and all the other anxieties that are an inevitable part of growing up, the most significant factor that has to be considered is that of gender difference. There have been a number of important discussions on the topic of gendered constructions of sexuality over the past decade (e.g. Lees, 1993; Thomson and Holland, 1998; Holland *et al.*, 1998). Hillier *et al.* (1998) get to the heart of the matter in their article entitled: '"When you carry condoms all the boys think you want it"'. As many of these writers make clear, a double standard operates in the sexual arena, whereby sexual prowess for men is something to be proud of, while for women it is something to keep quiet about. Indeed, young women who are known to be sexually active are often called the most derogatory names within the peer group. No doubt closely associated with this is the fact that women have less power than men in relation to decision-making over contraceptive use. Thus, they are more likely to defer to men, and to be influenced by the fact that condom use is less pleasurable for men than the use of other types of contraceptive. The use of safer-sex practices depends on trust between partners, as well as on a degree of planning and communication. Research over the past decade has illustrated that there is a wide range of obstacles to safer sex in this age group. A greater recognition of the social and psychological factors operating in sexual encounters is necessary, as is a more holistic approach to sex education.

Lesbian and gay sexuality in adolescence

During the past ten years there has been a much greater recognition of the place of lesbian and gay sexuality in adolescence. In the previous edition of this book this topic was hardly mentioned, and yet in the intervening years public perceptions have changed, and there has been a growing acknowledgement of the fact that no consideration of sexual development during the teenage years can be complete without some discussion of sexual orientation. Before turning to the substantive issues, we should perhaps mention one or two points about terminology. The terms 'gay' and 'lesbian' have been used rather than 'homosexual', since they are generally seen as carrying more positive evaluations of same-sex behaviour and identity. Many discussions of this topic also include some consideration of bisexual youth. This topic is important too, since it is clear that some young people's feelings are not necessarily or exclusively oriented solely to one sex or the other. There are some who have sexual feelings directed to both men and women, and these individuals may identify themselves as 'bisexual'.

One key issue which has received considerable attention in the literature is the development of a gay or lesbian identity. There are commentators who believe that it is helpful to identify a number of stages in this process (see e.g. Cass, 1984; Goggin, 1995). Writers such as these point to four stages in the identity-development process. First, there is the stage of 'sensitisation'. During this stage the child or young person begins to be aware that he or she may be different from others. He or she may have different interests, or may begin to recognise sexual feelings that are not the same as those experienced by others of the same gender. The second stage is that of 'identity confusion'. Here, the individual experiences an altered awareness of the self, sexual arousal associated with those of the same gender, a sense of stigma surrounding gay or lesbian behaviour, and inaccurate information concerning homosexuality. The third stage is that known as 'identity assumption'. Here, the young person begins to take on the identity of someone who is either gay or lesbian, and is able to express that identity to others, at least to close friends. The final stage is that of 'commitment'. At this point the individual can make a commitment to an intimate relationship with someone of the same gender, and is also able to disclose to family and other important people.

It has to be noted that some writers (e.g. Coyle, 1998), have serious concerns about the identification of stages of identity development. First, the notion of stages implies that individuals all go through the same processes in the same sequence, yet clearly this will not be so. Also, we know that there is great variability in the way young people come to the realisation of their gay or lesbian identity. Some may know from an early age, while others will remain confused and uncertain throughout adolescence. It will be most helpful to consider the stages outlined above as examples of the tasks and issues faced by young people who may be gay or lesbian, rather than seeing them as an unvarying framework for identity development. One young man describes his own personal identity development thus:

'I suppose I started having sexual feelings – I didn't categorise them in any way – from the age of 11 I suppose, and those feelings carried on until I was 14 or 15. It was only then, through watching television and talking to friends, that I would categorise some of them, not all of them, as gay thoughts. The actual process of realising that I was one of those 'poof' things that everybody had been talking about at school, was a very long process. It didn't really finish until I was 16, maybe 17, very late on really. I just thought they were ordinary sexual feelings, which in fact they were. It's just through images and things in the media, and social pressures, that our sexual feelings get channelled in one direction or another, and in mainstream society one of those feelings is good and okay and normal, and the other types are bad and to be got rid of and evil.'

(20-year-old man, quoted in Coleman, 1995)

One of the key issues facing any young person in this situation is homophobia. While it is undoubtedly true that there have been significant changes in attitude among professional adults, there is still an enormous degree of stigma associated with homosexuality, especially among young people themselves. Thus, any individual who begins to feel that he or she may be gay or lesbian has to develop coping strategies to deal with the hostility and ignorance that surrounds the subject. Of course, the most common strategy is to keep one's feelings private, and this has critical implications for young people in this situation. If there is no forum to discuss homosexuality, and no easy means to obtain information about gay and lesbian life-styles, then naturally individuals will feel even more uncertain and confused, as well as feeling that their sexuality is 'bad' or 'wrong'.

Social attitudes towards homosexuality have a lot to do with the problems of disclosure. In the research carried out by Coyle (1991) it was apparent that for young gay men first disclosures were most likely to be to close friends, of either gender. Breaking the news to parents and other family members is perhaps the most difficult hurdle, although Coyle reported that in most cases the result was relief for the young person, and reassurance rather than rejection from parents. The mother of a young gay man describes her experience as follows:

'So he sat down and he said: "I've got something to tell you". So I said: "Alright, what is it?" So he said: "Well your two friends would understand." And then it suddenly dawned on me which two friends he meant. And it was the gay friends we had. And I just said: "So you think you are?" And I didn't use the word. And he said yes. So I said: "What makes you think that?" And he said: "I just know". So I said okay, you know that's okay. And I could see the relief in his face, the absolute relief in his whole body. And I just went up to him and he burst into tears. And I put my arms around him, and I said: "It's alright, you know, don't worry about it." I said: "I still love you, you're my son, and nothing's going to make any difference to how I feel. You're no different now than a minute ago before you told me, so it's alright, don't worry."'

(mother of two boys, quoted in Coleman, 1995)

Nonetheless, there are certainly young people who have less satisfactory experiences disclosing to their parents, and, indeed, some may not be able to do so until they are well into adulthood. The role of parents is critical in allowing an individual to come to terms with their sexual identity. Here, again, there is a great need to tackle the ignorance which surrounds this subject, in order that young people may be able to disclose their sexuality to their parents without encountering the stereotypes and prejudice still pervasive in our society.

There has been considerable debate in the literature over the mental health of young people who are gay or lesbian (Savin-Williams and Rodriguez, 1993). Some studies have reported no differences between homosexual and heterosexual individuals, but today there appears to be a growing consensus that there is a serious mental health issue here. In a well-designed study in the UK (Coyle, 1993), it was found that young gay men had significantly poorer mental health than a control group. In the USA, D'Augelli and Hershberger (1993) found that 42 per cent of the gay and lesbian young people they studied had attempted suicide in the previous year. Similar figures were reported by Rotheram-Borus *et al.* (1994). Bridget (1995) found that of twenty relatively isolated lesbian adolescents, fourteen had either attempted or seriously contemplated suicide. Mental health problems are important in relation to sexual orientation, yet they are not easy to tackle. Many professionals are concerned with the issue of stereotyping that we have referred to, while young people themselves will be reluctant to be classified as in any way needing special help.

Coyle (1998) makes the point that it is not a gay or lesbian identity itself which is the cause of any difficulty. Rather, it is the situation in which young people find themselves, under pressure to conceal their feelings, with no outlet for support or assistance, and usually unable to share the burden of their anxieties with their families. The combination of isolation and the sense of stigma associated with homosexuality often creates intolerable stress. There is no doubt that educators and others have a substantial challenge before them. It is essential, therefore, that we take a proactive approach to this subject. More readily accessible support is essential, as is a new look at the sex education curriculum. Homophobia, especially in the school setting, needs to be confronted. Attitudes have to change if we are to give young gay and lesbian individuals the same chance as others to develop a sane and healthy sexual identity.

Teenage parenthood

Over the past decade there has been a growing concern with the topic of early parenthood. This has been especially marked in the USA, which has the highest teenage-pregnancy rate in the world, as well as in Britain, which has the highest rate among European countries (Coleman, 1997a). However, a clear understanding of teenage parenthood is hindered by a variety of factors. First, it is misleading to talk of teenage parenthood as a general concept. It is apparent that parenthood for a 19 year old is a completely different experience from parenthood for a 14 or 15 year old, yet in discussion on the subject there is all too rarely a recognition of the significance of the developmental stage of the young parent. We will here be referring primarily to those under 16.

A second problem is the process of stereotyping that has so affected teenage parents over the past decade or so in Britain and the USA. When politicians and other commentators describe this group as scroungers on the state, or as individuals who become pregnant in order to jump housing queues, then a climate is created that makes it difficult to consider the needs of young parents in a rational and constructive manner. It is not only politicians, however, who are responsible for the negative stereotype. Almost all research on this group of adolescents looks at the disadvantages of early parenthood (see e.g. reviews by Lask, 1994; Coley and Chase-Lansdale, 1998). While some work highlights the poorer outcomes for children of teenage parents, other studies concentrate on the characteristics of young people who become parents at an early age. Such studies often compare the parenting skills of young people with those of older parents, almost always to the detriment of the teenage group. Whether explicitly or implicitly, the great majority of research on this subject espouses what might be called a 'deficit model' of teenage parenthood. Such a model does a disservice not only to the young people concerned, but to the research endeavour itself (Coleman and Dennison, 1998).

A third problem is the limited research data available on teenage parenthood in the UK and in Europe generally. While there have been a few good studies, the majority of research on this subject originates from the USA. It is clear that populations of young parents from different countries are not comparable, and there is a real danger in using conclusions from one country and applying them in another. One example of this is that almost all the studies in North America have been based on African-American populations, yet in the UK only a small number of teenage parents come from minority backgrounds (Dennison and Coleman, 1998a).

Of course, all young women are not equally likely to become teenage parents. As we have indicated above, some are more at risk of unintended pregnancy than others, and then among this group some will continue with the pregnancy, while others will decide to have a termination. It is important to note, therefore, that the incidence of teenage pregnancy differs between geographical regions of a country. In the UK, conception rates are highest in urban areas, while rural localities have lower rates (Babb, 1993). Several studies have shown a strong association between socio-economic status and the incidence of teenage pregnancy and maternity. As Babb says: 'the highest levels of teenage births occur to the most socio-economically disadvantaged young women.' In addition to these broad demographic factors, there are other variables which play a part. So, for example, a number of commentators have documented an association between pregnancy in adolescence and similar experiences among the mothers of such young women (e.g. Simms and Smith, 1986). In addition, it would appear that especially vulnerable teenagers, such as those brought up in the care of local authorities, are more likely than others to become parents at an early age (Quinton and Rutter, 1988; Corlyon and McGuire, 1997). One young woman describes her motivation to become a parent in the following way:

'I don't think I missed out on me childhood because I never really had a childhood anyway. Because I was kicked out when I was three, and my mum walked out on me, and my dad was beating me around, and I was sexually assaulted when I was five, so I never had a childhood of me own anyway, so I don't miss it cos I've never had it. And when I got to around 14 I was in a children's home and all I felt was that no one loved me, no one ever loved me, no one would ever love me, and that's when I decided I wanted me own family, and so that's what I done.'

(young mother, aged 16, participant in the study reported in Dennison and Coleman, 1998b)

One of the questions most often addressed in research on this topic concerns the characteristics of young mothers. Some studies focus on the psychological profiles of such teenagers, while others look at parenting skills, knowledge of child development, and attitudes towards motherhood. Studies carried out in the USA are likely to highlight negative attributes associated with this group of parents. To take an example, the work of Osofsky and her colleagues has shown that young mothers are more depressed, more labile in their affect, and less emotionally available to their babies than older mothers (Osofsky et al., 1993). In another major study – the Baltimore Multi-Generational Study – the authors document a variety of risk factors among teenage mothers, including low educational attainment, behavioural problems and poor health (Furstenberg et al., 1989).

Not all British studies have avoided a deficit perspective, but there is evidence of a more balanced approach among some writers in this country. A good example of this may be found in the work of Phoenix (1991). She examined the experiences of eighty young women who became pregnant between the ages of 16 and 19. She found that they formed a heterogeneous group in terms of ethnicity, education and employment, and in their reasons for having children. They were, however, all linked by a common experience of poverty, and a determination to do the very best for their child, often in extremely difficult circumstances. Phoenix argued that, in comparison with older women in similar socio-economic situations, these young women were coping just as well. Their opportunities and life chances had, in any event, been limited, so that becoming a parent could be seen to have been a constructive and realistic path to choose.

The family background of teenage parents has received less attention, relatively speaking, than other topics in this field. However, since the early 1990s there has been a growing interest in this aspect of teenage parenthood, and studies in the USA have begun to identify the key role played by the grandmother (Chase-Lansdale *et al.*, 1991; East and Felice, 1996), while Dennison and Coleman (1998b) report the first such study in the UK of the family context of teenage parenthood. There are a number of issues to be addressed. First, the question arises as to whether co-residence, that is, teenage mother and grandmother living together, is of benefit to the young mother. Second, we may ask whether the grandmother can offer a valuable role-model for the young woman in the early stages of parent-hood, and in what circumstances support is best provided. Third, it may be of interest to look at the grandmothers' parenting styles, and to consider whether there are particular styles which are more empowering than others. One young woman describes her anxieties over her mother's role in childcare:

'Well, looking after her, I did most of it really. Well, I did it all really, my mum just helped all the time. Because I went back to school when I'd had her, it was just that I thought my mum was going to take over, you know, as though it were her baby, but she didn't. She was like, she had her when I went to school, and when I came home, I'd take over then, you know. And I were worried at first that the baby would start thinking that my mum were her mum, if you see what I mean. She wouldn't know who I were, like, but she does, so.'

(young mother aged 15, participant in the study reported in Dennison and Coleman, 1998b)

In terms of co-residence, a good review is provided by Brooks-Gunn and Chase-Lansdale (1995). They point out that, while early studies reported a number of benefits of co-residence, more recent research has emphasised the fact that the multi-generational family environment may not necessarily be supportive either to the young mother or to her baby. In particular, they note that mothers co-residing with their own mothers report high levels of stress (Chase-Lansdale *et al.*, 1994), and that babies and young children living in such circumstances do less well intellectually. Brooks-Gunn and Chase-Lansdale conclude that the conflicting re-sults may, in part, be explained by the different ages of the young mothers in the various studies. Thus, they suggest that co-residence may be beneficial for teen-agers in the younger age group, while it will be less beneficial for those who are older. Such a conclusion makes sense, and is consistent with findings reported by Dennison and Coleman (1998b). In this study a comparison of younger and older teenagers living with the grandmother shows better adjustment in the younger group.

In terms of mother–grandmother relationships, Wakschlag *et al.* (1996) led the way by developing a Scale of Intergenerational Quality for the study of this topic. Dennison and Coleman (1998b) revised the scale to make it more appropri-ate for a British context, and identified five dimensions of the relationship, includ-ing emotional closeness, validation of the young mother's parenting skills, maturity of the young mother, independence and conflict. Results from a sample of sixty mother–grandmother pairs show a high level of emotional closeness, relatively low levels of conflict and moderate degrees of validation. Findings indicate that the best relationships depend on the grandmothers' validation of her daughters' parent-ing ability, and an acknowledgement of her maturity and need for independence.

Further work is needed in this area, since it is clear that family relationships play a key role in facilitating adolescents to develop the necessary skills and confidence to become effective parents.

On the theme of family relationships, it is striking how little attention is paid to the place of the partner in the consideration of teenage parenthood. Most writers on this subject contribute to the overall impression that young fathers are either invisible or absent. That said, it is important not to underestimate the difficulty of involving young men in the research process. They may be suspicious of an unknown interviewer, or lacking in confidence in respect of their role. Because of this it is commonly assumed that young men do not want to take any responsibility for, or play an active part in, the upbringing of their child.

Recent findings do not support this view (Voran, 1991; Speak, 1997). Large numbers of teenage fathers do maintain contact with their children and do play a role in the child's upbringing. However, there are a number of obstacles, some of which at times seem unsurmountable to young men who are themselves still uncertain of their place in society. First, the great majority of relationships formed in the middle teenage years do not survive. Thus, problems of access to the child, resentment and/or conflict between the partners, and attitudes of grandmother and other extended family all have to be overcome. In addition, economic factors play their part too, since the young man may be looking for work or be on a training scheme in another area, making visiting difficult. In spite of all this, the evidence shows that where there is a positive involvement with the father a better outcome for the child may be expected (Robinson, 1988). More research is needed, as well as an acknowledgement by professionals that the young father has an important role to play. One young woman describes her partner as follows:

'Well, he was pretty positive, yeah really because we were only 17 at the time. We saw our friends, but I thought, what'll he think of being tied down with a baby? His friends are going to give him hassle, and one day he might turn around and say: "I've had enough, I don't see my friends, I don't go anywhere, I'm sat here with you and that baby." But he were always, he weren't always out with his friends, but he was with them. But at the same time he spent quite a lot of time with me. He found time for us both. It has brought us a bit closer than we were. At first we were really close, he were doing things for her, wouldn't let me do owt, but it's not gone on like that. Still he's great, I must say. We argue a bit of course, when she cries and that, and he is a bit rough with her, and then I start shouting, but I think we're closest we'll ever be.'

(young mother aged 18, participant in the study reported in Dennison and Coleman, 1998b).

Effective sex education

It seems appropriate to conclude this chapter with a consideration of sex education, and to look at some of the ways in which it might be modified to take into account the real needs of young people. First, it is clear that sex education cannot focus only on the biology. While biology must be an important component, it is those elements which concern the social context of sexuality, together with relationships and the ethics of sexual behaviour, which are most needed by young people. Teaching the biology of sex is relatively easy, but creating a sex education programme which allows young people to explore the dilemmas and contradictions inherent in sexual behaviour, and to develop the necessary relationship skills is much more difficult. It is in this direction that new thinking should be directed.

A second element of good sex education has to do with the importance of addressing the needs of both young men and young women, as well as those from minority cultures, and those who are gay, lesbian or bisexual. In terms of gender, it is a fact that sex education programmes rarely consider the significance of good communication between men and women, nor do they give young people an opportunity to explore the conventional notions of masculinity and feminity. Furthermore, the two sexes almost certainly need somewhat different things from sex education classes, so that for some of the curriculum there may be the need for single-sex groups in order that open discussion is made possible. As far as the needs of other groups is concerned, the key here is for sex education programmes to be proactive in recognising minorities, and valuing their experiences. The needs of these groups cannot be met unless such young people feel safe from prejudice and the possibility of harassment, whether of a racist or sexist nature. The responsibility to create a safe environment must rest with the professional adult.

A third factor which is essential for effective sex education is a recognition of the varying levels of knowledge among pupils. As indicated earlier, young people show considerable variation in their knowledge of sexuality. Both age and gender are factors, but equally important is the finding (Winn *et al.*, 1995) that pupils are more knowledgeable about some topics than about others. Thus, young people's understanding of fertility is relatively poor in contrast to their knowledge of HIV/AIDS. Such information should inform sex education programmes, and should help teachers give more attention to the need for the evaluation.

Mitchell (1998) makes an important point when she argues that we do not need sex education programmes that pre-empt decisions that young people are likely to make in the realm of sexual behaviour. Sex education should not be prescriptive, nor should it give a moral message about what is right or wrong. The most effective sex education programmes will provide young people with information as well as interpersonal skills, so that they can make informed choices about what is right for them. Of course, this viewpoint is not shared by all who take an interest in this subject. Since 1997, in the USA enormous amounts of money have been made available by the federal government to fund programmes which put forward the message that abstinence from sexual intercourse is the right way forward for young people. Such an approach has not been evident in government policy in European countries, but nevertheless the avoidance of a moral message does appear to be essential if programmes are to have credibility with young people.

Finally, as Reiss (1993) indicates, it is important to ask what are the goals for any sex education programme. Effective sex education will not prevent teenage pregnancy. Although ignorance may sometimes play a part in leading to an unwanted pregnancy, it will rarely be the sole factor involved. If the intention is to prevent, or at least reduce, the number of unintended conceptions among young people there will need to be a variety of strategies, including more accessible and acceptable sexual-health services, and a wider range of educational and employment opportunities for young women. Such strategies will, of course, need to be combined with more effective sex education, but it is essential to recognise that education alone will not reduce teenage pregnancy. What, then, is meant by effective sex education? In our view, this means the development and delivery of programmes which provide young people with both the knowledge and the relationship skills to take control over their lives in the sphere of sexual behaviour. Ideally, such programmes would become part of a more comprehensive 'skills for living' curriculum which would be introduced into all secondary schools. Evidence provided in this chapter demonstrates the potential value of such a policy.

Implications for practice

1. There have undoubtedly been profound changes in the sexual behaviour of young people since the 1960s. Most important of all is the increase in sexual activity among those in early and middle adolescence. From the evidence available, we can be reasonably confident that today more young people engage in sexual activity, and that they do so at an earlier age than in previous decades. This change is closely linked to changes in the pattern of adult sexual behaviour, and cannot be seen in isolation from other social trends. It does, however, have particular implications for educators and parents, and underlines the crucial importance of the timing of effective health and sex education.

2. The impact of HIV/AIDS on young people has been considerable, in spite of the fact that, as the century draws to a close, there is less adolescent concern about this sexually transmitted disease than there was at the beginning of the 1990s. The phenomenon of AIDS has led to a widespread focus on 'safer sex', including an interest in young people's knowledge about sexual matters, their attitudes to contraceptive practice, and the accessibility of condoms. 'Safer sex' is determined by a variety of factors, and health professionals working in the field have come to recognise that age, attitude, gender, type of sexual relationship and the social context of sexual activity will all play their part. As a result of AIDS much has been learnt about risk and sexuality in young people.

3. There has been a growing recognition of the circumstances which affect young people who develop as gay, lesbian or bisexual during their adolescent years. In particular, attention has been paid to the stages of identity development among this group. Many writers have pointed to the difficulties faced by gay and lesbian young people, especially the isolation experienced as a result of prejudice and negative stereotyping. It is clear that more support is needed, as well as a change in attitude, so that this subject can become an accepted part of the sex education curriculum in schools.

4. Teenage parenthood has received a high degree of attention, particularly in the USA and in the UK, where rates of teenage pregnancy are higher

than in other Western countries. While much research tends to concentrate on what might be called the 'deficit' model, comparing young parents unfavourably with older parents, such research overlooks the resources of adolescent parents. It is clear that, given appropriate support, young people can be effective mothers and fathers, and it is imperative that practitioners concentrate on strategies that facilitate parenting skills among young parents, rather than emphasising their limitations.

5. We have devoted the concluding section of this chapter to a consideration of effective sex education. Above all, it is essential to recognise that sex education cannot be seen as a subject on its own in the school curriculum, nor can it be seen as a strategy isolated from other sexual-health services. To be effective, sex education has to be conceptualised in a holistic manner, incorporated into a 'healthy living' curriculum in schools, or integrated with other health provision in the community. If there is one lesson to be learnt from research into adolescent sexuality, it is that sex education in the narrow, biological sense is not what is required by young people, nor is it likely to have any substantive effect on attitudes or behaviour.

Further reading

Coleman, J and Roker, D (Eds) (1998) *Teenage sexuality: health, risk and education.* Harwood Academic. London.
An edited collection of essays on a range of topics, including sexual knowledge, contraception, sex education, gay and lesbian identities and so on. Many of the essays challenge accepted thinking, and pose useful questions for discussion and debate.

Gullotta, T, Adams, G and Montemayor, R (Eds) (1993) *Adolescent sexuality.* Sage. London.
An edited collection of essays by North American writers on the topic. There is an emphasis on biological and behavioural perspectives.

Holland, J, Ramazanoglu, C, Sharpe, S and Thomson, R (1998) *The male in the head.* Tufnell Press. London.
This book contains accounts of young people talking frankly about their experiences of sexual risk. These accounts are used as a basis for a theory of male-dominated heterosexuality. The book also summarises the main findings from the 'Women, Risk and AIDS' and the 'Men, Risk and AIDS' projects carried out by the authors over the past decade.

Moore, S and Rosenthal, D (1995) *Sexuality in adolescence.* Routledge. London.
An excellent and accessible review of research on sexuality in this age group. The book has been reprinted twice, and is a very popular choice of students and health professionals wanting an introduction to this topic.

Moore, S, Rosenthal, D and Mitchell, A (1996) *Youth, AIDS, and sexually transmitted diseases.* Routledge. London.
A book by the same authors, looking in particular at the topic of STDs (sexually transmitted diseases). Again, readable and very worthwhile.

Adolescent health

In this chapter we look at various aspects of adolescent health, including health risks. Of course, there are some fairly obvious forms of risk over which young people have little control: growing up in poverty (Dennehy *et al.*, 1997; Roker, 1998); the effects of war and refugee status; victimisation and abuse by adults; hunger and political oppression (Gibson-Kline, 1996). In various parts of the world all these factors can, and do, offer health risks for young people, but here we will concentrate on aspects more often considered to be 'personal health' (though across the chapter we will examine how adults and wider society in general impinge on adolescent health behaviours).

As Hurrelmann and Losel (1990) have suggested, personal behaviours in adolescence can contribute to morbidity and mortality, so that smoking, drinking, drug use and other risky activities impinge on the health of the young person. While, on the one hand, adolescents may be considered to be a healthy sector of the population, since they make less use of health services than those in other age groups, on the other, they are also highly likely to take risks of various sorts with their health. It is this dilemma which we will be considering in this chapter. We will be exploring the following topics:

1   adolescent health risks which concern adult society;
2   young people's own health concerns;
3   mental health in adolescence;
4   sports and physical activities.

The adolescent years are a period when great adjustments have to be made by young people to changes both in themselves and in society, and in relation to the expectations which society places on them. Many young people make the transition to adulthood with relative ease but some are handicapped by economic and structural forces which make their passage to adult status very difficult. Others have the misfortune to have to cope with too many challenges to their self-esteem and identity at one time. For some young people in these positions anti-social behaviour or self-destructive behaviour can be the consequence of their need to find either status or solace. Yet this 'deficit' theory is not sufficient in itself to explain the attraction of taking risks, and an understanding of the very positive attraction of thrilling and potentially dangerous behaviours for some adolescents, and the promises and denials held out to youth by the various sectors of adult society, are important to understand. It also appears that the quest for excitement is symbolic in the sense that young people 'use' these behaviours to identify, however misguidedly, with adult patterns of behaviour.

Adult concern has focused, in particular, on drug and alcohol use, cigarette smoking, sexual behaviour and delinquency. Most of these behaviours would not be alarming if seen in adults but are perceived as being inappropriate for young people in the process of growing up. Silbereisen *et al.* (1986), for example, propose that a number of so-called 'anti-social' activities are in fact purposive, self-regulating and aimed at coping with aspects of adolescent development. They can play a constructive developmental role, at least over a short term. While such behaviours can be symbolic (i.e. usually engaged in because of a desire to create a self-image of maturity or as a perceived means of attaining attractiveness and sociability), they nevertheless can put adolescents at risk. Like adults, teenagers typically adopt behaviours in the belief that they will help achieve some desired end, such as giving pleasure or gaining peer acceptance. In doing so, they are likely to ignore or discount evidence that particular behaviours may pose a potential threat to them.

The concept of risk-taking is ill defined. Is it part of the psychological make-up of youth – a thrill-seeking stage in the developmental transition – or a necessary step to the acquisition of adult skills and self-esteem? Or is it a consequence of a societal or cultural urge by adults to marginalise youth, because in their transitions from controllable child to controlled adult they are seen as troublesome and a threat to the stability of the community? Before we consider such questions, we need clearer definitions of what is meant by risk-taking. Hendry and Kloep (1996) offer the following three categories of risk-taking behaviour.

First, there are thrill-seeking behaviours. These are exciting or sensation-seeking behaviours which arouse and test the limits of one's capacities. Such behaviours can be observed in children as well as in adolescents and adults. What distinguishes adolescent thrill-seeking behaviour is a combination of frequency (they engage in these activities more often than adults to test themselves and learn), and resources (they have more access than children to money and time; and as a result of limited experience, they lack judgement of their own capacities and the extent of risk they are undertaking).

Second, there are audience-controlled risk-taking behaviours. In order to be accepted, to find a place in a peer group and to establish a social position, people have to demonstrate certain qualities and abilities. Thus, it is obvious that most risky behaviours need an audience. This may be the reason why adults do not engage so often in demonstrative risk-taking: they have symbolic means of displaying their status, in titles, expensive clothes or sports cars. There is a special sub-category of audience-controlled risk-taking behaviour that young people engage in with the intention of impressing or provoking other people. Adults restrict many adolescent behaviours and activities, and defying norms is for many adolescents a step in the development of independence. Eager to break adults' dominance by refusing to obey their commands and prohibitions, adolescents may not always be able to discriminate between which were made to suppress them and which were in their best interests. This can lead to risk-taking (i.e. norm-breaking) behaviours, reinforced by adults' negative reactions.

Third, there are risk-taking behaviours which are irresponsible behaviours. These are not performed because of the risk they imply, but in spite of it, in order to achieve other desired goals. Such irresponsible behaviours demonstrate the inability of individuals to see long-term consequences, or, if these are apparent, to be unwilling to abstain from such activities because of perceived short-term advantages. Examples of such behaviours are smoking and drinking, abstaining from exercise, or engaging in unprotected sex. It is obvious that behaviours such as getting drunk or failing to use condoms are not attractive because of the risks they imply, but are pursued for other reasons that are temporarily more important than these consequences. As Arnett (1998) has suggested, cultures must accept a trade-off in socialisation between promoting individualism and self-expression, on the one hand, and in promoting social order, on the other. Societies such as ours

pay the price for promoting individualism and achievement by having higher rates
of adolescent risk-taking in response to adult culture.

Cigarette smoking

Golding (1987) noted that the decrease in smoking in industrialised countries has
been dramatic. In three decades, smoking prevalence among adult United Kingdom males, for example, has fallen from 70 per cent to 40 per cent. However,
within this general trend a number of themes in relation to gender, social class
and age gradients in smoking prevalence can be noted. Strong socio-economic
group gradients were noted in the adult population, the prevalence of smoking
being highest in the 'unskilled manual' and lowest in the 'professional' groups.
Gender and regional differences also existed. How far are these characteristics
replicated in the adolescent population? Cigarette smoking is often established in
adolescence and has significant long-term consequences in terms of morbidity
and mortality in adulthood (Holland and Fitzsimons, 1991). Approximately 10 per
cent of teenagers aged 11–15 are regular smokers, and there has been little change
over the past 12 years (Diamond and Goddard, 1995). However, data from the
General Household Survey in the UK suggests a decline in smoking rates among
16 to 19 year olds between 1972 and 1992 (Coleman, 1997a).

Numerous studies have shown a gender difference in the adolescent population, with girls being more likely to smoke than boys. So, for example, in Britain a
Health Education Authority survey found that 24 per cent of girls aged 15–16
smoked on a daily basis compared with 15 per cent of boys (Turtle *et al.*, 1997).
Lloyd and Lucas (1997) looked at this difference in more detail, showing that the
disparity between boys and girls starts to become apparent at age 13, and increases during the following years up to the age of 16. This finding is illustrated in
Figure 7.1. Similar patterns of cigarette smoking are reported in other countries,
for example, in Australia (Heaven, 1996) and in the United States and other European countries (Seiffge-Krenke, 1998).

Holland and Fitzsimons (1991), Jacobson and Wilkinson (1994), and Lloyd
and Lucas (1997) have all noted that teenagers who smoke tend to reveal certain
general characteristics: they have family members and friends who smoke; they
are more likely to come from single-parent families; they may have low self-
esteem, less confidence, more anxiety, and poor educational aspirations; and their
leisure time is spent in part-time working or 'hanging out'. In a study of schoolchildren, Goddard (1989), found that adolescents were much more likely to be
smokers if other people at home smoked. Brothers and sisters appeared to have
more influence in this respect than parents. These results are confirmed in a
study of Scottish adolescents undertaken by Glendinning *et al.* (1992). Although
the greatest incidence of regular smoking appears to start at age 14, this is pre-
ceded by a stage of experimentation at a younger age (Holland and Fitzsimons,
1991). A Trent Lifestyle Survey asked regular smokers to indicate where they
were most likely to smoke. The most frequently identified places were at parties,
on the way to school and in the street (Roberts *et al.*, 1995).

Percentages

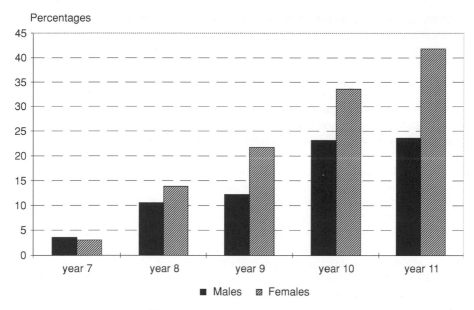

Figure 7.1 Percentage of boys and girls who are regular cigarette smokers by school year in England, 1996.

Source: Lloyd and Lucas (1997).

Coggans *et al.* (1990) undertook a large-scale prevalence study as part of a national evaluation of drug education. The young people in this study were aged from 13–15 years and were identified as representative of the range both of social class and drug-education experience typifying school pupils in these age groups though the pupil sample was drawn entirely from the Central Belt of Scotland. Something like 15 per cent of the Coggans sample smoked at the 'regular' level (defined as at least one cigarette a week). Davies and Coggans (1991) noted a strangely bimodal distribution of smoking in the adolescent population, one size-able group smoking very infrequently (19 per cent), and the other group (14 per cent) being frequent smokers. In other words, older adolescents are more likely to smoke than younger ones, females are more likely to smoke than males, and young people from lower socio-economic groups are more likely to smoke than their counterparts in higher socio-economic groups.

Further evidence on the link with social class comes from the Young People's Leisure and Lifestyle study (Hendry *et al.*, 1993), in which 19 per cent of 13 to 24 year olds considered themselves to be smokers. Overall, a clear trend with age is discernible in the data, with the proportions of smokers rising to a peak in the early twenties and then falling slightly. Of most interest, however, is the fact that social-class differences, when measured in the traditional way by social class of head of household, were non-significant, though the trend was in the same direction noted in other studies ('non-manual' adolescents providing 11 per cent of regular smokers, and those from a manual background providing 14 per cent of regular smokers). However, for the oldest four cohorts it was possible to measure current social class rather than class of origin (e.g. in full-time education, employed in semi-skilled occupation, etc.). Using this measure, we see significant differences in smoking status between groups of young people engaged in different types of economic activity. For example, only 11–13 per cent of young people in further education or professional and intermediate categories were 'regular' smokers, compared with 28 per cent of the unemployed.

School-based interventions aimed at reducing smoking rates among teenagers may improve knowledge but do not necessarily influence behaviour (Nutbeam *et al.*, 1993). Teenagers already have high levels of knowledge about the risks of smoking (Macfarlane *et al.*, 1987; Turtle *et al.*, 1997). The majority of teenagers who smoke indicate that they would like to give up (Turtle *et al.*, 1997), and in one study individual advice in the general practice setting has been shown to result in agreements for smoking cessation (Townsend *et al.*, 1991). However, the effect of individual health-promotion activity with respect to smoking may be minimal compared with wider societal influences of advertising, pricing, peer-group pressures, parental imitation and chemical addiction, indicating the necessity of a multi-faceted health-education approach (Townsend *et al.*, 1994; Macfarlane, 1993).

Drinking alcohol

In present-day society alcohol consumption among teenagers is common. Data from Goddard (1996) show that, in England, nearly 45 per cent of young men and approximately 35 per cent of young women have an alcoholic drink at least weekly by the age of 15. These findings are illustrated in Figure 7.2. The literature on young people's drinking describes such behaviour as part of the socialisation process from child to adult (e.g. Sharp and Lowe, 1989). In England and Wales the majority of adolescents have had their first 'proper' drink by the age of 13 (82 per cent of boys and 77 per cent of girls). In Scotland, schoolchildren start drinking a little later, but catch up with their English and Welsh peers by the age of 15 (Marsh *et al.*, 1986). It needs to be pointed out, however, that the majority of adolescents only drink alcohol a few times a year, and for most young people their early drinking is done at home with parents. Only as adolescents grow older does the context for their drinking spread to parties, or to the streets (Hendry *et al.*, 1998), then clubs and discos, and lastly pubs (Turtle *et al.*, 1997). Again, international comparisons can be found in Heaven (1996) and Seiffge-Krenke (1998).

While the long-term health consequences of regularly drinking large amounts of alcohol are well understood, there are also short-term health and social consequences of infrequent but very heavy drinking. Consequently, some of the data on 'drunkenness' may actually be of more interest. In the survey carried out by Marsh *et al.* (1986) about 30 per cent of the youngest boys and 23 per cent of the youngest girls who drank in Scotland admitted to being 'very drunk' once or more than once. It is important to note that these figures do not include young people who were not drinkers. Bearing in mind the caveat that such measurements are very subjective, it would seem that such behaviour peaks for both boys and girls at age 15, but declines more rapidly for girls thereafter.

Percentages

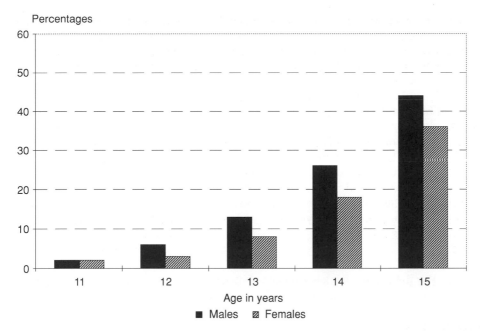

Age in years

■ Males   ▨ Females

Figure 7.2 Percentage of boys and girls drinking alcohol at least once a week in England, by age, in 1994.

Source: Goddard (1996).

Alcohol is readily available to teenagers by direct purchase. Balding (1997) suggests that approximately one-quarter of 15-year-old pupils reported having purchased alcohol from a supermarket or off-licence in the previous week, and 10 per cent had bought alcohol in a pub. A study in the mid-1980s showed that most young people's drinking was done at weekends and in relation to quantities, girls in every age group drank less than boys (Marsh *et al.*, 1986). Boys' consumption grows with age, with some very high levels being reached by age 17, whereas girls' consumption peaks in the last year of compulsory schooling (i.e. 16 years of age). Pub-going seemed to peak in the late teens and thereafter 'tail off' in early adulthood. The majority of adolescents associate drinking with positive reactions, but Marsh *et al.* (1986) noted that linked to such specific bouts of drunkenness were not only the inevitable physical symptoms but also drinking-related problems such as vandalism and attracting the attention of the police.

In Hendry *et al.*'s (1998) study of rural youth participants talked a good deal about drinking and the role that alcohol played in contemplating health concerns. Young people drank for a variety of reasons, including the availability and acceptability of drinking within the general cultural milieu. Like adults, these young people talked about drinking to relax, to increase their sociability, and for the sensory and cognitive changes it produced. For some, drinking had delivered a 'transformational' experience that allowed them to transcend their normal perceptual scope; for others it represented an escape. There was some indication that stages might exist in the way young people thought about drinking: from excessive early-age drinking, with loss of control, to 'sensible' patterns, and drinking according to one's 'limits'. Sometimes, older siblings or friends would act as mentors, advising on how to drink or looking out for younger adolescents at parties. Hangovers and other ill effects were accepted as part of the learning process. As one young man put it:

> 'I used to drink every second weekend. When I first started drinking, I was drinking every weekend. This year I've no really been out much. I've stopped. I'm trying to have just a couple of drinks and even that is too much some-times. (How do you find out what your limit is?) It's knowing how to drink . . . .
>
> Yeah, just through experience I think. I got drunk a few times! But now I only drink some, and I do not drink too much, because I don't like getting drunk. (How do you find out your limits?) You must do this. Try to. You do it because if you are going to drink it is essential. It is part of growing up.'
>
> (quoted in Hendry *et al.*, 1998)

For the young, drink is a means of making a shift into a world of heightened sensations. Their reasons for drinking – sociability, relaxation, companionship, excitement and so on – are the same as adults', and they perceive such behaviour as their growing acceptance into 'the drinking society'. What is clear is that health education aimed at young people on the subject of alcohol consumption has to attack the meanings invested in such activities and the fundamental changes iden-tified both in patterns of drinking and their reasons for drunkenness.

Illegal drugs

Another major concern of adult society is adolescent drug misuse. Surveys of this behaviour indicate an increase among young people during the last decade in all Western countries (Measham *et al.*, 1994; Sullivan and Thompson, 1994; Parker *et al.*, 1998). In terms of illegal drugs the most commonly used is cannabis. Roker and Coleman (1997) showed that up to 40 per cent of those in the 14–16 age group had used cannabis in England, and these figures are similar to findings in other countries. In an extensive study in the north-west of England Parker *et al.* (1998) looked at those between the ages of 14 and 18, and findings indicated an increase from 30 per cent using cannabis at 14 to nearly 60 per cent at age 18. Other illegal drugs were also being used, though not nearly to the same extent. Ecstasy, for example, is used by 19 per cent of 18 year olds. Some data from the Parker *et al.* (1998) study are illustrated in Table 7.1.

One of the forms of drug misuse associated with the youngest adolescents is solvent misuse. British studies (Ives, 1990) suggest that between 4 and 8 per cent of secondary-school pupils have tried solvents, and that sniffing peaks around 13–15 years. In Davies and Coggans' (1991) sample, nearly 11 per cent of the sample had used solvents at least once, a figure which is closer to the one indic-ated in the Parker *et al.* (1998) study. It should be noted that many who use solvents do so only once or a few times. However, despite the low incidence of

Table 7.1 Lifetime prevalence of illicit drug-taking (age 14–18 inclusive) by individual drug.

	Age 14 (n = 776) %	Age 15 (n = 752) %	Age 16 (n = 523) %	Age 17 (n = 536) %	Age 18 (n = 529) %
Amphetamines	9.5	16.1	18.4	25.2	32.9
Amyl nitrite	14.2	22.1	23.5	31.3	35.3
Cannabis	31.7	41.5	45.3	53.7	59.0
Cocaine	1.4	4.0	2.5	4.5	5.9
Heroin	0.4	2.5	0.6	0.6	6.0
LSD	13.3	25.3	24.5	26.7	28.0
Magic mushrooms	9.9	12.4	9.8	9.5	8.5
Ecstasy	5.8	7.4	5.4	12.9	19.8
Solvents	11.9	13.2	9.9	10.3	9.5
Tranquillisers	1.2	4.7	1.5	3.9	4.5
At least one	36.3	47.3	50.7	57.3	64.3

Source: Parker *et al.* (1998).

continued misuse, it is clear that the fashion for solvent misuse has not necessarily gone away despite attracting less media attention in recent years. Part of the concern rested in the fact that published guidelines to retailers on the sale of glues – the most well-known solvent – have led to a trend towards misuse of more dangerous products such as aerosols (Ives, 1990; Ramsey, 1990). An account of a group of 'sniffers' comes from a study carried out by O'Bryan (1989). It makes the point that health-education interventions have to tackle the issue – in this case, solvent abuse – according to the meaning and role it has for participants. All the solvent users were boys of around 14. Little sniffing was done in female company; in fact, these seemed to be boys who were particularly awkward with girls. Girls, anyway, are not part of the culture of hanging about on the streets in which sniffing flourishes.

No direct question was asked about personal drug-taking behaviours in Hendry *et al.*'s (1993) study, but young people were asked both about their attitudes to drug-taking and about the proportion of young people in their peer group who used drugs. Boys were more likely than girls to state that some of their close friends used drugs. Age 17 to 18 was the peak period for drug use, with 41 per cent of this age group claiming that some of their close friends used drugs. There was a significant link between those claiming a close friend as a drug user and social class, with 32 per cent of young people from professional or intermediate social classes making this claim compared with 23 per cent of those from semi-skilled or unskilled social classes. Significant differences also emerged, with the highest (48 per cent) declarations of drug use among peers in affluent areas of private housing. One could postulate that this puts the lie to theories about use of drugs in general and social deprivation, and highlights the advent of expensive designer drugs or the predominance of cannabis. Of particular interest from this study are the data on this topic for the oldest cohorts analysed by the current social class of the respondents themselves. The results demonstrate a distinctly bimodal distribution, in which the highest claims for drug use among friends are in the groups currently engaged in higher education and those who are unemployed.

What has been argued in this section from the key aspects of adult concerns over young people's health is that both legal and illegal drugs are used by young people to create transformational experiences. Additionally, for adolescents, they can be symbolic (e.g. looking 'cool' or 'grown up'). Therefore, there is ample evidence that illegal drug use by teenagers has been, and is, increasing. Drugs are more readily accessible and available, and drug use is becoming part of wider society and culture. Parker *et al.* (1998) make the point in the title of their book: *Illegal leisure: the normalisation of adolescent recreational drug use.*

Nevertheless, society in general expresses a great deal of concern over this issue. Such voiced concern may actually make adolescent drug-taking more dangerous and attractive. Dangerous, by criminalising 'soft' drugs and thus labelling and 'stigmatising' users, and making usage attractive to some groups by creating the thrill of illegality and an 'audience-controlled' risk (e.g. Hendry and Kloep, 1996). In turn, such over-exposure, often via the mass media, makes information-based prevention campaigns problematic for teenagers, and thus renders harm-reduction policies less effective. Prevention programmes based on information-giving alone do not seem to result in measurable changes in behaviour (e.g. Robson, 1996). Roker and Coleman (1997) report the results of a study in which 2,100 young people aged 11–16 were interviewed about drug education and information. The young people indicated that they would like to receive drugs education from someone with personal experience of illegal drugs, and from more private resources such as books and leaflets. Certainly, there is great dissatisfaction with current offerings from health-education programmes (e.g. Shucksmith and Hendry, 1998).

The majority of drug use among teenagers is experimental and short term, without any evidence of appreciable long-term harm or involvement. However, experimentation at an early age and high frequency of cannabis use are all suggested to be associated with higher-risk problems (Robson, 1996). Therefore, it is important that approaches to young people are sensitive to the meanings surrounding their involvement and their motivations for participating. We should try to see the situation from the young person's perspective as well as taking a wider cultural and legal view.

Young people's concerns

Until now in this chapter we have been looking at adults' concerns about adolescent health. What concerns young people? As we have noted, teenagers are generally considered to be a healthy population because of their relatively low contact with health services. Yet in a school-based questionnaire survey of teenagers aged 13–15 in nine London comprehensive schools young people demonstrated that their main health concerns were about weight, acne, nutrition and exercise (Epstein *et al.*, 1989). In addition, as a number of studies have shown, there appears to be an unmet need to discuss sexual development, sexually transmitted diseases and contraception (see e.g. Shucksmith and Hendry, 1998). Teenagers are generally shown to have less interest in discussing smoking, alcohol or drugs – all the adult concerns – with health professionals. Further in a postal survey of 16–20 year olds registered with an inner London general practice, 30 per cent of girls and 15 per cent of boys reported that there was something wrong with their health and, in particular, that they were overweight (Bewley *et al.*, 1984). A series of interviews by Aggleton *et al.* (1996) with children and teenagers aged 8–17 years support the view that the health concerns of young people extend beyond issues relating to smoking, drugs and sexual health. In addition to worries about diet and weight, there were clear concerns about relationship problems and the influence of these on emotional and psychological well-being.

Having the basic skills to 'get along with others' was seen as an essential component to a sense of health and well-being. It was felt that few adults appreciated either the nature of teenagers' needs for learning such social skills or the importance of the developmental task involved, and, more generally, it was felt that adults could learn to empathise better in relation to young people's concerns. In Hendry *et al.*'s (1998) study the opinion was expressed frequently that adults – and this included parents, teachers and the community of adults in general – did not necessarily understand what young people's health-related concerns were, nor did they understand how important certain kinds of experiences are in building up or damaging self-esteem and influencing 'resources' that might assist young people in developing healthier attitudes and behavioural practices. Further evidence was gathered from the interviews for the need to educate about depression and other affective illnesses. Young people also believed that they should receive a kind of 'emotional education', which would include learning how to cope with anger and to understand (i.e. recognise) emotions, moods and what to do with them, including working through issues of grief and loss (Perschy, 1997).

Churchill *et al.* (1997) stated that attitudes towards health can be categorised according to whether a person believes that they have control over their own health, or whether they believe that health is more related to chance. Such attitudes may then influence health-related behaviour and risk-taking. Such categorisation forms the basis of a 'health locus of control' measure (Norman and Bennett, 1996). Macfarlane *et al.* (1987) found that 13 per cent of teenagers expressed the view that health is a matter of luck, while 85 per cent agreed with the statement that 'there are many things that you can do to be healthy and avoid illness'. Balding (1992) incorporated the internal-external locus of control scale in a schools survey. There was little change in attitudes between ages 11 and 15, but boys scored more highly towards the internal locus of control than girls, who thus appear to perceive themselves as having less control over their own health. Approximately one-third of both boys and girls expressed varying degrees of 'helplessness' in the face of external influences on their health, and Balding suggests that such attitudes will act as a filter to any health-promotion messages. Similarly, in an extensive study of Scottish teenagers Hendry *et al.* (1993) found that young people had fairly positive views of their own health, that young women considered themselves to be less healthy and had more health problems than young men, and that, while some viewed health as a matter of luck or genetics, most considered that they could influence their health by the pattern of their chosen life-style.

Lewin (1980) suggested that it is adolescents' status as neither child nor adult that contributes to their emotional and behavioural problems. Although there may be difficult periods, including moments of despair, confusion, loneliness and self-doubt, the majority of young people cope with these feelings and try to correct the adverse situations that cause them (Plancherel and Bolognini, 1995). It can be argued that mental health is positively influenced by achieving the developmental tasks involved in the adolescent transition. Kleiber and Rickards (1985) state that 'the primary agenda of adolescents is to establish themselves as individuals with a sense of self and with some legitimacy, by exercising their expanding abilities in ways which make them effective in the larger society'. This point is also emphasised by Nurmi (1997), in an excellent paper showing the links between self-definition and positive mental health. Furthermore, external factors also play their part, since a number of differing contexts impact upon development, particularly family and school contexts, which, together with individual characteristics, have been found to be associated with health and behavioural risks (Resnick *et al.*, 1997).

Mental health

Most diagnosed mental-health problems are reported to have their onset in adolescence (Kosky, 1992; D. Steinberg, 1987). Generally, however, this period may be seen as a time of adapting to many changes, and providing opportunities for growth and development. Contemporary research also argues that a 'mismatch' between the needs of developing adolescents and their experiences at school, home and other contexts may negatively influence psychological and behavioural development (Eccles *et al.*, 1996). This is particularly so if young people lack the resources to cope with challenges (Petersen and Hamburg, 1986). Thus, it is the more socially and psychologically vulnerable adolescents who are likely to experience this period as difficult, which may manifest in psychological disturbances (Leffert and Petersen, 1995; Rutter, 1995). Many factors contribute to adolescent susceptibility to increased risk of mental-health problems, including social-risk factors such as increased life stress (Costello, 1989) and familial factors such as family breakdown or parenting structures (Maccoby and Martin, 1983).

It has been estimated that psychiatric disorders or handicapping abnormalities of emotions, behaviour or relationships are present in a substantial proportion (10–20 per cent) of children and young people in the general population (Hunter *et al.*, 1996). Three broad types of stressor have been associated with mental-health problems in this age group (Hodgson and Abbasi, 1995). These include normal, or normative, stress such as moving to a new school, severe non-normative stress, such as, for example, parental divorce, and severe chronic stress, which would be exemplified by living in serious poverty. The nature of stress will be discussed in more detail in Chapter 12.

Dennehy *et al.* (1997) wrote that mental health is generally assumed to cover a wide range of problems including suicide, depression and schizophrenia. However, mental health should be thought of as being more than simply the absence of mental illness (Wilson, 1995). This is particularly significant for young people whose state of mental health is essentially dependent on their emotional well-being, which is often linked to the realm of interpersonal relationships and the social environment rather than having its origins in medical or cognitive factors. Mental health must also be considered within the cultural context, because each culture has its own ideas about ideal states of mind or well-being (Wilson, 1995).

Rutter and Smith (1995) argue that a combination of a more insular youth culture (with more reliance on the influence of the peer group and less on adults) together with a movement towards more individualistic societal values over the past fifty years has generated a huge increase in psychosocial problems among young people. As we have noted, some mental-health problems will be experienced by 10–20 per cent of young people in any one year, although the majority will not need specialist professional help (Williams, 1996). The prevalence of depression rises during childhood and young adulthood, and major depression is found in between 2 and 8 per cent of young people, with the predominance of cases being found among females. In Hendry et al.'s (1998) study, over 25 per cent of young people interviewed talked about concerns related to depressive symptoms and other emotional upsets. Both the degree to which feeling depressed became a health concern and the serious worry and discomfort associated with these experiences was surprising, and stood in contrast to a stereotype of the rural adolescent as a contented and emotionally uncomplicated personality. It is not uncommon for young people with depressive disorders to have co-morbid conduct and/or anxiety disorder (Hunter et al., 1996), which may conceal their depression (Harrington, 1995). It is important to distinguish between depression, which we all suffer from at some point in our lives, and clinical depression, which is a persistent and often devastating disorder.

Unemployment is an important risk factor for mental-health problems (Bartley, 1994), and has been found to be strongly correlated with psychiatric admission rates (Gunnell et al., 1995). Financial problems resulting from unemployment are an important cause of mental-health problems, but a more important reason may be the effects of losing the non-financial benefits that work provides. Most of these are due to a 'loss of status, purpose and social contacts, and a time structure to the day' (Smith, 1985). A study of young women aged 15–20 showed that the rate of self-reported mood disturbance among the unemployed was significantly higher than the rate among the employed (Monck et al., 1994). These differences have also been shown to emerge among young people entering the labour market when no differences existed at school (Bartley, 1994).

The risk of insecure and unsatisfactory jobs can be just as depressing as unemployment itself (Bartley, 1994; Monck et al., 1994). Parental depression, particularly on the maternal side, has been consistently linked to depression in children (Monck et al., 1994). Environmental factors outside the family, such as friendship difficulties and bullying, are also likely to be relevant factors in increasing depressive disorders among young people (Harrington, 1995). As well as being affected by poverty, unemployment and other adverse social circumstances, young people are also highly susceptible to the impact of family events. Family poverty, parental unemployment, psychiatric disorder in parents, and physical and emotional neglect have consistently been shown to have a negative influence on child development and increase the risks of psychiatric, and particularly conduct, disorder (Goodyer, 1994).

To turn now to suicide and self-harm, deliberate self-harm is the commonest reason for acute hospital medical admission in young people, with an estimated 18–19,000 episodes per year requiring hospital treatment in England and Wales (Hawton *et al.*, 1996). The highest rates are found in 15–19-year-old females, with the most frequent reasons being difficulties in interpersonal relationships, unemployment and employment difficulties, substance abuse and eating disorders (Hawton, 1992). Thus, attempted suicide is three times more common among young women than their male counterparts, although as Hawton *et al.* (1999) show, there have been increases in the incidence of this behaviour among both sexes in the last decade. In cases of attempted suicide, relationship difficulties appear to be the most frequently quoted problem (Hawton *et al.*, 1996), with unemployment and substance abuse also being common, especially in males (Macfarlane *et al.*, 1987). Those who have attempted suicide are significantly more at risk of eventually dying by suicide than the rest of the population (Coleman, 1996). Deliberate self-harm becomes increasingly common from 12 years of age, remaining more widespread among girls (Hawton *et al.*, 1996). Reasons for gender differences may include earlier puberty in girls, and young girls facing more problems at this age than their male counterparts. Boys are also seen to have other means of expressing emotional problems, including aggressive behaviour and delinquency (Hawton *et al.*, 1996).

As far as completed suicide is concerned, the rate for 15–24-year-old males increased by more than 80 per cent in England and Wales during the years 1980–92 (Hawton *et al.*, 1996). This is contrary to trends in other age groups (Charlton, 1995) and youth suicide in the UK has increased at a greater rate than that in other European countries (Pritchard, 1992; Seiffge-Krenke, 1998). Rates of increase have been greater in Scotland than in England and Wales, with the lowest rates found in Northern Ireland (Coleman, 1997a). Possible explanations for the general rise include unemployment, alcohol and drug abuse, increased availability of methods for suicide, AIDS, marital breakdown, media influences and social changes (Hawton, 1992). There has been little change in the suicide rate among females over the same period. After accidents, suicide is the second most common cause of death in young males, although it is rare among boys under 15 years of age.

Sports and physical activities

One other aspect of adolescent life-styles which interests adult society is young people's involvement in physical activity and sport. This is, at least partly, because of the high incidence of cardiovascular disease in the adult population generally and a desire to inculcate active life-styles to counter this in the young, which has led to intensive promotion of leisure sports, epitomised by the notion of 'Sport for All' (European Sports Charter, 1975). The studies of Macintyre (1989), Hendry *et al.* (1993), and Kremer *et al.* (1997) have all indicated high involvement of school-age children in fairly regular physical activity and sport, yet differences obtain in relation to age and gender. Put simply, younger adolescents and male adolescents are most likely to be involved in physical activities and sports. There is a 'drop off' in involvement in the last few years of secondary schooling, particularly when young people made the transition from school towards work, training or

Table 7.2 Total hours spent on activities – summary statistics.

Activity	Mean	Standard deviation	Median	Minimum	Maximum
Television	5.52	4.10	4.95	0	25.2
Sport	3.74	3.98	3.00	0	28.2
Other	3.07	3.32	2.08	0	22.3
Homework	2.85	3.02	2.00	0	19.7
Work	2.41	4.43	0.00	0	23.0
Computing	1.02	1.99	0.00	0	14.2
Church	0.74	0.91	0.75	0	8.5
Music	0.94	1.88	0.00	0	24.0

Source: Trew (1997).

higher education. Beyond the school years, the social-class position of young people derived from their occupational status produces clear differences in health and fitness levels (Hendry *et al.*, 1993). The bulk of such national studies indicate a high involvement of school-age children in fairly regular physical activity. Trew (1997) illustrates how involvement with sport compares with other leisure activities, and hours spent in such activities among young people in Northern Ireland are illustrated in Table 7.2.

Work with young people perceived to be 'at risk' has often used sport and outdoor adventure as a mechanism to enhance self-esteem, develop skills and foster relationships between young people and adults (Jeffs and Smith, 1990). It is assumed that by setting and achieving challenges at the optimum level, young people will develop skills, self-discipline and the ability to make appropriate decisions, as well as a sense of responsibility and leadership. In turn, these will assist them in other spheres of their lives. Outdoor adventure pursuits such as hill walking, mountaineering, canoeing or skiing have long been used in this way (Cotterell, 1996). Mountain (1990) has outlined an alternative approach to working with young women at risk, which incorporates their specific needs within an overall framework of diversion. This involved an extensive period of time making contact with potential group members in a variety of settings, prior to setting up informal meetings and collaborating over a programme which involved a mix of practical activities and discussion.

Hence, sport is an activity which is socially approved and can provide self-control, sensation-seeking and peer approval. Yet, if sport is experienced as the only way of gaining peer acceptance and/or adult approval, the adolescent may invest too much time and effort, to the neglect of other achievements, like scholastic endeavour, or else 'success' may be enhanced by cheating and illegal means, creating a 'hidden curriculum' in sports (e.g. Hendry, 1992). If sport is the only way of experiencing 'thrill', the young person may take higher risks, influenced by the 'negative' elements inherent in many sport activities: high skill demands, parental pressure, 'insensitive' coaches or physical education teachers focusing only on talented athletes (Hendry, 1992).

Further, there is a lack of definitive evidence on physical activity and its association with the physical health of youth. Blair *et al.* (1989) have stated that the specific goal of exercise promotion in children is not the production of health outcomes. Rather, it is to establish regular exercise habits that will persist throughout life. Only regular exercise which is conducted over many years into adulthood can be expected to produce long-term effects (Rowland, 1991). As Wold and Hendry (1998) stated, physically active role models such as parents, siblings and peers, as well as figures in the mass media, influence young people to participate in physical activity. While cultural norms and values define gender differences in physical activity, so participation of girls is higher in countries with high equality between men and women than in countries low on gender equality. Importantly, these authors argue that young people from lower socio-economic status are less likely to engage in lifetime physical activity, hence physical activity contributes to the production of social inequality and, thus, to the social inequalities in health. Involvement in sport for young Black people is cited as a means of 'getting up and out' but there is little insight into how this relates to other aspects of their lives. Willis (1990), for example, found little evidence of ethnic differences in sports activity.

Long-term goals associated with cardiovascular health do not seem to be sufficiently potent as an impetus for young people's participation. For example, some time ago, Hendry and Singer (1981) found that a sample of adolescent girls had very positive attitudes towards physical activity for health reasons, but assigned low priority to their actual involvement in these pursuits because of 'conflicting' interests and saliences – usually of a social nature, related to visiting friends and going out. However, casual fun-oriented sports can be popular, especially with young women, when there is more focus on sociability, enjoyment and competence rather than on competition. For instance, Kloep (1998) found that the only sports activity with increasing participation among girls was jazz dance. Hence it may be important to stress the idea of 'sport as leisure', rather than as a competitive activity, and – especially for girls – as a vehicle for social interaction and fun.

Conclusion

It would appear that young people's developmental health quest is, in part, symbolic, in the sense that young people 'use' certain risky behaviours to identify with adult patterns of life-style. Like adults, teenagers typically adopt behaviours in the belief that they will achieve some desired end, such as giving pleasure or gaining peer acceptance. In doing so, they are likely to ignore or discount evidence that particular behaviours may pose a potential threat to them. Thus, as noted in this chapter, health is not seen by young people as a major life concern in the same way as adults perceive their health status. Adults' personal concerns relate to feelings of general well-being and maintenance of good health. Therefore, health is influenced by various socio-cultural influences across the life course (Backett and Davison, 1992). As we have seen, young people's perceptions are more centred, for example, on their personal and physical appearance, diet and the maintenance of a slim physique, though they also focus on decisions around drinking, smoking and drug use, and relational issues.

It is important to recognise that young people often learn from what, on the surface, may appear to be unhappy or negative experiences. In resolving not to repeat such an experience in the same manner, they can develop a range of psychosocial skills (Kloep and Hendry, 1999), and gain from what have been called 'steeling experiences', if, somehow, the situation contains within it elements rewarding to the individual. Rutter and Smith (1995) have talked about such 'steeling' experiences, which assist in the development of resilience and of coping mechanisms for future use in later adolescence. This ability to make choices for the self despite possible peer-group pressures reflects both the learning of positive social skills from relatively negative experiences and the development of maturity and independence in decision-making and behaviour which will have important consequences for adult life.

A number of issues seem relevant here. First, experimentation is an important process in gaining independence and responsibility for self-action in health and other life events. It is a step on the way to becoming more mature and adult-like, and in learning to make choices and come to decisions. It is important to learn from one's *own* experience. Second, adult society often gives adolescents conflicting messages and different sets of expectations about health behaviours. Hence, young people struggle to gain independence and self-agency in a society riddled with many inconsistencies, few social 'signposts' to maturity, and major anomalies regarding health, thereby allowing many adults to be unhealthy without the disapproval reserved for adolescents. Third, with regard to risk and risky health behaviours, adults can become very concerned – and over-anxious – on behalf of their adolescent offspring when 'catastrophes' occur. Gore and Eckenrode (1994) suggest that any event in a young person's life can be a challenge or a near-immovable obstacle to further psychosocial development. The important elements of success or failure, according to Gore and Eckenrode (1994) are: the young person's competencies in perception, planning, decision-making, learning capacities and interpersonal skills that can be brought to bear on the issue, together with the prioritisation of key aspects of the tasks involved, and the appearance or absence of other concurrently stressful events. One would want to add that these qualities are equally relevant for adults. Therefore, perhaps the role of the various health agencies which young people consult – including schools – should make a more integrated effort to enable young people to develop such competencies. What is required is acceptance and mutual respect, honesty and shared concerns – not power 'games', where 'health' is used as an argument for suppression, and 'unhealthy behaviour' is seen as a privilege for adult society.

Implications for practice

1. The first point to make is that an understanding of what lies behind young people's risk-taking behaviour will be helpful in any health intervention. While risk-taking is normally perceived by adults as a 'bad' thing, for adolescents risky behaviour carries with it a number of rewards. In particular, it may be that risk-taking assists in securing recognition in the peer group

or enables the young person to push against adult boundaries, and thereby to contribute to identity development.

2. In some respects, the adolescent population is a healthy group in comparison with other age groups. This is partly because childhood illnesses no longer impact on young people to the same extent, but the perception of health is also caused by the fact that adolescents do not use conventional health services to the extent that other age groups do. We have come to recognise that this is a somewhat misleading perception, and there is no doubt that health is a significant issue for some young people. First, because those living in disadvantaged circumstances do in fact suffer serious health problems, but, second, because research tells us that all young people do have health concerns. These are likely to be to do with questions of sexual behaviour, weight and body image, skin problems, and emotional difficulties.

3. It is essential for adult health professionals to recognise that adolescent concepts of health and health risk are not the same as those understood by older people. Young people may not worry about the future, and may not avoid all risks, but this does not mean that they are not concerned about their health. In terms of health interventions, these will be most effective if appropriate weight is given to the factors which influence young people, rather than to those which exercise the minds of adults.

4. One of the areas of health concern for young people is in the realm of mental or emotional health. It is clear that a significant number of adolescents experience a range of difficulties in this area, and yet there is too little support available to deal with these issues. In particular, problems around bullying, conflict at home or with close friends, feelings of depression or even suicide, and so on are common in adolescence. Health professionals would do well to attend to the needs of young people in this area.

5. Lastly, it is common to find that health services and interventions for young people have been planned by adults with little reference to the needs of those most concerned. Where resources exist which have been planned jointly with young people there is always a much higher rate of success. As this chapter has shown, health is an area where, all too often, adult concerns obscure the real needs of young people.

Further reading

Dennehy, A, Smith, L and Harker, P (1997) *Not to be ignored: young people, poverty and health*. Child Poverty Action Group. London.
A worthwhile review of mainly British research on poverty and other forms of disadvantage, and its impact on the health of young people.

Heaven, P (1996) *Adolescent health: the role of individual differences*. Routledge. London.

A useful review of research on this topic. The author is Australian, and this gives an international slant to the coverage.

Rutter, M and Smith, D (Eds) (1995) *Psychosocial disorders in young people*. John Wiley. Chichester.

This book became a classic almost as soon as it appeared. The chapters are by recognised experts in their fields, and the overall conclusion of the book, namely that psychosocial disorders have been increasing in the Western world since the 1950s, has led to wide-ranging debate. It will be in every library.

Schulenberg, J, Maggs, J and Hurrelmann, K (Eds) (1997) *Health risks and developmental transitions*. Cambridge University Press. Cambridge.

An important look at health from the perspective of the developmental social scientist. The various chapters explore concepts of risk, and show how these may be related to notions of adolescent health.

Seiffge-Krenke, I (1998) *Adolescents' health: a developmental perspective*. Lawrence Erlbaum. London.

A recent review of the literature on adolescent health. Because of the author's interest in coping and adjustment there is a strong emphasis on mental health and emotional well-being.

Shucksmith, J and Hendry, L (1998) *Health issues and adolescents: growing up and speaking out*. Routledge. London.

This book is based on a study of young people in Scotland, and considers whether health messages are more a form of social control than health protection. Adolescents speak out in the book, revealing how they absorb, adapt or ignore the health messages directed at them.

Friendship and
peer groups

Peer groups are not unique to adolescence, nor do they first appear in the teenage years. Nevertheless, they do have a special role in adolescence, and in this period of the lifespan are given great attention by adult society. In this chapter, we consider various aspects of friendships and peer groups, together with some of the other kinds of social networks and settings in which adolescents meet and interact. Thus, in general, we will explore what is known about the friendships and peer groups of young people growing up in present-day Western societies. More specifically, we will look at:

1   the genesis of adolescent social relationships;
2   the dynamics of friendship and peer groups;
3   families and friends;
4   the larger crowd;
5   rejection and isolation.

Twenty-seven years ago Dunphy (1972) suggested that youth groups form in societies where families or kinship groups – groups we have little or no choice in joining – cannot provide young people with the skills and roles they need to function effectively in the wider social setting. He maintained that participation in youth groups was necessary in becoming self-regulating and for constructing an adult identity. In this way, adolescents become embedded in a complex network of relationships which form a continuum, involving best friends, close friends, acquaintances, peer groups and romantic relationships. These groups all allow the young person a certain degree of choice in deciding whether or not to join. Based on his study of Australian youth, Dunphy (1972) distinguished three groupings of adolescents, namely, *cliques*, *crowds* and *gangs*. This is not the whole picture. Young people are embedded in a wider social network that extends from family members through friends of siblings, adults in the community, adults who organise clubs and activities, to adult mentors and so on. Further, they can associate themselves with interest groups whose participants cover all age stages, and be involved in, for example, religious or political groups, and even be in networks via the Internet. However, peer groups are important in adolescence for young people to acquire and learn the interpersonal skills that are valuable for living in complex ever-changing societies. These skills are also important so that adolescents can 'socially navigate' the relationships they develop in the process of growing up, from childhood to adulthood.

Here, we focus on friendship groups and peer groups. Friends represent the small close-knit groups which give support, companionship and re-affirm self-identity. This is what Dunphy called the 'clique'. Beyond friendship 'cliques', peer groups can be considered in (at least) two forms. First, there is the widest category, that of same-age and gender peers. Within this, there is a broad categorisation of 'types' or (sub-cultures) such as 'punks', 'druggies', 'religious' or 'sporty' youths. These peer groups set the general norms of adolescent behaviour for those who are attracted to identify with their values 'at a distance', and perceive – and receive – their norms, not necessarily face to face but perhaps via media 'images'. At a local level, there are the peer groups, which are more akin to Dunphy's (1972) 'crowds'. These groups reflect wider peer norms in the community. Again, they may be fairly 'impersonal' in terms of contact, but are visible within the local 'scene'. Both these types of groups offer values for the adolescent to choose, and, if chosen, they demand that signs and symbols of identification are worn. They exert pressure towards conformity to the group's norms, and these are accepted by young people because they represent the necessary entrance ticket to the group.

This situation can be as relevant to adults as it is to adolescents. For instance, in terms of deciding to join – or hoping to be accepted as a member of – a local golf club or rotary club. To draw an analogy with the Scottish clan system, within the structural boundaries of the clan system (i.e. age and gender norms) each of the clans (i.e. sub-cultures) possess their own local 'tribes' (i.e. crowds), and within these are situated a variety of friendship groups. All these, in various ways, present the young person with a framework of norms for behaviour and values at different levels of salience. To complicate matters a little further, Maffesoli (1996) has claimed that in present-day society adults and adolescents are involved in dipping into, or sampling, a range of varied groupings, which meet regularly, but can all possess different values and behaviours. In this chapter we will offer a relatively simple examination of peers by concentrating upon friendship groups and 'local' peer groups (i.e. 'crowds'), though the wider context of peer norms will be touched on from time to time.

The genesis of adolescent social relationships

As children grow up they learn that relationships with adults are essentially vertical relationships, in that adults are the power holders and young people have to learn to obey and conform to, for example, parental wishes. With their peers they learn horizontal relationships, which are more equal and less hierarchical. Further, in the period of pre-adolescence the sexes draw apart to create the single-sex groupings so apparent in primary school play-grounds. In these same-sex groupings different gender roles and games are enacted. Many years ago Elkin (1960) wrote that socialisation by peers supported the efforts of family and school, mediated the values of the adult world and gave the child contact with a more egalitarian type of relationship, passed on current trends and even fashions in the wider society, expanded horizons, and helped develop the ability to act independently of adult authority. Thus, in its extreme form, the peer group in middle childhood is both single sex and somewhat conformist. This is the time when the sexes appear to draw apart to rehearse rather traditional, stereotypic sex roles in preparation for puberty and the adolescent relationships which are to follow.

As a consequence of these different socialisation patterns, peer relationships have a different meaning for young men and women. Golombok and Fivush (1994) suggest the following development of boys' and girls' peer relationships. During the first years of primary school boys and girls play separately. Girls have a best friend with whom they talk a lot and share small secrets. They also play, but games as such are not of great importance to them. If a conflict arises they end the game in order to regain harmony in the relationship. Boys, on the other hand, play in groups and often do not have a single best friend. They play competitive games with clear rules. If conflicts arise, they are resolved in order to continue the game. Boys do not have long conversations with their peers; if they talk, they talk about the game and its rules. Thus, boys learn to negotiate, to cooperate with a group and to compete. By contrast, girls learn to communicate, to listen and to keep a relationship going. These different gender relationships can be observed for the rest of their lives. Girls have deeper, more emotional and personal relationships, while boys have more instrumental, action-centred relationships (Griffin, 1993; Shucksmith and Hendry, 1998). If boys or men are interested in deeper conversations – they seek a woman to talk to.

Close friendships are the rule during the teenage years. Almost all young people are eager to participate in shared activities and to exchange ideas and opinions with their friends (Youniss and Smollar, 1985). This leads to the formation and maintenance of fairly stable groups and the development of mutual similarity (e.g. Savin-Williams and Berndt, 1990). The quality of relationship that adolescents are able to establish with their friendship group is important. To the extent that individuals can identify and integrate with a group they will derive corresponding benefits in terms of emotional support, assistance and social learning, and this in turn is likely to be reflected in their self-esteem (Kirchler et al., 1995). Perhaps the most distinctive feature of adolescent relationships across the teenage years is the disintegration of the gender segregation that is so typical of middle childhood. Although there is still a good deal of initial teasing, and awkward social approaches to initiate friendships, adolescence does see a progression towards the establishment of cross-gender friendships and romantic relationships. Mirroring earlier social patterns, these changes do not necessarily occur evenly in the adolescent's psychosocial development.

Usually during early to mid-adolescence personal needs and social pressures direct adolescents towards at least one friendship group because the alternative is loneliness and isolation. Although friends typically live in the same community and are similar in ethnic and socio-economic backgrounds, friendships occasionally cross boundaries of gender, race, age and social class. Friendships usually begin in school, while time spent together outside of school strengthens the bond. Some young people find it difficult to establish out-of-school friendships because they lack confidence or the necessary social skills. How well young people get along with friends partly reflects what they have learned about close relationships at home. Every-day family life provides children with many learning situations around self-disclosure, trust, loyalty, conflict, compromise and respect (e.g. Collins and Repinski, 1994). Lack of transportation as well as race and gender differences are potential obstacles to out-of-school friendships (DuBois and Hirsch, 1993), and friendship networks become more exclusive with increasing age (Urberg et al., 1995). Compared with younger children, who are normally more flexible and less self-conscious, many adolescents feel awkward about meeting and joining established groups (e.g. Vernberg, 1990). This may be partly due to the fact that in adolescence young people link to a range of groups, for example, having a school-based friendship group, a community-based group, and one built around a leisure activity, such as a sports club. These different groups demand different roles, have different norms, and may be difficult for some teenagers to penetrate as newcomers. Brown (1990) distinguished between friendship cliques, which consist of self-chosen friends, and activity-based cliques, such as a sports team. He also noted that young people can typically identify with a reference group to which they may not in fact belong.

By comparison with adolescent young men, young women are more concerned with forming emotional, intimate relationships with just one, or a few, 'best' friends. Nevertheless, they do not seem to differ from males in the actual number of friends they possess. For adolescent young women, the larger peer group or crowd is seen primarily as a network of intimate friendships, a place to find a friend, and a source of support and confidences. By comparison with adolescent boys, girls rate their friendships as higher in affection, intimacy, companionship and satisfaction (Jones and Costin, 1995). They are in more frequent contact with, and are more likely to, possess an intimate knowledge of their close friends than are boys (Belle, 1989), and there is an increasing ability among girls to seek constructive solutions to problems through negotiation and the generation of alternatives to create consensus (Leyva and Furth, 1986).

The dynamics of friendship and peer groups

Members of friendship groups usually are similar to begin with and influence each other in the direction of greater similarity (Mounts and Steinberg, 1995). The benefits that accrue to the individual as a result of being part of such a group can result in pressures to conform to group norms. Although the influence of peers during the teenage years is usually positive and constructive, the notion of peer pressure remains a convenient (if simplistic) way for adults to explain anti-social behaviour. While some adolescent groups support and sustain delinquent and anti-social behaviour, their importance for most adolescents is frequently over-estimated, especially by worried parents. Contrary to popular belief, however, in many areas of adult concern, such as sexual behaviour or drug use, the normative pressures from the group may not be particularly powerful, or can be in the *desired* (adult) direction. Indeed, in early adolescence at least, group pressures are often against such activities and may be more positive than negative (Berndt and Zook, 1993). When encouragement to engage in smoking, drinking, sex and drugs does start to feature in adolescence, this may largely be an acceptance of adult values and norms rather than teenage rebellion or experimentation.

Many writers have stressed the need in mid-adolescence for peer acceptance, and comments about peer pressure by young people were particularly noticeable in Shucksmith and Hendry's (1998) study. 'Peer pressure' was used to explain inappropriate, 'risky' activities. So, in a sense, the wider peer network within which young people have their friendship groups can act as a hazard, creating unfavourable norms both by providing incorrect, or indeed false, information, and by producing inaccurate expectations about behaviour. However, it was clear from their comments that many young people do go through an experimental stage, perhaps in response to crowd expectations and pressures, which passes as they mature and become more confident in their independence and self-agency (Shucksmith and Hendry, 1998). Conformity to the adolescent friendship group appears to increase towards mid-adolescence and then gradually lessens. This pattern has been explained as resulting from the individual's increasing romantic interests, which moves the focus of their social attention outside of the group. However, it is equally possible to explain this decline in terms of lower levels of required conformity in later adolescence (Durkin, 1995; Hendry *et al.*, 1993), or because older adolescents have clarified their sense of identity, social roles and social status, and thus are less dependent on the affirmation and support of their peers. As adolescence progresses, conformity to the clique lessens as the social opportunities to be had in dyads and small friendship groups outside the 'crowd' begin to occur. Jaffe (1998) has proposed that similarities among friends are due to the following processes and conditions:

1   *socio-demographic conditions* that bring children into proximity with each other;
2   *differential selection*, whereby individuals seek out as friends those who are similar to them;
3   *reciprocal (mutual) socialisation*, whereby peers become similar to friends by interacting with them;
4   *a contagion effect*, whereby people in highly cohesive groups sometimes do things that they would not do on their own; and
5   *selective elimination*, whereby non-conforming members are forced to leave the group or leave voluntarily.

These processes may operate simultaneously or at different times during a group's existence, and indicate the flexible nature of friendships during adolescence (Hogue and Steinberg, 1995; Hartup, 1996).

It would be wrong to assume that all young people are equally susceptible to peer influence. Most are somewhat susceptible to certain peer influences at certain times, under specific conditions. Additionally, adolescents are more likely to experience subtle pressure to conform to group values and standards ('gentle persuasion') than overt attempts to control or manipulate them (Shucksmith and Hendry, 1998; Hendry *et al.*, 1998). Further, small groups of close friends seem to wield more influence on adolescent behaviour than individual friends (McIntosh, 1996). Young people themselves are clear that friendship groups and crowds are not the same thing. For girls, in particular, a friendship group can provide a supportive, protective environment against perceived hostile 'forces' emanating from the broader peer group. Earlier portrayals of the clique as an inescapable force generating group norms which pushes young people into trouble, is now giving way to a reformulation which lays more stress both on young people's self-agency and their competence to choose their companions by shared interests (Coggans and McKellar, 1994). Shucksmith and Hendry's (1998) findings support the notion that young people make clear choices in the knowledge that participation in different social networks will involve them in different specific behaviours.

Close friendship groups develop by choice and by mutual preference for characteristics and collaborative activities, and in a sense allow the young person a reaffirmation of chosen identity in mid-adolescence. They further enable young people to perceive, understand and accept the values of their chosen groupings. This in turn allows them to be fairly critical, and even scathing, of the fashion styles, behaviours and general social conduct of other groups. In this there is clear evidence in 'in-group/out-group' perceptions which further strengthen and affirm life-style and identity choices (Shucksmith and Hendry, 1998). Social reinforcement around a cluster of behaviours and attitudes allows greater cohesion and selection of friends by preference and by similarity of hobbies, dress, leisure interests, attitudes to school, pop music, group allegiances and so on. Friendship groups emerge as important settings for learning appropriate forms of behaviour, policing of behaviour, devising of strategies of resistance, and the giving and receiving of social support (Phoenix, 1991; Lees, 1993). Interactions among peer groups, friendships and social institutions, especially the school, reveal complex webs of meanings, reputations and identities (Lees, 1993). Approaches to the study of friendship have shown continuities throughout the life course, from the adolescent years to old age (e.g. Ginn and Arber, 1995).

Being popular is highly valued during adolescence. Whereas friendship refers to a close bond between two or more people, popularity reflects the way an individual is regarded within the wider peer structure and the way she/he is treated by the crowd. Popular individuals typically are friendly, sensitive and have a sense of humour. Successful athletes can also gain considerable prestige in communities that value competition and winning (e.g. Lerner et al., 1991; Wentzel and Erdley, 1993). Other attributes that are important to adolescents' popularity include, for instance, being 'smart', wearing fashionable clothing and following particular popular musical styles. Being physically attractive is important to popularity. Attractive individuals benefit from a 'halo effect'. They are assumed to have pleasing personalities that match their physical appearance. One disadvantage of the halo effect, however, is that popular adolescents, assumed to be competent and self-reliant, often find it harder to get support from peers when they do need help (Munsch and Kinchen, 1995).

Physique and body image are major concerns of many adolescents. Being over- or underweight can substantially impact on adolescent self-images and affect their social opportunities (Seiffge-Krenke, 1998). The importance and consequences of physical attractiveness may be greater for girls than boys, because it is a more significant part of the feminine gender role and self-concept in many cultures (Freedman, 1984). The more intimate relationships of girls also enable them to engage in a more detailed analysis and evaluation of their relative standing on attributes such as physical attractiveness (Felson, 1985). For some adolescent girls, an attractive appearance is so central to their gender role that this may cause severe adjustment problems, including a negative body image, eating disorders, self-consciousness, feelings of low self-esteem and withdrawal (Freedman, 1984). Paradoxically, these adjustment problems may be greater for more, rather than less, attractive adolescents as their appearance is often a more significant component of their self-esteem (Zakin et al., 1984).

There is generally a friendship selection among similar adolescents (Clark and Ayers, 1992). Similar levels of attractiveness may be used as a cue that the other person is also likely to hold similar attitudes and values (Erwin and Calev, 1984). As such relationships progress, other psychosocial aspects are likely to become important. These include important personal characteristics and behaviours, such as school interests, music, fashion, smoking, drug usage, personal needs and personality (Gavin and Furman, 1996). However, opposites can attract, and asymmetrical relationships blossom when one partner possesses skills – rather than beauty – or provides supports that are rewarding to the other. In turn, this may allow access to a popular crowd. Having high-status friendships contributes to one's popularity (Perry, 1987). For example, Eder (1985) noted that being friends with a popular girl gave other girls access to the 'cool' crowd. However, jealousy of these very popular girls sometimes leads to accusations of their being 'stuck up' and conceited. Thus, adolescents can be popular and lonely at the same time, and frequent contact with peers does not necessarily guarantee them satisfying relationships (Savin-Williams and Berndt, 1990).

Family relationships and friendships

Friendships, as Youniss and Smollar (1985) pointed out, are based on a completely different set of structural relationships than those with parents. They are more symmetrical, involve reciprocity and are evolutionary through adolescence. While friendships are also important to younger children, there is a change at the beginning of adolescence – a move to intimacy that includes the development of a more exclusive focus, openness to self-disclosure and the sharing of problems and advice. Youniss and Smollar (1985) comment that the central notion is that friends tell one another, and get to know, just about everything that is going on in one another's lives. Friends literally reason together in order to organise experience and to define themselves as persons.

During adolescence clear changes take place in relationship patterns and social contexts. Greater significance is given to peers as companions, as providers of advice, support and feedback, as models for behaviour and as sources of comparative information concerning personal qualities and skills. Relationships with parents alter in the direction of greater equality and reciprocity (Hendry *et al.*, 1993), and parental authority comes to be seen as an area which is itself open to discussion and negotiation (Youniss and Smollar, 1985) and within which discrimination can be made (Coleman and Coleman, 1984). Interactions with parents become increasingly concerned with daily aspects of life such as tidiness, times of going out and coming in, volume of music and so on (Smetana and Asquith, 1994), and teenagers increasingly challenge parental control as they begin to desire equality in their relationships.

However, relationships with parents remain important at times of transition and in future-oriented domains such as education and career, although peers have greater influence regarding current events, fashions and leisure-time activities (Hendry *et al.*, 1993). Importantly, Ochiltree (1990) also suggested that adolescents take their major values in life from their parents, while they consult both parents and friends about relationship and personal problems (Meeus, 1989). Over time most teenagers come to prefer the companionship of peers to that of their family (Blyth *et al.*, 1982; Larson *et al.*, 1996). Friends are less likely than parents to coerce, criticise and lecture, and are more willing to give each other personal validity, social status and shared interests. Further, peer relationships are more egalitarian than adult–child relationships (e.g. Hartup, 1996), while explanations and understandings are more complete (Hunter, 1985). Decreased frequency of contact with the family does not necessarily mean lessened closeness or poorer quality relationships (Hendry *et al.*, 1993; O'Koon, 1997), and much diminished family time is replaced by time spent alone at home – usually in the bedroom listening to music or playing computer games (Larson, 1997; Smith, 1997). Hence, most adolescents acknowledge that some of their closest relationships are with family members, including parents, siblings and grandparents (Hendry *et al.*, 1992; Bo, 1996; Philip and Hendry, 1997). While peers are the major sources of support in day-to-day matters, the social support provided by parents is crucial in emergency situations. Nevertheless, for most adolescents, the pull of the peer group and outside interests (part time job, sports, romance) is stronger than that of being with the family (Hendry *et al.*, 1993; Larson *et al.*, 1996). However, both types of relationships are of importance for coping successfully with developmental tasks. This is supported by research carried out by Palmonari *et al.* (1989). Part of this work involved examining how adolescents use different relationships in order to deal with various types of problem they encountered. A traditional (storm-and-stress) model would predict a straightforward change from 'reference to parents' to 'reference to peers' as adolescence progresses. In fact, Palmonari *et al.* were able to show that young people acted in a selective way. Depending on the type of problem, reference might be made to parents, to peers or to both.

Similar findings have been demonstrated in studies by Meeus (1989) and by Hendry *et al.* (1993). In a cross-cultural study, Claes (1998) showed that the family played a more central role in the relational world of Italian adolescents, whereas friends were found to occupy a more important place for Canadian youth, with Belgian adolescents adopting a middle position between these two extremes. The project also revealed the importance of friends in the lives of teenagers in all three countries, and the key position of mothers within family life. The findings were interpreted as showing the importance of cultural variations and practices in influencing the emphases in adolescents' relationships. In most countries, within the family, mothers are typically described as fulfilling a supportive function for both sexes (Williamson and Butler, 1995; Philip and Hendry, 1997). Yet the transition from mothers to friends as sources of advice are revealed by Treboux and Busch-Rossnagel (1995) in examining young women's sexual behaviour. They found that the effects of discussions with mothers and parental approval of sexual behaviour operated indirectly through sexual attitudes, with the effects of discussions with mothers being strongest around 15 years of age, whereas the indirect influence of friends' approval of sexual behaviour via sexual attitudes reached a peak of influence around 17 years. Williamson and Butler stated that over a quarter of respondents in their study held a strong conviction that they would talk to no-one.

> Many other children and young people said that they would only very reluctantly discuss their personal circumstances with others ... but 'mums' were most frequently described as the person within the family network with whom they would share confidences and talk through anxieties ... any one else trusted was because there were specific reasons ... overall young people had lost faith in the possibility that adults might be able to understand them in ways which they considered to be appropriate.
>
> (Williamson and Butler, 1995, p. 303)

147

This view is strongly supported by the comments made by young people in an investigation of adolescents and adult mentors carried out by Philip and Hendry (1997). Nevertheless, in general terms, parental and peer influences complement each other in ways that prepare adolescents for more mature relationships in their future lives. Family relationships during childhood provide a strong emotional foundation for peer relationships during adolescence. Peers usually model and reinforce in each other the behaviours and values that they learn from their parents (Fuligni and Eccles, 1993; Gavin and Furman, 1996; Dekovic and Meeus, 1997). In this connection it is interesting to mention a questionnaire study by Durbin *et al.* (1993) on 3,407 European-American adolescents. They found that teenagers who characterised their parents as *authoritative* were more likely to be oriented towards peer groups (crowds) that rewarded both adult- and peer-supported norms (i.e. 'brainy', 'popular'). Girls, and to a lesser extent boys, who characterised their parents as *uninvolved* were more likely to be oriented towards groups that did not endorse adult values (i.e. 'druggies'). Boys who characterised their parents as *indulgent* were more likely to be oriented towards crowds with a 'fun-culture' orientation (i.e. 'party-goers'). These findings are mirrored to some extent by the work of Shucksmith *et al.* (1995).

Yet parents are sometimes concerned about their offspring's choice of friends in adolescence, because young people actively select friends on the basis of similar interests, characteristics and behaviours. In part, this may be because in adolescence friends and peers are encountered in settings other than the family home and, therefore, some friends are 'unknown' to parents. At adolescence young people move into negotiating and claiming sets of relationships on their own terms, beyond parental control. Thus, similarities among friends in cigarette smoking or drinking alcohol, for example, may depend more on friendship selection than on peer influence (Berndt and Zook, 1993).

The larger crowd

Peer relationships begin to extend beyond the dyad or small clique of friends to larger, more loosely knit groups (or 'crowds': Dunphy, 1972) consisting of several cliques that regularly associate in the school or home neighbourhood (Urberg *et al.*, 1995). They often have male and female members, and are most common during mid-adolescence. The main function of the crowd, according to Dunphy, is to facilitate contact between the two sexes so that heterosexual behaviours can be learned and practised. Crowds are created when two to four cliques come together. Thus, cliques are often the gateway to crowd membership. Nevertheless, some adolescents – perhaps particularly lonely adolescents – take up activities or interests as a way of belonging to a group (e.g. religious groups or horse-riding clubs) in which friendships might be made. Whereas cliques are usually activity based, crowds are 'reputation' based. Membership implies certain attitudes and activities associated with crowd members. Whereas clique norms develop within the friendship group itself, crowd norms sometimes are imposed by 'outsiders' who view the crowd stereotypically (Brown *et al.*, 1994). During middle adolescence, a loosely connected network of dating couples begins to emerge, as illustrated in

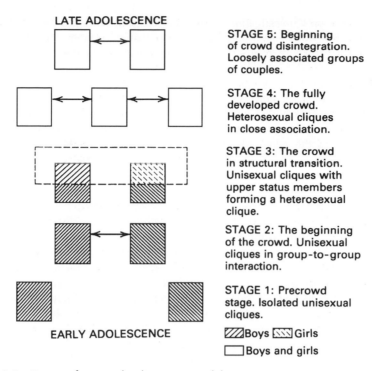

LATE ADOLESCENCE

STAGE 5: Beginning
of crowd disintegration.
Loosely associated groups
of couples.

STAGE 4: The fully
developed crowd.
Heterosexual cliques
in close association.

STAGE 3: The crowd
in structural transition.
Unisexual cliques with
upper status members
forming a heterosexual
clique.

STAGE 2: The beginning
of the crowd. Unisexual
cliques in group-to-group
interaction.

STAGE 1: Precrowd
stage. Isolated unisexual
cliques.

EARLY ADOLESCENCE

Boys ⟍⟍ Girls

Boys and girls

Figure 8.1 Stages of group development in adolescence.
Source: Dunphy (1972).

Figure 8.1. Thus, adolescents in middle school and high school usually begin to leave their close-knit cliques to become members of larger and more diverse crowds of boys and girls. This provides them with an even greater sense of belonging (e.g. Brown *et al.*, 1994). Gradually, by mid- to late-adolescence, these mixed-sex cliques begin to replace the same-sex cliques as opposite-sex peers start to assume importance as companions (Buhrmester and Furman, 1987).

In American studies, crowds are characterised by general dispositions or shared interests – their clothing, preferred music and activities, interest in achievement and so on. Students do not join a crowd 'so much as they are thrust into one by virtue of their personality, background, interests and reputation among peers' (Brown, 1990, p. 183). Each crowd has a set of hard-core members, a set of peripheral members, and those who 'float' from one crowd to another (Brown, 1996). Not everyone is pleased about the crowd with which he or she is identified, particularly those who aspire to belong to a higher-status crowd. In Brown and Mounts' (1989) study of multi-ethnic high schools, between one-third and one-half of minority pupils were in ethnically defined crowds – 'rappers' (Blacks), Asians, Hispanics and so on – but the rest were classified as belonging to reputation-based groups such as 'populars' or 'druggies'. It is difficult to interpret why ethnicity was the defining characteristic in the eyes of peers for some minority pupils, whereas activities, interests or social standing among peers stood out for others. In Brown's investigations many high-school students reported belonging to several crowds – some single-sex, some cross-gender groups – and it is impressive that the core groups were identified by students in many different high schools.

In the later years of secondary school, the boundaries that separate different crowds begin to break down as members of these crowds begin to adopt new perspectives towards higher education and careers, and as some members leave school to start a job (e.g. Brown, 1990; Youniss *et al.*, 1994; Hendry *et al.*, 1998). At this stage of the adolescent years, individualism, and dating dyads, assert themselves as young people move closer to seeing themselves as 'adult' and being accepted by others as being adult (Hendry *et al.*, 1993).

Crowds provide secondary-school pupils with frequent opportunities to experiment with their identity while maintaining a sense of group belonging (Pombeni *et al.*, 1990; McIntosh, 1996). For example, some groups display a subtle, yet distinctive, style of dressing and hairstyle (the crowd 'uniform') that indicates their membership of a particular crowd and their 'separateness' from other crowds (Eicher *et al.*, 1991). (Some adolescents may even apply cosmetics or change into their peer 'uniform' between home and school to avoid detection by disapproving parents.) Given that pupils in large high schools cannot know all their peers individually, crowds help clarify the 'rules of engagement' with same-sex and opposite-sex peers (e.g. Brown, 1996). The dominant crowds in most schools are perceived as socially and academically competent. Groups with the lowest level of involvement in school activities, such as the 'druggies', are viewed more negatively by other groups (Downs and Rose, 1991; Brown *et al.*, 1993). This is equally true in rural settings. Hendry *et al.* (1998) have shown that school, for example, provided one setting for group differentiation. There were recognised groupings of young people often related to perceived peer status and, sometimes, to a pecking order within the peer group. A 'high-status' group was identified and defined as 'cool', and associated with consumption, youth culture and expensive designer clothes.

> There's the 'cool' crowd, which think they're cool. I don't know if they really are better off or richer like, but they all seem to have a lot more expensive clothes. Designer crew. And then there's the 'medium' lot. And the 'sad' bunch. The yokels. It's just the way they are. There's groups of people who just don't go out. They are really childish. . . .
>
> (Hendry *et al.*, 1998, p. 42)

Different groupings were influential in different aspects of school life – both within the formal school structure and within extra-curricular activities.

> The school council . . . there's no point in going in for that. It's just a popularity contest. Everybody in the popular crowd, they've just got it. It's just like, did anybody else get a chance? They just do it for the status, like they don't do it to do anything. It's just a mark about their name. All the 'cool' crowd.
>
> (Hendry *et al.*, 1998, p. 64)

Leisure groupings were also clearly visible in the ways they were described by young people. There were groupings that were differentiated because of particular behaviours, for example, those that were seen as 'bad' and, sometimes, as a threat. There was also a tendency for those interviewed to see themselves as normal and to categorise other groupings as 'deviant'.

> There's the drinkers, and the ones with the drugs, and there's us lot. There's the people hanging around on the streets, sitting on the benches, and waiting for the cars to go past and they jump in the cars and go spinning and that's just it. Some people are in one car and then in the other . . . it's like that the whole night until they go home.
>
> (Hendry *et al.*, 1998, p. 114)

When young people gathered in various leisure contexts there was an awareness of being in the company of like-minded peers, and of identifying other groupings as different.

> He thinks it's a drug hole. It is, if you're in that group, but they stick to themselves, and we stick to ourselves. There's cruisers and skaters. . . . And there's the spivvy lot. They just stand about smoking fags. And there's us lot. We just stand behind the station, and go to the pub. We're normal. We're the only sane ones around here. And there's the druggie-hippie lot. And then there's people who just stay at home and just watch TV. And there's the druggie lot and the cruiser lot, and they have big fights together. They hate each other.
>
> (Hendry *et al.*, 1998, p. 96)

Social activities and contexts were also seen as marking young people out from each other – going out to dances and to commercial night-clubs or hanging around outside late at night in groups at designated places within the community. Against this backdrop of social and leisure activities, some young people were grouped together as 'low status', as socially isolated or immature, often serving as a reference point for others in the peer group. In general terms, however, the friendship groups who participated in Hendry *et al.*'s (1998) study regarded themselves as 'normal' in their interests and activities and, by comparison, the other groupings that they spoke of were typically seen as either 'loud', 'bad' or 'sad'.

Another aspect of peer groups is that large amounts of the adolescent's free time are spent in cliques and crowds, discussing topics of major interest, such as the activities of other members of the group, aspects of popular culture, the latest fashions, recent record and film releases, and television programmes. Adolescents report spending more time simply talking to peers than on any other activity. 'Fooling around' and laughter that may seem aimless and pointless to an outsider, is perceived as among the most fulfilling of their activities by the adolescents themselves (Csikszentmihalyi *et al.*, 1977). When friends cannot meet face to face the telephone is much in use to enable the talking to continue. This is particularly true of youths in rural areas (Hendry *et al.*, 1998).

Many venues serve as meeting points for adolescent groups. Popular urban venues are shopping malls and amusement arcades, though a street corner, park or other convenient assembly point may also serve this function (Fisher, 1995). Thus, adolescent crowds are a common sight around many streets, parks or other public places, and represent important settings for the sexes to meet. Older adolescents and those seeking dates may make more use of these meeting places. Conversely, those feeling threatened or frustrated in their hopes of romantic relationships may retreat from such places of high exposure (Silbereisen *et al.*, 1992). However, it is important to note that the problem for rural youths is that there is no street corner at which to meet, and friends are spread over a wide geographic area, so that the school becomes an essential social venue and meeting point – even though it may not be an ideal context from the adolescent's perspective (Kloep and Hendry, 1999). It is also interesting, from a developmental point of view, to note that the 'crowd stage' often occurs somewhat later for boys than girls, perhaps as a feature of young women's earlier social maturity and their association with older male companions.

Rejection and isolation

Because of the centrality of peers in the adolescent's social life, this is a time when loneliness is a common experience. Sensing what behaviours are offensive is important for avoiding peer rejection. Young people believe that being sincere and caring contribute to successful friendships (e.g. Jarvinen and Nicholls, 1996). Such social strategies require the ability to recognise people's needs and interpret people's verbal and non-verbal cues. Adolescents who are actively disliked and rejected by their peers may be deficient in these social skills and thus are difficult to get along with, or they may be perceived as being somehow 'different' from their peers (Merten, 1996). Rejected adolescents have few, if any, friends in their neighbourhood or school. Anxiously trying to connect with peers, socially unskilled teenagers often withdraw or 'come on too strong'. Some adolescents are not aggressive or alienated. They are simply unpopular, ignored – and shy (Parkhurst and Asher, 1992; George and Hartmann, 1996). Because of their avoidance of social encounters they miss out on the very psychosocial experiences they need to become more skilful in social situations. When they try to interact with peers, the quality of the relationship is not satisfying to either party (Roscoe and Skomski, 1989; Hansen *et al.*, 1995). They tend to be too 'clingy'. Further, they often tend to be the victims of bullying. By teaching rejected or shy adolescents assertiveness and other social skills, and giving them opportunities to practise these skills, they might be enabled to re-integrate with their peers and acquire a range of important life-skills (e.g. Christopher *et al.*, 1993). Some teenagers who do not have supportive friends may only need to interact with peers and adults who encourage them to form friendships. However, others may need training in skills that contribute to forming and maintaining friendships (Savin-Williams and Berndt, 1990).

Some young people are unable to maintain cooperative and friendly relations with anyone and develop a reputation for aggressive behaviour, which reinforces their 'differences' from their peers (Coie and Dodge, 1983; Asher and Coie, 1990). Their interpersonal problems often emerge from emotionally deprived, socially unskilled family relationships that leave them unable to 'read' social cues or adapt their behaviour. Without supportive peer relationships, these children become increasingly isolated and alienated (Buhrmester, 1990; Savin-Williams and Berndt, 1990; East *et al.*, 1992; Levitt *et al.*, 1993). Some rejected children are antagonistic, some withdrawn, some attempt to dominate peers, and others act appropriately but are still rejected (e.g. Merten, 1996). Adolescents who are spurned by their peers are at risk in terms of social adjustment, the seriousness of which depends on the intensity and frequency of rejection (DeRosier *et al.*, 1994).

At the extreme end of the 'unpopularity' continuum are excluded, rejected adolescents. They have few, if any, friends and are perceived as withdrawn, hostile or aggressive. They are caught in a cycle of rejection, harassment and aggression that often begins during childhood. Lacking positive qualities, these young people try too hard to gain attention or admiration, often through anti-social behaviours like boasting or bullying. When their peers reject them, some become angry and over-react. Relationships that they manage to establish are confrontational, and, unlike adolescents with sound relationships, they have few opportunities to learn the social skills that they need to develop close friendships (Bierman *et al.*, 1993; Savin-Williams and Berndt, 1990). Once they are labelled, it is almost impossible for rejected children to improve their situation unless they can change schools and make a clean start (Evans and Eder, 1993; Kinney, 1993). Attempts by rejected and neglected adolescents to reach out to peers during stressful times can sometimes be successful (Munsch and Kinchen, 1995), but trying to change their behaviour to please their peers is usually unsuccessful.

One important aspect of this is bullying. When interviewed, bullies claim that they don't know why they harass their peers (Merten, 1996), and it is possible that earlier many of them have been victims of such harassment in their own families or peer groups. The research of Olweus (1984) with thousands of Nordic youths demonstrated that bullies tend to be anxious, passive and insecure. They feel ashamed, unattractive, abandoned, without friends. Thus, the bully's popularity is often only 'on the surface', their followers only doing so out of fear. Both victim and bully are lonely, and depression is high for both; but whereas the victim's self-esteem is low, the bully's is sometimes high (Kloep, 1998).

Bronfenbrenner (1979, 1989) claimed that the breakdown in adolescents' social networks leads to impairments in their mental health, social behaviour and academic performance. In relation to the social adjustment of young people, and despite the importance of such skills in adult life and relationships, social development in adolescence is not given the significance it should merit in young people's educational experiences (though see e.g. Dornbusch *et al.*, 1996; Kloep and Hendry, 1999). Interestingly, there are some suggestions that programmes for developing interpersonal and social skills can be effective for academic learning (e.g. Nisbet and Shucksmith, 1984; Kloep and Hendry, 1999). Making learning collaborative rests on the idea that peers may be a potential educational resource. Cowie and Ruddock (1990) believed that, given experience and support on the part of teachers and peers, 'pupils can develop the qualities which will help them to solve problems, to complete tasks and to interact effectively with others'. Hendry (1993) has proposed a similar approach in preparing young people for integration into rapidly changing technological societies.

Conclusion

In summary, the role of friendship groups increases during adolescence as young people's ability to form more mature relationships increases (Crockett *et al.*, 1984). Friends act as a source of support, provide mutual activity involvement, and influence. Friendships at this age are distinctive, in that they usually occur between young people of the same age, educational background and interests, whose current life experiences are similar (e.g. Grunebaum and Solomon, 1987; Reisman, 1985). Adolescents report that they enjoy activities more with friends than, say, with adults or casual acquaintances. This participation is largely experienced in the context of leisure (e.g. Csikszentmihalyi and Larson, 1984; Hendry *et al.*, 1993). Heaven (1994), among others, has suggested that boys' friendships are formed through mutual activities, while close interpersonal communication is more central to the friendships of girls. Adolescents report spending time talking with friends about themselves and life events, and in establishing companionships that enable them to experience a sense of belonging. This sharing creates loyalty and intimacy in friendships (e.g. Savin-Williams and Berndt, 1990). In adolescence, being accepted or rejected by peers is proposed as being a possible predictor of mental-health status (e.g. Parker and Asher, 1987). Hartup (1996), for example, has suggested that the impact of friends may vary in that relationships between socially skilled young people may be advantageous, while confrontational relationships could be potentially harmful. Hence, friendships in adolescence, and experiences within the broader crowd structure, are generally believed to play a significant role in psychosocial development.

A number of points can be made from this chapter in relation to young people growing up in changing Western societies. First, close relationships are essential during adolescence. Friends seek shared understanding, openness, trust and acceptance. In addition, emotional and social needs are met, and problems worked out. Because the process requires equality in give and take, friends are the key to understanding the social world through a mutual exchange of ideas, feelings and thoughts that are offered for comment and evaluation. The ultimate developmental outcome should be a feeling of individuality, and yet of being connected to others. Therefore, we should perhaps give more attention to the development of friendship-enhancing skills, along the lines noted in our discussion of Selman's work in Chapter 3.

The second point to make is that, at present, these skills are not acknowledged for their value in working life and in interpersonal relationships across the lifespan. They may become vital in a rapidly changing social milieu. These social skills have importance for life in democratic societies, and should have a more significant place in the developmental experiences of young people. If Maffesoli (1996) is correct about the extended range of groupings we will occupy in modern and future societies, we may have to develop a different view of the value of adolescent peer-group involvement. For instance, one major point to emerge from this chapter is that, in the main, adolescent peer groups are not in opposition to parental wishes or demands. Further, some adults see adolescent groups as different or deviant, yet if one considers adult groups comparatively, it is often easier to see similarities than differences, so long as one can look beyond the obvious variations in dress and activities. A business convention, for example, can be just as conformist as a group of young people at a pop concert. Once again, the point being made is that adolescents cannot learn soon enough the interpersonal and social skills needed for living in a modern society.

Finally, how might we make a start towards such a 'learning' society? We might try harder to remove age segration in many sectors of our societies, in order to develop more horizontal relationships with young people. In turn, this would enable adults to act as role models and mentors, rather than as teachers and supervisors. Also, we might look more seriously at developing venues and facilities where young people could work, play and associate away from adults, in order to practise their social skills. One aspect of modern societies is that social divisions create inequalities, which offer future scenarios of increased risk of crime and social exclusion. To have truly democratic societies, adults need to involve young people in group processes in a more genuine and open way, creating situations of partnership for the benefit of these societies, which one day young people will inherit and govern.

Implications for practice

1. It is not always recognised by parents and other adults, but in adolescence friends and the wider peer group play an especially significant role as contributors to development. Friends are important in childhood, but they become more central during the adolescent years as the young person seeks social support outside the family. In addition, the peer group provides an alternative set of values and opinions, and acts as a useful barometer of fashion and taste. Peers also offer an arena for the development of social skills, and assist in key aspects of identity formation.

2. Issues of popularity and status in the peer group matter greatly during this stage of development. As a result, young people may appear to be conformist in their dress, their choice of music and leisure activities, and in their opinions. This conformity reflects the need to be accepted within the salient social grouping of the moment. As young people develop their own self-confidence and assurance, the need to be like everyone else will diminish, and more individualistic forms of behaviour will become apparent.

3. It is often believed that, during adolescence, the peer group becomes the most influential reference group, and that parents no longer have any part to play. Research shows this to be incorrect. Parents and peers are not necessarily in opposition to each other, but rather the two groups may be influential in different arenas. Thus, young people will listen to their friends when it comes to questions of fashion or social convention, but will refer to their parents over school issues, careers, morality and so on. It is also important to note that young people often choose friends who have views similar to those of their parents, even though it may be essential for them to deny any such similarities.

4.   Because friendship and acceptance in the peer group is so important during this stage, those who are isolated or rejected are at a particular disadvantage. Loneliness can be difficult to deal with, especially when everyone else appears to be part of a group. For practitioners this group need special attention, and, as we have shown, there is a lot that can be done to assist those who find friendship problematic during adolescence.

Further reading

Brown, B (1990) Peer groups and peer culture. In Feldman, S and Elliott, G (Eds) *At the threshold: the developing adolescent*. Harvard University Press. Cambridge, MA.

A review chapter in the Feldman and Elliott text from one of the acknowledged experts on this topic. An excellent summary of the literature.

Cotterell, J (1996) *Social networks and social influences in adolescence*. Routledge. London.

This book by an Australian author covers the research on the social context in which friendship and the peer group operate. It looks at notions of conformity and influence, as well as exploring the difficulties of those who have problems in their social relationships.

Jackson, S and Rodriguez-Tome, H (1993) *Adolescence and its social worlds*. Lawrence Erlbaum. London.

A valuable exploration of the social world of the young person from a European perspective.

Montemayor, R, Adams, G and Gullotta, T (Eds) (1994) *Personal relationships during adolescence*. Sage. London.

An edited collection of chapters by North American writers. It contains some key reviews of interesting subjects in this area.

Nestmann, F and Hurrelmann, K (Eds) (1994) *Social networks and social support in childhood and adolescence*. De Gruyter. New York.

This book contains chapters based on a conference on this topic. Unusually, the conference papers have combined to make a worthwhile book, so credit is due to the editors here. Somewhat different from other books on this list because of the broader age range being considered, and the developmental perspective which this provides.

Work, unemployment and leisure

Many young people today make their social, employment and leisure transitions within rapidly changing Western consumer cultures, characterised by an expectation that individual needs and desires can be gratified through purchase of different commodities. Given the nature of these increasingly consumer-oriented societies, commercial influences on young people's lives have grown and this has had, and is having, a profound impact on adolescence and young people's transitions. Thus the life experiences of young people in modern industrialised societies have changed significantly over the past two decades. In view of these social changes, this chapter examines schooling; transitions to the labour market; work and unemployment; unemployment and well-being; and young people's life-styles and leisure.

Writing about adolescents, Maffesoli (1996) suggests that the more permanent and 'visible' variety of youth sub-cultures of the 1970s and 1980s differentiated by social-class membership, ethnicity and gender, which were described by Brake (1985) and others, have given way to other forms of social gatherings. For young people, supporting soccer teams, discos, pubs, night clubs, youth organisations of various types, raves and so on may represent the social networks of these youthful tribes. Yet for some young people involvement in these tribal networks may be more problematic in terms of opportunities and the availability of cash to 'tune in' to these life-styles. As Coles puts it:

> The transitions of youth . . . can be regarded as being akin to a rather vicious game of snakes and ladders. Main transitions are the ladders through which young people gradually move towards adult statuses. . . . Those disadvantaged by social class background; those brought up in localities in which the labour market offer few opportunities for employment; those brought up in care; those who suffer problems with their health or have special needs; those who become involved in the criminal justice system; all these are prone to sliding down the 'snakes' in the transition game and suffer serious set-backs in their attempt to move towards adult status and relative independence and autonomy. For if youth has been restructured in the last quarter of a century, it is the vulnerable who have suffered the most in coping with the transitions associated with these changes. The costs of adequately addressing [these] youth policy areas are considerable. But the costs of not doing so are also huge.
>
> (Coles, 1995, pp. 24–5)

Schooling and transitions to the labour market

Over one generation radical changes have occurred in the pattern of schooling and higher education. Young people from all social classes tend to remain in full-time education until a later age, and higher education is becoming an experience for many rather than for a relatively small elite (Egerton and Halsey, 1993). Routes through the educational system have become more diverse as young people experience a greater range of academic and vocational courses (Chitty, 1989). Yet, while educational experiences have become more varied, social class and gender remain important determinants of educational pathways and attainment. Jones and Wallace (1990, p. 137) have argued that 'paths to adulthood, far from being individualised, can still be predicted from social class origins to a great extent in both Britain and West Germany', while Bourdieu (1977) predicted that the social and cultural advantages possessed by middle-class children would have a greater impact on levels of attainment as meritocratic educational policies became widespread, a theory which is supported by Zinneker's (1990) view that 'cultural capital' has in fact become increasingly central to the reproduction of social advantage. Ball *et al.* (1996) have argued that parental choice and the introduction of competition between schools have led to social class and ethnic polarisation (e.g. Brown and Lauder, 1996). Additionally, education has been 'packaged' as a consumer product with 'league tables' to encourage parental 'clients' to shop around for the most appropriate school for their children (e.g. Furlong and Cartmel, 1997).

In considering adolescents and schooling, German, Swedish and British data, for instance, all reveal the same picture. Though the level of education has risen across the whole population, 'inequality of educational chances has simply consolidated at a higher level of education' (Apel, 1992, p. 368). Swedish data show that children of manual workers attend university to a significantly lesser degree than those of non-manual workers; they are less likely to complete secondary school or to receive work-related further education; they get less help from their parents with school assignments; and their parents' aspirations for their educational achievements are lower (SOU, 1994). Intergenerational class mobility in relation to education and work investigated by Hendry *et al.* (1993) in a large sample of young people in Scotland in the age range 17–22 years, revealed a powerful effect of social origin in determining the current educational and economic status of modern youth. Apel (1992) reported similar data regarding parental educational level after interviewing 3,142 German youth in the age range 13–29 years. Over 70 per cent of the pupils at higher secondary school (*Gymnasium*) had parents who themselves had completed higher secondary school. On the other hand, over 80 per cent of those aiming for the lowest educational level (*Hauptschule*) had parents with the same educational qualifications as themselves, while only 6 per cent of children whose parents completed higher secondary school were to be found in this type of school.

Inequalities in education seem to start early in life. Jonsson and Arnman (1991), for example, followed 3,600 children on their way through the Swedish school system. What they found was a clear social-class segregation from the start of their school career. There were typically high-academic-status classes comprising a majority of upper-class children (75 per cent living in private housing), and a very low proportion of immigrant children (1 per cent). By contrast, there were typically low-academic-status classes with a majority of working-class children (only 10 per cent living in a private house), and a high proportion of immigrant children (25 per cent). Inequalities at primary school left their traces: the types of secondary school that provide the best preparation for later university studies were 'chosen' by 59 per cent of boys and 48 per cent of girls from upper and middle social classes, but by only 16 per cent of boys and 15 per cent of girls from the working classes.

In a large-scale longitudinal British study, Hendry *et al.* (1993) considered young people's attitudes to various social institutions. The principal elements of young people's interactions with their surrounding social environment were found

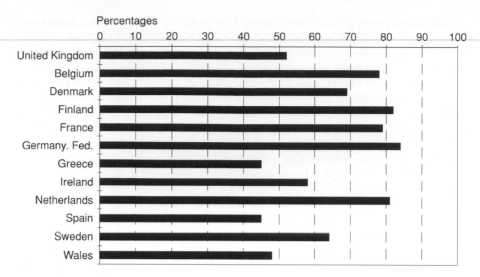

Figure 9.1 Participation in education and training of 18 year olds in European countries in 1991–92.

Source: Coleman (1997a).

to relate to disaffection with school, integration into the peer group, relationship with parents and attitudes to adult authority. In middle adolescence, different combinations of these elements would appear to represent three distinct types of young people, namely, conventional, school and family-oriented youth; peer-oriented youth; and disaffected, peer-oriented youth. Hendry *et al.*'s (1993) findings suggested that the majority of young people may be described as 'conventional', while a substantial minority of young people could be described as 'disaffected'. Examining young people's background, Hendry and colleagues showed that different youth 'types' were linked to the socio-economic status of the family. For example, young people from the 'disaffected' group were more likely to come from 'manual' households and were much more likely to leave school with few educational qualifications and to be economically inactive in later adolescence.

The decline in job opportunities for 'early' school-leavers has led to many deciding to follow post-compulsory educational courses. Although rates of participation in post-compulsory education have increased substantially, compared with many other developed countries' levels of participation in Britain remain relatively low. In the early 1990s between 80 per cent and 90 per cent of young people remained in education or training in many European countries, while in Britain the proportion was only just over 50 per cent. Comparative figures are illustrated in Figure 9.1.

In an attempt to encourage higher rates of educational participation in Britain, a range of vocational courses (such as TVEI and GNVQ) were introduced in schools and colleges of further education. The evidence suggests that vocational options are popular with pupils (e.g. Lowden, 1989). But, because vocational education tends to have a lower status, it has been suggested that this newer form of differentiation would increase inequalities associated with class, gender and race (e.g. Blackman, 1987; Brown, 1987). Vocational options in the school have mainly been taken up by working-class pupils in the lower-attainment bands, leaving the traditional academic curriculum to be followed by middle-class pupils.

With regard to ethnic differences, Drew *et al.* (1992) have shown that at the age of 16 the scholastic performance of White young people was around twice as high as that of Afro-Caribbeans, with the attainment of Asians being fairly close to the White majority. Some studies have also highlighted significant gender differences. Cross *et al.* (1990), for example, show that among Afro-Caribbeans, as among the White population, girls outperform boys. In general terms, young women seem to have benefited most from recent educational changes. By the mid-1990s adolescent young women:

> were maintaining their primary school lead over boys throughout secondary and into higher education. Girls today outperform boys in GCSEs, do better at A-levels, and are more likely to enter higher education. Girls have also been making inroads into traditionally male subjects. They now do better than boys in GCSE maths and are a growing proportion of sixth form and higher education students in science and medicine. More young women than men are currently in medical schools training to be doctors.
>
> (Roberts, 1995, p. 47)

Social 'shifts' and educational changes have also had effects on higher education. The continued expansion of qualified school-leavers, together with raised quotas for admissions to higher education have also led to an increase in admissions to degree courses (e.g. Smithers and Robinson, 1995; Surridge and Raffe, 1995). Increased university education has occurred in most industrial countries world-wide, though increases in the UK have been particularly rapid since the late 1980s. Despite these changes, social-class differentials in access to higher education have been maintained (Halsey, 1992; Blackman and Jarman, 1993). Prospects of graduates have become increasingly stratified, with former students of the 'new' universities in Britain facing the greatest problems in the labour market (Brown and Scase, 1994). As Brown (1995) suggested, a degree from Oxford or an American Ivy League University has greater 'capital' value than one from a lesser known institution. In this respect, an increase in university places generally is unlikely to lead to an equalisation of employment opportunities.

Leaving home: a status transition

Along with the protraction of the school-to-work transition, there has been an extension of the period in which young people remain dependent on their families, and it has become difficult for them to make successful housing and domestic transitions (e.g. Jones, 1995; Coles, 1995). The extension of compulsory schooling, the collapse of the youth labour market, changing household arrangements and forms of family organisation, changing welfare and social policy towards the family and youth have combined to reframe notions of responsibility and rights in relation to young people over recent decades in a number of European countries. These structural concerns alone cannot explain the context of contemporary youth but must be linked to some analysis of developmental issues (Jones and Wallace, 1992). For example, Jones (1995) has examined how patterns of leaving home for young people reflect some of the dilemmas of transitions to adulthood.

> Outside Britain, as within, the timing of most young people's departure from the family home is often only partially a matter of individual choice. The structures of opportunity continue to allow for some and impose constraints for others.
>
> (Jones and Wallace, 1992, p. 28)

These authors concluded that across Europe, a decreasing link has been established between young people leaving home to set up a partnership, although leaving to marry is still more likely for southern European young people.

Part of the process of transition to adult status involves disengagement from parental influence. For most young people in the UK this is a gradual process. Hendry *et al.* (1993) found that only 6 per cent of 17–18 year olds had left their parental home. After this age gender differences appear. Girls are much readier to 'fly the nest' than their male counterparts. Even by 23–24 years, half of the male population are still living with parents, while a third of the girls are in this situation. Only a small proportion of young people feel that parents forced them to leave, and these are mostly in the younger age groups (17–18 years) and among those from manual households. Other studies have shown that the majority of young people moving away from the parental home continue to live locally, often deriving help from an extended kin network (Harris, 1993). It is those who do not enjoy this family support who are at risk of homelessness. The pervasive influence of unemployment has created a shifting population of homeless people who have inhabited the 'cardboard cities' in the streets of central London and other cities. Voluntary organisations estimate that 200,000 young people experience homelessness in Britain each year (Killeen, 1992).

State support for the transition to adulthood has been withdrawn, so that the responsibility of families to provide avenues for young people's development of citizenship has been stressed and extended. As Jones and Wallace (1992) state, young people's access to an employment income or access to the state safety net of social security, access to family support and access to independent housing all interact with the young person's 'personal resources' to affect the transition to independence. Consequently, those young people experiencing family conflict, those living in deprived areas, those having 'special needs', those leaving school early with poor qualifications, or those leaving care are particularly at risk in progressing towards independent living.

Work and unemployment

Present-day society is characterised by a shrinking manufacturing sector and the dominance of the service sector, and the post-industrial era has been characterised by a dramatic decline in the demand for unskilled labour. In the modern labour market, employment contexts are increasingly differentiated, and with increased competition for jobs. Individual academic performance has become a prerequisite for economic survival. Over the past two decades entry to the labour market has become more difficult, and unemployment has become a typical part of the transition for many young people – including university graduates. In the 1970s young people made fairly direct transitions from school to full-time employment. From the mid-1980s to the late 1990s the transitions from school to work have become extended, fragmented and less predictable (e.g. Roberts and Parsell, 1992a).

With an increase in all-age unemployment caused by the economic recession, minimum-aged school-leavers increasingly face difficulties securing work, and by the mid-1980s, the majority of 16-year-old leavers were spending time on government sponsored training schemes (e.g. Furlong and Raffe, 1989). These industrial changes led to a fundamental restructuring of the youth labour market (Ashton *et al.*, 1990) and had a radical impact on transitions from school to work. As a consequence, the number of young people leaving school to enter the labour market at 16 years of age declined sharply. In 1988, around 52 per cent of the school-year cohort entered the labour market at the minimum age, compared with 42 per cent in 1990 and 34 per cent in 1991 (Payne, 1995). The increase in numbers of young people continuing in full-time education post-16 can be seen in Figure 9.2.

According to MacDonald (1997), many young people who join the workforce on leaving school become engaged in the 'marginal' economy and take up 'fiddly jobs', because of the shortage of mainstream job opportunities and because of the difficulties in surviving economically on benefits. Although self-employment among young people has risen, most of those who become self-employed have few qualifications and their businesses have a high failure rate (see Park, 1994; MacDonald, 1997). Thus, across Europe, whether a young person can find employment, and what kind of employment, is greatly dependent on type and length of education. For example, in Germany, only 6 per cent of unemployed youth have completed higher secondary school (*Gymnasium*), while 74 per cent have completed the lowest level of education (*Hauptschule*), two-thirds of them coming from working-class families (Kruger, 1990). This disadvantage remains throughout life. Between 1992 and 1994, the unemployment rate among workers with low qualifications rose significantly in Germany, but it rose least among those with good academic qualifications (Bundesanstalt für Arbeit, 1994). In Britain, Hendry *et al.* (1993) found a strong relationship between school qualifications and labour-market position. At 17–18 years of age, those remaining in full-time education were best qualified; whereas those in training schemes and manual employment tended to be less qualified; and the young unemployed were most likely to have the poorest qualifications. At 19–20 years of age, this differentiation was even more marked. Furthermore, youths coming from homes where the head of household was out of work were twice as likely to be unemployed themselves, while young people coming from a family with a non-manual background were least likely to be unemployed. Similarly, in Sweden, a higher percentage of young manual workers than non-manual workers reported having experienced unemployment during the

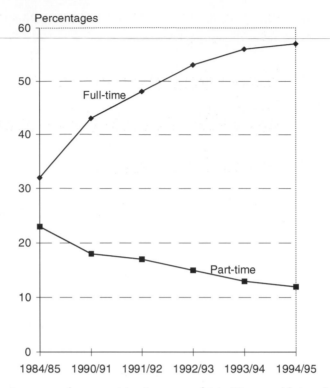

Figure 9.2 Post-compulsory participation rates of 16–18 year olds in education in the UK, 1984/85–94/95. Full- and part-time shown separately.

Source: Coleman (1997a).

previous five years and at the time of the study had no full-time employment (Vogel *et al.*, 1987). Consequently, more young people from working-class backgrounds express concern about unemployment than middle-class young people (68.5 vs. 55.9 per cent of 16–29 year olds; SOU, 1994). For young people, unemployment and the threat of unemployment has had a strong impact on labour-market experiences. As Mizen (1995) wrote: 'Today, in the 1990s, far from being easy, finding a job directly from school has been the exception rather than the rule and many young workers are now forced to confront realities of a hostile labour market in a way unimaginable even 20 years ago' (Mizen, 1995, p. 2). With the collapse of the youth labour market and the subsequent withdrawal of social security and unemployment benefit, 16 year olds tend to face a choice between remaining in further full-time education or finding a place on a training scheme. In some areas where the range of training opportunities has been limited, young people have been sceptical about the value of the programmes and hostile towards the low allowance provided. When it comes to securing jobs, the *context* of youth training, which includes contact with local labour markets and informal recruitment networks, is much more significant than the *content* of the training, including the skills and competencies gained (e.g. Raffe, 1990). Roberts and Parsell

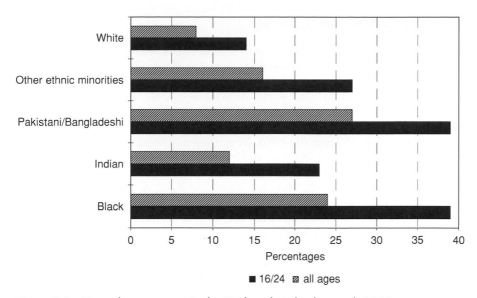

Figure 9.3 Unemployment rates in the UK by ethnic background, 1995.

Source: Focus on Ethnic Minorities (1996). Crown Copyright. Reproduced by permission of the Controller of HMSO and of the Office for National Statistics.

(1992b) stated that the stratification of youth training results in a diversity of experiences, with some young people (primarily working-class trainees with few qualifications and members of ethnic minorities) being trained in contexts where the chances of employment are virtually nil. Although all young people have become increasingly vulnerable to unemployment, in recent years there has been a disproportionate increase in male unemployment, which has been noted in a number of European countries (e.g. Hammer, 1996).

Among the Black population unemployment rates tend to rise faster than among the White majority (e.g. Ohri and Faruqi, 1988), while those who are employed are over-represented in poorly paid occupations (Skellington and Morris, 1992). Differences in levels of unemployment among various ethnic groups are even more significant among older age youth groups. For young adults in Britain between the ages of 16 and 24 years, unemployment is significantly higher among Afro-Caribbeans (40 per cent), and Pakistanis and Bangladeshis (35 per cent), while the unemployment rate among the Indian population is similar to that of the White population (20 per cent). These figures are illustrated in Figure 9.3.

Once a young person gives up hope of finding a job, labour-market withdrawal may represent an option which provides positive benefits. For young women, especially those who are married or have children, withdrawal may be a socially acceptable alternative to long-term unemployment. As Furlong and Cartmel (1997) noted, some young people who experience unemployment after completing education or training, subsequently withdraw from the labour market. Most of those who withdraw have substantial experience of unemployment, with young women being twice as likely to withdraw than males.

Unemployment and well-being

It has been claimed that the incidence of mental illness, eating disorders, suicide and attempted suicide have increased as young people develop a sense of having 'no future' (West and Sweeting, 1996). These trends are also affected by an increasing isolation from the adult world. As Winefield (1997) has noted, it is recognised that the psychological distress experienced by young unemployed people is less severe than that experienced by unemployed older people (Rowley and Feather, 1987; Broomhall and Winefield, 1990). Nevertheless, the continuing high level of youth unemployment is perceived as a major social problem for a number of reasons. First, and most obviously, is the higher rate of youth unemployment, compared with that of adults. Second, there are theoretical reasons, based on lifespan developmental theory to suppose that unemployment during adolescence may retard healthy psychosocial development (see Hendry et al., 1993). Third, there is the fear that widespread youth unemployment may lead to social alienation, manifested by an increase in criminal activity and other forms of anti-social behaviour (Thornberry and Christenson, 1984), and to increased risk of self-harm and suicide (Platt, 1984). Fourth, there is concern in some sectors of adult society that it may have a detrimental effect on work values, so that unemployed youths come to reject the work ethic and prefer a life of idleness supported by the dole to paid employment (Carle, 1987). However, it is important to point out that, into the future, societies may need to consider the development of leisure skills in their citizens as much as a continuance of a work ethic for all.

For the present, Winefield (1997) has commented that those who are unemployed display lower self-esteem and are more emotionally depressed than those in jobs. Two explanations have been proposed to explain this association. First, it has been suggested that unemployment causes a decline in psychological well-being. This hypothesis is known as the 'exposure' (or 'social causation') hypothesis. Second, it has been suggested that people whose psychological well-being is low are less likely to be offered jobs (and/or are more likely to be sacked). This hypothesis is known as the 'selection' (or 'drift') hypothesis. Both theories, however, can co-exist and be relevant within one study (e.g. Nasstrøm and Kloep, 1994).

As Winefield (1997) pointed out, the complexity of these interpretations is demonstrated by the fact that even studies conducted within the same country at around the same time report conflicting findings. For example, several prospective longitudinal studies of school-leavers were carried out in Australia around 1980 (Tiggemann and Winefield, 1984; Patton and Noller, 1984; Feather and O'Brien, 1986). Although all the studies found that psychological well-being was better in the employed than in the unemployed, the evidence as to how the difference arose is conflicting. The study by Tiggemann and Winefield reported improved well-being in those who gained employment after leaving school but no change in those who became unemployed. On the other hand, the studies by Feather and O'Brien (1986) and Patton and Noller (1984) showed no change in those who gained employment, but a decline in those who became unemployed. Winefield et al. (1993) were among the first to demonstrate persuasively that young people employed in jobs with which they were dissatisfied were consistently as badly off in terms of mental health as their unemployed peers. Prause and Dooley (1997) have taken this notion further – both conceptually and empirically – with their call for thinking in terms of a 'continuum of employment statuses', which include continuing unemployment, intermittent unemployment, involuntary part-time employment and full-time employment. As Fryer (1995) notes:

> Many people have careers of labour market disadvantage consisting of moving from school or insecure, psychologically dissatisfying, stressful jobs within the secondary labour market via training schemes into further unemployment or other insecure psychologically dissatisfying or mental health threatening employment or sickness and so on in a cycle of adverse labour market experience. All this takes place, for many, in the context of living in communities hard hit by unemployment, with a disproportionate likelihood of family and friends also being unemployed or in psychologically poor quality jobs in a nation in which the real value of benefits, wages and working conditions are deteriorating, where the labour market is being increasingly casualised, part-time, short-contract and insecure employment increasing, full time, secure, employment decreasing and where the gap between the relatively poor and the relatively well-off is widening.
>
> (Fryer, 1995, p. 269)

In a context of locally low unemployment, however, the experience of unemployment is likely to be more distressing (Jackson and Warr, 1987). It follows that those who become unemployed because of mental-health problems (individual drift) are at risk of having their problems exacerbated or compounded (cumulatively or by multiplying) by social causation (Fryer, 1997). Further, there is increasing reason to believe that pre-unemployment and post-unemployment psychological distress is high for many in the labour market and will increase still further. The anticipation of unemployment has been shown to be particularly distressing. Ullah and Brotherton (1989) reported levels of psychological distress in UK secondary school pupils as high as those in unemployed people. They attributed this distress to concern about high levels of unemployment. As Wilkinson (1990, p. 405) wrote: 'Our environment and standard of living no longer impact on our health primarily through direct physical causes, regardless of our attitudes and perceptions, but have come to do so mainly through social and cognitively mediated processes.' The social and cognitively mediated processes by which unemployment causes mental ill health are important to understand.

Some simple resolutions to these issues can be found by referring back to an earlier theoretical model proposed by Hendry (1987). Here, it was suggested that the consequences of unemployment could be considered in a similar way to the focal model which we described in Chapter 1. The focal model of psychosocial concerns in adolescence explained how some young people can find the teenage years stressful, while the majority cope well. Sources of stress, such as identity crisis or role development, rarely occur at the same time; they can usually be dealt with separately and cause the adolescent little or no distress. Sometimes, however, several sources of stress affect the adolescent concurrently, making it increasingly difficult to cope with the pressures. Similarly, the unemployed adolescent will usually undergo a mixture of positive and negative experiences. It is only when a number of negative factors impinge on the individual concurrently, and cumulatively, that unemployment becomes an ordeal like other adolescent crises. Often, the influence of several positive factors can allow the unemployed youth to cope relatively easily with the experience. For instance, a supportive family, enjoyable leisure and good time structure create the potential for an individual to cope with unemployment even after a fairly lengthy period without work.

It is being suggested that these apparent paradoxes may be resolved by interpreting the experience of unemployment for young people in terms of positive and negative 'trade-offs'. Rather, as the focal model suggests, the reality of the process of unemployment can be viewed as a series of different psychological and social issues hitting the individual sequentially. Problems occur when several issues overlap. These factors, in combination, produce the elements around which coping strategies develop or a growing state of distress emerges in the face of unemployment continuing. There is strong evidence to show that young people continue to retain very high levels of employment commitment even after long periods of unemployment. This may be to their disadvantage, since higher levels of employment commitment are associated with higher levels of distress among unemployed people. This results in young people continuing to compete for the few jobs available, thus functioning as a reserve army of youth labour.

Young people, leisure and life-styles

The 'affluent teenager' was initially a phenomenon of the post-war boom in western Europe (Davis, 1990). A period of stable and relatively full employment of youth led to high earnings and a new market for consumer goods. Davis, however, has pointed out that this picture tends to gloss over differences between different groups of young people – for example, those in full-time education or those in full-time employment and the unemployed, young White men and their Black counterparts, and young women. More recently, Stewart (1992) has suggested that the overall spending power of adolescents was not very significant compared with other consumer groups, but the difference lay in the 'discretionary' element, so that purchasing was largely concentrated in the 'non-essential' or leisure markets. Further, citizenship rights are inconsistent, as Coleman and Warren-Adamson (1992) have pointed out in relation to the UK context. Thus, some rights can be claimed at 16 years (the heterosexual age of consent), while others will not be assumed until 26 years of age (classed as an adult entitled to housing benefit).

Ziehe (1994) commented that family background, social class and regional origin have become less significant for the future life-style of the individual, and that modern society confronts youth with both the option of and the pressure towards life-style choice. In other words, it can be argued that there is a fostering of individualism in society. It is possible for people to portray a range of 'styles', since there can be a variety of overlapping groups with which they can identify and within which they can play roles associated with everyday social networks. Maffesoli (1996) makes this point when he discusses 'neo-tribes' in present-day society. Yet, it is also possible to suggest that these tribal 'styles', however fluid and relatively transient, can contain within them 'embedded' values which influence the developing adolescent's life-style.

Hendry *et al.* (1993) found that in Britain social class *does* impact on young people's leisure interests, in the sense that middle-class adolescents are more likely to be involved in organised adult leisure pursuits and clubs and less likely to be engaged in peer-oriented casual leisure. Additionally, in late adolescence, around the ages of 18–20 years, economic status had a particular effect on young people's leisure, creating the situation where unemployed young people took less part in commercial forms of leisure and were more involved in attending youth clubs and 'hanging around on street corners'. Many of these unemployed adolescents resented the fact that they could not afford the same entertainment as their peers who were working. They felt trapped in a limbo between youth clubs they had outgrown and 'adult leisure' provision that was too expensive for them. The leisure patterns in other European countries reflect similar class biases. For example, Swedish youth of non-manual parents participate in all kinds of leisure-time activities (with the exception of fishing and gardening) to a higher degree than offspring of working-class parents (SOU, 1994). This is particularly true for organised activities, such as joining sports clubs, visiting the local library or reading a daily newspaper. Working-class young people also travel less and are more likely to have never been abroad (Vogel *et al.*, 1987). Young people attending the German *Hauptschule*, or adolescent children of parents who have lower levels of education, are less likely to participate in organised leisure-time activities than those from higher secondary school or with parents with a higher educational background.

In general terms, Hendry (1983) has theorised that the leisure patterns of both boys and girls move through three age-related stages: 'organised leisure', 'casual leisure' and 'commercial leisure', with boys making transitions from one phase to the next slightly later than girls. Organised leisure includes sports participation and adult-led activities, which tend to decline from 13 to 14 years of age. Casual leisure includes 'hanging around' with friends, and this tends to be less common after the age of 16. Commercial leisure becomes the predominant form after the age of 16 and includes cinema attendance as well as visiting discos, clubs and pubs: on average, 75 per cent of 16 to 24 year olds, for example, visit pubs four times a week (Willis, 1990).

Using a different empirical approach from Coleman (1974), with a representative sample of Scottish adolescents, Hendry *et al.* (1993) found the same general age trends in relational issues as in the original study, which formed the background to the formulation of the focal model. This may seem surprising, given the many societal changes that have occurred since the original theory was presented a number of years ago. The results confirmed the age trends in adolescent leisure transitions proposed by Hendry (1983), and suggested that casual and informal leisure activities outwith the home, such as 'hanging about with friends' in the local neighbourhood, are at a peak in middle adolescence and fall away rapidly thereafter, while commercial leisure venues, such as cinemas, discos, clubs and pubs, steadily increase in importance across the adolescent years to reach a peak in later adolescence. Gender differences were evident in these leisure transitions, with a decline in the use of the local neighbourhood seen to be more marked among young women, and an increase in pub attendance more marked among young men. The results certainly suggest that young people's leisure involvement is linked to social-class background (where social-class differences relate to casual rather than commercial leisure involvement), but the key finding is that age trends in leisure involvement are broadly similar for all social groupings.

Irrespective of the transitional routes followed by young people, strong differences are evident between males and females (Furlong *et al.*, 1990). At all stages, women's leisure participation has been constrained by gender relations (Griffin, 1993; Lees, 1993). In the past two decades there have been changes in the leisure patterns of young women, yet gender has remained a strong predictor of participation in 'active' pursuits (see e.g. Glyptis, 1989; Wold and Hendry, 1998). In particular, leisure opportunities are restricted through conventions governing the use of 'space'. Coakley and White (1992) cited conventions tending to prevent young women from entering snooker halls alone, while accepting women who accompany a boyfriend or brother as spectators. By contrast, there are fewer conventions which restrict the activities of young males. Hendry *et al.* (1993) have reported that many leisure settings are male preserves, and that this lack of access to leisure 'space' for girls means that they often retreat into home-based activities. They suggested that female cultures tend to emphasise 'best friends' and close relationships in small groups, and that this results in some 'psychological' discomfort with collective team situations. Future participation patterns may, however, reveal fewer gender biases.

Coakley and White (1992) argued that young men regard sporting activity as congruent with the masculine role and gain kudos from engaging in competitive activities. On the other hand, young women are less likely to connect sports activity with the process of becoming a woman, and may avoid participating in leisure activities which may be perceived as threatening to their femininity. Focusing on sports participation, Hendry and colleagues (1993) found that among 13 to 20 year olds, around three-quarters of males but less than half of females participated in sports on a weekly basis. Coakley and White (1992, p. 32) suggested that 'the decision to participate in sport was integrally tied to the way young people viewed themselves and their connection in the social world'. Throughout adolescence, young people's involvement in sporting activities declines, with young women 'dropping out' at an earlier stage than men (Hendry *et al.*, 1993).

Participation in many home-based leisure pursuits also varies by gender – with the exception of watching television and videos and listening to the radio and popular music (Furnham and Gunter, 1989). Figures from the General Household Survey in Britain (OPCS, 1995) show that young males are more likely to spend time on DIY (Do-It-Yourself) projects and gardening, while females spend time dressmaking and knitting. In terms of gender differences in leisure activities, little change in patterns of participation over the past decade are discernible. Fitzgerald *et al.* (1995) interviewed adolescents in Ireland about their leisure pursuits. The most popular activities of boys and girls matched those of adolescents in the United States and Britain – watching television and listening to the radio, visiting friends, listening to music, having friends visit, and reading newspapers and magazines (Trew, 1997).

To turn now more generally to leisure, Jaffe (1998) tells us that about 40 per cent of the waking hours of adolescents in the United States are spent in casual, non-directed leisure, compared with 29 per cent in 'productive' time and 31 per cent in 'maintenance' activities such as eating and performing chores (Csikszentmihalyi and Larson, 1984; Larson and Richards, 1989). Jaffe states that teenagers in other countries spend far more time than those in the United States doing schoolwork and family chores. How adolescents spend their free time depends partly on their family situation. For example, young women who live in single-parent families are more likely to have a part-time job and thus less leisure time (Zick and Allen, 1996). Many young people, like adults, are more content than younger children to spend time alone – reading, sleeping or listening to music. Young men are more likely than young women to go out (Woodroffe *et al.*, 1993), engage in and watch sport, play video games and to spend time alone. Young women spend more time than young men shopping with and talking to their friends, and reading books and magazines (Bruno, 1996). They are more likely to go out for meals, to cinemas, theatres, concerts and churches, and to visit friends and relations. Young women are less leisure active than boys; they are expected to spend more of their free time helping out in the home and are often required to return home earlier in the evening. Moreover, they receive lower wages and less pocket money and have higher 'self-maintenance costs' (Roberts *et al.*, 1989; Furlong *et al.*, 1990). Van Roosmalen and Krahn (1996) found that Canadian youth culture is heavily gendered regarding household chores, part-time jobs and sports participation.

Hedonism for 'hard times'?

Parker *et al.* (1998) have argued that the transition from childhood through adolescence and on towards adulthood and full citizenship is now a longer, more uncertain journey. While objectively the levels of risk of 'failure' are still differentiated by race, gender, wealth, parental background, educational qualifications and neighbourhood, almost all young people subjectively experience this as a long period of uncertainty in a 'risk society' (Beck, 1992). Under such social conditions, where developmental processes and 'signposts' are problematic, it is hardly surprising that from time to time young people seek pleasurable, if risky, transformational experiences as an escape from the harsh realities of everyday life – hedonistic interludes in times of psychosocial hardship. It is clear that the process of growing up has become more complicated, and in this state of rapid societal flux adolescents take risks and weigh up enjoyment and the functional advantages of their various social habits against the dangers and pitfalls. This 'cost–benefit risk' assessment, as Parker *et al.* (1998) call it, is an elaborate psychosocial process in which they decide how far to go to get a 'buzz' or to get 'out of it' via alcohol or drugs.

In relation to this uncertainty and risk, Parker *et al.* (1998) have suggested that there has been a 'normalisation' of recreational drug use, in the sense that risk management has become routinised for many young people. Additionally, Gofton (1990) examined the practices of young drinkers and contrasted these with older drinkers who disapproved of the patterns adopted by these younger drinkers. This was related less to the amount of intake, but rather to the rituals and patterns adopted by both groups. For these young drinkers the aim was principally to 'get out of it' at the weekend and lose control. Sex was an important possible outcome of this and discourses of spontaneity and 'getting carried away' were drawn on to excuse risky behaviours. To this end, high-alcohol designer beer was preferred in order to get drunk as quickly as possible in a restless moving from pub to pub. The search was for a 'high' and for a 'magical' transformation of reality.

For some young people the desire for flow, for a transformation of reality, or for a sense of belonging to a social group may be important and is often compared with adults' rationalisations for use of alcohol (e.g. Klee, 1991; McKenna, 1993). The rave and club culture seems to epitomise this 'hedonism for hard times', where the over-riding imperative is the search for flow and escapism. Further, Mackay (1996) considered the origins of the rave culture as a selective harking back to the 1960s and a rejection of the 'punk' ethos. He saw hedonism as being 'back with a vengeance', with the focus on Ibiza, a traditional hangout for hippies in the 1960s, offering historical resonances in relation to drugs and alternative cultures.

> A fortnight's holiday in the sun became packed into a single weekend, then the next weekend and the next. Tanned youth queuing up in dreary London streets to get into the club, to get out of it, dance floor as beach, beachwear as night-club garb in British winter – why not? The British parody themselves abroad on package tours – why wouldn't sharp youth offer a parody of themselves as parodies abroad when they get home? In Ibiza the Balearic beat took dance rhythms and mixed them with eclectic tracks to produce an intriguing and fresh sound on the dance floor, which British DJs and audiences were quick to pick up on and take home.
>
> (Mackay, 1996, p. 105)

Mackay went on to examine how regional movements, for example, 'Scallydelia' in Liverpool and 'Madchester' in Manchester, have offered particular regional 'takes on' of style and 'hipness', challenging the notion of London as the epicentre. Moreover, it is clear that, unlike many other youth 'scenes', club cultures do accommodate young people of different ages, social backgrounds and race under their roof (e.g. Rietveld, 1994; Thornton, 1997). Drugs played a central part in the development of the club scene and continue to provide a central focus and help build up the feeling of transformation.

Another dimension of young people's involvement with technological society has been investigated by Griffiths (1995). Discussing adolescent gambling and playing slot machines, where the elements of escapism, excitement, uncertainty and transformational flow occur, he has pointed out that this can lead on to 'technological' addictions which involve human–machine interactions. He proposes a developmental model of gambling in which there can be transformations from passive viewer (television addict) to active participant (pathological gambler) over

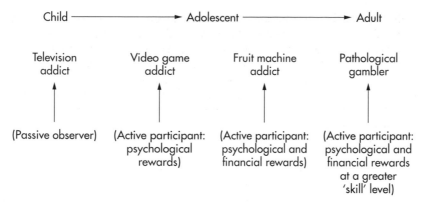

Figure 9.4 A developmental model of a possible route from a television viewer to pathological gambler.

Source: Griffiths (1995).

time. This may have important implications into the future with the development of telephone chat-lines, Internet and video games. One survey of early adolescents revealed that boys spent over four hours a week and girls spent about two hours a week playing video games (Funk, 1993). Some teenagers spend fifteen or more hours a week playing video games at home or in arcades. Most video games have violence as their major theme. Thus, a large number of children and teenagers gain pleasure each day from symbolic acts of violence, often with women as victims (Strasburger, 1995). It has been suggested that violent games sometimes increase players' hostility, anxiety and aggression (e.g. Anderson and Ford, 1987).

Adolescents have become massive consumers of media products and materials – films, television programmes, CDs, tapes, records, computer games, comics, magazines, newspapers and the Internet (Palladino, 1996). Arnett (1995) viewed these changes in the cultural environment as a new and important source of socialisation for adolescents, since to a large extent they select their own media materials and programmes. Arnett stated that adolescents use media for entertainment, identity formation, stimulation, coping and as a way of identifying with youth culture. Roe (1995) extended this to include 'killing time', atmosphere creation and mood control. Watching television becomes 'an opportunity to turn off the self . . . by turning on the TV adolescents are able to turn off the stressful emotions they experience during a long day of school and interactions with peers . . . compared to children, adolescents begin to use TV viewing more deliberately as a response to negative emotional states' (Roe, 1995, p. 544). All of these uses, except entertainment, Arnett maintained, have particular developmental significance for adolescents. The media materials they choose 'reflect important aspects of themselves and their views of the world . . . in their pursuit of information about the possibilities of life' (Arnett *et al.*, 1995, p. 514).

What is being suggested here in general terms is that young people's responses to the vagaries of 'risk society' (Beck, 1992), with the challenges and excitement available in a blossoming leisure sector, allow adolescents to 'transform' from the uncertainties of the everyday world to a 'leisure sphere', wherein risk management appears to be more individually controllable – at times vicariously – even though the intentions are, in some cases, towards mood-altering experiences. This is consistent with Maffesoli's (1996) ideas of the many and varied, if transient, allegiances to different social groups, which may cut across gender and class boundaries, that individuals will adhere to. In turn, such apparent personalised choices will still be influenced by the traditional factors of gender, social class, education and wealth. The significant difference in present-day society, however, is that all these factors are filtered through the various prisms of a technological, consumer-oriented society.

Conclusion

In this chapter we have attempted to examine the effects of rapid social and economic changes on young people's transitions to adult society. Having considered the various aspects of societal change which impinge on adolescents' development, we studied the educational system to demonstrate the ways in which 'traditional' inequalities of gender, social class and race may still be in evidence, albeit in altered form. Working-class young people, and those from certain ethnic groups are disadvantaged, while young women have achieved relative success in late modernity. The issue of gaining independence and developing self-agency across the teenage years was then explored in relation to leaving home. It has been shown that the labour market and governmental policies combine to 'force' young people to greater dependency on their families, at a time when independency and identity are said to be crucial developmental issues. The varied, individual routes that young people take into youth schemes, employment and unemployment have been considered, and again, underlying inequalities are evident. This led to some discussion of the possible impact of unemployment on adolescents' psychosocial development and mental health. Young people's leisure pursuits have been looked at in relation to gender, social class and the leisure transitions from 'organised', through 'casual' to 'commercial' activities which coincide with certain relational issues as adolescents develop. The chapter concluded by examining some of the reasons why adolescents pursue 'risky' leisure pursuits as responses to the ethos of modern technological societies (Beck, 1992). Thus, one thing adults could do to help young people's transitions to adulthood would be to encourage and enable them to develop an appropriate repertoire of psychosocial life-skills. This repertoire might encompass basic living skills for societies such as ours, like computing, reading, writing, personal economy, understanding directions and timetables, domestic capacities and interpersonal social skills. Adolescents should also acquire a wide range of skills to ensure satisfying leisure-time and occupational life, given that across the lifespan employment may not be a consistent state. Clausen (1991) emphasised that a 'socialisation for competence' should enhance knowledge, abilities and controls: knowing something about one's own intellectual abilities, social skills, and about available options and how to maximise or expand them, together with the ability to make accurate assessments of the actions and reactions of others. Most importantly, one should be able to apply these 'competencies' to everyday living.

We cannot teach every life-skill. So what is proposed is that young people develop 'learning to learn' strategies – meta-skills which enable young people to learn whatever they need by organising their learning themselves (e.g. Hendry, 1993). Usually, adolescents are not taught to take responsibility for monitoring the way or the contexts in which skills can be used. Thus, they have trouble applying them again in new situations on their own initiative. Nisbet and Shucksmith (1984) suggested a hierarchical (classroom) learning model which distinguishes task-oriented, highly specific skills from learning strategies. Strategies represent superordinate skills, generalised procedures or sequences of activities such as self-monitoring, reviewing and self-evaluating. Many of these strategies are meta-cognitive in character, that is, they involve individuals in being aware of their own preferred learning and thinking styles, orientations to learning contexts, and awareness of alternative strategies, thus placing them in a position of choice within a framework of 'learning to learn'. As Furntratt and Moller (1982) described them, these are skills 'that support task-solution'.

This is in line with Gardner's (1984) broad definition of intelligence as a set of 'appropriate skills' related to exploring and solving problems, not only in the cognitive domain, but also in the psychomotor, artistic, musical, leisure and social spheres, as well as other aspects of life. Therefore, we should add to interpersonal social skills other 'learning to learn' strategies such as self-management (skills like planning, time-management, setting objectives, self-reinforcement) and the skills of general problem-solving (e.g. operationalisation of goals, information-seeking, decision-making). Then, these meta-skills, together with a high degree of process-awareness, should enhance the acquisition of more specific skills needed for everyday life, in leisure and working life (Kloep and Hendry, 1999). These would provide young people with an arsenal of tools to meet whatever challenges they may encounter on their way to becoming an adult in modern society.

Implications for practice

1. In considering the employment situation of young people today, we have to take into account the wide-ranging changes that have occurred during the late 1980s and the 1990s. The delay in entry into the labour market has had profound implications for education and training, as well as for young people's views of their opportunities of gainful employment in late adolescence and early adulthood. This situation has had an especially powerful effect on those from less advantaged backgrounds.

2. Research shows that unemployment may have less of a detrimental impact on young people than on adults. This may be because it is perceived as being short term, or because more resources are available to assist. It is clear that social support plays a key role in determining psychological adjustment to unemployment in this age group. It is also important to note that adolescents and young adults retain a remarkable commitment to the

value of work, and continue to pursue employment opportunities, even under very adverse conditions.

3. It is apparent that leisure patterns follow developmental trajectories, with a typical pattern involving a gradual evolution from home- and school-based activities to those located in the wider social setting. Leisure patterns are determined both by gender and by social background, and have been much affected by the shift in employment patterns and opportunities in the late twentieth century. The more limited the work prospects for an individual, the more salient leisure becomes. It has been suggested that, where there is little satisfaction to be had from employment, a hedonistic leisure pattern may be discerned. Hard times may lead young people to seek pleasure in the 'here and now', since there appears to be little hope in the future.

Further reading

Furlong, A and Cartmel, F (1997) *Young people and social change*. Open University Press. Milton Keynes.
This excellent book charts the shifts in society over recent decades and shows how these have affected the lives of adolescents and young adults. Policy issues are addressed in the context of the UK and other European countries, and, as an overview of the position of young people in a rapidly changing world, the book can be strongly recommended.

Hendry, L, Shucksmith, J, Love, J and Glendinning, A (1993) *Young people's leisure and lifestyles*. Routledge. London.
The research documented in this book was carried out in Scotland, and is based on a large sample of young people from various backgrounds. The research looked not only at leisure, but at the general pattern of activities and achievements of this group of adolescents. Numerous findings from this study are referred to in the course of the 'Nature of Adolescence'.

MacDonald, R (Ed.) (1997) *Youth, the 'underclass', and social exclusion*. Routledge. London.
Over the last few years there has been a growing concern about the idea that marginalised young people may become part of an underclass, permanently excluded from adult society. This book explores the notion of an 'underclass' through a series of well-written essays, and convincingly shows the improbability of this idea. A landmark book in the literature on disadvantage and youth.

Roberts, K (1995) *Youth and employment in modern Britain*. Oxford University Press. Oxford.
Here, the author looks at the changing nature of the labour market, and the way in which this has influenced the lives of young people. An important contribution to an understanding of the way employment lies at the heart of the transition to adulthood in our society.

Winefield, A, Tiggeman, M, Winefield, H and Goldney, R (1993) *Growing up with unemployment: a longitudinal study of its impact*. Routledge. London.
In this book, the authors report the results of a longitudinal study of unemployment in Australia. One of the few studies of this sort, this book's conclusions make a significant contribution to the literature on the impact of unemployment on young people.

Young people and anti-social behaviour

In the public mind, crime, vandalism, car theft, football hooliganism and other anti-social behaviours are closely associated with images of young people. For this reason, it is particularly important to include a short review of this topic here, covering issues such as the prevalence of anti-social behaviour, the characteristics of those involved in crime and other types of problem behaviour, as well as evidence on prevention and treatment. As Rutter *et al.* (1998) point out, it is a particularly good time to carry out such a review, since the past ten years have seen advances on two fronts. First, the results of a number of key longitudinal studies of anti-social behaviour have become available, giving a new developmental perspective on this problem, and, second, some important meta-analyses of treatment options have provided a better notion of what works with young offenders. We will be discussing these findings in the course of this chapter.

It will be as well to say a brief word about terminology here, since a number of different phrases are in use, and their meaning is not always clear. Terms which need to be distinguished are 'anti-social behaviour', 'psychosocial disorder', 'problem behaviour' and 'behaviour disorder'. In this chapter we will be considering the first of these, namely 'anti-social behaviour'. This term is usually taken to refer to behaviour that is criminal, although it may not necessarily result in a prosecution. The terms 'offending behaviour' or 'delinquency' are also used. It is important to note that children and young people below the age of criminal responsibility may engage in anti-social behaviour – an appearance in court is not necessary for behaviour to fall into this category. The phrase 'psychosocial disorder' is used to describe a wider range of behaviours, and tends to include not only criminal behaviour, but behaviours which we have considered in Chapter 7, such as depression, suicidal behaviour and so on. Rutter and Smith's classic text *Psychosocial disorders in young people* (1995) dealt with crime, substance misuse, depression, suicide and eating disorders.

Next, the term 'problem behaviour' is one associated with Jessor and his colleagues. Jessor has used the term to describe individuals who are tolerant of deviance, and who are likely to engage in a high number of risk-taking behaviours. While some of these behaviours will involve offending, others, such as promiscuous sexuality, will not necessarily do so (Jessor and Jessor, 1977). This concept is similar to the notion of an 'anti-social tendency' described by Farrington and his colleagues. They developed a scale to measure this (see Farrington, 1995), and believe that both offending and other risk-taking behaviours cluster together. Lastly, the phrase 'adolescent behaviour disorder' is also used, but in more of a clinical context (for review see Gaoni *et al.*, 1998). Thus this syndrome covers such things as attention-deficit disorder, conduct disorder and oppositional defiant disorder. It is more difficult to define precisely, and includes such things as aggressiveness, loneliness and isolation, lying, bullying and other behaviours which are not normally included in any definition of anti-social behaviour.

Prevalence of anti-social behaviour

Every review of this topic (see e.g. Smith, 1995; Steinberg, 1996; Rutter *et al.*, 1998) reports a rise in anti-social behaviour over recent decades, whether in

European countries or in North America. Thus, for example, Rutter *et al.* (1998) illustrate this with figures showing a five-fold increase in recorded offences in the UK over the period 1950–90, and point out that the great majority of such offences will have been committed by those under 25. Similarly, Steinberg reports a steady rise in crime among those under 18 in the USA, and notes in particular a dramatic rise in violent crime among this age group. Smith (1995) reports similar trends in European countries. However, there are a number of factors to take into account here. First, most of these analyses take a long historical perspective, usually over thirty or forty years. Yet, in the more recent past things do not look quite the same. Thus, in Britain, there was actually a slight fall in the numbers of juveniles found guilty or cautioned for indictable offences between the years 1980 and 1990. In addition to this, the actual level of recorded crime is subject to variations in police procedure and in methods of data collection. It is certainly true that official statistics give only a partial picture of anti-social behaviour in young people.

Concerns such as these have led a number of investigators to use self-report procedures in order to assess actual levels of offending behaviour in this age group. When such methods were first used the results caused some surprise. Thus, in the Cambridge study (West and Farrington, 1977) 96 per cent of young men from London admitted to having committed at least one of ten common offences (including theft, violence, burglary, vandalism and drug abuse). However, only 33 per cent had been convicted for any of these offences (Farrington, 1989). Other studies (e.g. Huizinga and Elliott, 1986) have also reported very high levels of offending behaviour, although most have found levels to be between 60 per cent and 80 per cent depending on the sample. In the UK, the most recent research project of this type was carried out by Graham and Bowling (1995). They report that 55 per cent of males and 31 per cent of females between the ages of 14 and 25 admitted to having committed at least one criminal offence in their lives, and that in the year of the study 28 per cent of males and 12 per cent of females had committed an offence.

Such figures give a picture of higher levels of offending than would be expected from official statistics, although, as Farrington (1995) notes, there is a strong correlation between self-report and official records when the more serious offences are considered. Looking at the worst offenders (by seriousness and frequency) in the Cambridge study, we see that 62 per cent of those who reported serious criminal activity were also convicted of these offences in the courts (West and Farrington, 1977). Self-report studies also point up another important conclusion. While those from ethnic minorities show up more frequently in official statistics than those from White, mainstream cultures, they do not appear to be more anti-social when self-report data are considered. Indeed, both in the USA (Krisberg *et al.*, 1986) and in the UK (Graham and Bowling, 1995) the evidence shows clearly that there is very little difference between cultures in offending rates. The most likely explanation for the discrepancy between official statistics and self-report data is the way adolescents from minority communities are treated by the police. All self-report studies describe the police to be less tolerant, to give out harsher treatment, and to be more likely to arrest young people from ethnic minorities than those from White communities. Data on comparisons between ethnic groups in relation to property offences are illustrated in Figure 10.1.

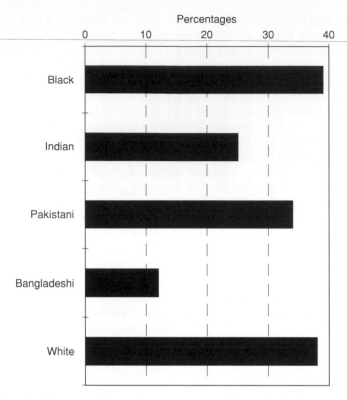

Percentages

Figure 10.1   14–25 year olds committing property offences in England and Wales, by ethnic background, 1993.

Source: Focus on Ethnic Minorities (1996). Crown Copyright. Reproduced by permission of the Controller of HMSO and of the Office for National Statistics.

To turn now to another feature of anti-social behaviour, the evidence indic-ates that such behaviour is not equally distributed across age groups. Most recent statistics show the peak age of offending for males to be 18, and for females to be 15. The age distribution is illustrated in Figure 10.2. This phenomenon has given rise to a number of debates about the causes of anti-social behaviour. Why is it so closely associated with the adolescent period, and why does it decrease so markedly as young people reach adulthood? While there are no clear answers to these questions, writers have advanced a variety of suggestions. Thus, some argue that the social bonds which encourage law-abiding behaviour are weaker during adolescence than at other times (Gottfredson and Hirshi, 1990), while others believe that processes in the peer group or an inevitable confrontation with authority underlie anti-social behaviour at this stage (Emler and Reicher, 1995). Most agree that more work is needed before a satisfactory answer can be found. As Smith puts it: 'It seems likely that the age-crime curve largely reflects pro-cesses of biological development and maturation, but if so the specific processes involved have not been identified, and why they should result in a pattern of fairly abrupt desistance is not understood' (Smith, 1995, p. 173).

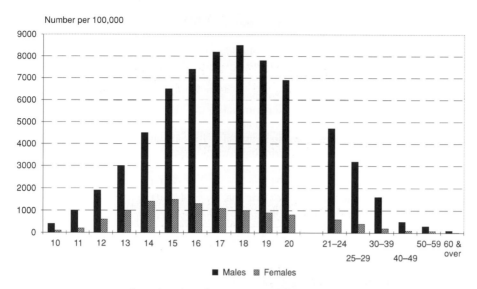

Figure 10.2 Persons found guilty of, or cautioned for, indictable offences per 100,000 population by age, 1995, in England and Wales.

Source: Criminal Statistics, England and Wales, 1995. London: HMSO (1996).

When considering the prevalence of anti-social behaviour, it is also important to recognise that there is a wide degree of variation in the types of behaviour being considered. This is a point strongly underlined by Rutter and colleagues (1998), in their recent review of the field. These authors believe that the longitudinal evidence allows a clear distinction to be drawn between three broad types of anti-social behaviour. First, there is anti-social behaviour which has an overlap with hyperactivity. This usually starts sometime in childhood, is associated with cognitive and social problems, is likely to persist into adulthood, and shows a beneficial response to medication, at least in the short term. A second type is anti-social behaviour which has a very early onset. In some studies onset of 'problem' behaviour is shown to be present even before school age. This type of anti-social behaviour is likely also to persist into adolescence and adulthood, and has come to be called 'life-course persistent'. Finally, there is anti-social behaviour which arises in adolescence, and is, by and large, limited to this stage of development. It is this latter group which is by far the largest of the three. It should be noted that a number of studies have shown a degree of overlap between the first and second types, for example, by indicating that both have more cognitive deficits and higher rates of social problems. As Rutter and colleagues note: 'Acknowledging the hetereogeneity of anti-social behaviour has obvious consequences for the way it is studied and dealt with. Different causal pathways may relate to different subgroups, and different interventions will be appropriate depending on what we know about the alternative pathways in and out of such behaviour' (1998, p. 377).

One of the most valuable longitudinal studies in this field has been that carried out in Stockholm by Magnusson and Stattin and their colleagues

Table 10.1 The flow of criminal activity over time (709 males).[a]

Childhood (0–14)	Adolescence (15–20)	Early Adulthood (21–29)	Obtained N	% of Subjects	Expected N
1. Criminal	Criminal	Criminal	38 (t)	5.4	4
2. Criminal	Criminal	Noncriminal	17	2.4	16
3. Criminal	Noncriminal	Criminal	8	1.1	13
4. Criminal	Noncriminal	Noncriminal	18 (at)	2.5	48
5. Noncriminal	Criminal	Criminal	41	5.8	33
6. Noncriminal	Criminal	Noncriminal	81 (at)	11.4	123
7. Noncriminal	Noncriminal	Criminal	64 (at)	9.0	100
8. Noncriminal	Noncriminal	Noncriminal	442 (t)	62.3	371
P(c)[b] = 11.4%	P(c) = 25.0%	P(c) = 21.3%			

[a] Significance tests for the respective cells are adjusted for the fact that multiple comparisons were performed.
[b] Percentage of subjects who were registered for some offence.
Note: t = type, significant at the 5% level; at = antitype, significant at the 5% level.
Source: Stattin and Magnusson (1996).

(Magnusson and Bergman, 1990; Stattin and Magnusson, 1996). This study looked at 700 males from childhood through to age 30, and documented patterns of criminal behaviour which fit closely with those described by Rutter *et al.* (1998). Eight possible variations are set out in Table 10.1, together with the proportions of the sample which fall into the eight categories. It will be noted that 5 per cent are classified as anti-social at all stages, while 11 per cent are anti-social during adolescence only. Approximately 38 per cent of the sample engage in some form of anti-social behaviour in at least one of the three stages. Of particular interest is the finding that the males in the first sequence (i.e. anti-social at all stages) represent 14 per cent of those who are at some time involved in offending behaviour. However, this group accounts for approximately 60 per cent of all offences committed by the whole sample. Thus, it is undoubtedly the group who are 'life-course persistent', in Rutter's words, who are the most serious offenders.

Risk factors in anti-social behaviour

Research has indicated that anti-social behaviour can be shown to have associations with a number of variables. These include gender, family background, housing, schools and neighbourhood, and anti-social peer groups. It is important to note a distinction here between a discussion of risk factors and one about causes of anti-social behaviour. We are currently still far from clear about the exact reasons which lie behind this type of behaviour, and, indeed, as is indicated in the paragraphs above, it may be that different types of anti-social behaviour will prove to have quite different causes. For the present, therefore, we are on safer ground if we avoid a discussion of causes, and look rather at the risk factors associated with anti-social behaviour. We will look at each of these in turn.

The trends illustrated in Figure 10.2 show two important features of anti-social behaviour. Not only is age an obvious factor influencing the prevalence of this behaviour, but, in addition, offences are committed much more frequently by men than by women. Indeed, gender is considered to be one of the key variables associated with anti-social behaviour (Lyon, 1997). The great majority of crime is committed by males, and this raises a central question about its nature. Why should anti-social behaviour be so predominantly a behaviour of males rather than females? Many different explanations have been put forward to explain this phenomenon. Thus, for example, it may be that boys' and girls' peer groups function differently, with boys engaging in more risk-taking, competitive and distinctly macho behaviour, thereby facilitating anti-authority and delinquent activity (Maccoby, 1990, 1998). An alternative view is that taken by Emler and Reicher (1995). They suggest four reasons for the gender imbalance, focusing specifically on gender identity. First, they believe that girls are less likely to be out and about on the streets where crime is committed. Second, the very fact that girls lead less public lives reduces the need to have delinquent identities for protection in unsafe environments. Third, girls will have fewer confrontations with authority, and thus have less need to demonstrate an ability to challenge that authority. Finally, girls spend more time at home, leading to closer links with parents and a greater opportunity for parents to know friends and to monitor peer-group activities.

An entirely different explanation is given by those who believe that males are more aggressive than females, and that this characteristic is closely associated with criminality (for review see Smith, 1995). In addition, as Rutter *et al.* (1998) point out, hyperactivity and conduct disorders are more common in boys, both of which are characteristics linked with at least one type of anti-social behaviour. Others have suggested that young men and young women are treated differently by youth-justice authorities, leading to higher rates of conviction for men. It is important to note that self-report studies show less of a discrepancy between the genders than is evident from official statistics (e.g. Junger-Tas *et al.*, 1994), so that it may be that the attitudes of magistrates and the police do play some part in explaining the size of the difference between males and females. Graham and Bowling (1995) also explored the gender discrepancy, concentrating on desistance from crime. In their view, the fact that young women are likely to leave home earlier, to have families earlier, and to make the transition to adult roles at a younger age all contribute to the fact that not only do women commit less crime, but they desist from this behaviour at an earlier stage in their development.

Before leaving the subject of gender, we should note that the gap between males and females is believed to have narrowed in the recent past. There has been much talk of girl gangs, and of young women being more assertive on the streets and more prone to getting involved in fights and other forms of public disorder. The hard evidence of this is difficult to come by, but official statistics in the UK do indicate some rise in the number of young women being convicted or cautioned, in comparison to the figures for males, which show little change over the past decade. These figures are illustrated in Figure 10.3.

To turn now to the role of the family, every study carried out on the subject of anti-social behaviour has identified family factors as being highly significant. In a meta-analysis of a large number of British, American and Scandinavian studies

Numbers per 100,000

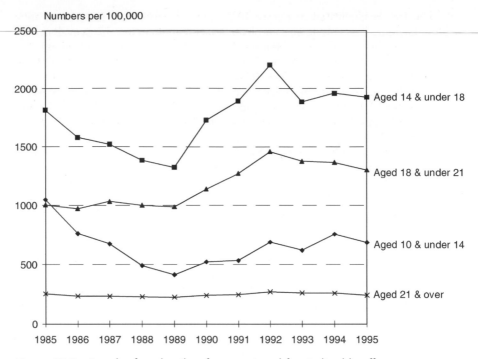

Figure 10.3 Females found guilty of, or cautioned for, indictable offences per 100,000 population by age group, 1985–95.

Source: Criminal Statistics, England and Wales, 1995. HMSO, London (1996).

Loeber and Stouthamer-Loeber (1986) outlined four ways in which the family might be associated with anti-social behaviour. First, they pinpointed the role of neglect, whereby parents spend too little time with their children and are therefore unaware of what they are doing, and with whom they associate. Two elements of neglect may be important here: parents may be neglectful in failing to supervise their children, or they may simply be uninvolved in the lives of their sons and daughters. To take some examples, using data from the Cambridge-Somerville study in Boston, McCord (1979) reported that poor parental supervision was the best predictor of both violent and property crimes. Robins (1978), in her long-term follow-up studies in St Louis, also found that poor supervision was consistently related to later offending.

The second point that Loeber and Stouthamer-Loeber make is that conflict in the home appears to be a key factor, either through direct aggression, disharmony or violence, or because of harsh, erratic or inconsistent discipline. Numerous studies have provided evidence to support this argument, including West and Farrington's (1977) Cambridge research, Kolvin *et al.*'s (1990) Newcastle Thousand Family Study, and many others. The next variable to consider is the deviant behaviour or values of the parents themselves. Thus, for example, Hagell and Newburn's (1996) study of persistent offenders showed that one of the most significant predictors of whether a young person will acquire a criminal record is whether they have a parent who had been convicted. The fourth issue to consider is what Loeber and Stouthamer-Loeber call the 'disruption paradigm'. By this they mean that neglect and conflict may arise in the family because of marital discord, or because of separation, parental illness or the absence of one parent. Again, there is a wealth of evidence to support this, although many writers make the point that it is not the event itself – the separation or the illness – which is associated with anti-social behaviour. Rather, it is the consequences which flow from the event, such as neglect, inadequate parenting or chronic conflict, which are significant here.

The meta-analysis showed that, while all four factors were associated with anti-social behaviour in young people, it was the first of these – neglect – that had the strongest relationship. In addition, there appeared to be a cumulative effect, so that the greater the number of family handicaps, the greater the chance of anti-social behaviour being in evidence. Before we leave this subject it is interesting to note that, just as family factors are highly significant in predicting the onset of offending, they also have a role to play in predicting desistance. Thus, improved parental relationships can have a critical impact on anti-social behaviour, and there is some evidence in the literature that marriage is associated with a reduction in criminal behaviour. In the Cambridge study West (1982) showed that young men who got married by the age of 22 were less likely to reoffend than others in the sample who were not married by this age.

We will spend relatively little time on the peer group here, since this is a topic we considered in some detail in Chapter 8. For the moment it is important to note that for many writers an association with an anti-social peer group is a significant factor in explaining offending behaviour. However, the picture is not entirely clear, since we cannot be sure whether young people encourage each other, or whether it is simply the case that offences are likely to be committed in groups rather than alone. Indeed, there may be a third explanation, namely that young people with deviant attitudes cluster together, so that those with similar propensities and interests are drawn together, without anyone exerting an anti-social influence on anyone else. That said, there seems little doubt that there is a close relationship between the delinquent activities of a young person and those of his friends. In the American National Youth Survey (Elliott *et al.*, 1985) it was shown that having delinquent peers was the best independent predictor of self-reported offending behaviour. Similarly, Agnew (1991), drawing on the same data, concluded that this relationship was strongest for young people who were most attached to their peers, and who felt most peer pressure. As Farrington (1995) notes, however, there is still a problem of interpretation. If offending behaviour is a group activity, then delinquents will inevitably have delinquent friends. This does not mean that the peer group necessarily leads others to offend; it is safer to conclude that having delinquent friends is an indicator of delinquency, rather than a cause of it.

We will turn now to the links between social and environmental factors and anti-social behaviour. While it used to be a common assumption that social class and offending were related, today commentators are more likely to point to other factors associated with living in disadvantaged circumstances. Thus, for example, it is probable that poverty, rather than social class, is critical in affecting the

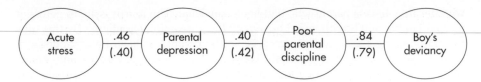

Figure 10.4 Coefficients for family stress and related factors.

Note: Coefficients for father measures above those for mother measures (in parentheses).
Source: Data from Oregon study, adapted from Conger *et al.* (1995).

behaviour and experiences of young people. First, when families live in impoverished neighbourhoods parents are less effective in providing support and in monitoring the behaviour of their children (Sampson and Lamb, 1994). Second, poverty
undermines the social fabric of a neighbourhood, making it more difficult for
adults to provide role models, leisure activities and avenues for young people to
move into adulthood (Bolger *et al.*, 1995). Third, poverty and unemployment are
closely related, and unemployment makes it more difficult for young men to find
appropriate roles, as well as encouraging aggressive behaviour as an alternative
mark of status and power in the community (Fergusson *et al.*, 1997). Finally, there
is a high incidence of violence in areas of great poverty, and exposure to this, either
in the home or the neighbourhood, has an impact on the behaviour of young people.

While there seems little doubt that social disadvantage is associated with
anti-social behaviour in young people, research over the last decade or so has
provided some perspective on how these associations work. Conger and colleagues
(Conger *et al.*, 1994) carried out a longitudinal study of 378 families in rural Iowa,
in the USA, looking at the impact of economic pressure on the parents and their
adolescent children. The results show that economic pressure does have an impact, but an indirect one. The impact is mediated by parental depression, marital
conflict and hostility. In a further study in Oregon, Conger *et al.* (1995) looked at
family stress (as indicated by a drop in income or serious illness or injury), and
showed again that the influence of stress was mediated by parental depression
and poor parental discipline. Results from this study are illustrated in Figure 10.4.
In considering social disadvantage, therefore, it seems probable that factors within
the family are as important as the impact of neighbourhood and the social milieu
of impoverished communities.

Interventions in relation to anti-social behaviour

The risk factors considered above should help to point the way to interventions
which might be effective in reducing engagement in anti-social behaviour. In particular, the role of the family, the peer group and the neighbourhood have all been
identified as contexts in which interventions can be developed. Before looking at
these, however, we will consider two other modalities in which treatment programmes have been located. There is substantial research to show that both
impulsivity and low intelligence are risk factors for the development of anti-social
behaviour (see Rutter *et al.*, 1998), and some important intervention programmes

in these areas are worth noting. First, in relation to impulsivity, it has been clear for some years that young people involved in anti-social behaviour show deficits in cognitive and interpersonal skills. Ross and colleagues believe that delinquents can be taught the social skills which are linked to an avoidance of offending, and thereby lessen the risk of further offending behaviour (Ross et al., 1988). The aims of the programmes are to modify the impulsive, egocentric thought which is characteristic of this group, to teach the ability to stop and think before acting, to encourage alternative approaches to problem-solving, and to enhance moral reasoning. The programmes have been developed in Canada, where they are called 'Reasoning and Rehabilitation', and they are also now being used in Britain and other countries, sometimes called 'Enhanced Thinking Skills Programmes'. The evidence for the effectiveness of the approach is encouraging, although it seems likely that it will not necessarily be appropriate for all young offenders (McGuire, 1995).

To turn now to intellectual development, one of the most successful interventions to reduce the risk of offending has been the Perry Preschool project carried out in Michigan, and described in Schweinhart and Weikart (1980). This was essentially a Head Start initiative, targeted at disadvantaged young Black children, who attended an enriched daily pre-school programme. While the short-term gains in intelligence did not appear to last into the school years, there were long-term effects on motivation, social behaviour and offending. The children involved have now been followed up into their twenties, and the gains shown in adolescence were still present, with the experimental group being involved in less anti-social behaviour and more likely to be in employment than the control group (Schweinhart et al., 1993). The Perry project is only one small study of the effects of pre-school enrichment, but it should be noted that ten other Head Start programmes have been evaluated by the Consortium for Longitudinal Studies (see Farrington, 1995), all of which show beneficial effects in terms of school success, better employment prospects, and fewer special educational placements. Despite the number of years intervening between pre-school experiences and adolescence, there is compelling evidence that this approach could pay real dividends for disadvantaged families. At the time of writing, it had just been announced that the Government is to introduce a similar scheme in Britain, entitled 'Sure Start'. It will be instructive to follow its progress.

We will now consider interventions in the family context, and in relation to this topic the most promising work here has come from the Oregon Social Learning Centre, and the efforts of Patterson and his colleagues. He has focused particularly on the parenting practices of mothers and fathers whose children appear to be at risk, and has argued that monitoring and supervision, the consistent enforcement of rules, and the use of appropriate punishments can all make a considerable difference. Patterson and others (Dishion et al., 1992; Patterson et al., 1992) have developed programmes to train parents in effective parenting, and have shown considerable success in reducing anti-social behaviours, such as stealing and drug abuse, over short periods. The ideas of Patterson and his colleagues have been developed further by others in the field. Thus, Webster-Stratton (1996) has included the use of video to assist parents in improving their skills, as well as broadening the programme to include parental involvement with homework, the teaching of social skills to the young people involved, and engaging teachers in classroom management and the facilitation of better home–school links. Results show that interventions which focus on both parents and young people are more likely to have an impact on anti-social behaviour than programmes which focus on one generation only (Webster-Stratton and Herbert, 1994). In Montreal a study by Tremblay and colleagues (Tremblay *et al.*, 1992) also involved both parents and children, and included both an experimental and a control group. In this case the treatment programme lasted two years. Three years after the completion of the programme 44 per cent of the control group were reported by teachers to be involved in anti-social behaviour or to be in difficulty in school, while only 22 per cent of the target intervention group were in these categories. Such findings are encouraging, although in a further follow-up three years later (Tremblay and Craig, 1995) a number of the gains had faded.

Other areas in which interventions have been targeted include the peer group and the wider social environment. In relation to the peer group Botvin (1990) summarises the results of programmes aimed at increasing resistance to peer-group pressure, and developing social skills. Findings show that adult teachers are rarely effective in such programmes, while same-age individuals have more success. Peers of high status may be used as role models, combined with the sort of cognitive reappraisal approaches already mentioned. In the view of Tobler (1986) such approaches are especially successful in reducing substance abuse, and less successful in relation to offending behaviour. Other strategies which have been used to reduce offending include modification of the environment, such as increased lighting on housing estates or the use of closed-circuit television, or the reduction of opportunity, such as paying wages by cheque rather than cash. In a review of such approaches Clarke (1992) notes some successes, but also sounds a warning note in saying that many offenders may simply move on to other environments where controls are less effective.

What seems clear from our review of this field is that anti-social behaviour is not a single category of behaviour, but may have a variety of causes and involve different developmental pathways. In view of this, interventions are likely to be most effective if they are multi-modal or target very specific behaviours. As an example of a multi-modal approach, Hengeller *et al.* (1996) describe a multi-systemic programme which involves the family, the school, as well as the wider community. In this model it is envisaged that all systems which might play a role in maintaining delinquent behaviour should become part of the intervention. The authors believe that only in this way can we expect to make a serious impact on anti-social behaviour. Hengeller's argument receives some support from a review by Lipsey (1995) of the treatment effectiveness of 400 programmes designed for young offenders. Based on the results of this review, it can be shown that, apart from employment, which is clearly the most effective form of intervention, multi-modal and behavioural approaches appear to have the greatest impact. Lipsey's findings are illustrated in Figure 10.5.

In conclusion, we can see that anti-social behaviour is a characteristic of a significant number of young males. While figures vary, it is evident that, at the very least, more than a third of young men have been involved in some form of offending before they reach the age of 30. Such behaviour is less prevalent in young women, although there is evidence that the gap between the genders in the

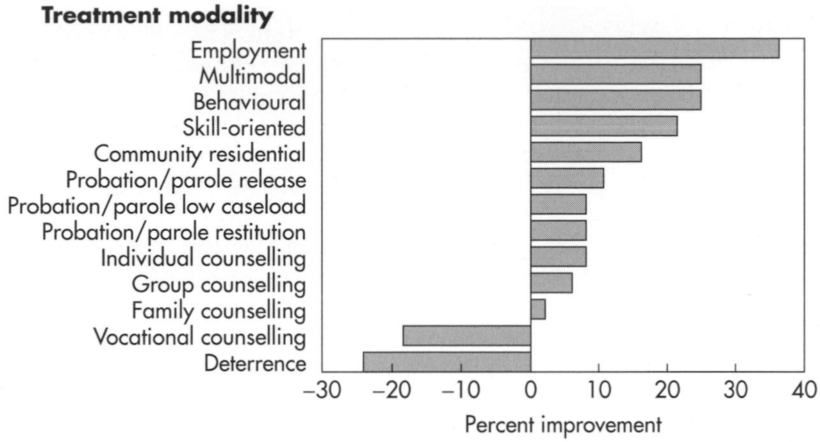

Treatment modality

Figure 10.5 Juvenile justice treatments: percentage improvement over control group by modality.

Source: Lipsey (1995). Copyright © John Wiley. Reproduced with permission.

incidence of these types of behaviours is narrowing. As Lyon (1996) makes clear, both interventions and policy must be based on good-quality research, and in this regard it is interesting to note that the past few years have seen the publication of many important new findings in the field of offending behaviour. This is especially striking in respect of the reports based on major longitudinal studies in Cambridge, Stockholm, Dunedin and the USA. While many questions remain, particularly in the area of interventions, there is a sense in which we can say that a better understanding of the nature of anti-social behaviour has developed in the recent past.

Implications for practice

1. One of the most powerful findings to emerge from research over the past decade has been the conclusion that there are different types of anti-social behaviour, with different developmental trajectories. In particular, it is important to make a distinction between anti-social behaviour which is life-course persistent and that which is adolescence limited. The factors underlying these behaviours will not be the same, and thus interventions will need to be tailored to the specific type of anti-social behaviour in question.
2. We have learnt a considerable amount about risk factors associated with anti-social behaviour from research. While the field is very broad, we have attempted to summarise the findings in this chapter. Young men are significantly more likely to engage in anti-social behaviour than young women, and particular family experiences, including having a family member already involved in crime, are strongly associated with offending. Parental neglect is also a powerful risk factor, as are certain environmental circumstances, including poverty and social disadvantage.

3. As far as race is concerned, it would appear from conventional crime stat-
    istics that young people from ethnic-minority backgrounds are more likely
    to offend than are young people from majority cultures. However, it is very
    important to note that self-report studies of offending behaviour show no
    differences between these groups. It seems most probable that the explana-
    tion lies in the harsher treatment of adolescents who are from ethnic
    minorities by the police and youth-justice authorities. This is a matter of
    serious concern, having profound implications for race relations and for
    the development of ethnic-minority young men in particular.

4. Much has been learnt about the possible interventions available for those
    involved in anti-social behaviour. Interventions include the development of
    social and cognitive skills, the enhancement of parenting abilities, the modi-
    fication of disadvantaged environments, and the support of positive peer
    groups. Studies of interventions show that opportunities for employment
    are possibly the most powerful of all options, but that in addition those
    interventions which are multi-modal are more likely to be successful than
    those which concentrate on one modality at a time.

Further reading

Emler, N and Reicher, S (1995) *Adolescence and delinquency*. Blackwell. Oxford.
This book won a prize for its contribution to our understanding of adolescence. It
looks at delinquency from the perspective of a social psychologist, and presents a
new and challenging view of delinquent behaviour.

Farrington, D (1996) The challenges of teenage anti-social behaviour. In Rutter, M
    (Ed) *Psychosocial disturbances in young people: challenges for prevention*. Cam-
    bridge University Press. Cambridge.
An excellent review article, summarising among other things the work of the
Cambridge studies of delinquency carried out in Britain by West and Farrington.

Haines, K and Drakeford, M (1998) *Young people and youth justice*. Macmillan. London.
A short and readable book summarising the state of youth justice in Britain today.
It has a strong emphasis on policy, as well as looking at practice in relation to
prevention.

Rutter, M and Smith, D (Eds) (1995) *Psychosocial disorders in young people*. John
    Wiley. Chichester.
This book has already been described in Chapter 7. A milestone text.

Rutter, M, Giller, H and Hagell, A (1998) *Anti-social behaviour by young people*.
    Cambridge University Press. Cambridge.
This is possibly the most important book to appear on this subject in the 1990s. It
is an essential read for anyone interested in the subject. It reviews most of what is
known about anti-social behaviour, drawing particularly on new evidence from key
longitudinal studies carried out around the world. It will stand as the seminal book
on the subject for a number of years to come.

Chapter 11

Politics, altruism and social action

A number of factors have contributed to a growing interest in the themes to be explored in this chapter, namely politics, altruism and social action. First, political events, as, for example, the fall of communism, have encouraged social scientists to look more closely at the impact of political change on adolescent development. In addition, as noted in other chapters, the growing focus on Europe as a political entity has led to a new collaboration between countries in the way youth is supported and understood. Next, the very difficulties that young people have experienced, such as delayed entry into the labour market, have encouraged a concern with the adolescent transition, and have fostered innovative research in areas such as participation and citizenship. Indeed, as an example, in the UK the Economic and Social Research Council has, commencing in 1998, established a five-year research programme entitled 'Youth, citizenship and social change'. Related to this is a growing anxiety over the possibility that some young people, particularly those who suffer severe poverty and disadvantage, will become socially excluded, and thereby disconnected from the democratic political process. Finally, the concept of altruism itself has been the subject of new research, with important work emerging on the development of caring (Chase-Lansdale et al., 1995) and on altruistic behaviour (Roker et al., 1999).

This chapter will be divided into two main sections. In the first we will consider cognitions relating to both political and pro-social reasoning. We will consider the development of thinking in these spheres, and ask whether certain levels of reasoning are necessary for behaviour of a political or altruistic nature. In the second section we will discuss social action in its broadest sense. Here will be included participation in organisations and non-school activities, volunteering and engagement in community service, citizenship and involvement in political activity, as well as other types of pro-social behaviour. It should be noted that the dividing line between many of these activities is an artificial one, and there will inevitably be considerable overlap between the different areas of participation. The chapter will conclude with some reflections on the relation between thought and action, and on the nature of the research endeavour in this politically sensitive area of adolescent behaviour.

Political thought and political reasoning

Those with an interest in the development of thinking in these areas have, not unnaturally, looked first to theorists such as Piaget, Kohlberg and Selman in order to gain a perspective on the nature of cognition during adolescence. It will be recalled from our descriptions in Chapter 3 that each of these theorists proposed a series of stages, either in relation to thinking in general, in relation to moral reasoning, or in relation to perspective-taking in social situations. It seems unlikely that we can say that one type of reasoning – let us say Kohlberg's moral reasoning – is a necessary precondition for other types of thought. In her review of the field, Torney-Purta (1990) argues that different domains of thinking appear distinct but related. Eisenberg (1990) believes that Kohlberg's research concerned one particular type of moral judgement; a judgement about moral dilemmas where rules, laws and formal obligations are central. By contrast, Eisenberg herself has

been interested in moral dilemmas where there are no formal guidelines or obligations, and where one person's needs conflict with those of other people. She calls
this pro-social moral reasoning, and sees the two types of reasoning as being
separate, although possibly related. She does, however, report correlations between pro-social moral thought and social perspective-taking, as outlined by Selman.
Work on political reasoning in adolescence is seen by most as having less of an
overlap with other theoretical positions, and in view of this we shall look first at
political thought, and then consider the work of those, such as Eisenberg, who are
interested in the development of pro-social reasoning.

One of the most imaginative research projects in the field of political reasoning has been that carried out by Adelson and his colleagues (Adelson and O'Neill,
1966; Adelson *et al.*, 1969). They approached the issue of the growth of political
ideas by posing for young people of different ages the following problem: 'Imagine
that a thousand men and women, dissatisfied with the way things are going in
their own country, decide to purchase and move to an island in the Pacific; once
there they must devise laws and modes of government.' These authors then
explored the adolescent's approach to a variety of relevant topics. They asked
questions about how a government would be formed, what its purpose would be,
whether there would be a need for laws and political parties, how you would
protect minorities, and so on. The investigators proposed different laws, and
explored typical problems of public policy. The major results may be discussed
under two headings – the change in modes of thinking and the decline in authoritarianism with age. As far as the first is concerned, there was a marked shift in
thinking from the concrete to the abstract, a finding which ties in with the work of
Piaget and his successors. Thus, for example, when asked: 'What is the purpose
of laws?' one 12 year old replied: 'If we had no laws people could go around killing
each other.' By contrast, a 16 year old replied: 'To ensure safety, and to enforce
the government.' Another commented: 'They are basically guide-lines for people. I
mean, like this is wrong and this is right, and to help them understand' (Adelson,
1971).

The second major shift observed was a decline in authoritarian solutions to
political questions. The typical young adolescent of 12 or 13 years of age appeared
unable to appreciate that problems can have more than one solution, and that
individual behaviour or political acts are not necessarily absolutely right or wrong,
good or bad. The concept of moral relativism was not yet available for the making
of political judgements. When confronted with law-breaking or even mild forms of
social deviance, the younger adolescent's solution was, characteristically,

> . . . simply to raise the ante: more police, stiffer fines, longer gaol sentences,
> and if need be, executions. To a large and varied series of questions on
> crime and punishment, they consistently proposed one form of solution:
> punish, and if that does not suffice, then punish harder. . . . At this age the
> child will not ordinarily concede that wrongdoing may be a symptom of
> something deeper, or that it may be inhibited by indirect means. The idea of
> reform and rehabilitation through humane methods is mentioned only by a
> small minority at the outset of adolescence.
>
> (Adelson, 1971, p. 1023)

By contrast, the 14 or 15 year old is much more aware of the different sides of any argument, and is usually able to take a relativistic point of view. Thinking begins to be more tentative, more critical, and more pragmatic.

> Confronting a proposal for a law, or for a change in social policy, he scrutinizes it to determine whether there is more to it than meets the eye. Whose interests are served, and whose are damaged? He now understands that law and policy must accommodate competing interests and values, that ends must be balanced against means, and that the short-term good must be appraised against latent or long-term or indirect outcome.
>
> (Adelson, 1971, p. 1026)

While Adelson and his colleagues did not propose a stage theory relating to growth in political thought, it will be apparent from what has been outlined above that the move from concrete to abstract, and from absolute to relativistic reasoning is consistent with research findings described in Chapter 3. It has to be noted that, following the work of Adelson, there have been only a few scattered studies in the literature on this topic, and little of particular interest emerged during the 1970s or 1980s, a point underlined by Torney-Purta's (1990) review. However, the political events in Europe relating to the fall of communism and the reunification of Germany have provided a stimulus for social scientists in the 1990s. This process has led to some important collaborative and cross-cultural work, and has reinvigorated the field.

Questions addressed by researchers include comparisons between young people from East and West Germany in their perceptions of social change (Noack et al., 1995), a concern with the origins of right-wing ideologies and anti-foreigner attitudes (Kracke et al., 1998), an exploration of pro-social and anti-social attitudes in different countries (Tromsdorff and Kornadt, 1995), and investigations into authoritarian attitudes in Germany and the USA (Rippl and Boehnke, 1995). Broadly speaking, findings indicate that there are fewer differences between countries and political contexts than there are between generations and between young men and young women. Thus, for example, Noack et al. (1995) conclude that comparisons between adolescents and their parents in attitudes to social change yielded greater differences than comparisons between families from East and West Germany. Young people were more optimistic about the process of reunification than were their parents. Similarly, Rippl and Boehnke (1995) found few differences in authoritarianism in their comparison between the USA, East Germany and West Germany. They conclude:

> The central results of this study are as follows: an authoritarian character seems to exist in all three cultures included in the present study, there is no persuasive evidence that state socialism produced distinctly more authoritarian personalities than Western democracies do, gender-specific socialization practices are more influential than the educational intentions of the political system, and adolescence seems to be a 'hot phase' for changes in the level of authoritarianism.
>
> (p. 66)

These findings showed that boys were more authoritarian than girls, and that, just as Adelson had indicated, authoritarian thinking declines during the adolescent years. Many of the studies of East and West Germany have focused on the role of the family as an agent of socialisation in relation to political change. Thus, for example, it was interesting to see that one factor influencing the health of young people during the reunification of Germany was the degree of uncertainty experienced by their parents in response to this event (Noack and Kracke, 1997). Clearly, families are one of the key agents of socialisation, yet there is no direct transmission of attitudes or values in this area. Jennings and Niemi (1971) showed that there are similarities between parents and young people in their political affiliations, and that these similarities are stronger in some cultures than in others (Jennings and Niemi, 1981). However, it is also apparent from the European research quoted above that there will be differences between the generations, and that other variables, such as gender, may in some circumstances be more powerful than parental influence.

Other agents of socialization include the media, and the school curriculum. Investigators have looked at the impact of both these sources of influence, with varying results. Connell (1971) showed that the impact of the media was greatest when it concerned local events which were of more interest to young people than national events, while Sigel and Hoskin (1981) reported that social-studies courses had differential effects on political knowledge, depending on the student's past experience and interest in the subject. In Britain, as well as in other countries, research has generally shown that age is a major determinant of political knowledge. The older the student, the better informed he or she will be, although it is also true that young men do better in tests of political knowledge than young women (for a review see Fraser, 1999). A further factor that needs to be considered is educational attainment, since the higher the educational attainment, the greater the knowledge, interest and participation in politics (Banks *et al.*, 1992). Finally, it would appear that young people's knowledge of political issues is very mixed. There is an assumption that adolescents know very little about politics, but recent research by Niemi and Junn (1996) in the USA shows that although students have poor knowledge of political parties and political history, they do well when asked about civil rights, criminal justice and local government. Thus, as might be expected, individuals will have greater knowledge about topics which are personally salient to them.

Having considered political knowledge and political thought, we can now give some consideration to the development of pro-social reasoning. As already noted, Eisenberg and her colleagues (Eisenberg, 1990; Eisenberg *et al.*, 1995) have explored pro-social reasoning in contexts where there are no formal structures or guidelines. Thus, one story concerns a girl who very much wants to go to a party, but cannot get there without the help of another girl, Mary. The respondent is asked to say why Mary should or should not help the needy person. Responses are scored in five categories:

1   Hedonism. 'It depends how much fun Mary expects the party to be.'
2   Needs-oriented. 'It depends whether the girl really needs help or not.'
3   Approval-oriented. 'It depends whether Mary's parents and friends think she has done the right thing.'

4   Stereotyped response. 'It depends if Mary thinks it is a decent thing to do or not.'

5   Sympathetic, perspective-taking. 'It depends on how Mary would feel about herself if she helped or not.'

Eisenberg and her colleagues report a longitudinal study throughout adolescence and into early adulthood, and are able to show significant changes across the age span in types of reasoning. In summary, hedonistic reasoning decreased during adolescence, but showed a slight increase in early adulthood. Needs-oriented and stereotypic reasoning declined in use as a function of age, while several modes of higher-level reasoning, such as perspective-taking, increased in use across adolescence and early adulthood. The overall level of reasoning in women was of a higher level than in men, and there was some correlation between different measures of pro-social reasoning and perspective-taking.

A similar approach, using a different instrument, has been employed in cross-national studies by Boehnke et al. (1989) and by Silbereisen et al. (1991). The Prosocial Motivation Questionnaire, developed by Silbereisen et al. (1986), uses stories such as the following: 'It's a nice day. After school you go and visit a friend. He's helping his parents to clean up the house. Because it is going to take some time before it is done, you decide to help your friend clean up. What would have been some of the reasons for you to do so?' Responses are scored in much the same way as in the Eisenberg methodology, with a distinction being made between hedonism and self-interest, conformity, and orientation either to the task or to the needs of the other. Young people between the ages of 11 and 18 were studied in four countries: Poland, West Germany, Italy and the USA. Results showed that what were called 'extrinsic' motives (hedonism and self-interest) were least preferred, while intrinsic motives (task and other-orientation) were most popular. Conformity fell between these two extremes. Both hedonism and conformity decreased with age, while only task orientation showed a developmental increase.

Gender differences became apparent from the age of 12 onwards, with girls showing a higher level of intrinsic motivation, in line with the results of Eisenberg. Finally, results also showed strong similarities among the four countries in the developmental patterns and types of response at various ages. The authors make the point that cross-national consistency in pro-social reasoning would appear to support normative developmental trends, rather than ones dependent on a political or social context. Much the same argument was used above when considering the comparisons between political thought in young people from East and West Germany.

Lastly in this section we will consider the question of whether certain levels of thought or reasoning are associated with engagement in pro-social behaviours. Eisenberg et al. (1995) looked at the relation between such things as volunteering, helping others and giving money to charity with pro-social moral reasoning. Results show an overall correlation between these helping behaviours and scores of sympathetic, perspective-taking responses on the reasoning task. However, correlations were weaker at some ages than at others, and there is undoubtedly more work to do in this area, as Eisenberg readily admits. There have been other studies on this topic, as Yates and Youniss (1999) indicate. However, most focus on undergraduates, rather than adolescents, and all use widely varying methodologies. There is no doubt that the link between thought and action is one which requires further investigation. While it may be relatively easy to ask young people to give a response to a hypothetical story situation, it is clearly more difficult to show that such responses have any bearing on actual behaviour. There is a growing body of research which tells us a considerable amount about those who participate and engage in social action. Yet whether the types of thinking studied by developmental psychologists relate to this behaviour remains an open question.

Social action

The involvement of adolescents in social action or political activity is an emotionally charged subject. On the one hand, adults worry about the level of apathy and alienation among the young, believing that this reflects poorly on the health of our democratic institutions. There are also those who believe that engagement in some form of pro-social behaviour is an essential element in any comprehensive education programme. At the outset we noted a growing anxiety over the possibility that some groups of disadvantaged young people might suffer social exclusion, and there is certainly a determination among policy-makers to address this issue. In addition, there are some who believe that young people today are more racist, or anti-authority or self-centred than ever before, and who feel that a greater degree of participation in community service or in the political process may moderate these divisive attitudes. On the other hand, there are those who focus on young people who are activists, protesters and campaigners, and see such involvement as likely to undermine political stability. While all these opinions are significant for the role that young people are able to play in this arena, we will concentrate here on some of the research that has been carried out, and on the views of those concerned with increasing the participation of young people in their communities.

We will first consider the body of evidence on community service, or what is known in the USA and some other countries as 'service learning'. Three questions have been addressed by investigators in this area. The first concerns the characteristics and motivations of the participants, the second has to do with the effects of participation, and the third relates to the process of engagement in some form of service activity. We will look at each of these in turn. As far as the characteristics of the participants are concerned, the most consistent finding is an association between family attitudes and young people's behaviour. Flanagan *et al.* (1999) studied volunteers across seven countries, and showed that there were few crossnational differences in level of volunteering, but that the one variable which distinguished the volunteers from non-volunteers was the ethics of the family. The greater the belief that parents had in service to others, the more likely it was that their children would become involved in pro-social activity. In addition, a number of writers (e.g. Yates and Youniss, 1999) have indicated that young people who engage in pro-social behaviours are more likely than others to have parents who do the same.

An interesting study by Hart and Fegley (1995) took this theme further by studying a group of African-American and Latin-American young people who were described as being 'care exemplars'. These young people were nominated as having demonstrated unusual commitment to community service, usually in deprived neighbourhoods. Results showed that, although there were no differences between the care exemplars and others in terms of level of moral judgements, there were big differences in the way the care exemplars thought about themselves. This group had more articulated thoughts about their personal beliefs and philosophies, and were more likely to incorporate their ideals and parental role models into their images of themselves.

To turn now to the question of the effects of participation, a useful review of this topic is provided by Keith (1994). In this volume, various papers explore the impact of school-based community service. Thus, Batchelder and Root (1994) reported gains in decision-making, pro-social reasoning and identity development among those who experienced a service-learning programme, Giles and Eyler (1994) indicated an increase in a sense of agency among participants in service programmes, and Brill (1994) showed how such participation could reduce isolation among disabled adolescents. Other studies have reported increases in personal competence, grade-point average, and social relatedness (for reviews, see Conrad and Hedin, 1982, Johnson *et al.*, 1998; Yates and Youniss, 1999). Thus, it is clear that the experience of participation in service learning of various types has an impact on the young person's social and psychological skills. Research also indicates that the process of participation has an influence on the way the adolescent develops. Numerous writers make the point that participants report experiencing new challenges, increased responsibility and a sense of achievement during engagement in service activities (e.g. Hart *et al.*, 1996). In one of the few longitudinal studies Johnson *et al.* (1998) were able to show that those who participated in a volunteering activity had developed enhanced community values and experienced a lessening of the importance of personal career goals when interviewed some time after this participation.

Yates (1995, 1999) carried out research on the effects on young people of working in a soup kitchen in Washington, DC. Through the use of quantitative and qualitative material she conveys the marked changes that occur both in identity development and in the young person's world view. There is no doubt that the experience is not only intensely educational, but also influential in raising key questions for the individual about the nature of society, and their own place in it, as the following quotes graphically illustrate.

> I felt a certain spark of joy when a nice fellow named G came over when I was serving the sandwiches and said that he really appreciated my classmates and I to take time out of our life to be bothered with homeless people. It seemed like every time I gave a sandwich away and received a thank you from one of the people I served, I felt respected and I also felt like I had a place in the world as a human being just like those homeless people. I mean a person like Chris, he has a lot of potential, and a desire for comfort and help, yet there he is. . . . The soup kitchen was a good experience for me because it makes me feel a lot more fortunate.
>
> (Yates, 1995, p. 68)

Any type of person can be put in the situation that they have to go to the soup kitchen, old, young, black, white, dark skin, light skin, clean faces, dirty faces, beards, mustaches, any types at all. At the soup kitchen the question I ask myself is why. Why does a man in a suit with a tie come to the soup kitchen, for the company or for the need? Either way I don't think anybody should be at the soup kitchen. There should not be a need, but because of job cuts and lack of hope people are forced to do things they do not want to do. Today I saw a man who I remembered from before. He did not talk to me, just waved a fist. I don't know if that meant he remembered me, but if he did it is a sign. It is a sign that I touched someone's life . . . the sad part was that he was still there in line being fed . . . I just thought a lot about the faces and the people I saw. I was more aware of who comes in. It struck me that anything can happen to the best of us.

(Yates, 1995, p. 72)

In a useful review of the effects of participation, Quinn (1995) emphasises the possibility that engagement in community activity can reduce levels of high-risk behaviours, especially in disadvantaged communities. A study in the USA by Larson (1994) provides empirical evidence of such an effect. Larson looked at three possible measures of participation: engagement in sports, involvement in arts and hobbies, and membership of non-school organisations and clubs. The most striking finding from this research was the negative correlation which the author demonstrated between organisational participation and delinquency, especially for those in the older age groups. This relation is illustrated in Figure 11.1, from which it can be seen that involvement in delinquency and participation in organisations remains relatively stable over time, while the negative relation between the two is strongest at ages 16 and 17 (US school grades 11 and 12). Similar findings were reported for sports activity, but at a weaker level. It would appear from this research that participation has a beneficial impact for young people, possibly in acting as a buffer against engagement in anti-social behaviour.

Let us turn now to involvement in political activity. One index of participation in this realm is voting behaviour, and it is evidence on this issue more than any other that encourages the attachment of the 'apathy' label to today's young people. Recent research in the UK indicates that 45 per cent of those under 25 did not vote in the 1992 election (Wilkinson, 1996), while 50 per cent in this age group did not vote in 1997 (British Youth Council, 1998). As many writers have pointed out, however, an interest in conventional party politics is not the same as being concerned with political issues. Both Bynner et al. (1997) and Roker et al. (1999) emphasise the fact that young people today are interested in, and actively engaged with, environmental, welfare and rights issues, without seeing the process of government as being particularly relevant to their lives. While many report that they are not interested in politics (Banks et al., 1992), or that they do not know enough to talk confidently about the subject (Bhavnani, 1991), the fact is that there is a high level of idealism and engagement in single-issue politics among adolescents, as we shall see below.

Hackett (1997) makes a number of important points about the participation of young people in the political sphere. First, she notes that participation is inevitably related to levels of knowledge and awareness of the political process. In her view,

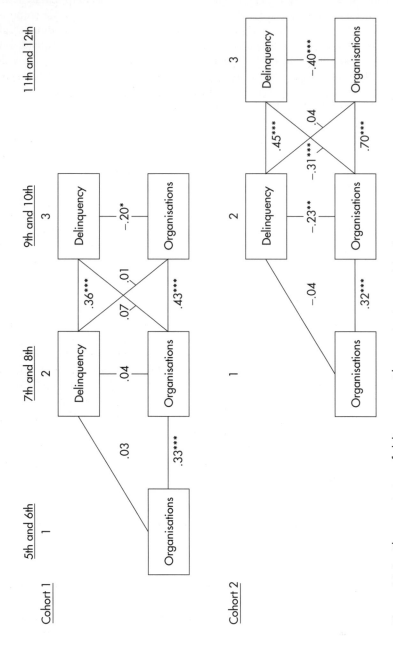

Figure 11.1 The association of delinquency with organisation participation.

Source: Larson (1994).

a lot could be done to increase knowledge of political issues that are relevant to the concerns of young people, a point to which we will return when we consider Roker's research on altruism below. Hackett's second point is that recent changes in education and in employment have meant that adolescents have less time for participation in their communities. Many have part-time jobs in addition to involvement in training or further education, and the constraints of both time and finance limit the opportunities which are available. Finally, Hackett notes that one of the problems of youth participation from the adult perspective is that it requires a shift in the balance of power. If adults are to allow young people to participate in any meaningful way it means handing over some degree of control, and for many this is hard to do. However, the rewards, for both adults and teenagers, are enormous, as is evidenced by a quote from a young man who participated in a Youth Rights group:

> Then it came to me. It was the direction of the group. Before the group started, the idea of self-direction was simply theoretical. It wasn't until the group put this into practice that we realised that the destiny of this group lay in our hands, not the workers', not Save the Children's, not the Children's Rights Alliance, but ours. And for me that was an awe-inspiring feeling. At the tender age of seventeen I was making decisions with minimal adult influence. I felt in charge and how good it felt!
>
> (Hackett, 1997, p. 86)

An important study which crosses many of the boundaries between different categories of participation and social action is that carried out by Roker and her colleagues (Roker *et al.*, 1997, 1999). In this study young people aged 14–16 from three schools in different geographical and social locations in the UK took part. Over 1,000 teenagers were involved in the study, and the findings illustrate a high level of participation in some form of pro-social activity. Table 11.1 shows that, during the last year, over 40 per cent had signed a petition, 70 per cent had given money to a charity, and more than 30 per cent had helped out with a charity. While some of the activities were organised or supported through the school, many were not, and the results show few differences between the three schools in level of participation.

A small but important group, 155 young people who represented approximately 13 per cent of the sample, were members of campaigning organisations. These organisations were very diverse, and included the League Against Cruel Sports, Amnesty International, the Royal Society for the Protection of Birds and World Vision. Some 146 young people were involved in regular, weekly voluntary activity. Such activities included being a volunteer youth worker, helping with Oxfam, doing conservation work, and working with younger children. Approximately a quarter of this group said that they had become involved because of parents or siblings, 17 per cent cited a friend as the main reason for involvement, and a further 20 per cent had become involved because of membership of an organisation such as a church, youth club or something similar. Results showed that, while there were gender differences, with females being more active than males, some boys showed high levels of commitment. In addition, the question of image was more salient for boys, so that it was easier to be discouraged because of the possibility of criticism or teasing by the peer group. Those from ethnic

Table 11.1 Frequency of voluntary and campaigning activities undertaken in the last year (valid % per activity).

Activity	More than once		Once		Never	
	No.	%	No.	%	No.	%
Signed a petition	476	41.1	332	28.7	349	30.2
Helped out at a charity event	383	33.1	386	33.3	388	33.5
Attended a public meeting	112	9.7	212	18.3	833	72.0
Given money to charity	813	70.3	221	19.1	122	10.6
Delivered leaflets	214	18.5	227	19.7	714	61.8
Joined in with Red Nose Day	338	29.2	407	35.2	410	35.4
Gone on a march/rally	66	5.7	128	11.1	961	83.2
Written to an MP/Councillor	53	4.6	133	11.5	971	83.9
Joined in with environmental group activity	77	6.6	180	15.5	901	77.8
Joined in with an event for a third world charity	166	14.4	339	29.3	651	56.4
Helped out with younger children	239	20.7	276	23.8	641	55.4
Boycotted something	408	35.3	278	24.0	471	40.7
Campaigned for something at school	249	21.6	443	38.4	463	40.0
Campaigned for something in local area	155	13.4	397	34.3	605	52.3

Source: Roker *et al.* (1997).

minorities also experienced particular difficulties, either through family resistance, or because of the possibility of racial harassment or abuse. Finally, location proved to be important, with those from rural communities finding it more difficult to become engaged because of problems with travel and distance.

The findings of the study illustrate that pro-social behaviour is not only influenced by personal variables but by cultural, social and practical variables as well. Future research will need to take into account such factors if community service and social action in adolescence is to be fully understood. What is clear is that engagement in pro-social activity has a marked impact on the individual's self-concept, as has been reported in research outlined above. Two young people make the point well.

> ... for me it just makes me feel good. I'm not very ... you know ... like I'm not very good at school work. But at the Club [teaching sports to younger children] I'm the expert, I'm the one who knows. The younger kids look up to me, which really makes me feel good. And you know, I have to do things like organising them, helping them, encouraging them. It's a real skill.
>
> (15-year-old young man, in Roker *et al.*, 1997, p. 199)

> My stuff, activities with Amnesty had a big effect on me. I felt good being with a group of people who were all working for the same thing, who were all caring about others in some way. But it made me feel that I mattered too,

like how many people my age have had to write to the King of Indonesia and ask him about political prisoners?

(15-year-old young woman, in Roker *et al.*, 1997, p. 199)

Engagement in these forms of activity is important for all young people, especially for those who are marginalised in some way. Roker *et al.* (1998) extended their work to a group of disabled adolescents, exploring the opportunities for social action available to them, and indicating much the same effects. As one disabled young woman, campaigning for a Disability Rights group, put it: 'I feel bigger, that I can do things, try things, that I've never done before. Like I'd not have talked to you (the interviewer) before, never talked about myself, like this . . .' (Roker *et al.*, 1998, p. 737).

We said at the beginning of this chapter that we would conclude with some comments on the relationship between thought and action. There is certainly a divergence of interest between those who wish to explore a cognitive process, that is, the development of moral and pro-social reasoning in adolescence, and those who are concerned with social action. While the two bodies of enquiry have both made progress in recent years, it remains the case that there have been few attempts to coordinate the two areas of work. As a result, we still know relatively little about the links between reasoning and action. One obvious gap has to do with the impact of participation on pro-social reasoning. Does this experience enhance cognitive development? It is clear that personal agency, a sense of competence, and identity and self-esteem are affected by engagement in social action, yet what about pro-social reasoning? Similarly, comparisons between volunteers and non-volunteers in respect of intellectual development are also sparse. The field would benefit from a greater collaboration between those with a social and an individual focus. There seems little doubt that thought and action are closely linked. The challenge for research is to explore the links in a more systematic manner.

Implications for practice

1. Recent research has illustrated the fact that more young people are engaged in pro-social activities than is generally realised. Indeed, in some circumstances teenagers are taking part in such activities for personal or idealistic reasons, without necessarily informing their parents or teachers at school. The fact that a significant number of young people become involved in projects which are for the benefit of others or for the community should be more widely publicised. The extent of altruistic or pro-social behaviour in this age group could do something to counteract the negative stereotype usually ascribed to adolescents.

2. It is clear that involvement in such activities has considerable benefits for young people. In the short term it enhances self-esteem, aids the development of identity, and opens the door to new opportunities in terms of both education and work. Research indicates that there are also long-term advantages for adolescents in becoming engaged in volunteering,

especially with respect to the formation of a more community-oriented and less person-centred value system.

3. Research in this field indicates that the family plays a key role in fostering involvement in volunteering and campaigning activities. However, it is also clear that schools and community agencies have a part to play in providing the opportunities and openings for young people to engage in such activities. Where schools and community agencies are active in providing opportunities and in publicising their availability, there will be a greater engagement of young people in pro-social behaviour.

4. Involvement in volunteering and campaigning is of benefit to all young people, irrespective of their circumstances or ability. Studies of young people who are disabled and also engaged in pro-social activity show that there is as much, if not more, benefit to be gained from such activities for those who feel themselves to be marginalised. We can conclude that the greater opportunities there are for adolescents to be of service to others, the greater are the benefits in terms of their own personal and social development.

Further reading

Bynner, J, Chisholm, L and Furlong, A (Eds) (1997) *Youth, citizenship and social change in a European context*. Ashgate. Aldershot.
A collection of essays looking at citizenship, participation, identity and the marginalisation of youth in a European context. The book offers an important overview of key social issues for those growing up in Europe today.

Hackett, C (1997) Young people and political participation. In Roche, J and Tucker, S (Eds) *Youth in society*. Sage. London.
A chapter in a book for Open University students, it provides a useful discussion of participation and its effects on young people.

Johnson, M, Beebe, T, Mortimer, J and Snyder, M (1998) Volunteerism in adolescence: a process perspective. *Journal of Research on Adolescence*. 8. 309–332.
An excellent journal article, setting volunteering in the context of the developmental process. A good summary of research on volunteering.

Torney-Purta, J (1990) Youth in relation to social institutions. In Feldman, S and Elliott, G (Eds) *At the threshold: the developing adolescent*. Harvard University Press. Cambridge, MA.
Once again this essay in the Feldman and Elliott text provides a comprehensive survey of the topic by one of the major figures in the area.

Yates, M and Youniss, J (Eds) (1999) *Roots of civic identity: international perspectives on community service and activism in youth*. Cambridge University Press. Cambridge.
A collection of articles reporting new research in this burgeoning field. Authors are an international mix, and include British, European and North American scholars. Much of the research breaks new ground, making this an especially interesting book.

Stress, coping and adjustment

To some people adolescence may appear to be a stressful time. Such people could point to the stress of examinations, peer pressure in relation to drugs or sex, anxieties about jobs and qualifications, and to a variety of other factors which make life difficult for young people today. Yet communities and neighbourhoods are full of adolescents getting on with their lives, coping with problems that adults might find daunting, enjoying their leisure, preparing for and taking exams, and entering into the world of work with enthusiasm. Even those growing up in disadvantaged circumstances frequently demonstrate resilience and a capacity for coping in spite of having the odds stacked against them. At first sight, this may seem to be something of a paradox. While there are many stresses inherent in the adolescent life stage, there is also more than enough evidence to reflect the resources and capabilities of young people. It is this paradox which we will be exploring in this final chapter.

While we consider it very important indeed to underline the adaptive abilities of young people, we would not want to underestimate the impact of stress, nor to minimise in any way the difficulties and obstacles faced by some adolescents as they move towards adulthood. As we shall be indicating below, there are a variety of types of stress, ranging from relatively minor daily irritants to acute stress, such as the loss of a parent, or to chronic stress, such as ongoing bullying or living in poverty. These stressors affect different people in different ways, and although some may cope well, others will not, and may as a result of stress develop emotional or physical disorders of varying severity.

Nonetheless, the evidence which has accumulated on the coping skills of young people has led to a new way of thinking about adolescence. No longer is it seen as a 'problem stage'. Today, we are more concerned to identify risks and stressors, and to attempt to understand the processes of coping used by adolescents in their daily lives. Such an approach is especially important, since it is a reflection of a different perspective which emphasises adaptation rather than disorder. This approach fits well with the focal model outlined in Chapter 1, and with the emphasis on developmental contextualism. These concepts will be essential in our exploration of stress and the processes of coping in the rest of the chapter. We will be looking first at transitions in adolescence, and considering to what extent it can be said that these transitions are stressful in themselves. We will next discuss the nature of stress, and look at some of the factors which are associated with it in adolescence. Following this, we will explore the processes of coping, we will consider questions of risk and resilience, and we will conclude the chapter with a review of successful coping in adolescence.

Stress and transitions in adolescence

Traditional views of adolescence have often had associated with them a notion of stress, primarily because of what has become known as the 'storm and stress' concept. This concept originated with German writers of the nineteenth century such as Schiller and Goethe, but the first person to apply such a notion to adolescence in any systematic way was G. Stanley Hall, in his classic text of 1904. In this text he argued that young people experienced turmoil both in their emotions and in their relationships, to the extent that the period was one of continuing oscillation of contradictory tendencies. In particular, Hall noted how inertia and lethargy might be followed by exuberant gaiety, how altruism and selfishness co-exist side by side, and how the need for conformity is present at the same time as a wish to challenge existing values and modes of behaviour. A full summary of Hall's theory may be found in Muuss (1996).

Since the publication of Hall's work many other theorists have made use of the notion of storm and stress, and the belief that this phrase accurately summarises the adolescent experience is deeply embedded in our culture. However, the findings of empirical studies of adolescence, commencing in the 1950s, have shown that the concept of storm and stress may have serious limitations, and considerable time and effort on the part of the research community has been taken up in attempts to place the concept in a proper context. In particular, Bandura's well-known article entitled 'The stormy decade: fact or fiction?' (1964), and the major research of Douvan and Adelson (1966), had a particularly powerful impact, although this is not to underestimate the wealth of other publications addressing the same theme (e.g. Offer, 1969; Rutter *et al.*, 1976; Coleman, 1978; Feldman and Elliott, 1990; Jackson and Bosma, 1992; Rutter and Smith, 1995).

In essence, all such works have demonstrated much the same thing. It would appear that, while a minority of young people experience what might be called a stressful or turbulent adolescence, the majority adjust relatively well. Research demonstrates that the majority are not alienated from their families, do not have major psychiatric disorders, do not experience a total breakdown of communication with their parents, do not go through a serious identity crisis, and so on. A good example of a study which reflects this overall conclusion is that of Siddique and D'Arcy (1984), who looked at stress and well-being in this age group. They summarised their results as follows:

> In this study some 33.5% of the adolescents surveyed reported no symptoms of psychological distress, and another 39% reported five or fewer symptoms (a mild level of distress). On the other hand a significant 27.5% reported higher levels of psychological distress. For the majority the adolescent transition may be relatively smooth; however for a minority it does indeed appear to be a period of storm and turmoil. . . . The large majority of adolescents appear to get on well with adults, and are able to cope effectively with demands of school and peer groups. They use their resources to make adjustments with environmental stressors with hardly visible signs of psychological distress.
>
> (1984, p. 471)

Thus, we can see that empirical research has made it possible to gain a broader picture of large populations. From this evidence we may conclude that G. Stanley Hall's concept of adolescence as being a time of storm and stress is misleading, since serious turmoil is only experienced by a minority of young people. Adolescence as a life stage is not, in itself, intrinsically stressful. Yet, there are some individuals who experience it this way, so we now need to look more closely at why this should be so.

The first thing to note is that in the course of the adolescent period an individual will experience a wide variety of events, changes and transitions, some of which may be stressful in themselves. One helpful way of distinguishing these potential stressors is to classify them as falling into one of three categories (Hauser and Bowlds, 1990: Rice *et al.*, 1993). These categories are normative events, non-normative events and daily hassles. As far as normative events are concerned, this category refers to events that are experienced by all young people, and would include such things as pubertal development, a change of school at age 11 or 13, peer pressure, and so on. The important thing here is that these are events which all young people have to confront, but usually within a relatively predictable timescale. Whether such things are experienced as stressful or not will depend on a range of factors which we will be considering below. Non-normative events are different in that they concern individual young people, and can occur at any time. Such events could include illness, injury, friendship break-up, parental conflict or separation, difficulties related to parental employment, and so on. Lastly, there are the daily hassles which may appear to be relatively minor in scale, but which may have a cumulative impact, especially if there are many of them, and if they combine with normative and/or non-normative stressors.

In considering these three types of events, we may think about a number of dimensions which determine the degree to which they will be stressful to any individual. In a helpful paper, Rice *et al.* (1993) note that the number of events, the timing of the events, and the synchronicity of these events are all key features of any one person's experience. First, there is the question of how many changes a young person experiences. The sheer number of changes may have an impact on the way in which any individual copes at this time. A young person who has to adjust to parental divorce, to a change of school, and a loss of friends, on top of all the normative physical and psychological changes will clearly be at a greater disadvantage than someone who does not have these additional events to cope with.

Next, there is the question of timing. A good example of the way this might affect adjustment is the variation in pubertal development. As we noted in Chapter 2, young people enter puberty at different times, so that, while the majority are in-step with others, or 'on-time', as it is sometimes called, a smaller group will be either very young when they commence puberty, or much older than their peers. These early and late developers thus have to deal with the experience of puberty either before they are ready, or at a point when they are carrying with them a sense of having been left behind. Thus the timing of a normative event such as puberty will make a difference to the overall adjustment of the individual. The issue of timing links also to that of synchronicity. The way normative and non-normative events cluster together has always been seen as a critical factor in determining the ability of the individual to cope. The more potential stressors occur at or around the same time, the more difficult it will be for an individual to find the resources to manage these events.

It will be recalled that in Chapter 1 reference was made to the paper by Graber and Brooks-Gunn (1996), and their discussion of transitions and turning points. Essentially, they make the same points as Rice *et al.* (1993). The number of changes, the timing of the changes and their synchronicity are all notions that are agreed to be critical in understanding the coping process. They also relate

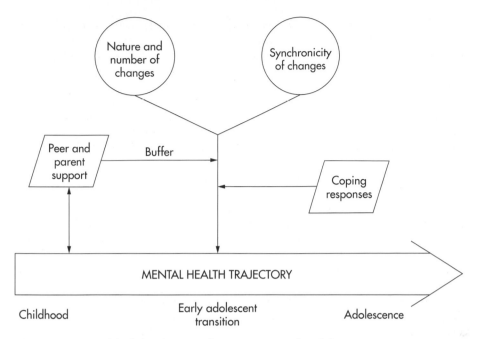

Figure 12.1 Model of developmental transition in early adolescence.

Source: Rice *et al.* (1993).

closely to the thinking behind the focal model outlined in Chapter 1. Rice *et al.* (1993) propose a model of development in early adolescence which summarises what has been said so far, and this is illustrated in Figure 12.1. From this it can be seen that each of these variables has a contribution to make in relation to the coping process, but that in addition to these factors we need also to consider the individual's coping responses, and the supports or buffers which are available. We will be turning to these factors once we have considered other models of stress.

It is important to note that other writers have used somewhat different classifications of potential stressors. One well-known example may be found in the work of Compas (Compas *et al.*, 1993; Compas, 1995). As he notes, stress will vary along a number of dimensions, including whether it is normative or atypical, large or small in magnitude, and chronic or acute in nature. He argues that it is most helpful to think of stressors in three broad categories, especially if we are wanting to consider the mental-health implications of these events in the adolescent period. These three categories are what he calls generic or normative stress, severe acute stress, and severe chronic stress.

As Compas points out, all adolescents will be exposed to some level of generic stress as they move through this stage of life, and we have explored this notion already in discussing normative events. However, Compas then goes on to make the distinction between acute and chronic stress, giving as examples of the former such things as the death of a parent or loved one, injury or accident, and so on. Where chronic stress is concerned he cites exposure to poverty and economic hardship, racism, parental psychopathology, and other long-standing

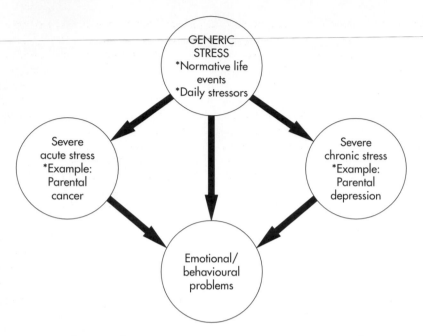

Figure 12.2 Sub-types of stress: generic stress, severe acute stress, and severe chronic stress.

Source: Compas (1995).

stressors. The key factor here is Compas' argument that different types of stress will have a differential impact on the mental health of young people. In addition, if interventions are to be effective they will need to be tailored to the particular stressor or combination of stressors. The sub-types of stress identified by Compas are illustrated in Figure 12.2.

So far we have been outlining examples of some of the stressors to which young people may be exposed, and considering factors, such as timing, which might affect adjustment. It is important to emphasise that the transitions of adolescence are not necessarily stressful events. If there is appropriate support, and if the potential stressors are reasonably spaced, then there is every likelihood that a young person will adapt to change in a relatively effective manner. The questions of timing, synchronicity and number of changes are critical here, and it is precisely these issues which are highlighted by the focal model. Other factors being equal, if events are reasonably spaced, and if there are not too many of them all occurring at the same time, then coping will be that much easier. It is only through a model such as this that we can comprehend the adaptive capabilities of the great majority of adolescents.

Causes and correlates of stress

As we have seen, there are many different types of stress, and in the section above we have begun to explore the range of stressors which affect young people. We now wish to look more closely at some additional factors which play their part in determining how various events are experienced in adolescence. One of the first of these is what are known as event parameters. In the literature on stress much has been made of the different parameters of a potentially stressful life event which will determine an individual's reaction to that event (Lazarus and Folkman, 1991). The four most commonly mentioned parameters are frequency, predictability, uncertainty and control. Essentially, it is argued that any event will vary in respect of these parameters, and that this variation will play a central role in determining how the stressor is perceived by the individual responding to it. To illustrate the point, we may look at being the victim of bullying as an example. Here, the event is relatively unpredictable, the individual is likely to feel that he or she has little control over it, and there will be uncertainty over the possible frequency. Thus, such an event is likely to have a high degree of stress associated with it.

Seiffge-Krenke (1995) emphasises the particular importance of event predicability as a determinant of stress. In her view, the more unpredictable an event, the more potentially stressful it is likely to be. The major reason for this is that in these circumstances there is no possibility of anticipatory coping. The most stressful event is one for which no preparation at all is possible, such as an unexpected death. However, if we return to bullying, it can be seen that, if the individual has been the subject of bullying once, then some anticipatory coping can be undertaken, either internally, or with outside help. However, it remains a fact that the timing of the next occurrence of bullying cannot be predicted, and thus planned coping will be difficult to put into operation.

It is clear from the results of much empirical research that the key variables of age, gender and ethnicity influence the types of stress experienced by different individuals. In relation to age, an interesting study by Larson and Asmussen (1991) showed that older adolescents were more likely to have negative emotions relating to the domains of opposite-sex friends and non-school activities (jobs, the environment, leisure time), while the level of negative emotions was higher in the family and school domains among younger adolescents. Where gender is concerned many writers have pointed to differences between young men and young women in their experiences of stress. Thus, for example, Compas and Wagner (1991) reported that females appear to find family, friendships and sexual relationships more stressful than males during adolescence. Some have wondered whether results such as this are reflective of greater honesty or insight on the part of women, while other writers (e.g. Heaven, 1996) have pointed to the likelihood that females are more sensitive than males to strains in interpersonal networks. We shall look at gender in relation to coping in more detail in the next section.

A further stress-related gender difference concerns the greater incidence of depression among young women in adolescence, a point noted in Chapter 7. Findings from studies by Brooks-Gunn (1991) and Petersen et al. (1991) support the conclusion that levels of depression are higher among females, possibly as a result of hormonal changes during and after puberty. However, it should be noted that in Brooks-Gunn's (1991) study it appeared that negative life events played at least an equal part in explaining the differences between the genders in levels of depression. In addition, it is possible that increased concern over height, weight and other physical characteristics among early adolescent girls, together with higher levels of body-image dissatisfaction, may be a partial explanation for these findings (Davies and Furnham, 1986). Ethnicity is a variable which also has an impact on experiences of stress. Munsch and Wampler (1993) showed that in the USA African-American adolescents perceived suspension from school, and having trouble with the teacher, as being significantly more stressful than did those from other ethnic groups. European-Americans experienced being chosen to perform tasks within the school setting as most stressful, while for Mexican-Americans failure in a test or exam rated as the most stressful school experience.

Having noted a range of possible stressors for young people, we should perhaps mention two other things – boredom and loneliness – that may be experienced as causing difficulty during adolescence. Let us first consider boredom. Frydenberg (1997) reported that boredom surfaced frequently in her interviews with teenagers in Australia as something which caused them stress. For some boredom stemmed from literally having nothing to do, but for others it reflected a need for stimulation and excitement, possibly as a defence against an inner emptiness which is not uncommon at this stage. Frydenberg (1997, p. 23) quotes a number of young people.

'The only problem I have is boredom. I can't stand the thought of another day. I just try and make the best of it, and I get out and I think one day I am just going to get out and do one thing I really want to do.'

(15-year-old boy)

'I get bored very easily. Like I'll be talking to someone on the phone, and I will be baking a cake at the same time. I can't just sit there and do nothing. In class I'm usually the one who makes the smart-arse comments.'

(15-year-old girl)

As far as loneliness is concerned a number of writers have attended to this as a possible stressor. In research carried out on attitudes to relationships at various ages Coleman (1974) reported that the highest levels of anxiety about solitude were found in the 11–13 age group, with a significant decrease from then on. Subsequent studies have explored various aspects of the experience of being alone, although one of the problems that has become apparent is that it is essential to distinguish between voluntary solitude and enforced isolation from family or friends. Some studies, such as that of Inderbitzen-Pisaruk *et al.* (1992), have looked at the correlates of loneliness, where it is assumed that loneliness is enforced rather than voluntary. These authors showed that loneliness in the middle-adolescent period was associated with low self-esteem and with self-perceptions of poor social skills. Some gender differences were found, with males being more likely to have low levels of perceived personal control, while females were more likely to have high levels of social anxiety.

Larson (1997) has explored the constructive dimension of solitude, arguing that as young people move from childhood to adolescence they are better able to make good use of being on their own. In particular, he shows that time alone becomes more voluntary with increasing age, and that a moderate level of solitude in early and middle adolescence is likely to be associated with positive adjustment outcomes. As he says: 'while continuing to be a lonely time, in early adolescence solitude comes to have a more constructive role in daily life as a strategic retreat that complements social experience' (1997, p. 80). By contrast, a different approach has been taken by Goossens and his colleagues (Goossens *et al.*, 1998; Goossens and Marcoen, 1999b), who have related loneliness to personality characteristics such as attachment style. They show that adolescents who are rated as 'securely attached' are more positive about loneliness, while those who are 'dependently attached' find loneliness more difficult to cope with. This work is important in showing that a number of factors in addition to age, self-image and perceived social skills may relate to the experience of loneliness in adolescence.

It will be apparent from the above that stress is a complex concept. There are a variety of categories and parameters to be considered if any clear picture is to be gained of the manner in which we can relate the process of coping to the experience of stress in adolescence. A useful schema is proposed by Seiffge-Krenke (1995) in her book on the subject. She suggests four main areas which need to be identified and elaborated if we are to give proper attention to the field. These are the nature of the stressors, the internal resources of the individual, the type of social supports available, and finally the coping process itself. Seiffge-Krenke sees these four as being related sequentially, in other words, we need first to attend to the stressors, then to look at the internal resources of the individual, and so on. The schema is illustrated in Figure 12.3. Not everyone will agree that a diagram of this sort accurately reflects all the issues, and it should be noted that the author is herself aware of the limitations inherent in portraying the situation in this graphic manner. Nonetheless, we believe it is very helpful indeed in clarifying the major issues contributing to the complexity of the topic.

Coping in adolescence

Having considered the topic of stress, and with Seiffge-Krenke's schema in mind, we can now turn to the subject of coping. It is first important to note that there have been a number of attempts to classify coping, and before any detailed discussion can take place it will be necessary to outline the main contributors in this area. We will start with the views of Compas, who has already been mentioned above. Compas (1987) applies to this age group a distinction, first suggested by Lazarus (1966), between emotion-focused and problem-focused coping. The function of both types of coping is to modify the relationship between the stressor and the individual, but in problem-focused coping one attempts to alter, reduce or get rid of the stress, while in emotion-focused coping one can attempt to change the emotional state which is created by the stressor. In a useful review of a large body of research on the two types of coping (Compas *et al.*, 1993), the authors show that although there is clear evidence of an increase in emotion-focused coping with age (see e.g. Band and Weisz, 1988; Altschuler and Ruble, 1989), it appears that there is no increase in problem-focused coping throughout childhood and adolescence. In addition, it is also suggested (see Compas, 1995) that the two types of coping serve different functions, with emotion-focused coping being more

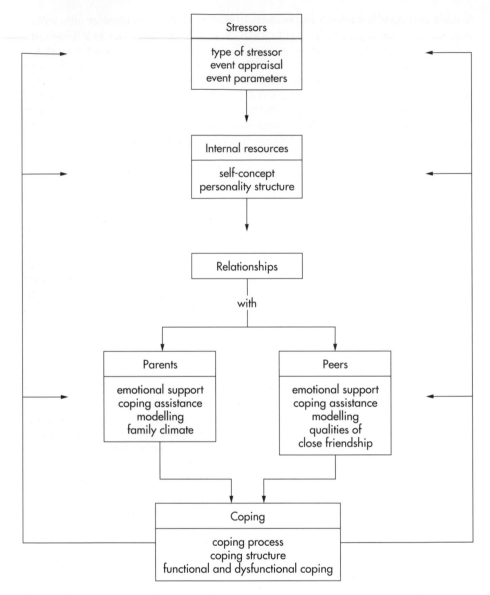

Figure 12.3 Conceptual issues and major questions in relation to stress and coping.
Source: Seiffge-Krenke (1995).

likely in situations of perceived threat and high anxiety arousal, while problem-focused coping would be used in circumstances where it was likely that the stressor could be controlled or changed.

Another possible classification of coping approaches is that outlined in Seiffge-Krenke (1993, 1995). This is not dissimilar to that utilised by Compas but includes a third category, which allows for the possibility of stress avoidance. In Seiffge-Krenke's terminology there are three modes of coping: active coping, internal coping and withdrawal. The first two are comparable to emotion-focused and problem-focused coping, and are considered to be functional, while the third covers behaviour which involves turning away from the stressor, and is considered to be dysfunctional. In terms of measurement Seiffge-Krenke developed the Coping Across Situations Questionnaire (CASQ), which includes twenty possible strategies. These include such things as turning to friends, turning to parents, compromising, refusing to worry, expecting the worst, using alcohol or drugs to forget the problem, and so on.

A very similar approach is that which has been taken by Frydenberg and her colleagues (Frydenberg and Lewis, 1993; Frydenberg, 1997). These authors believe that coping depends on being able to make use of a wide repertoire of behaviours. In their view, there are an infinite number of coping actions, so that if a valid picture is to be obtained of any individual's coping skills a range of options needs to be set out. With this in mind they have developed a scale, similar to the CASQ, termed the Adolescent Coping Scale (ACS), which comprises eighteen different coping strategies. Their work is based on the development of scales such as the A-COPE (Patterson and McCubbin, 1987). The eighteen categories of the ACS include such things as seeking social support, worrying, investing in close friends, tension reduction, ignoring the problem, self-blame, seeking professional help, focusing on the positive, and so on. Approaches such as these, which allow the individual respondent a range of options, are undoubtedly preferable to those which impose a particular classification of coping responses. However, methodological problems are created because of the recognition that coping can include such a variety of behaviours.

We will now turn to a consideration of developmental trends in the use of coping strategies. We have already noted the review by Compas and others, which shows no change in the use of problem-focused strategies with age, but a clear increase in the use of emotion-focused strategies. Numerous studies using Frydenberg's ACS have looked at developmental change in coping strategies among Australian adolescents (Frydenberg, 1997). The conclusions contrast somewhat with those of Compas. Although there is no disagreement that emotion-focused coping increases with age, the Frydenberg studies also highlight a greater use of dysfunctional modes of coping in the latter years of adolescence. In particular, the authors report more use of tension-reduction strategies such as drug and alcohol use, as well as increased self-blame in this older group.

In the work carried out by Seiffge-Krenke (1995) much is made of the finding that age 15 appears to be a turning point in respect of the use of certain coping strategies. It is reported that there was a marked increase in young people addressing directly the person who was creating the stress, as well as a growing tendency to turn to others who might have experienced similar problems. As she puts it:

> We observed that after the age of 15, the perspective of significant others was increasingly adopted, which led to increases in compromising and giving in. Also a higher frequency in reflecting about possible solutions led to a

> richer inner picture of coping options, although not necessarily to more actions. Knowledge about social conventions and higher impulse control are partly responsible for constraint on acting. Moreover, increased acceptance of one's own limits enhances a stronger reality orientation.
>
> (1995, p. 221)

Gender differences have also been a focus of much interest in the literature on coping (for reviews see Hauser and Bowlds, 1990; Seiffge-Krenke, 1993; Frydenberg, 1997). The question at the heart of any debate on this subject is neatly expressed in the title of Frydenberg and Lewis' (1993) paper: 'Boys play sport and girls turn to others'. In fact, the situation is, as might be expected, somewhat more complex than this, although it is clear that there are stereotypical differences between the genders in their choice of coping strategies. Broadly speaking, males make more use of active coping, being more inclined to go out and meet the problem head-on, more likely to seek further information to assist in problem-solving, and more often using aggressive or confrontational techniques to deal with interpersonal difficulties. In addition, a number of studies have shown that males use denial more often than females.

By contrast, it is consistently reported that girls are more affected by stress than are boys and are more likely to disclose a greater number of stressful events in their lives. Girls see setbacks and difficulties as more threatening than boys, and are more likely to expect the worst in stressful situations. In Seiffge-Krenke's (1995) study girls, in comparison with boys, saw identical stressors as four times more threatening. In terms of coping with stress females use social support more than males. Girls and young women are more likely to be dependent on parents and other adults for assistance, and are more sensitive to the expectations of others. In a study by Schonert-Reichl and Muller (1996), which compared males and females in their help-seeking behaviour, results showed that young women were significantly more likely to seek assistance from parents, friends and professionals than were young men. Two graphs are shown in Figure 12.4, which illustrate a combination of gender and age effects in relation to two approaches to coping, seeking comfort from others and compromising. Results are from Seiffge-Krenke (1995).

While comparisons between young men and young women may in some respects be too broad to be helpful, in that there will obviously be wide variation within genders, it is undoubtedly important to recognise these major differences. It is also essential to consider the implications of this diversity. Seiffge-Krenke asks whether females are more at risk than males. As she puts it:

> Females appear to be caught in a special dilemma. On the one hand it appears that females feel more stressed than males by the same event – entailing interpersonal conflicts with significant others. On the other hand, they more often applied coping strategies that required using these same social relations. We would suggest that this social and psychological dependency of females causes an irresolvable dilemma for them. Possibly the greater dependency in female adolescents is one factor which may account for the nature of their stress perception, and its relation to symptomatology.
>
> (1995, p. 223)

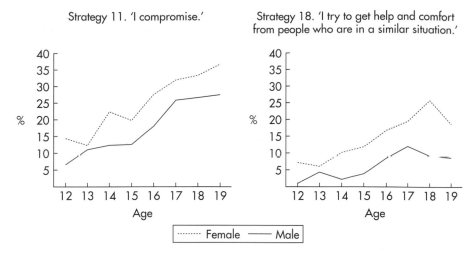

Figure 12.4 Gender differences in 6 of the 20 coping strategies assessed (males: n = 479; females: n = 549).

Source: Seiffge-Krenke (1995).

Coping is affected not only by age and gender, but also by the social support available to the individual. This was a point illustrated by the diagram in Figure 12.3. We will now consider some of the relevant evidence. To look first at support from within the family, it is widely accepted that high levels of such support assist in the coping process (Hauser and Bowlds, 1990; Heaven, 1996). If parents are available to offer information and assistance in a non-judgemental manner this is supportive in itself, but it also offers a model of relationships which would encourage the use of social support more generally. Where support from parents is limited one might expect to see the use of more dysfunctional coping strategies. In an important study of this subject Shulman (1993) looked at four types of family climate, and showed how each climate was associated with the use of different coping styles. Young people growing up in families which were unstructured and in which there were high levels of conflict displayed poor coping skills, especially passivity and withdrawal. Families which were highly structured tended to have adolescents with dependent styles of coping, while adolescents in families which were oriented towards independence or the open expression of feelings demonstrated coping skills which included planning and the use of others for social support. The findings of the study are summarised in Table 12.1.

These findings are supported by a further study in this area by McIntyre and Dusek (1995). These authors classified parenting styles within the paradigm originating from the work of Maccoby and Martin (1983), and described in Chapter 6. The four styles are authoritative, authoritarian, neglectful and permissive. Results showed that those whose parents were seen as authoritative (i.e. warmth and nurturance coupled with close monitoring and age-appropriate demandingness) were most likely to use social support and to employ problem-focused coping. The authors suggest that the central mediating factor between parenting styles and

Table 12.1 Relationships between family climate and coping behaviours.

Family climate	Coping behaviours
1. Unstructured conflict oriented E.g. High degree of conflictive interaction; lack of support within family; no support for personal growth	High level of dysfunctional coping characterised by withdrawal and passivity
2. Control oriented E.g. Structured family activities; explicit family rules; emphasise achievement; supportive family, but do not express emotions	Rely on family decisions; tend to be passive
3. Unstructured expressive-independence oriented E.g. Cohesive and unified; express feelings; support individual independence; no pressure to achieve	Turn to others for advice and information; adolescents plan course of action
4. Structured expressive-intellectual oriented E.g. Emphasis on family relationships; independence encouraged; clear rules	Turn to others for advice and information; adolescents plan course of action

Source: Shulman (1993).

coping behaviour may have to do with feelings of personal control. Authoritative parenting promotes a sense of competence, and thus facilitates feelings of personal control in stressful situations. It is also of note that studies such as those of Compas *et al.* (1991) have demonstrated a link between problem-focused coping and high levels of personal control. As McIntyre and Dusek put it:

> The relation between parental rearing practices and coping dispositions, then, appears to be indirect. Parental rearing practices influence control beliefs, that, in turn, influence coping dispositions. Increasingly researchers are finding that during the adolescent years parental influences on offspring are more indirect than they are during childhood.
>
> (1995, p. 507)

Peers too play a key role in providing social support where stress is concerned. As noted in Chapter 8, young people increasingly turn to their contemporaries as they grow older, and, as research such as that of Seiffge-Krenke (1995) has confirmed, the strategy 'I try to solve the problem with the help of my friends' is one of the two most common coping strategies, together with discussing the problem with parents. Indeed, Seiffge-Krenke's (1995) study shows that dependence on friends increases markedly during adolescence, equalling the importance of parents at age 15–16, and being clearly more salient at age 17–19.

The work of Hirsch *et al.* (1990) has shown how important friends, especially those who are seen out of the school context, can be for dealing with

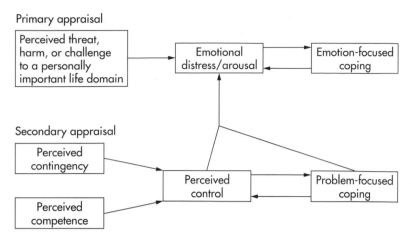

Figure 12.5 Model of control-related beliefs, coping, and emotional distress.
Source: Compas (1995).

stressful situations. Young people in early and middle adolescence reported seeing their friends out of school as being central in providing support with ongoing hassles and problems. The findings showed 55 per cent saw friends daily, while a further 27 per cent saw friends more than once a week. In a further study, Hirsch and Dubois (1989) tried to determine what obstacles inhibited the use of peer support outside the school setting. They looked at whether such obstacles were situational or person focused. They found that the obstacles included such things as social-skills deficits, competing activities, home conflicts and moral concerns. As Frydenberg (1997) points out, if those who do better in adolescence are those who are able to make use of social support, it is important that we know more about these obstacles. Thus those with social-skills deficits reported feelings such as 'I'm not sure what to ask them to do', and 'I'm not sure how to go about asking'. It may be that social-skills training could be appropriate and helpful for those falling into this group. In an interesting study Kuhl *et al.* (1997) reported the development of an instrument to measure barriers to help-seeking, an indication that more social scientists are recognising the importance of the issue.

So far, we have not given much attention to the place of appraisal, and it is now time to look at this more closely. In the writings of Lazarus, Compas, Frydenberg and others it is argued that the appraisal process has a critical role to play in the way in which an individual responds to any stressor. Indeed, it was suggested by Lazarus (Lazarus and Folkman, 1991) that it is necessary to distinguish between primary and secondary appraisal, as illustrated in Figure 12.5. From this model it can be seen that primary appraisal is concerned with the emotional impact of the stressful event or challenge, while secondary appraisal has to do with a more cognitive assessment of the relevance of the threat and the competence of the individual to deal with it. It is generally believed that successful coping is closely linked with the appraisal process. Two people may view exactly the same stressor in very different ways. Alternatively, the same person may view an identical stressor quite differently on two occasions, as a result perhaps of mood, previous stresses on that day, a perception of available resources at that time, and so on. Whether an individual will go on to cope with a stressor will depend first on the results of the appraisal process.

An excellent example of the role of appraisal is given in the work of Beardslee and Podorefsky (1988), who studied resilience in adolescents facing the depression of a parent. They noted that resilient young people were those who had gone through a realistic appraisal of the stress associated with their parents' depressive disorder, and acted in a manner which was consistent with this appraisal. The authors observed that these adolescents had at first wanted to change or cure their parents' depression, but had come to recognise over time that this was not a realistic goal. Such young people then turned their attention to providing support for the depressed parent and for other family members in whatever way they could. It was noted that this response was more congruent with the objective nature of the situation, and enabled the adolescents to acknowledge that their parents' situation was beyond their control. By contrast, those whose appraisal did not include the possibility that there was likely to be no change in their parents' condition proved to be less resilient to the ongoing stress of the family situation.

Another central feature of successful coping has to do with personal control. As is apparent in the diagram illustrated in Figure 12.5, personal control is linked to the secondary-appraisal process, and results from a combination of perceived contingency and perceived competence. As Frydenberg puts it: 'Whether or not a stressor is controllable seems to determine how one copes' (1997, p. 35). In support of this she quotes a study by Compas et al. (1988), who looked at the relative controllability of a range of stressors for adolescents. They found that academic stressors were perceived as more controllable than interpersonal stressors, and that as a result more problem-focused coping was used with academic stressors, while more emotion-focused coping was used with interpersonal stressors. Compas and his colleagues also showed that the greater the perceived personal control, the more likely the individual is to use problem-focused coping. This point is illustrated in the diagram in Figure 12.5. Compas (1995) outlines his argument thus:

> Control beliefs and problem-focussed coping are related in a reciprocal fashion. A high sense of personal control will lead to a greater use of problem-focussed coping, and problem-focussed coping efforts may enhance feelings of control if they are effective in changing the environment. Emotion-focussed coping efforts are unrelated to control beliefs, but instead are used to a greater or lesser degree in response to levels of emotional distress or arousal.
> (p. 259)

In summary, if we are to ask how these distinctions relate to successful coping, it is suggested by Compas and others that problem-focused coping strategies are more adaptive when they are directed at aspects of the environment that are perceived as changeable, whereas emotion-focused coping strategies are more adaptive when a situation is recognised as uncontrollable. Thus, it may be concluded that a key developmental task would be to learn to distinguish between situations where some change is possible, and situations where it is not. It could be argued that perceptions of control may play a central part here, since the changeability of any event or circumstance which causes stress will be influenced not only by the nature of the event, but also by the resources and capabilities of the individual faced with the stressful event. Returning to Frydenberg's statement, which we quoted above, successful coping is unlikely without a sense of control.

As we have seen in this section, coping can be classified in a number of different ways. The most common classification is that which distinguishes emotion-focused and problem-focused coping. Many factors determine the use of coping strategies, and we have noted the part played by age, gender and family climate. We have also looked at the role of appraisal and personal control. It is now time to turn to the body of literature which has looked at similar issues from a slightly different perspective. This field of work has used the terms 'risk' and 'resilience', rather than stress and coping, although, as will become apparent, the questions posed are closely related.

Risk and resilience

Broadly speaking, those who study risk and resilience, rather than coping, tend to come from a clinical background, which may partly explain the different terminology. Key texts in this area are Garmezy and Rutter (1983), Haggerty et al. (1994) and Rutter (1995). If we look at both the empirical and the theoretical work which underpins concepts of risk and resilience, it is apparent that the major concern has been with severe chronic stressors. Thus, for example, one of the first substantive studies in this field was that of Werner and others (Werner and Smith, 1982), who studied a sample of young people growing up in Hawaii who were considered to be at risk of psychosocial disorder because of their early life experiences. These individuals were born into poverty, and had parents with little education, or problems of alcoholism or psychiatric disorder. Such risk factors are similar to the ones mentioned earlier in this chapter and cited by Compas as examples of severe chronic stress.

There have been two primary questions at the heart of the risk and resilience research. First, there has been a wish to identify the childhood variables associated with later behavioural and emotional problems. In addition, however, there has also been an interest in how some individuals, in spite of exposure to a number of adverse experiences in their early years, manage to escape any serious harm. It is this question that relates to the notion of resilience. To take the first question for the moment, it is clear that certain factors are associated with increased risk for poor adjustment in later life, and these include poverty and economic difficulties, parental deviance or disorder, impaired parenting, abuse, family conflict and family breakdown. However, it is also clear from the literature that the links between specific risk factors and outcomes have been shown to be relatively weak, so that single risk factors explain little of the variation between individuals. In the main longitudinal studies, such as that carried out in Hawaii, and the Christchurch, New Zealand study (Fergusson et al., 1994; Fergusson and Lynskey, 1996), results indicate that poor outcomes for young people are most likely to be associated with a combination of risk factors. As an example, Fergusson and his colleagues, as part of a long-term study of risk, examined the childhoods of the most disadvantaged 5 per cent of their cohort. They reported that this 5 per cent had risks of becoming multiple-problem teenagers that were 100 times greater than the risks for those in the most advantaged 50 per cent of the sample.

There has been, as noted, an interest in the literature in the factors that may protect against or mitigate the effects of early disadvantage. The findings indicate that there are at least five factors which appear to play a part in fostering resilience:

1   Intelligence and problem-solving skills. Numerous studies have shown that higher intellectual ability is associated with resilience. Thus, Fergusson and Lynskey (1996) reported that in the Christchurch study resilient teenagers were significantly more likely than others to have an average or above average IQ. Herrenkohl *et al.* (1994) reported similar findings. It can be concluded that at least average intelligence is a necessary but not sufficient condition for adolescent resilience.

2   External interests or attachments. Many studies have indicated that those who develop strong interests outside the home, or who are able to form attachments to adults outside the immediate family are more resilient in the face of family adversity. Both Jenkins and Smith (1990) and Werner (1989) reported results which emphasise the place played by external factors in the development of resilience.

3   Parental attachment and bonding. It has been suggested that a warm and supportive relationship with at least one parent may act to protect the child or young person against other types of disadvantage, or to limit the impact of such things as severe economic hardship. Again the Hawaii study (Werner, 1989) shows this to be the case, as do Herrenkohl *et al.* (1994), and Jenkins and Smith (1990).

4   Early temperament. In spite of questions over the validity of measures of childhood temperament, a number of studies have pointed out that those who could be classified as having an easy temperament were more likely to become resilient teenagers. Support for this conclusion can be found in the Hawaii study, as well as in that reported by Wyman *et al.* (1991).

5   Peer factors. Although relatively less attention has been paid to this variable, Fergusson and Lynskey (1996) show that the resilient adolescents in their sample had significantly lower affiliations with delinquent peers. It may be that positive peer relationships can play their part in counteracting adverse family influences, and Werner reports this to be the case in his Hawaiian sample.

To conclude this section on risk and resilience, it is of interest to consider circumstances in which risk itself can have a positive impact. Gore and Eckenrode (1994) point out that there may be situations in which what appears to be an adverse experience may have the opposite effect. They mention the possibility that where parents divorce the adolescent might be given greater responsibility in the home, thus fostering enhanced emotional and social maturation. In Elder's (1974) classic study of the Great Depression in the USA, he showed that, at least for older teenagers, family hardship propelled them into the role of wage earner, and thereby into social independence. In at least some of the families he studied, this accelerated autonomy and responsibility led to positive outcomes.

Elder and Caspi (1988) talk of an 'accentuation process', whereby the stressor facilitates the potentially healthy tendencies already present in environments or personalities. As an example of this Gore and Eckenrode (1994) report a study in which they showed that adolescents living in chronically stressed families did better, and were less depressed, if they could reorient themselves away from the family and turn towards the peer group. Behaviour which at first appeared dysfunctional – rejecting the family – actually led to more adaptive outcomes. Thus, as Masten *et al.* (1990) point out, the older adolescent brings to stressful situations increasing control and knowledge of coping options, and the ability to seek protective relationships if others fail. This notion of active coping ties in well with the theoretical position we outlined in Chapter 1, and links neatly with the focal model described there.

Conclusion

In looking back over the topics covered in this book, we see a number of themes emerge. First, it is clear that we cannot understand adolescence without taking into account the social changes which have impacted on Western society. The alterations in the labour market, the shifts in family functioning, the political and attitudinal changes that we have all experienced during the 1980s and 1990s have had a profound influence on those growing up in these times. In addition, we need to recognise that the adolescent transition has also altered, since it has become a much longer process. In some respects those of 9 or 10 years of age are experiencing the beginnings of adolescence, while young adults of 19, 20 and 21 remain economically dependent, and thus take longer to leave adolescence behind.

These factors are the background to any serious study of the adolescent stage of development. This stage is an extended one, and one in which a range of major emotional, physical and social transformations occur. In view of this, it is right that the topic of coping and adjustment is the subject of the final chapter in this book. We have put forward the view that adolescence is not, by definition, a stage of trauma and disorder. Theories which suggest such an idea do not accord with the empirical evidence. It seems that the majority of young people cope reasonably well with the normative stresses which are inherent in the adolescent transition. Nonetheless, there are, of course, those who experience difficulty, and an understanding of what makes coping problematic is equally important as recognising that most adjust reasonably well.

There is general agreement among those who have written about this subject (e.g. Feldman and Elliott, 1990; Rice *et al.*, 1993; Graber and Brooks-Gunn, 1996) that the timing of stresses, the extent or number of changes experienced by the young person, and the synchronicity of changes all contribute to whether the individual will cope well or not. In addition, the role of social support is critical, as is the impact of environmental factors. It hardly needs to be pointed out that coping when a young person is growing up in poverty or disadvantage, when he or she is living in a family with a dysfunctional parent, or experiencing violence, abuse or racial harassment, will be quite different from coping in a supportive, settled and economically stable environment. It is here that theoretical notions of developmental contextualism, which we outlined in Chapter 1, can be seen to have an obvious contribution.

In addition to these questions, we believe the focal model adds one more factor, namely, the concept of agency. It is our view that the young person plays a part in the coping process. Although many of the issues discussed above are outside the control of the individual, we cannot ignore the role the young person plays in adapting to circumstances. It will be recalled that many of the writers mentioned in this chapter (e.g. Compas, Seiffge-Krenke and Frydenberg) all point to a sense of personal control as being critical in the coping process. We would go further. The young person makes a personal contribution to managing the changes he or she experiences through the adolescent transition. As Feldman and Elliott (1990, p. 495) put it, young people 'shape the context in which they operate'. It is possible to deal with one change or stress at a time. It is possible to space things out, to tackle one issue at a time. We suggest that adolescents cope as well as they do by being active agents in their own development.

Implications for practice

1. As might be expected, there are a range of implications for practice stemming from the material reviewed in this chapter. First, it is important to distinguish different types of stress. A distinction which is often used is that between normative stresses, non-normative stresses and daily hassles. This distinction was carried further by Compas, who argued that it is also necessary to differentiate chronic and acute stress. By chronic stress he refers to poverty and other ongoing environmental factors, while acute stress might be caused by parental illness, divorce or other types of trauma.

2. Seiffge-Krenke makes the point that in considering stress there are four main components to take into account. These are the nature of the stressor, the internal resources of the individual, the social supports available, and the coping process itself. This breakdown is helpful in assisting practitioners to evaluate a young person's circumstances, and to assess the range of interventions which might be appropriate.

3. In terms of the coping process, much attention has been paid to the distinction between problem-focused and emotion-focused coping. Essentially, the former refers to actions which might be taken to modify the stress or its source, while the latter applies to an alteration of the feelings which are engendered by the stressor. Seiffge-Krenke called these two types of coping active coping and internal coping. In addition, she added a third reaction to stress – withdrawal. This she considered to be in the main dysfunctional, although there are clearly circumstances when to withdraw from or to avoid stress would be the most functional thing to do. It would appear that emotion-focused coping increases with age, although problem-focused coping remains at much the same level in different age groups.

4. There are clear gender differences in coping during adolescence. Boys are most likely to use active coping, but they are also more likely to deny a problem, or to withdraw from the stress. Girls, on the other hand, are more likely to use social support as a means of coping, and to utilise emotion-focused coping strategies. In addition, girls and young women are more affected by stress, and perceive events as being more stressful than their male counterparts.

5. Finally, the distinction between problem-focused coping and emotion-focused coping assists us in identifying a key developmental task. Research indicates that problem-focused strategies are more adaptive in situations when the stressor can be modified. Emotion-focused strategies are of more help when stressors cannot be altered. For this reason, a goal for those working with young people on the development of coping skills should be to facilitate learning about whether stressors can be changed or not. Thus, enabling young people to classify sources of stress, to think about types of coping, and to develop skills around event appraisal can all contribute to emotionally healthy development during adolescence.

Further reading

Frydenberg, E (1997) *Adolescent coping: theoretical and research perspectives.* Routledge. London.
This text provides a summary of research in the field, and includes chapters on coping in gifted young people and in those suffering illness. A clear and comprehensive analysis of thinking in this important area. A good start for anyone looking for an introduction to the topic.

Gore, S and Eckenrode, J (1994) Context and process in research on risk and resilience. In Haggerty, R, Sherrod, L, Garmezy, N and Rutter, M (Eds) *Stress, risk and resilience in children and adolescents.* Cambridge University Press. Cambridge.
A thoughtful and detailed article drawing conclusions from recent research on risk and resilience. Strongly recommended.

Hauser, S and Bowlds, M (1990) Stress, coping and adaptation. In Feldman, S and Elliott, G (Eds) *At the threshold: the developing adolescent.* Harvard University Press. Cambridge, MA.
Again the high standard of the Feldman and Elliott text is exemplified by this chapter. Both authors are well-known figures, and the article is very worthwhile.

Rutter, M (Ed.) (1995) *Psychosocial disturbances in young people: challenges for prevention.* Cambridge University Press. Cambridge.
In this book Rutter draws together a range of contributions from distinguished authors, who write about strategies for prevention in the context of emotional disturbance. An unusual collection of articles, the result is a book which can be recommended to anyone interested in preventive work in the field of mental health.

Seiffge-Krenke, I (1995) *Stress, coping, and relationships in adolescence.* Lawrence Erlbaum. Mahwah, NJ.

The author is responsible for much innovative work on this topic, and this book summarises her research, and sets the findings in the context of other theoretical and empirical approaches to coping and adjustment. A valuable report of empirical investigations over a number of years, as well as a contribution to the theory of coping in adolescence.

References

Abell, S and Richards, M (1996) The relationship between body shape satisfaction and self-esteem: an investigation of gender and class differences. *Journal of Youth and Adolescence.* 25. 691–703.

Adams, G and Fitch, S (1982) Ego stage and identity status development: a cross-sequential analysis. *Journal of Personality and Social Psychology.* 43. 574–583.

Adams, G and Jones, R (1983) Female adolescents' identity development: age comparisons and perceived child-rearing experience. *Developmental Psychology.* 19. 249–256.

Adams, G, Gullotta, T and Montemayor, R (Eds) (1992) *Adolescent identity formation.* Sage. London.

Adams, G, Montemayor, R and Gullotta, T (Eds) (1996) *Psychosocial development during adolescence: progress in developmental contextualism.* Sage. London.

Adelson, J (1971) The political imagination of the young adolescent. *Daedalus.* Fall. 1013–1050.

Adelson, J, Green, B and O'Neill, R (1969) Growth of the idea of law in adolescence. *Developmental Psychology.* 1. 327–332.

Adelson, J and O'Neill, R (1966) The development of political thought in adolescence. *Journal of Personality and Social Psychology.* 4. 295–308.

Aggleton, P, Hart, G and Davies, P (1991) *AIDS: responses, interventions and care.* Falmer Press. London.

Aggleton, P, Whitty, G, Knight, A, Prayle, D and Warwick, I (1996) *Management summary of promoting young people's health: the health concerns and needs of young people.* Health Education Authority. London.

Agnew, R (1991) The interactive effects of peer variables on delinquency. *Criminology.* 29. 47–72.

REFERENCES

Alexander, C, Somerfield, M, Ensminger, M, Johnson, K and Kim, Y (1993) Consistency of adolescents' self-report of sexual behaviour in a longitudinal study. *Journal of Youth and Adolescence*. 22. 455–472.

Allison, P and Furstenberg, F (1989) How marital dissolution affects children: variations by age and sex. *Developmental Psychology*. 25. 540–549.

Alsaker, F (1992) Pubertal timing, overweight, and psychological adjustment. *Journal of Early Adolescence*. 12. 396–419.

Alsaker, F (1995) Timing of puberty and reactions to pubertal changes. In Rutter, M (Ed.) *Psychosocial disturbances in young people: challenges for prevention*. Cambridge University Press. Cambridge.

Alsaker, F (1996) The impact of puberty. *Journal of Child Psychology and Psychiatry*. 37. 249–258.

Alsaker, F and Flammer, A (1998) *The adolescent experience: European and American adolescents in the 1990s*. Lawrence Erlbaum Associates. London.

Alsaker, F and Olweus, D (1992) Stability and global self-evaluations in early adolescence: a cohort longitudinal study. *Journal of Reseach in Adolescence*. 47. 123–145.

Altschuler, J and Ruble, D (1989) Developmental changes in children's awareness of strategies for coping with uncontrollable stress. *Child Development*. 60. 1337–1349.

Amato, P and Keith, B (1991) Parental divorce and the well-being of children: a meta-analysis. *Psychological Bulletin*. 110. 26–46.

Anderson, C and Ford, C (1987) Affect of the game player: short-term effects of highly and mildly aggressive video games. *Personality and Social Psychology Bulletin*. 12. 390–402.

Apel, H (1992) Intergenerative Bildungsmobilitat in den alten und neuen Bundeslandern. In Jugendwerk der Deutschen Shell (Ed.) *Jugend '92*. Vol. 2, pp. 353–370. Leske & Budrich. Opladen.

Archer, S (1982) The lower age boundaries of identity development. *Child Development*. 53. 1551–1556.

Archer, S (1993) Identity in relational contexts. In Kroger, J (Ed.) *Discussions on ego identity*. Lawrence Erlbaum. Hillsdale, NJ.

Archer, S and Waterman, A (1990) Varieties of identity diffusions and foreclosures: an exploration of subcategories of the identity statuses. *Journal of Adolescent Research*. 5. 96–111.

Arnett, J (1995) Adolescents' use of the media for self-socialisation. *Journal of Youth and Adolescence*. 24. 519–534.

Arnett, J (1998) The young and the reckless. In Messer, D and Dockrell, J (Eds) *Developmental psychology: a reader*. Arnold. London.

Arnett, J and Taber, S (1994) Adolescence terminable and interminable: when does adolescence end? *Journal of Youth and Adolescence*. 23. 517–538.

Arnett, J, Larson, R and Offer, D (1995) Beyond effects: adolescents as active media users. *Journal of Youth and Adolescence*. 25. 511–518.

Asher, S and Coie, J (1990) *Peer rejection in childhood*. Cambridge University Press. Cambridge.

Ashton, D, Maguire, M and Spilsbury, M (1990) *Restructuring the labour market: the implications for youth*. Macmillan. Basingstoke.

Babb, P (1993) Teenage conceptions and fertility in England and Wales: 1971–1991. *Population Trends*. 74. 12–22.

Babb, P and Bethune, A (1995) Trends in births outside marriage. *Population Trends*. 81. HMSO. London.

Back, L (1997) 'Pale shadows': racisms, masculinity and multiculture. In Roche, J and Tucker, S (Eds) *Youth in society*. Sage. London.

Backett, K and Davison, C (1992) Rational or reasonable? Perceptions of health at different stages of life. *Health Education Journal*. 51. 55–59.

Balding, J (1992) *Young people in 1991*. Schools Health Education Unit. Exeter.

Balding, J (1997) *Young people in 1996*. Schools Health Education Unit. Exeter.

Ball, S, Bowe, R and Gerwirtz, S (1996) School choice, social class and distinction: the realisation of social advantage in education. *Journal of Education Policy*. 11. 89–113.

Bancroft, J and Reinisch, J (1990) *Adolescence and puberty*. Oxford University Press. Oxford.

Band, E and Weisz, J (1988) How to feel better when it feels bad: children's perspectives on coping with everyday stress. *Developmental Psychology*. 24. 247–253.

Bandura, A (1964) The stormy decade: fact or fiction? *Psychology in the Schools*. 1. 224–231.

Banks, M, Breakwell, G, Bynner, J, Emler, N, Jamieson, L and Roberts, K (1992) *Careers and identities*. Open University Press. Milton Keynes.

Barber, B and Eccles, J (1992) Long-term influence of divorce and single parenting on adolescent family and work-related values, behaviours and aspirations. *Psychological Bulletin*. 111. 108–126.

Barenboim, C (1981) The development of person perception in childhood and adolescence. *Child Development*. 52. 129–144.

Bartley, M (1994) Unemployment and ill health: understanding the relationship. *Journal of Epidemiology and Community Health*. 48. 33–37.

Batchelder, T and Root, S (1994) Effects of an undergraduate program to integrate academic learning and service: cognitive, prosocial cognitive, and identity outcomes. *Journal of Adolescence*. 17. 341–356.

Bhattacharyya, G and Gabriel, J (1997) Racial formations of youth in late twentieth century England. In Roche, J and Tucker, S (Eds) *Youth in society*. Sage. London.

Baumrind, D (1971) Current patterns of parental authority. *Developmental Psychology Monographs*. 4. 1–102.

Baumrind, D (1991) The influence of parenting style on adolescent competence and substance misuse. *Journal of Early Adolescence*. 11. 56–95.

Beardslee, W and Podorefsky, D (1988) Resilient adolescents whose parents have serious affective and other psychiatric disorders: importance of self-understanding and relationships. *American Journal of Psychiatry*. 145. 63–69.

Beck, U (1992) *Risk society: towards a new modernity*. Sage. London.

Belle, D (1989) Gender differences in children's social networks and social supports. In D Belle (Ed.) *Children's social networks and social supports*. John Wiley. New York.

Berndt, T J and Zook, J M (1993) Effects of friendship on adolescent development. *Bulletin of the Hong Kong Psychological Society*. 30–31. 15–34.

Berry, J (1990) Psychology of acculturation. In Berman, J (Ed.) *Cross-cultural perspectives*: *Nebraska Symposium on Motivation*. University of Nebraska Press. Lincoln, NB.

Berzonsky, M (1992) A process perspective on identity and stress management. In Adams, G, Gullotta, T and Montemayor, R (Eds) *Adolescent identity formation*. Sage. London.

Bewley, B, Higgs, R and Jones, A (1984) Adolescent patients in an inner London general practice: their attitudes to illness and health care. *Journal of the Royal College of General Practitioners*. 34. 543–546.

Bhavnani, K-K (1991) *Talking politics: a psychological framing for views from youth in Britain*. Cambridge University Press. Cambridge.

Bierman, K L, Smoot, D L and Aumiller, K (1993) Characteristics of aggressive-rejected, aggressive (non-rejected), and rejected (non-aggressive) boys. *Child Development*. 64. 139–151.

Blackman, R and Jarman, J (1993) Changing inequalities in access to British universities. *Oxford Review of Education*. 9. 197–215.

Blackman, S (1987) The labour market in school: new vocationalism and issues of socially ascribed discrimination. In Brown, P and Ashton, D (Eds) *Education, unemployment and labour markets*. Falmer. London.

Blair, S, Clark, D, Cureton, K and Powell, K (1989) Exercise and fitness in childhood: implications for a lifetime of health. In Gisolfi, C and Lamb, D (Eds) *Perspectives in exercise science and sports medicine*. Benchmark Press. Indianapolis, IN.

Block, J and Robins, R (1993) A longitudinal study of consistency and change in self-esteem from early adolescence to early adulthood. *Child Development*. 64. 909–923.

Blyth, D, Hill, J and Thiel, K (1982) Early adolescents' significant others. *Journal of Youth and Adolescence*. 11. 425–450.

Blyth, D, Simmons, R and Zakin, D (1985) Satisfaction with body image for early adolescent females: the impact of pubertal timing within different school environments. *Journal of Youth and Adolescence*. 14. 207–226.

Bo, I (1996) The significant people in the social networks of adolescents. In Hurrelman, K and Hamilton, S (Eds) *Social problems and social contexts in adolescence*. Aldine De Gruyter. New York.

Boehnke, K, Silbereisen, R, Eisenberg, N and Palmonari, A (1989) Developmental patterns of prosocial motivation. *Journal of Cross-Cultural Psychology*. 20. 219–243.

Bogenshneider, K and Stone, M (1997) Delivering parent education to low and high risk parents of adolescents via age-paced newsletters. *Family Relations*. 42. 26–30.

Bolger, K, Patterson, C, Thompson, W and Kupersmidt, J (1995) Psychosocial adjustment among children experiencing persistent and intermittent family economic hardship. *Child Development*. 66. 1107–1129.

Bosma, H (1992) Identity in adolescence: managing commitments. In Adams, G, Gullotta, T and Montemayor, R (Eds) *Adolescent identity formation*. Sage. London.

Botvin, G (1990) Substance abuse prevention: theory, practice and effectiveness. In Tonry, M and Wilson, J (Eds) *Drugs and crime*. University of Chicago Press. Chicago.

Bourdieu, P (1977) Cultural reproduction and social reproduction. In Karabel, J and Halsey, A (Eds) *Power and ideology in education*. Oxford University Press. Oxford.

Brake, M (1985) *Comparative youth culture*. Routledge. London.

Breakwell, G and Fife-Shaw, C (1992) Sexual activities and preferences in a United Kingdom sample of 16–20 year olds. *Archives of Sexual Behaviour*. 21. 271–293.

Breakwell, G and Millward, L (1997) Sexual self-concept and sexual risk-taking. *Journal of Adolescence*. 20. 29–42.

Bridget, J (1995) *Lesbian and gay youth and suicide*. Paper presented at the National Children's Bureau, London. Quoted in Coyle (1998).

Brill, C (1994) The effects of participation in service-learning on adolescents with disabilities. *Journal of Adolescence*. 17. 369–380.

British Youth Council (1998) *State of the young nation*. British Youth Council. London.

Brody, G, Moore, K and Glei, D (1994) Family processes during adolescence as predictors of parent-young adult attitude similarity: a six-year longitudinal analysis. *Family Relations*. 43. 369–373.

Bronfenbrenner, U (1979) *The ecology of human development: experiments by nature and design*. Harvard University Press. Cambridge, MA.

Bronfenbrenner, U (1989) Ecological system theories. *Annals of Child Development*. 6. 187–249.

Brooks-Gunn, J (1991) How stressful is the transition to adolescence for girls? In Colten, M and Gore, S (Eds) *Adolescent stress: causes and consequences*. Aldine De Gruyter. New York.

Brooks-Gunn, J and Chase-Lansdale, L (1995) Adolescent parenthood. In Bornstein, M (Ed.) *Handbook of parenting: Vol. 3*. Lawrence Erlbaum Associates. Hillsdale, NJ.

Brooks-Gunn, J and Warren, M (1985) The effects of delayed menarche in different contexts: dance and non-dance students. *Journal of Youth and Adolescence*. 14. 285–300.

Brooks-Gunn, J, Petersen, A and Eichorn, D (Eds) (1985) The time of maturation and psycho-social functioning in adolescence: Parts 1 and 2. *Journal of Youth and Adolescence*. 14(3). 149–264 and 14(4). 265–372.

Brooks-Gunn, J, Attie, H, Burrow, C, Rosso, J and Warren, M (1989) The impact of puberty on body and eating concerns in athletic and non-athletic contexts. *Journal of Early Adolescence*. 9. 269–290.

Broomhall, H and Winefield, A (1990) A comparison of the affective well-being of young and middle-aged unemployed men matched for length of unemployment. *British Journal of Medical Psychology*. 63. 43–52.

Brown, B (1990) Peer groups and peer culture. In Feldman, S and Elliott, G (Eds) *At the threshold: the developing adolescent.* Harvard University Press. Cambridge, MA.

Brown, B (1996) Visibility, vulnerability, development, and context: ingredients for fuller understanding of peer rejection in adolescence. *Journal of Early Adolescence*, 16. 27–36.

Brown, B and Mounts, N (1989) *Peer group structure in single vs multi-ethnic high schools.* Paper presented at the Society for Research in Child Development conference. Kansas. April.

Brown, B, Mory, M and Kinney, D (1994) Casting adolescent crowds in a relational perspective: caricature, channel and context. In Montemayor, R, Adams, G and Gullotta, T (Eds) *Personal relationships during adolescence.* Sage. London.

Brown, B, Mounts, N, Lambert, S and Steinberg, L (1993) Parenting practices and peer group affiliation in adolescence. *Child Development.* 64. 467–482.

Brown, P (1987) *Schooling ordinary kids.* Tavistock. London.

Brown, P (1995) Cultural capital and social exclusion: some observations on recent trends in education, employment and the labour market. *Work, Employment, and Society.* 91. 29–51.

Brown, P and Lauder, H (1996) Education, globalisation and economic development. *Journal of Education Policy.* 11. 1–27.

Brown, P and Scase, R (1994) *Higher education and corporate realities.* UCL Press. London.

Bruno, J (1996) Time perceptions and time allocation preferences among adolescent boys and girls. *Adolescence.* 31. 109–126.

Buchanan, C (1991) Pubertal development, assessment of. In Lerner, R, Petersen, A and Brooks-Gunn, J (Eds) *Encyclopedia of adolescence.* Garland Publishing. New York.

Buchanan, C, Maccoby, E and Dornbusch, S (1996) *Adolescents after divorce.* Harvard University Press. London.

Bugenthal, D *et al.* (1989) Perceived control over care-giving outcomes. *Developmental Psychology.* 25. 532–539.

Buhrmester, D (1990) Intimacy of friendship, interpersonal competence, and adjustment during pre-adolescence and adolescence. *Child Development.* 61. 1101–1111.

Buhrmester, D and Furman, W (1987) The development of companionship and intimacy. *Child Development.* 58. 1101–1113.

Bulcroft, R (1991) The value of physical change in adolescence. *Journal of Youth and Adolescence.* 20. 89–106.

Bundesanstalt für Arbeit (1994) *Arbeitmarkst: 1994.* Amtliche Nachrichten der Bundesanstalt für Albeit, 43, Sondernummer. Nurnberg: BfA.

Bynner, J, Chisholm, L and Furlong, A (Eds) (1997) *Youth, citizenship and social change in a European context.* Ashgate Publishing. Aldershot.

Capaldi, D and Patterson, G (1991) Relation of parental transitions to boys' adjustment problems. *Developmental Psychology.* 27. 489–504.

Carle, J (1987) Youth unemployment – individual and societal consequences, and new research approaches. *Social Science and Medicine.* 25.

Cass, V (1984) Homosexual identity: a concept in need of definition. *Journal of Homosexuality.* 9. 105–126.

Chao, R (1994) Beyond parental control and authoritarian parenting style: understanding Chinese parenting through the cultural notions of training. *Child Development.* 65. 1111–1119.

Charlton, J (1995) Trends and patterns in suicide in England and Wales. *International Journal of Epidemiology.* 24. 45–52.

Chase-Lansdale, L, Brooks-Gunn, J and Paikoff, B (1991) Research and programmes for adolescent mothers: missing links and future promises. *Family Relations.* 40. 396–404.

Chase-Lansdale, L, Brooks-Gunn, J and Zamsky, E (1994) Young African-American multi-generational families in poverty: quality of mothering and grand-mothering. *Child Development.* 65. 373–393.

REFERENCES

Chase-Lansdale, L, Wakschlag, L and Brooks-Gunn, J (1995) A psychological perspective on the development of caring in children and youth: the role of the family. *Journal of Adolescence*. 18. 515–556.

Chisholm, L and Hurrelmann, K (1995) Adolescents in modern Europe: pluralized transition patterns and their implications for personal and social risks. *Journal of Adolescence*. 18. 129–158.

Chitty, C (1989) *Towards a new educational system: a victory for the new right?* Falmer. London.

Christopher, J, Nangle, D and Hansen, D (1993) Social-skills interventions with adolescents: current issues and procedures. *Behaviour Modification*. 17. 314–338.

Churchill, R, Allen, J, Denman, S, Fielding, K, Williams, D, Hollis, C, Williams, J, von Fragstein, M and Pringle, M (1997) *Factors influencing the use of general practice based health services by teenagers*. School of Medicine, University of Nottingham. Nottingham.

Claes, M (1998) Adolescents' closeness with parents, siblings, and friends in three countries: Canada, Belgium and Italy. *Journal of Youth and Adolescence*. 27. 165–184.

Clark, M, and Ayers, M (1992) Friendship similarity during early adolescence. *Journal of Psychology*. 126. 393–405.

Clarke, R (Ed.) (1992) *Situational crime prevention*. Harrow & Heston. New York.

Clausen, J (1975) The social meaning of differential physical and sexual maturation. In Dragastin, S and Elder, G (Eds) *Adolescence in the life cycle*. John Wiley. New York.

Clausen, J (1991) Adolescent competence and the shaping of the life course. *American Journal of Sociology*. 96. 805–842.

Coakley, J and White, A (1992) Making decisions: gender and sport participation among British adolescents. *Sociology of Sport Journal*. 9. 20–35.

Cockett, M and Tripp, J (1994) *The Exeter family study*. University of Exeter. Exeter.

Coggans, N and McKellar, P (1994) Drug use among peers: peer pressure or peer preference? *Drugs: Education, Prevention and Policy*. 1. 15–26.

Coggans, N, Shewan, D, Henderson, M, Davies, J and O'Hagan, F (1990) *National evaluation of drug education in Scotland: final report*. Scottish Education Department. Edinburgh.

Coie, J and Dodge, K (1983) Continuities and changes in children's social status: a five year long longitudinal study. *Merrill-Palmer Quarterly*. 29. 261–282.

Coleman, J (1974) *Relationships in adolescence*. Routledge & Kegan Paul. London.

Coleman, J (1978) Current contradictions in adolescent theory. *Journal of Youth and Adolescence*. 7. 1–11.

Coleman, J (1990) *Teenagers and divorce*. Trust for the Study of Adolescence. Brighton, Sussex.

Coleman, J (1995) *Teenagers and sexuality*. Hodder & Stoughton. London.

Coleman, J (1996) Adolescents and suicide. In Williams, R and Morgan, G (Eds) *Suicide prevention: the challenge confronted*. HMSO. London.

Coleman, J (1997a) *Key data on adolescence*. Trust for the Study of Adolescence. Brighton, Sussex.

Coleman, J (1997b) The parenting of adolescents in Britain today. *Children and Society*. 11. 45–52.

Coleman, J and Coleman, E (1984) Adolescent attitudes to authority. *Journal of Adolescence*. 7. 131–141.

Coleman, J and Dennison, C (1998) Teenage parenthood: a review. *Children and Society*. 12. 306–314.

Coleman, J and Roker, D (Eds) (1998) *Teenage sexuality: health, risk and education*. Harwood Academic Press. London.

Coleman, J and Warren-Adamson, C (Eds) (1992) *Youth policy for the 1990s*. Routledge. London.

Coles, B (1995) *Youth and social policy*. UCL Press. London.

234

Coles, B (1997) Vulnerable youth and processes of social exclusion. In Bynner, J, Chisholm, L and Furlong, A (Eds) *Youth, citizenship and social change in a European context.* Ashgate Publishing. Aldershot.

Coley, R and Chase-Lansdale, L (1998) Adolescent pregnancy and parenthood: recent evidence and future directions. *American Psychologist.* 53. 152–166.

Collins, W and Repinski, D (1994) Relationships during adolescence: continuity and change in interpersonal perspective. In Montemayor, R, Adams, G and Gullotta, T (Eds) *Personal relationships during adolescence.* Sage. London.

Compas, B (1987) Coping with stress during childhood and adolescence. *Psychological Bulletin.* 101. 393–403.

Compas, B (1995) Promoting successful coping during adolescence. In Rutter, M (Ed.) *Psychosocial disturbances in young people.* Cambridge University Press. Cambridge, UK.

Compas, B and Wagner, B (1991) Psychosocial stress during adolescence: intrapersonal and interpersonal processes. In Colten, M and Gore, S (Eds) *Adolescent stress: causes and consequences.* Aldine De Gruyter. New York.

Compas, B, Malcarne, V and Fondacaro, K (1988) Coping with stressful events in older children and young adolescents. *Journal of Consulting and Clinical Psychology.* 56. 405–411.

Compas, B, Orosan, P and Grant, K (1993) Adolescent stress and coping: implications for psychopathology in adolescence. *Journal of Adolescence.* 16. 331–349.

Compas, B, Banez, G, Malcarne, V and Worsham, N (1991) Perceived control and coping with stress: a developmental perspective. *Journal of Social Issues.* 47. 23–34.

Conger, R, Patterson, G and Ge, X (1995) It takes two to replicate: a mediational model for the impact of parents' stress on adolescent adjustment. *Child Development.* 66. 80–97.

Conger, R, Ge, X, Elder, G and Simmons, R (1994) Economic stress, coercive family process, and developmental problems of adolescents. *Child Development.* 65. 541–561.

Connell, R (1971) *The child's construction of politics.* Melbourne University Press. Carleton, Virginia.

Conrad, D and Hedin, D (1982) The impact of experiential education on adolescent development. In Conrad, D and Hedin, D (Eds) *Youth participation and experiential education.* Haworth Press. New York.

Cooper, C (1994) Cultural perspectives on continuity and change in adolescent relationships. In Montemayor, R, Adams, G and Gullotta, T (Eds) *Personal relationships during adolescence.* Sage. London.

Corlyon, J and McGuire, C (1997) *Young parents in public care.* National Children's Bureau. London.

Costello, E (1989) Child psychiatric disorders and their correlates: a primary care paediatric sample. *Journal of the American Academy of Child and Adolescent Psychiatry.* 28. 851–855.

Cote, J (1996) Sociological perspectives on identity formation: the culture–identity link and identity capital. *Journal of Adolescence.* 19. 417–428.

Cote, J (1997) An empirical test of the identity capital model. *Journal of Adolescence.* 20. 577–598.

Cotterell, J (1996) *Social networks and social influences in adolescence.* Routledge. London.

Cowie, H and Rudduck, J (1990) Learning from one another: the challenge. In Foot, H, Morgan, M and Shute, R (Eds) *Children helping children.* John Wiley & Sons. Chichester.

Coyle, A (1991) The construction of gay identity. Unpublished PhD. University of Surrey.

Coyle, A (1993) A study of psychological well-being among gay men using the GHQ-30. *British Journal of Clinical Psychology.* 32. 218–220.

Coyle, A (1998) Developing lesbian and gay identity in adolescence. In Coleman, J and Roker, D (Eds) *Teenage sexuality: health, risk and education.* Harwood Academic Press. London.

Crockett, L, Losoff, M and Petersen, A (1984) Perceptions of the peer group and friendship in early adolescence. *Journal of Early Adolescence.* 4. 155–181.

Crockett, L, Bingham, C, Chopak, J and Vicary, J (1996) Timing of first sexual intercourse: the role of social control, social learning and problem behaviour. *Journal of Youth and Adolescence*. 25. 89–112.

Cross, M, Wrench, J and Barnett, S (1990) *Ethnic minorities and the careers service*. Department of Employment. London.

Csikszentmihalyi, M and Larson, R (1984) *Being adolescent: conflict and growth in the teenage years*. Basic Books. New York.

Csikzentmihalyi, M, Larson, R and Prescott, S (1977) The ecology of adolescent activity and experience. *Journal of Youth and Adolescence*. 6. 281–294.

Damon, W and Lerner, R (Eds) (1998) *Handbook of child psychology: Vol. 1*. John Wiley. New York.

D'Augelli, A and Hershberger, S (1993) Lesbian, gay and bisexual youth in community settings. *Americal Journal of Community Psychology*. 21. 421–448.

Davies, E and Furnham, A (1986) The dieting and body shape concerns of adolescent females. *Journal of Child Psychology and Psychiatry*. 27. 417–428.

Davies, J and Coggans, N (1991) *The facts about adolescent drug abuse*. Cassell. London.

Davis, J (1990) *Youth and the condition of Britain: images of adolescent conflict*. Athlone Press. London.

Dekovic, M and Meeus, W (1997) Peer relations in adolescence: effects of parenting and adolescents' self-concept. *Journal of Adolescence*. 20. 163–176.

Dennehy, A, Smith, L and Harker, P (1997) *Not to be ignored: young people, poverty and health*. Child Povery Action Group. London.

Dennison, C and Coleman, J (1998a) Teenage motherhood: experiences and relationships. In Clement, S (Ed.) *Psychological perspectives on pregnancy and childbirth*. Churchill Livingstone. Edinburgh.

Dennison, C and Coleman, J (1998b) *Adolescent motherhood: the relation betweeen a young mother and her mother*. Research report. Trust for the Study of Adolescence. Brighton.

Department for Education and Employment (DfEE) (1993) International statistical comparisons of the participation in education and training of 16 to 18 year olds. *Statistical Bulletin*. 19–93. London.

Department for Education and Employment (DfEE) (1994) *Employment Gazette*. 102. London.

DeRosier, M, Kupersmidt, J and Patterson, C (1994) Children's academic and behavioural adjustment as a function of the chronicity and proximity of peer rejection. *Child Development*. 65. 1799–1813.

Diamond, A and Goddard, E (1995) *Smoking among secondary school children in 1994*. HMSO. London.

Dishion, T, Patterson, G and Kavanagh, K (1992) An experimental test of the coercion model: linking theory, measurement, and intervention. In McCord, J and Tremblay, R (Eds) *Preventing anti-social behaviour*. Guilford. New York.

Dohrenwend, B and Dohrenwend, B (Eds) (1974) *Stressful life events, their nature and effects*. John Wiley. New York.

Dornbusch, S, Herman, M and Morley, J (1996) Domains of adolescent achievement. In Adams, G, Montemayor, R and Gullotta, T (Eds) *Psychosocial development during adolescence: progress in developmental contextualism*. Sage. London.

Dornbusch, S, Ritter, P, Liederman, P and Fraleigh, M (1987) The relation of parenting style to adolescent school performance. *Child Development*. 58. 1244–1257.

Douvan, E and Adelson, J (1966) *The adolescent experience*. John Wiley. New York.

Downs, W and Rose, S (1991) The relationship of adolescent peer groups to the incidence of psychosocial problems. *Adolescence*. 26. 473–492.

Drew, D, Gray, J and Sime, N (1992) *Against the odds: the education and labour market experiences of black young people*. Employment Department. Sheffield.

Drury, J, Catan, L, Dennison, C and Brody, R (1998) Exploring teenagers' accounts of bad communication: a new basis for intervention. *Journal of Adolescence*. 21. 177–196.

DuBois, D and Hirsch, B (1993) School/non-school friendship patterns in early adolescence. *Journal of Early Adolescence.* 13. 102–122.

Dunne, M, Donald, M, Lucke, J, Nilson, R and Raphael, B (1993) *National HIV/AIDS Evaluation and Survey in Australian secondary schools.* Commonwealth Department of Health. Canberra.

Dunphy, D (1972) Peer group socialisation. In Hunt, F (Ed.) *Socialisation in Australia.* Angus & Robertson. Sydney.

Durbin, D, Darling, N and Steinberg, L (1993) Parenting style and peer group membership. *Journal of Research on Adolescence.* 3. 87–100.

Durkin, K (1995) *Developmental social psychology.* Blackwell. Oxford.

East, P and Felice, M (1996) *Adolescent pregnancy and parenting.* Lawrence Erlbaum. Hillsdale, NJ.

East, P, Lerner, R, Lerner, J, Soni, R and Jacobson, L (1992) Early adolescent–peer group fit, peer relations, and psychological competence: a short-term longitudinal study. *Journal of Early Adolescence.* 12. 132–152.

Eccles, J, Flanagan, C, Lord, S, Midgley, C, Roeser, R and Yee, D (1996) Schools, families and early adolescents: what are we doing wrong and what can we do instead? *Developmental and Behavioural Paediatrics.* 17. 267–276.

Eder, D (1985) The cycle of popularity: interpersonal relations among female adolescents. *Sociology and Education.* 58. 154–165.

Egerton, M and Halsey, A (1993) Trends in social class and gender in access to higher education in Britain. *Oxford Review of Education.* 19. 183–196.

Eicher, J, Baizerman, S and Michelmann, J (1991) Adolescent dress, Part II: a qualitative study of suburban high school students. *Adolescence.* 26. 678–686.

Eisenberg, N (1990) Prosocial development in early and mid-adolescence. In Montemayor, R, Adams, G and Gullotta, T (Eds) *From childhood to adolescence.* Sage. London.

Eisenberg, N, Carlo, G, Murphy, B and Van Court, P (1995) Prosocial development in late adolescence: a longitudinal study. *Child Development.* 66. 1179–1197.

Elder, G (1974) *Children of the Great Depression.* University of Chicago Press. Chicago.

Elder, G and Caspi, A (1988) Human development and social change: an emerging perspective on the life course. In Bolger, N, Caspi, A, Downey, G and Moorehouse, M (Eds) *Persons in context: developmental processes.* Cambridge University Press. Cambridge.

Elkin, F (1960) *The child and society: the process of socialisation.* John Wiley. New York.

Elkind, D (1966) Conceptual orientation shifts in children and adolescents. *Child Development.* 37. 493–498.

Elkind, D (1967) Egocentrism in adolescence. *Child Development.* 38. 1025–1034.

Elkind, D and Bowen, R (1979) Imaginary audience behaviour in children and adolescents. *Developmental Psychology.* 15. 38–44.

Elliott, D, Huizinga, D and Ageton, S (1985) *Explaining delinquency and drug use.* Sage. Beverley Hills, CA.

Emler, N and Reicher, S (1995) *Adolescence and delinquency.* Blackwell. Oxford.

Enright, R, Shukla, D and Lapsley, D (1980) Adolescent egocentrism – sociocentrism and self-consciousness. *Journal of Youth and Adolescence.* 9. 101–116.

Epstein, R, Rice, P and Wallace, P (1989) Teenagers' health concerns: implications for primary health care professionals. *Journal of the Royal College of General Practitioners.* 39. 247–249.

Erikson, E (1968) *Identity, youth and crisis.* Norton. New York.

Erwin, P and Calev, A (1984) Beauty: more than skin deep? *Journal of Social and Personal Relationships.* 1. 359–361.

European Sports Charter (1975) *'Sport for all' charter.* European Sports Ministers' Conference. Brussels.

Evans, C and Eder, D (1993) 'No exit': processes of social isolation in the middle school. *Journal of Contemporary Ethnography.* 22. 139–170.

Eveleth, P and Tanner, J (1977) *Worldwide variation in human growth*. Cambridge University Press. Cambridge.

Eveleth, P and Tanner, J (1990) *Worldwide variation in human growth: 2nd Edition*. Cambridge University Press. Cambridge.

Facio, A and Batistuta, M (1998) Latins, Catholics and from the far south: Argentinian adolescents and their parents. *Journal of Adolescence*. 21. 49–68.

Farrell, C (1978) *My mother said . . . the way young people learn about sex and birth*. Routledge & Kegan Paul. London.

Farrington, D (1989) Self-reported and official offending from adolescence to adulthood. In Klein, M (Ed.) *Cross-national research in self-reported crime and delinquency*. Kluwer. Dordrecht.

Farrington, D (1995) The challenge of teenage antisocial behaviour. In Rutter, M (Ed.) *Psychosocial disturbances in young people: challenges for prevention*. Cambridge University Press. Cambridge.

Feather, N and O'Brien, G (1986) A longitudinal study of the effects of employment and unemployment on school-leavers. *Journal of Occupational Psychology*. 59. 121–144.

Feiring, C (1996) Concepts of romance in 15-year-old adolescents. *Journal of Research on Adolescence*. 6. 181–200.

Feiring, C and Lewis, M (1993) Do mothers know their teenagers' friends? Implications for individuation in early adolescence. *Journal of Youth and Adolescence*. 22. 337–354.

Feldman, S and Elliott, G (1990) *At the threshold: the developing adolescent*. Harvard University Press. Cambridge, MA.

Feldman, S, Rosenthal, D, Brown, N and Canning, R (1995) Predicting sexual experience in adolescent boys from peer rejection and acceptance during childhood. *Journal of Research on Adolescence*. 5. 387–412.

Felson, R (1985) Reflected appraisal and the development of self. *Social Psychology Quarterly*. 48. 71–78.

Fergusson, D and Lynskey, M (1996) Adolescent resiliency to family adversity. *Journal of Child Psychology and Psychiatry*. 37. 281–292.

Fergusson, D, Horwood, L and Lynskey, M (1994) The childhoods of multiple problem adolescents: a 15 year longitudinal study. *Journal of Child Psychology and Psychiatry*. 35. 1123–1140.

Fergusson, D, Lynskey, M and Horwood, J (1997) The effects of unemployment on juvenile offending. *Criminal Behaviour and Mental Health*. 7. 49–68.

Ferri, E (1984) *Step children: a national study*. NFER-Nelson. Windsor.

Fisher, S (1995) The amusement arcade as a social space for adolescents. *Journal of Adolescence*. 18. 71–86.

Fitzgerald, M, Joseph, A, Hayes, M and O'Regan, M (1995) Leisure activities of adolescent schoolchildren. *Journal of Adolescence*. 18. 349–358.

Flanagan, C, Jonsson, B, Botcheva, L, Csapo, B, Bowes, J, Macek, P and Sheblanova, E (1999) Adolescents and the social contract: developmental roots of citizenship in seven countries. In Yates, M and Youniss, J (Eds) *Roots of civic identity*. Cambridge University Press. Cambridge.

Fletcher, A, Darling, N, Steinberg, L and Dornbusch, S (1995) The company they keep: relation of adolescents' adjustment and behaviour to their friends perceptions of authoritative parenting. *Developmental Psychology*. 31. 300–310.

Fogelman, K (1976) *Britain's 16 year olds*. National Children's Bureau. London.

Ford, N and Morgan, K (1989) Heterosexual lifestyles of young people in an English city. *Journal of Population and Social Studies*. 1. 167–185.

Fraser, E (1999) Introduction to Special Issue on Political Education. *Oxford Review of Education*. 25. 5–22.

Freedman, R (1984) Reflections on beauty as it relates to health in adolescent females. *Women and Health*. 9. 29–45.

Frydenberg, E (1997) *Adolescent coping: theoretical and research perspectives*. Routledge. London.

Frydenberg, E and Lewis, R (1993) Boys play sport and girls turn to others: gender and ethnicity as determinants of coping. *Journal of Adolescence.* 16. 253–266.

Fryer, D (1995) Benefit Agency? Labour market disadvantage, deprivation and mental health. *The Psychologist.* 8. 265–272.

Fryer, D (1997) International perspectives on youth unemployment and mental health: some central issues. *Journal of Adolescence.* 20. 333–342.

Fuhrman, T and Holmbeck, G (1995) A contextual-moderator analysis of emotional autonomy and adjustment in adolescence. *Child Development.* 66. 276–285.

Fuligni, A and Eccles, J (1993) Perceived parent–child relationships and early adolescents' orientation towards peers. *Developmental Psychology.* 29. 622–632.

Funk, J (1993) Re-evaluating the impact of video games. *Clinical Pediatrics.* 32. 86–90.

Furlong, A and Cartmel, F (1997) *Young people and social change.* Open University Press. Milton Keynes.

Furlong, A and Raffe, D (1989) *Young people's routes into the labour market.* Industry Department for Scotland. Edinburgh.

Furlong, A, Campbell, R and Roberts, K (1990) The effects of post-16 experiences and social class on the leisure patterns of young adults. *Leisure Studies.* 9. 213–224.

Furnham, A and Gunter, B (1989) *The anatomy of adolescence.* Routledge. London.

Furntratt, E and Moller, C (1982) *Lernprinzip erfolg.* Peter Lang. Frankfurt.

Furstenberg, F, Brooks-Gunn, J and Chase-Lansdale, L (1989) Teenage pregnancy and child-bearing. *American Psychologist.* 44. 313–320.

Gaoni, L, Couper Black, Q and Baldwin, S (1998) Defining adolescent behaviour disorder: an overview. *Journal of Adolescence.* 21. 1–14.

Gardner, H (1984) *Frames of mind.* Heinemann. London.

Garmezy, N and Rutter, M (1983) *Stress, coping and development in childhood.* McGraw-Hill. New York.

Garnefski, N and Diekstra, R (1997) Adolescents from one parent, stepparent, and intact families: emotional problems and suicide attempts. *Journal of Adolescence.* 20. 201–208.

Gavin, L and Furman, W (1996) Adolescent girls' relationships with mothers and best friends. *Child Development.* 67. 375–386.

Gecas, V and Seff, M (1990) Families and adolescents: a review of the 1980s. *Journal of Marriage and the Family.* 52. 941–958.

George, T and Hartmann, D (1996) Friendship networks of unpopular, average, and popular children. *Child Development.* 67. 2301–2316.

Gibson-Kline, J (1996) *Adolescence: from crisis to coping.* Butterworth-Heinemann. Oxford.

Gilani, N (1995) A study of mother–daughter relationships in two cultures. Unpublished PhD dissertation. University of Sussex.

Giles, D and Eyler, J (1994) The impact of a college community service laboratory on students' personal, social and cognitive outcomes. *Journal of Adolescence.* 17. 327–340.

Gilligan, C (1982) *In a different voice.* Harvard University Press. Cambridge, MA.

Gilligan, C and Belenky, M (1980) A naturalistic study of abortion decisions. In Selman, R and Yando, R (Eds) *Clinical-developmental psychology.* Jossey-Bass. San Francisco, CA.

Gilligan, C, Lyons, N and Hanmer, T (1990) *Making connections: the relational worlds of adolescent girls at Emma Willard School.* Harvard University Press. Cambridge, MA.

Ginn, J and Arber, S (1995) Only connect: gender relations and ageing. In Arber, S and Ginn, J (Eds) *Connecting gender and ageing: a sociological approach.* Open University Press. Milton Keynes.

Gjerde, P and Shimizu, H (1995) Family relationships and adolescent development in Japan. *Journal of Research on Adolescence.* 5. 281–318.

Glendinning, A, Love, J, Shucksmith, J and Hendry, L (1992) Adolescence and health inequalities: extensions to McIntyre and West. *Social Science and Medicine.* 35. 679–687.

Glyptis, S (1989) *Leisure and unemployment.* Open University Press. Milton Keynes.

Goddard, E (1989) *Smoking among secondary school children in 1988.* OPCS Social Survey Division. HMSO. London.

Goddard, E (1996) *Teenage drinking in 1994.* HMSO. London.

Gofton, L (1990) On the town: drink and the new lawlessness. *Youth and Policy.* 29. 33–39.

Goggin, M (1995) Gay and lesbian adolescence. In Moore, S and Rosenthal, D (Eds) *Sexuality in adolescence.* Routledge. London.

Golding, J (1987) Smoking. In Cox, B (Ed.) *The health and lifestyle survey.* The Health Promotion Research Trust. Cambridge.

Goldman, R and Goldman, J (1988) *'Show me yours' – understanding children's sexuality.* Penguin. Ringwood, Australia.

Golombok, S, and Fivush, C (1994) *Gender development.* Cambridge University Press. Cambridge.

Goodnow, J and Collins, A (1990) *Development according to parents.* Lawrence Erlbaum. Hillsdale, NJ.

Goodyer, I (1994) Development psychopathology: the impact of recent life events in anxious and depressed school-age children. *Journal of the Royal Society of Medicine.* 87. 327–329.

Goossens, L and Marcoen, A (1999a) Relationships during adolescence: constructive versus negative themes and relational dissatisfaction. *Journal of Adolescence.* 22. 49–64.

Goossens, L and Marcoen, A (1999b) Adolescent loneliness, self-reflection and identity: from individual differences to developmental processes. In Rotenberg, K and Hymel, S (Eds) *Loneliness in childhood and adolescence.* Cambridge University Press. New York.

Goossens, L, Seiffge-Krenke, I and Marcoen, A (1992) The many faces of adolescent egocentrism: a European replication. Paper presented at Society of Research on Adolescence conference, Washington, DC.

Goossens, L, Marcoen, A, Van Hees, S and Van de Woestijne, O (1998) Attachment style and loneliness in adolescence. *European Journal of Psychology of Education.* 13. 529–542.

Gore, S and Eckenrode, J (1994) Context and process in research on risk and resilience. In Haggerty, R, Sherrod, L, Garmezy, N and Rutter, M (Eds) *Stress, risk and resilience in children and adolescents.* Cambridge University Press. Cambridge.

Gottfredson, M and Hirshi, T (1990) *A general theory of crime.* Stanford University Press. Stanford, CA.

Graber, J and Brooks-Gunn, J (1996) Transitions and turning points: navigating the passage from childhood through adolescence. *Developmental Psychology.* 32. 768–776.

Graham, J and Bowling, B (1995) *Young people and crime.* Home Office Research Study No. 145. Home Office. London.

Greenberger, E (1984) Defining psychosocial maturity in adolescence. In Karoly, P and Steffen, J (Eds) *Adolescent behaviour disorders.* Heath. Lexington, MA.

Greenberger, E and O'Neill, R (1990) Parents' concerns about the child's development: implications for fathers' and mothers' well-being and attitudes to work. *Journal of Marriage and the Family.* 56. 621–630.

Griffin, C (1993) *Representations of youth.* Polity Press. London.

Griffiths, M (1995) *Adolescent gambling.* Routledge. London.

Grob, A (1998) Dynamics of perceived control across adolescence and adulthood. In Perrig, W and Grob, A (Eds) *Control of human behaviour: mental processes and awareness.* Lawrence Erlbaum Associates. Hillsdale, NJ.

Grotevant, H and Cooper, C (1985) Patterns of interaction in family relationships and the development of identity exploration in adolescence. *Child Development.* 56. 415–428.

Grotevant, H and Cooper, C (1986) Individuation in family relationships: a perspective on individual differences in the development of identity and role-taking skill in adolescence. *Human Development.* 29. 82–100.

Grotevant, H and Cooper, C (1998) Individuality and connectedness in adolescent development: review and prospects for research on identity, relationships and context. In Skoe, E and von der Lippe, A (Eds) *Personality development in adolescence: a cross-national and lifespan perspective.* Routledge. London.

Grunebaum, H and Solomon, L (1987) Peer relationships, self-esteem and the self. *International Journal of Group Psychotherapy*. 37.475–511.

Gunnell, D, Peters, T, Kammerling, R and Brooks, J (1995) Relation between parasuicide, suicide, psychiatric admissions and socio-economic deprivation. *British Medical Journal*. 311. 226–230.

Hackett, C (1997) Young people and political participation. In Roche, J and Tucker, S (Eds) *Youth in society*. Sage. London.

Hagell, A and Newburn, T (1996) Family and social contexts of adolescent re-offenders. *Journal of Adolescence*. 19. 5–18.

Haggerty, R, Sherrod, L, Garmezy, N and Rutter, M (Eds) (1994) *Stress, risk and resilience in children and adolescents: processes, mechanisms and interventions*. Cambridge University Press. Cambridge.

Hale, S (1990) A global developmental trend in cognitive processing speed. *Child Development*. 61. 653–663.

Halsey, A (1992) *Opening wide the doors of higher education*. Briefing Paper No. 6. National Commission on Education. London.

Hammer, T (1996) History dependence in youth unemployment. *European Sociological Review*. 13. 17–33.

Hansen, D, Giacoletti, A and Nangle, D (1995) Social interactions and adjustment. In Van Hasselt, V and Hersen, M (Eds) *Handbook of adolescent psychopathology: a guide to diagnosis and treatment*. Lexington Books. New York.

Hanson, S (1988) Divorced fathers with custody. In Bronstein, P and Cowan, C (Eds) *Fatherhood today: men's changing role in the family*. Wiley. Chichester.

Harlan, W, Harlan, E and Grillo, C (1980) Secondary sex characteristics of girls 12 to 17 years of age: the US Health Examination Survey. *Journal of Pediatrics*. 96. 1074–1078.

Harrington, R (1995) Depressive disorder in adolescence. *Archives of Disease in Childhood*. 72: 193–195.

Harris, C (1993) *The family and industrial society*. Allen & Unwin. London.

Hart, D and Fegley, S (1995) Prosocial behaviour and caring in adolescence. *Child Development*. 66. 1346–1359.

Hart, D, Yates, M, Fegley, S and Wilson, G (1996) Moral commitment in inner-city adolescents. In Killen, M and Hart, D (Eds) *Morality in everyday life: developmental perspectives*. Cambridge University Press. New York.

Harter, S (1988) The construction and conservation of the self: James and Cooley revisited. In Lapsley, D and Power, F (Eds) *Self, ego and identity*. Springer-Verlag. New York.

Harter, S (1989) Causes, correlates, and the functional role of global self-worth: a life-span perspective. In Kolligian, J and Sternberg, R (Eds) *Perceptions of competence and incompetence across the life-span*. Yale University Press. New Haven, CT.

Harter, S (1990) Self and identity development. In Feldman, S and Elder, G (Eds) *At the threshold: the developing adolescent*. Harvard University Press. Cambridge, MA.

Harter, S and Monsour, A (1992) Developmental analysis of conflict caused by opposing attributes in the adolescent self-portrait. *Developmental Psychology*. 28. 251–260.

Hartup, W (1996) The company they keep: friendships and their developmental significance. *Child Development*. 67. 1–13.

Haskey, J (1996) Population review 6: families and households in Great Britain. *Population Trends*. 85. 7–24.

Hatfield, E and Sprecher, S (1986) Measuring passionate love in intimate relationships. *Journal of Adolescence*. 9. 383–410.

Hauser, S and Bowlds, M (1990) Stress, coping and adaptation. In Feldman, S and Elliott, G (Eds) *At the threshold: the developing adolescent*. Harvard University Press. Cambridge, MA.

Hauser, S, Book, B, Houlihan, J, Powers, S and Noam, G (1987) Sex differences within the family: studies of adolescent and family interaction. *Journal of Youth and Adolescence*. 16. 199–213.

Hawton, K (1992) By their own hand: suicide is increasing rapidly in young men. *British Medical Journal*. 304. 1000.

Hawton, K, Fagg, J and Simkin, S (1996) Deliberate self-poisoning and self-injury in adolescents: a study of characteristics and trends in Oxford: 1976–1989. *British Journal of Psychiatry*. 169. 202–208.

Hawton, K, Fagg, J, Simkin, S and Bale, L (1999) Deliberate self-harm in adolescents in Oxford: 1985–1995. *Journal of Adolescence*. In Press.

Heaven, P (1994) *Contemporary adolescence*. Macmillan. London.

Heaven, P (1996) *Adolescent health: the role of individual differences*. Routledge. London.

Hendry, L (1983) *Growing up and going out*. Pergamon. London.

Hendry, L (1987) Young people: from school to unemployment? In Fineman, S (Ed.) *Unemployment: personal and social consequences*. Tavistock. London.

Hendry, L (1992) Sports and leisure. In Coleman, J and Warren-Adamson, C (Eds) *Youth policy in the 1990s*. Routledge. London.

Hendry, L (1993) Learning the new 3 Rs. *Aberdeen University Review*. 189. 33–51.

Hendry, L and Kloep, M (1996) Is there life beyond 'flow'? Proceedings of 5th Biennial Conference of the EARA, University of Liege, May 1996.

Hendry, L and Singer F (1981) Sport and the adolescent girl: a case study of one comprehensive school. *Scottish Journal of Physical Education*. 9. 19–29.

Hendry, L, Glendinning, A, Reid, M and Wood, S (1998) *Lifestyles, health and health concerns of rural youth: 1996–1998*. Report to Department of Health, Scottish Office. Edinburgh.

Hendry, L, Roberts, W, Glendinning, A and Coleman, J (1992) Adolescents' perceptions of significant individuals in their lives. *Journal of Adolescence*. 15. 255–270,

Hendry, L, Shucksmith, J, Love, J and Glendinning, A (1993) *Young people's leisure and lifestyles*. Routledge. London.

Hengeller, S, Cunningham, P, Pickrel, S and Brondino, M (1996) Multi-systemic therapy: an effective violence prevention approach for serious juvenile offenders. *Journal of Adolescence*. 19. 47–62.

Hermann-Giddens, M, Slora, E and Wasserman, R (1997) Secondary sexual characteristics and menses in young girls seen in office practice. *Paediatrics*. 99. 505–512.

Herrenkohl, E, Herrenkohl, R and Egolf, B (1994) Resilient early school-age children from maltreating homes: outcomes in late adolescence. *American Journal of Orthopsychiatry*. 64. 301–309.

Hetherington, M (1993) An overview of the Virginia longitudinal study of divorce and remarriage with a focus on early adolescence. *Journal of Family Psychology*. 7. 39–56.

Hetherington, M and Clingempeel, W (1992) Coping with marital transitions: a family systems perspective. *Monographs of the Society for Research in Child Development*. 57.

Hickman, P (1997) Is it working? The changing position of young people in the UK labour market. In Roche, J and Tucker, S (Eds) *Youth in society*. Sage. London.

Hill, J (1988) Adapting to menarche: familial control and conflict. In Gunnar, M and Collins, W (Eds) *21st Minnesota Symposium on Child Psychology*. Laurence Erlbaum. Hillsdale, NJ.

Hill, P (1993) Recent advances in selected aspects of adolescent development. *Journal of Child Psychology and Psychiatry*. 34. 69–100.

Hillier, L, Harrison, L and Warr, D (1998) 'When you carry condoms all the boys think you want it': negotiating competing discourses about safe sex. *Journal of Adolescence*. 21. 15–30.

Hirsch, B and DuBois, D (1989) The school–nonschool ecology of early adolescent friendships. In Belle, D (Ed.) *Children's social networks and supports*. John Wiley. New York.

Hirsch, B and DuBois, D (1991) Self-esteem in early adolescence: the identification and prediction of contrasting longitudinal trajectories. *Journal of Youth and Adolescence*. 20. 53–72.

Hirsch, B, Engel-Levy, A, DuBois, D and Hardesty, P (1990) The role of social environments in social support. In Sarason, B, Sarason, I and Pierce, G (Eds) *Social support: an interactional view.* John Wiley. New York.

Hodgson, R and Abbasi, T (1995) *Effective health prevention: literature review.* Health Promotion, Wales. Cardiff.

Hofstede, G (1983) Dimensions of national cultures in 50 countries and 3 regions. In Deregowski, J, Dzurnwiecz, S and Annis, R (Eds) *Explications in cross-cultural psychology.* Swets & Zeitlinger. Lisse, The Netherlands.

Hoge, D, Smit, E and Crist, J (1995) Reciprocal effects of self-concept and academic achievement in sixth and seventh grade. *Journal of Youth and Adolescence.* 24. 295–314.

Hogue, A and Steinberg, L (1995) Homophily of internalised distress in adolescent peer groups. *Developmental Psychology.* 31. 897–906.

Holland, J, Ramanazoglu, C, Sharpe, S and Thomson, R (1998) *The male in the head.* Tufnell Press. London.

Holland, W and Fitzsimons, B (1991) Smoking in children. *Archives of Disease in Childhood.* 66: 1269–1274.

Holmbeck, G, Paikoff, R and Brooks-Gunn, J (1995) Parenting adolescents. In Bornstein, M (Ed.) *Handbook of Parenting: Vol. 1.* Laurence Erlbaum. Mahwah, NJ.

Hope, S, Power, C and Rodgers, B (1998) The relationship between parental separation in childhood and problem drinking in adulthood. *Addiction.* 93. 505–514.

Huizinga, D and Elliott, D (1986) Reassessing the reliability and validity of self-report measures. *Journal of Quantitative Criminology.* 2. 293–327.

Hunter, F (1985) Adolescents' perception of discussions with parents and friends. *Developmental Psychology.* 21. 433–440.

Hunter, J, Higginson, I and Garralda, E (1996) Systematic literature review: outcome measures for child and adolescent mental health services. *Journal of Public Health Medicine.* 18. 197–206.

Hurrelmann, K and Losel, F (1990) *Health hazards in adolescence.* De Gruyter. New York.

Inderbitzen-Pisaruk, H, Clark, M and Solano, C (1992) Correlates of loneliness in midadolescence. *Journal of Youth and Adolescence.* 21. 151–168.

Inhelder, B and Piaget, J (1958) *The growth of logical thinking.* Routledge & Kegan Paul. London.

Ives, R (1990) Sniffing out the solvent users. In Ashton, M (Ed.) *Drug misuse in Britain: national audit of drug misuse statistics.* Institute for the Study of Drug Dependence. London.

Jackson, P and Warr, P (1987) Mental health of unemployed men in different parts of England and Wales. *British Medical Journal.* 295. 525.

Jackson, S and Bosma, H (1992) Developmental research on adolescence: European perspectives for the 1990s and beyond. *British Journal of Developmental Psychology.* 10. 319–338.

Jacobson, L and Wilkinson, C (1994) Review of teenage health: time for a new direction. *British Journal of General Practic*e. 44. 420–424.

Jaffe, M (1998) *Adolescence.* John Wiley. New York.

Jahnke, H and Blanchard-Fields, F (1993) A test of two models of adolescent egocentrism. *Journal of Youth and Adolescence.* 22. 313–326.

Jarvinen, D and Nicholls, J (1996) Adolescents' social goals: beliefs about the causes of social success, and satisfaction in peer relations. *Developmental Psychology.* 32. 435–441.

Jeffs, T and Smith, M (1990) *Young people, inequality and youth work.* Macmillan. London.

Jenkins, J and Smith, M (1990) Factors protecting children living in disharmonious homes: maternal reports. *Journal of the American Academy of Child and Adolescent Psychiatry.* 29. 60–69.

Jennings, M and Niemi, R (1971) *The political character of adolescence.* Princeton University Press. Princeton, NJ.

Jennings, M and Niemi, R (1981) *Generations and politics.* Princeton University Press. Princeton, NJ.

Jessor, R and Jessor, S (1977) *Problem behaviour and psychosocial development: a longitudinal study of youth.* Academic Press. New York.

Johnson, A, Wadsworth, K, Wellings, K and Field, J (1994) *Sexual attitudes and lifestyles.* Blackwell. Oxford.

Johnson, M, Beebe, T, Mortimer, J and Snyder, M (1998) Volunteerism in adolescence: a process perspective. *Journal of Research on Adolescence.* 8. 309–332.

Jones, D and Costin, S (1995) Friendship quality during pre-adolescence and adolescence. *Merrill Palmer Quarterly.* 41. 517–535.

Jones, G (1995) *Leaving home.* Open University Press. Milton Keynes.

Jones, G and Wallace, C (1990) Beyond individualisation: what sort of social change. In Chisholm, L, Buchner, P, Kruger, H-H and Brown, P (Eds) *Childhood, youth and social change: a comparative perspective.* Falmer. London.

Jones, G and Wallace, C (1992) *Youth, family and citizenship.* Open University Press. Milton Keynes.

Jonsson, I and Arnman, G (1991) Skolan och klassklyftorna. In Statens Ungdomsrad (Ed.) *Uppvactvilkor*, pp. 27–32. Stockholm. Statens Ungdomsrad.

Juang, L and Silbereisen, R (1998) Parenting in various ecological niches and across time. Presentation at the 6th Biennial Conference of the EARA, Budapest. June.

Junger-Tas, J, Terlouw, G and Klein, M (1994) *Delinquent behaviour among young people in the Western world: first results of the international self-report delinquency study.* Kugler. Amsterdam.

Kaffman, M (1993) Kibbutz youth: recent past and present. *Journal of Youth and Adolescence.* 22. 573–604.

Kail, R (1991) Developmental change in speed of processing during childhood and adolescence. *Psychological Bulletin.* 109. 490–501.

Kalakoski, V and Nurmi, J-E (1998) Identity and educational transitions: age differences in adolescent exploration and commitment. *Journal of Research on Adolescence.* 8. 29–47.

Katchadourian, H (1990) Sexuality. In Feldman, S and Elliott, G (Eds) *At the threshold: the developing adolescent.* Harvard University Press. London.

Keating, D (1990) Adolescent thinking. In Feldman, S and Elder, G (Eds) *At the threshold: the developing adolescent.* Harvard University Press. Cambridge, MA.

Keating, D and Sasse, D (1996) Cognitive socialisation in adolescence: critical period for a critical habit of mind. In Adams, G, Montemayor, R and Gullota, T (Eds) *Psychosocial development during adolescence: progress in developmental contextualism.* Sage. London.

Keith, N (1994) School-based community service. Special Issue of the *Journal of Adolescence.* 17. 311–409.

Kiernan, K (1997) *The legacy of parental divorce: social, economic and demographic experiences in adulthood.* Centre for the Analysis of Social Exclusion. London.

Killeen, D (1992) Leaving home. In Coleman, J and Warren-Adamson, C (Eds) *Youth policy in the 1990s.* Routledge. London.

Kinney, D (1993) From 'nerds' to 'normals': the recovery of identity among adolescents from middle school to high school. *Sociology of Education.* 66. 21–40.

Kirchler, E, Palmonari, A and Pombeni, M (1995) Developmental tasks and adolescents' relationships with their peers and their family. In Jackson, S and Rodriguez-Tome, H (Eds) *Adolescence and its social worlds.* Erlbaum. Hove.

Klee, H (1991) Sexual risk among amphetamime users: prospects for change. Paper presented at the 5th Social Aspects of OADs Conference, London. March.

Kleiber, D and Rickards, W (1985) Leisure and recreation in adolescence: limitation and potential. In Wade, M (Ed.) *Constraints on leisure.* Charles C Thomas. Springfield, IL.

Kloep, M (1998) *Att vara ung I Jamtland.* Uddeholt. Osterasen.

Kloep, M (1999) Love is all you need? Focussing on adolescents' life concerns from an ecological perspective. *Journal of Adolescence.* 22. 49–64.

Kloep, M and Hendry, L (1999) Challenges, risks and coping. In Messer, D and Millar, S (Eds) *Exploring developmental psychology.* Arnold. London.

Kohlberg, L (1970) Moral development and the education of adolescents. In Purnell, R (Ed.) *Adolescents and the American high school.* Holt, Rinehart & Winston. New York.

Kohlberg, L (Ed.) (1981) *The philosophy of moral development: Vol. 1.* Harper & Row. San Francisco, CA.

Kohlberg, L (Ed.) (1984) *The psychology of moral development: Vol. 2.* Harper & Row. San Francisco, CA.

Kohlberg, L and Gilligan, C (1971) Twelve to sixteen: early adolescence. *Daedalus.* 100. No.4. 1068–1072.

Kohlberg, L and Gilligan, C (1972) The adolescent as philosopher; the discovery of the self in a post-conventional world. In Kagan, J and Coles, R (Eds) *Twelve to sixteen: early adolescence.* Norton. New York.

Kohlberg, L and Nisan, M (1984) Cultural universality of moral judgement stages: a longitudinal study in Turkey. In Kohlberg, L (Ed.) *The psychology of moral development: Vol. 2.* Harper & Row. San Francisco, CA.

Kolvin, I, Miller, F, Scott, D and Fleeting, M (1990) *Continuities of deprivation.* Avebury. Aldershot.

Kosky, R (1992) Adolescents in custody: a disciplining or disabling experience. In Kosky, R, Eshkevari, H and Kneebone, G (Eds) *Breaking out: challenges in adolescent mental health in Australia.* Canberra: Australian Government Publishing Service.

Kracke, B and Noack, P (1998) Continuity and change in family interactions across adolescence. In Hofer, M, Youniss, J and Noack, P (Eds) *Verbal interactions and development in families with adolescents.* Ablex Publishing. Norwood.

Kracke, B, Oepke, M, Wild, E and Noack, P (1998) Adolescents, families and German unification: the impact of social change on anti-foreigner and anti-democratic attitudes. In Nurmi, J-E (Ed.) *Adolescents, cultures and conflicts.* Garland. New York.

Kraft, P (1993) Sexual knowledge among Norwegian adolescents. *Journal of Adolescence.* 16. 3–21.

Kremer, J, Trew, K and Ogle, S (Eds) (1997) *Young people's involvement in sport.* Routledge. London.

Krisberg, B, Schwartz, I, Fishman, G and Guttman, E (1986) *The incarceration of minority youth.* Hubert Humphrey Institute of Public Affairs. Minneapolis, MN.

Kroger, J (1985) Relationships during adolescence: a cross-national comparison of New Zealand and United States teenagers. *Journal of Youth and Adolescence.* 8. 47–56.

Kroger, J (Ed.) (1993) *Discussions on ego identity.* Lawrence Erlbaum. Hillsdale, NJ.

Kroger, J (1996) *Identity in adolescence: the balance between self and other. 2nd Edn.* Routledge. London.

Kroger, J and Green, K (1996) Events associated with identity status change. *Journal of Adolescence.* 19. 477–490.

Kruger, H (1990) Zwischen Verallgemeinerung und Zerfaserung: Zum Wandel der Lebensphase Jugend in der Bundesrepublik Deutschland nach 1945. In H H Kruger and L Chisholm (Eds) *Kindheit und jugend im interkulturellen vergleich*, pp. 113–123. Leske & Budrich. Opladen.

Kuhl, J, Jarkon-Horlick, L and Morrissey, R (1997) Measuring barriers to help-seeking behaviour in adolescents. *Journal of Adolescence.* 26. 637–650.

Kurdek, L and Fine, M (1994) Family acceptance and family control as predictors of adjustment in young adolescents: linear, curvilinear, or interactive effects? *Child Development.* 65. 1137–1146.

Lamborn, S and Steinberg, L (1993) Emotional autonomy redux: revisiting Ryan and Lynch. *Child Development.* 64. 483–499.

Lapsley, D (1992) Pluralism, virtues, and the post-Kohlbergian era in moral psychology. In Powers, F and Lapsley, D (Eds) *The challenge of pluralism, education, politics and values.* University of Notre Dame Press. Notre Dame, IN.

Larson, R (1994) Youth organisations, hobbies and sports as developmental contexts. In Silbereisen, R and Todt, E (Eds) *Adolescence in context: the interplay of family, school, peers and work in adjustment.* Springer-Verlag. New York.

Larson, R (1997) The emergence of solitude as a constructive domain of experience in early adolescence. *Child Development.* 68. 80–93.

Larson, R and Asmussen, L (1991) Anger, worry and hurt in early adolescence: an enlarging world of negative emotions. In Colten, M and Gore, S (Eds) *Adolescent stress: causes and consequences.* Aldine De Gruyter. New York.

Larson, R. and Richards, M (1989) The changing life space of early adolescence. *Journal of Youth and Adolescence.* 18. 501–509.

Larson, R, Richards, M, Moneta, G, Holmbeck, G and Duckett, E (1996) Changes in adolescents' daily interactions with their families from ages 10 to 18: disengagement and transformation. *Developmental Psychology.* 32. 744–754.

Lask, J (1994) Parenting in adolescence. *ACPP Review and Newsletter.* 16. 5. 229–236.

Lazarus, R (1966) *Psychological stress and the coping process.* McGraw-Hill. New York.

Lazarus, R and Folkman, S (1991) *Stress, appraisal and coping.* Springer. New York.

Lees, S (1993) *Sugar and spice: sexuality and adolescent girls.* Penguin. London.

Leffert, N and Petersen, A (1995) Patterns of development in adolescence. In Rutter, M and Smith, D (Eds) *Psychosocial disorders in young people.* John Wiley. Chichester.

Lerner, R (1985) Adolescent maturational changes and psychosocial development: a dynamic interactional perspective. *Journal of Youth and Adolescence.* 14. 355–372.

Lerner, R, Lerner, J and Tubman, J (1989) Organismic and contextual bases of development in adolescence. In Adams, G, Montemayor, R and Gullotta, T (Eds) *Biology of adolescent behaviour and development.* Sage. London.

Lerner, R, Lerner, J, Jovanovic, J, Talwar, R and Kucher, J (1991) Physical attractiveness and psychosocial functioning among early adolescents. *Journal of Early Adolescence.* 11. 300–320.

Levesque, R (1993) The romantic experience of adolescents in satisfying love relationships. *Journal of Youth and Adolescence.* 22. 219–252.

Levitt, M, Guacci-Franco, N and Levitt, J (1993) Convoys of social support in childhood and early adolescence: structure and function. *Developmental Psychology.* 29. 811–818.

Lewin, K (1980) Field theory and experiment in social psychology. In Muuss, R (Ed.) *Adolescent behaviour and society: 3rd Edn.* Random House. New York.

Leyva, F and Furth, H (1986) Compromise formation in social conflicts. *Journal of Youth and Adolescence.* 15. 441–451.

Lipsey, M (1995) What do we learn from 400 research studies on the effectiveness of treatment with juvenile delinquents? In McGuire, J (Ed.) *What works? reducing re-offending.* Wiley. Chichester.

Lloyd, B and Lucas, K (1997) *Smoking in adolescence: images and identities.* Routledge. London.

Loeber, R and Stouthamer-Loeber, M (1986) Family factors as correlates and predictors of juvenile conduct problems and delinquency. In Morris, M and Tonry, M (Eds) *Crime and justice: Vol. 7.* University of Chicago Press. Chicago.

Lowden, S (1989) *Three years on: the reaction of young people to Scotland's action plan.* Centre for Educational Sociology, University of Edinburgh. Edinburgh.

Lyon, J (Ed.) (1996) Adolescents who offend. Special Issue of the *Journal of Adolescence.* 19. 1–109.

Lyon, J (1997) Gender and crime. In Kremer, J and Trew, K (Eds) *Gendered psychology.* Arnold. London.

Maccoby, E (1990) Gender and relationships: a developmental account. *American Psychologist.* 45. 513–520.

Maccoby, E (1998) *The two sexes: growing up apart, coming together.* Belknap. Cambridge, MA.

Maccoby, E and Martin, J (1983) Socialisation in the context of the family: parent–child interaction. In Hetherington, E (Ed.) *Handbook of child psychology.* Wiley. New York.

McCord, J (1979) Some child-rearing antecedents of criminal behaviour in adult men. *Journal of Personality and Social Psychology*. 37. 1477–1486.

MacDonald, R (Ed.) (1997) *Youth, the 'underclass' and social exclusion*. Routledge. London.

Macfarlane, A (1993) Health promotion and children and teenagers (editorial). *British Medical Journal*. 306(6870). 81.

Macfarlane, A, McPherson, A, McPherson, K and Ahmed, L (1987) Teenagers and their health. *Archives of Disease in Childhood*. 62. 1125–1129.

McFarlane, A, Bellissimo, A and Norman, G (1995) Family structure, family functioning, and adolescent well-being: the transcendent influence of parenting style. *Journal of Child Psychology and Psychiatry*. 36. 847–864.

McGuire, J (1995) *What works? Reducing reoffending: guidelines from research*. John Wiley. Chichester.

McIntosh, H (1996) Adolescent friends not always a bad influence. *American Psychological Association Monitor*. 16.

McIntyre, J and Dusek, J (1995) Perceived parental rearing practices and styles of coping. *Journal of Youth and Adolescence*. 24. 499–509.

Macintyre, S (1989) West Scotland Twenty-07 Study: health in the community. In Martin, C and MacQueen, D (Eds) *Readings for a new public health*. Edinburgh University Press. Edinburgh.

Mackay, G (1996) *Senseless acts of beauty: cultures of resistance since the 1960s*. Verso. London.

McKenna, C (1993) *Drug use and related needs in East Lothian*. Scottish Drugs Forum. Glasgow.

McLoughlin, D and Whitfield, R (1984) Adolescents and their experiences of divorce. *Journal of Youth and Adolescence*. 7. 155–170.

Maffesoli, M (1996) *The time of the tribes*. Sage. London.

Magnusson, D and Bergman, L (1990) A pattern approach to the study of pathways from childhood to adulthood. In Robins, L and Rutter, M (Eds) *Straight and devious pathways from childhood to adulthood*. Cambridge University Press. Cambridge.

Magnusson, D and Stattin, H (1998) Person–context interaction theories. In Damon, W and Lerner, R (Eds) *Handbook of child psychology: Vol. 1*. John Wiley. New York.

Malmberg, L and Trempala, J (1997) Anticipated transition to adulthood: the effect of educational track, gender, and self-evaluation on Polish and Finnish adolescents. *Journal of Youth and Adolescence*. 26. 517–538.

Marcia, J (1966) Development and validation of ego-identity status. *Journal of Personality and Social Psychology*. 3. 551–558.

Marcia, J (1980) Identity in adolescence. In Adelson, J (Ed.) *Handbook of adolescent psychology*. Wiley. New York.

Marcia, J (1993) The relational roots of identity. In Kroger, J (Ed.) *Discussions on ego identity*. Lawrence Erlbaum. Hillsdale, NJ.

Marsh, H (1987) The big-fish-little-pond effect on academic self-concept. *Journal of Educational Psychology*. 79. 280–295.

Marsh, H (1989) Age and sex effects in multiple dimensions of self-concept. *Journal of Educational Psychology*. 81. 417–430.

Marsh, H, Byrne, B and Shavelson, R (1988) A multi-faceted academic self-concept: its hierarchical structure and its relation to academic achievement. *Journal of Educational Psychology*. 80. 366–380.

Marsh, H, Richards, G and Barnes, J (1986) Multidimensional self-concepts: the effect of participation in an outward bound programme. *Journal of Personality and Social Psychology*. 50. 195–204.

Marshall, S (1995) Ethnic socialization of African-American children: implications for parenting, identity development, and academic achievement. *Journal of Youth and Adolescence*. 24. 377–396.

Marshall, W and Tanner, J (1970) Variations in the pattern of pubertal changes in boys. *Archives of Disease in Childhood*. 45. 13–23.

Martinez, R and Dukes, R (1997) The effects of ethnic identity, ethnicity, and gender on adolescent well-being. *Journal of Youth and Adolescence*. 26. 503–516.

Masten, A, Best, K and Garmezy, N (1990) Resilience and development: contributions from the study of children who overcome adversity. *Development and Psychopathology*. 2. 425–444.

Mazor, A (Ed.) (1993) Kibbutz adolescents. Special Issue of the *Journal of Youth and Adolescence*. 22. 569–714.

Measham, F, Newcombe, R and Parker, H (1994) The normalisation of recreational drug use among young people in north-west England. *British Journal of Sociology*. 45. 287–313.

Meeus, W (1989) Parental and peer support in adolescence. In Hurrelmann, K and Engel, U (Eds) *The social world of adolescents: international perspectives*. De Gruyter. Berlin.

Merten, D (1996) Visibility and vulnerability: responses to rejection by non-aggressive junior high school boys. *Journal of Early Adolescence*. 16. 5–26.

Meschke, L and Silbereisen, R (1997) The influence of puberty, family process, and leisure activities on the timing of the first sexual experience. *Journal of Adolescence*. 20. 403–418.

Miller, B and Bingham, C (1989) Family configuration in relation to the sexual behaviour of female adolescents. *Journal of Marriage and the Family*. 51. 499–506.

Mirzah, H (1992) *Young, female and black*. Routledge. London.

Mitchell, A (1985) *Children in the middle*. Tavistock. London.

Mitchell, A (1998) Accentuating the positive: HIV/AIDS and STDs prevention and education. In Coleman, J and Roker, D (Eds) *Teenage sexuality: health, risk and education*. Harwood Academic Press. London.

Mizen, P (1995) *The state, youth training and young people*. Mansell. London.

Monck, E, Graham, P, Richman, N and Dobbs, R (1994) Self-reported mood disturbance in a community population. *British Journal of Psychiatry*. 165. 760–769.

Montagna, W and Sadler, W (Eds) (1974) *Reproductive Behavior*. Plenum. New York.

Montemayor, R and Brownlee, J (1987) Fathers, mothers and adolescents: gender based differences in parental roles during adolescence. *Journal of Youth and Adolescence*. 16. 281–291.

Montemayor, R, McKenry, C and Julian, P (1993) Men in midlife and the quality of father–adolescent communication. *New Directions in Child Development*. 62. 59–72.

Moore, S (1995) Girls' understanding and social constructions of menarche. *Journal of Adolescence*. 18. 87–104.

Moore, S and Rosenthal, D (1991) Adolescents' perceptions of friends' and parents' attitudes to sex and sexual risk-taking. *Journal of Community and Applied Social Psychology*. 1. 189–200.

Moore, S and Rosenthal, D (1995) *Sexuality in adolescence*. Routledge. London.

Moore, S and Rosenthal, D (1998) Adolescent sexual behaviour. In Coleman, J and Roker, D (Eds) *Teenage sexuality: health, risk and education*. Harwood Academic Press. London.

Moore, S, Rosenthal, D and Mitchell, A (1996) *Youth, AIDS, and sexually transmitted diseases*. Routledge. London.

Mountain, A (1990) *Lifting the limits*. National Youth Bureau. Leicester.

Mounts, N and Steinberg, L (1995) An ecological analysis of peer influence on adolescent grade point average and drug use. *Developmental Psychology*. 31. 915–922.

Munsch, J and Kinchen, K (1995) Adolescent sociometric status and social support. *Journal of Early Adolescence*. 15. 181–202.

Munsch, J and Wampler, R (1993) Ethnic differences in early adolescents' coping with school stress. *American Journal of Orthopsychiatry*. 63. 633–646.

Murphy, J and Gilligan, C (1980) Moral development in late adolescence and adulthood: a critique and reconstruction of Kohlberg's theory. *Human Development*. 23. 77–104.

Murray, F (1990) The conversion of truth into necessity. In Overton, W (Ed.) *Reasoning, necessity and logic: developmental perspectives*. Erlbaum. Hillsdale, NJ.

Muuss, R (1996) *Theories of adolescence: 6th Edn*. McGraw-Hill. New York.

Nakkula, M and Selman, R (1991) How people 'treat' each other: pair therapy as a context for the development of interpersonal ethics. In Kurtines, W and Gewirtz, J (Eds) *Handbook of moral behaviour and development: Vol. 3.* Erlbaum. Hillsdale, NJ.

Nasstrøm, A-C and Kloep, M (1994) The effect of job practicing on the psychological well-being of unemployed youth. *Arbete och Halsa.* 33. 79–88.

Nelson, J, Smith, D and Dodd, J (1990) The moral reaoning of juvenile delinquents: a meta-analysis. *Journal of Abnormal Child Psychology.* 18. 231–239.

Newcomer, S and Udry, J (1985) Oral sex in an adolescent population. *Archives of Sexual Behaviour.* 14. 41–46.

Niemi, R and Junn, J (1996) For a reinforced citizenship in the United States. *Prospects.* 26. 37–46.

Nisbet, J and Shucksmith, J (1984) *Learning strategies.* Routledge & Kegan Paul. London.

Noack, P and Kracke, B (1997) Social change and adolescent well-being: healthy country, healthy teens. In Schulenberg, J, Maggs, J and Hurrelmann, K (Eds) *Health risks and developmental transitions during adolescence.* Cambridge University Press. Cambridge.

Noack, P, Hofer, M, Kracke, B and Klein-Allerman, E (1995) Adolescents and their parents facing social change: families in East and West Germany after unification. In Noack, P, Hofer, M and Youniss, J (Eds) *Psychological responses to social change.* Walter De Gruyter. Berlin.

Noller, P and Callan, V (1991) *The adolescent in the family.* Routledge. London.

Norman, P and Bennett, P (1996) Health locus of control. In Conner, M and Norman, P (Eds) *Predicting health behaviour.* Open University Press. Milton Keynes.

Nucci, L and Webber, E (1991) The domain approach to values education: from theory to practice. In Kurtines, W and Gewirtz, J (Eds) *Handbook of moral behaviour and development: Vol. 3.* Erlbaum. Hillsdale, NJ.

Nurmi, J-E (1997) Self-definition and mental health during adolescence and young adulthood. In Schulenberg, J, Maggs, J and Hurrelmann, K (Eds) *Health risks and developmental transitions during adolescence.* Cambridge University Press. Cambridge.

Nutbeam, D, Macaskill, P and Smith, C (1993) Evaluation of two school smoking education programmes under normal classroom conditions. *British Medical Journal.* 306. 102–107.

O'Bryan, L (1989) Young people and drugs. In MacGregor, S (Ed.) *Drugs and British society: responses to the social problem in the 1980s.* Routledge. London.

Ochiltree, G (1990) *Children in Australian families.* Longman. Melbourne.

Offer, D (1969) *The psychological world of the teenager.* Basic Books. New York.

Offer, D, Ostrov, E, Howard, K and Dolin, S (1992) *The Offer Self-Image Questionnaire for Adolescents – revised.* Western Psychological Services. Los Angeles, CA.

Office of Populations Censuses and Surveys (OPCS) (1995) *General household survey.* HMSO. London.

Ohri, S and Faruqi, S (1988) Racism, employment and unemployment. In Bhat, A, Carr-Hill, R and Ohri, S (Eds) *Britain's black population: a new perspective.* Gower. Aldershot.

Olweus, D. (1984) Aggressors and their victims: bullying at school. In Frude, N and Gault, N (Eds) *Disruptive behaviour in schools.* John Wiley. London.

Osofsky, J, Hann, D and Peebles, C (1993) Adolescent parenthood: risks and opportunities for parents and infants. In Zeannah, C (Ed.) *Handbook of infant mental health.* Guilford. New York.

O'Koon, J (1997) Attachment to parents and peers in late adolescence and their relationship with self-image. *Adolescence.* 32. 471–482.

Paikoff, R, Brooks-Gunn, J and Carlton-Ford, S (1991) Effect of reproductive status changes on family functioning and well-being of mothers and daughters. *Journal of Early Adolescence.* 11. 201–220.

Palladino, G (1996) *Teenagers: an American history.* Basic Books. New York.

Palmonari, A, Pombeni, M and Kirchler, E (1989) Peer groups and the evolution of self esteem in adolescence. *European Journal of Psychology of Education.* 4. 3–15.

Papini, D and Clark, S (1989) Grade, pubertal status, and gender-related variations in conflictual issues among adolescents. *Adolescence.* 24. 977–987.

Papini, D and Sebby, R (1987) Adolescent pubertal status and affective family relationships: a multivariate assessment. *Journal of Youth and Adolescence.* 16. 1–16.

Park, A (1994) *England and Wales youth cohort study 4: young people 18–19 years old in 1991.* Employment Department. London.

Parker, H, Aldridge, J and Measham, F (1998) *Illegal leisure: the normalisaton of adolescent recreational drug use.* Routledge. London.

Parker, J and Asher, S (1987) Peer relations and later personal adjustment: are low-accepted children at risk? *Psychological Bulletin.* 102. 357–389.

Parkhurst, J and Asher, S (1992) Peer rejection in middle school: sub-group differences in behaviour, loneliness, and interpersonal concerns. *Developmental Psychology.* 28. 231–241.

Patterson, G, Reid, J and Dishion, T (1992) *Antisocial boys.* Castalia. Eugene, OR.

Patterson, G and Stouthammer-Loeber, M (1984) The correlation of family management practices and delinquency. *Child Development.* 55. 1299–1307.

Patterson, G, Dishion, T and Chamberlain, P (1993) Outcomes and methodological issues relating to treatment of antisocial children. In Giles, T (Ed.) *Handbook of effective psychotherapy.* Plenum. New York.

Patterson, J and McCubbin, H (1987) Adolescent coping style and behaviours: conceptualization and measurement. *Journal of Adolescence.* 10. 163–186.

Patton, W and Noller, P (1984) Unemployment and youth: a longitudinal study. *Australian Journal of Psychology.* 36. 399–413.

Payne, J (1995) *Routes beyond compulsory schooling.* Youth Cohort Paper No. 31. Employment Department. London.

Perry, T (1987) The relation of adolescents' self-perceptions to their social relationships. Unpublished doctoral dissertation, University of Oklahoma. Norman, OK.

Perschy, M (1997) *Helping teens work through grief.* Taylor & Francis. Washington, DC.

Petersen, A and Crockett, L (1985) Pubertal timing and grade effects on adjustment. *Journal of Youth and Adolescence.* 14. 191–206.

Petersen, A and Hamburg, B (1986) Adolescence: a developmental approach to problems and psychopathology. *Behaviour Therapy.* 13. 480–499.

Petersen, A, Sarigiani, P and Kennedy, R (1991) Adolescent depression: why more girls? *Journal of Youth and Adolescence.* 20. 247–271.

Philip, K and Hendry, L (1997) *Young people, lifestyles and health in the nineties: a literature review.* Centre for Education Research, University of Aberdeen. Aberdeen.

Phinney, J (1992) The multi-group ethnic identity measure: a new scale for use with adolescents and adults from diverse groups. *Journal of Adolescent Research.* 7. 156–176.

Phinney, J (1993) A three-stage model of ethnic identity development. In Bernal, M and Knight, G (Eds) *Ethnic identity: formation and transmission among Hispanics and other minorities.* State University of New York Press. Albany, NY.

Phinney, J and Devich-Navarro, M (1997) Variations in bicultural identification among African-American and Mexican-American adolescents. *Journal of Research on Adolescence.* 7. 3–32.

Phinney, J and Goossens, L (Eds) (1996) Identity development in context. Special issue of the *Journal of Adolescence.* 19. 401–500.

Phinney, J and Rosenthal, D (1992) Ethnic identity in adolescence: process, context and outcome. In Adams, G, Gullotta, T and Montemayor, R (Eds) *Adolescent identity formation.* Sage. London.

Phoenix, A (1991) *Young mothers?* Polity Press. London.

Piaget, J (1932) *The moral judgement of the child.* Routledge & Kegan Paul. London.

Plancherel, B and Bolognini, M (1995) Coping and mental health in early adolescence. *Journal of Adolescence.* 18. 459–474.

Platt, W (1984) Unemployment and suicidal behaviour: review of the literature. *Social Science and Medicine.* 19. 93–115.

Pombeni, M, Kirchler, E and Palmonari, A (1990) Identification with peers as a strategy to muddle through the troubles of the adolescent years. *Journal of Adolescence.* 13. 351–369.

Power, T and Shanks, J (1988) Parents as socializers: maternal and paternal views. *Journal of Youth and Adolescence.* 18. 203–220.

Prause, J and Dooley, D (1997) Effect of underemployment on school-leavers' self-esteem. *Journal of Adolescence.* 20. 243–260.

Pritchard, C (1992) Is there a link between suicide in young men and unemployment? A comparison of the UK with other European countries. *British Journal of Psychiatry.* 160. 750–756.

Pugh, G, De'Ath, E and Smith, C (1994) *Confident parents: confident children.* National Children's Bureau. London.

Quadrel, M, Fishoff, B and Davis, W (1993) Adolescent (in)vulnerability. *American Psychologist.* 48. 102–116.

Quinn, P (1995) Positive effects of participation in youth organisations. In Rutter, M (Ed.) *Psychosocial disturbances in young people.* Cambridge University Press. Cambridge.

Quinton, D and Rutter, M (1988) Parents with children in care: current circumstances and parenting skills. *Journal of Child Psychology and Psychiatry.* 25. 211–230.

Raffe, D (1990) The transition from school to work. Content, context and the external labour market. In Wallace, C and Cross, M (Eds) *Youth in transition.* Falmer. London.

Ramsey, B (1990) Dangerous games: UK solvent deaths 1983–1988. *Druglink.* 5. 8–9.

Rattansi, A and Phoenix, A (1997) Rethinking youth identities: modernist and post-modernist frameworks. In Bynner, J, Chisholm, L and Furlong, A (Eds) *Youth, citizenship and social change in a European context.* Ashgate. Aldershot.

Reisman, J (1985) Friendship and its implications for mental health or social competence. *Journal of Early Adolescence.* 5. 383–391.

Reiss, M (1993) What are the aims of school sex education? *Cambridge Journal of Education.* 23. 125–126.

Resnick, M, Bearman, P, Blum, R, Bauman, K, Harris, K, Jones, J, Tabor, J, Beurhring, T, Sieving, R, Shew, M, Ireland, M, Bearinger, L and Udry, J (1997) Protecting adolescents from harm: findings from the national longitudinal study on adolescent health. *Journal of the American Medical Association.* 278. 823–832.

Rest, J (1973) The hierarchical nature of moral judgement. *Journal of Personality.* 41. 86–109.

Rice, K, Herman, M and Petersen, A (1993) Coping with challenge in adolescence: a conceptual model and psycho-educational intervention. *Journal of Adolescence.* 16. 235–252.

Richards, M (1996) *The interests of children at divorce.* Edition Bruylant. Brussels.

Richards, M (1997) *The socio-legal support for divorcing parents and their children.* In Conference Papers of 'Teenagers and Divorce', a conference sponsored by Relateen, Belfast, 18 April 1997.

Rietveld, H (1994) Living the dream. In Redehead, S (Ed.) *Rave off: politics and deviance in contemporary culture.* Avebury. Aldershot.

Riley, T, Adams, G and Nielsen, E (1984) Adolescent egocentrism: the association among imaginary audience behaviour, cognitive development and parental support and rejection. *Journal of Youth and Adolescence.* 13. 401–438.

Rippl, S and Boehnke, K (1995) Authoritarianism: adolescents from East and West Germany and the United States compared. In Youniss, J (Ed.) *After the wall: family adaptations in East and West Germany.* New Directions for Child Development. No. 70. Winter. Jossey-Bass. San Francisco, CA.

Roberts, H, Dengler, R and Magowan, R (1995) *Trent Health Young People's Survey Results.* Trent Lifestyle Survey 1995 March; 1992–1994, 3. 51.

Roberts, K (1995) *Youth and employment in modern Britain.* Oxford University Press. Oxford.

Roberts, K (1997) Structure and agency: the new youth research. In Bynner, J, Chisholm, L and Furlong, A (Eds) *Youth, citizenship and social change in a European context.* Ashgate. Aldershot.

Roberts, K and Parsell, G (1992a) Entering the labour market in Britain: the survival of traditional opportunity structures. *Sociological Review.* 30. 727–753.

Roberts, K and Parsell, G (1992b) The stratification of youth training. *British Journal of Education and Work.* 5. 65–83.

Roberts, K, Brodie, D, Campbell, R and York, C (1989) *Fit for life.* Health Promotion Research Trust. London.

Robins, L (1978) Sturdy childhood predictors of adult antisocial behaviour: replications from longitudinal studies. *Psychological Medicine.* 8. 611–622.

Robinson, B (1988) *Teenage fathers.* Lexington Books. Lexington, MA.

Robinson, D (1995) *The impact of cognitive skills training on post-release recidivism among Canadian federal offenders.* Correctional Research and Development, Correctional Service of Canada. Ottawa.

Robson, P (1996) Young people and illegal drugs. In Macfarlane, A (Ed.) *Adolescent medicine,* pp. 131–138. Royal College of Physicians. London.

Rodgers, B and Pryor, J (1998) *Divorce and separation: the outcomes for children.* The Joseph Rowntree Foundation. York.

Rodgers, B, Power, C and Hope, S (1997) Parental divorce and adult psychological distress: evidence from a national birth cohort. *Journal of Child Psychology and Psychiatry.* 38. 867–872.

Roe, K (1995) Adolescents' use of socially disvalued media: towards a theory of media delinquency. *Journal of Youth and Adolescence.* 24. 617–631.

Roker, D (1998) *Worth more than this: young people growing up in family poverty.* The Children's Society. London.

Roker, D and Coleman, J (1997) Education and advice about illegal drugs: what do young people want? *Drugs: Education. Prevention and Policy.* 4. 71–81.

Roker, D and Coleman, J (1998) 'Parenting teenagers' programmes: a UK perspective. *Children and Society.* 12. 359–372.

Roker, D and Coleman, J (1999) Supporting parents of teenagers: a school-based intervention and evaluation. *Psychology of Education Review.* 23. 32–35.

Roker, D, Player, K and Coleman, J (1997) *Challenging the image: young people as volunteers and campaigners.* Trust for the Study of Adolescence. Brighton.

Roker, D, Player, K and Coleman, J (1998) Challenging the image: the involvement of young people with disabilities in volunteering and campaigning. *Disability and Society.* 13. 725–741.

Roker, D, Player, K and Coleman, J (1999) Exploring adolescent altruism: British young people's involvement in voluntary work and campaigning. In Yates, M and Youniss, J (Eds) *Roots of civic identity.* Cambridge University Press. Cambridge.

Roscoe, B and Skomski, G (1989) Loneliness among late adolescents. *Adolescence.* 24. 947–955.

Rosenberg, M (1965) *Society and the adolescent self-image.* Princeton University Press. Princeton, NJ.

Rosenberg, M (1979) *Conceiving the self.* Basic Books. New York.

Ross, R., Fabiano, E and Ewles, C (1988) Reasoning and rehabilitation. *International Journal of Offender Therapy and Comparative Criminology.* 32. 29–35.

Rotheram-Borus, M, Hunter, J and Rosario, M (1994) Suicidal behaviour and gay-related stress among gay and bisexual male adolescents. *Journal of Adolescent Research.* 9. 498–508.

Rowland, T (1991) Influence of physical activity and fitness on coronary risk factors in children: how strong an argument? *Paediatric Exercise Science.* 3. 189–191.

Rowley, K and Feather, N (1987) The impact of unemployment in relation to age and length of unemployment. *Journal of Occupational Psychology.* 60. 323–332.

Rutter, M (Ed.) (1995) *Psychosocial disturbances in young people: challenges for prevention.* Cambridge University Press. Cambridge.

Rutter, M and Smith, D (Eds) (1995) *Psychosocial disorders in young people.* John Wiley. Chichester.

Rutter, M, Giller, H and Hagell, A (1998) *Antisocial behaviour by young people.* Cambridge University Press. Cambridge.

Rutter, M, Graham, P, Chadwick, O and Yule, W (1976) Adolescent turmoil: fact or fiction? *Journal of Child Psychology and Psychiatry.* 17. 35–56.

Sampson, R and Lamb, J (1994) Urban poverty and the family context of delinquency: a new look at structure and process. *Child Development.* 65. 523–540.

Savin-Williams, R and Berndt, R (1990) Friendship and peer relations. In Feldman, S and Elliot, G (Eds) *At the threshold: the developing adolescent.* Harvard University Press. Cambridge, MA.

Savin-Williams, R and Rodriguez, R (1993) A developmental, clinical perspective on lesbian, gay and bisexual youths. In Gullotta, T, Adams, G and Montemayor, R (Eds) *Adolescent sexuality.* Sage. London.

Schofield, M (1965) *The sexual behaviour of young people.* Longman. London.

Schonert-Reichl, K and Muller, J (1996) Correlates of help-seeking in adolescence. *Journal of Youth and Adolescence.* 25. 705–732.

Schweinhart, L and Weikart, D (1980) *Young children grow up.* High/Scope. Ypsilanti, MI.

Schweinhart, L, Barnes, H and Weikart, D (1993) *The High/Scope Perry Preschool study through age 27.* Scope Educational Foundation. Ypsilanti, MI.

Seiffge-Krenke, I (1993) Stress and coping in adolescence. Special Issue of the *Journal of Adolescence.* 16. 225–349.

Seiffge-Krenke, I (1995) *Stress, coping, and relationships in adolescence.* Lawrence Erlbaum. Mahwah, NJ.

Seiffge-Krenke, I (1998) *Adolescents' health: a developmental perspective.* Lawrence Erlbaum. London.

Selman, R (1977) A structural-developmental model of social cognition. *Counselling Psychologist.* 6. 3–6.

Selman, R (1980) *The growth of interpersonal understanding: developmental and clinical analyses.* Academic Press. London.

Selman, R and Schultz, L (1990) *Making a friend in youth: developmental theory and pair therapy.* University of Chicago Press. Chicago.

Selman, R, Beardslee, W, Schultz, L, Krupa, M and Podorefsky, D (1986) Assessing adolescent interpersonal negotiation strategies. *Developmental Psychology.* 22. 450–459.

Sharp, D and Lowe, G (1989) Adolescents and alcohol – a review of the recent British research. *Journal of Adolescence.* 12. 295–307.

Shavelson, R, Hubner, J and Stanton, G (1976) Self-concept: validation of construct interpretations. *Review of Educational Research.* 46. 407–441.

Shayer, M (1979) *Science reasoning tasks.* National Foundation for Educational Research. Slough.

Shayer, M and Wylam, H (1978) The distribution of Piagetian stages of thinking in British middle and secondary school children: 2. *British Journal of Educational Psychology.* 48. 62–70.

Shayer, M, Kuchemann, D and Wylam, H (1976) The distribution of Piagetian stages of thinking in British middle and secondary school children. *British Journal of Educational Psychology.* 46. 164–173.

Shorter-Gooden, K and Washington, N (1996) Young, Black and female: the challenge of weaving an identity. *Journal of Adolescence.* 19. 465–476.

Shucksmith, J and Hendry, L (1998) *Health issues and adolescents: growing up and speaking out.* Routledge. London.

Shucksmith, J, Hendry, L and Glendinning, A (1995) Models of parenting: implications for adolescent well-being within different types of family context. *Journal of Adolescence.* 18. 253–270.

Shulman, S (1993) Close relationships and coping in adolescence. *Journal of Adolescence.* 16. 267–284.

Shulman, S and Seiffge-Krenke, I (1997) *Fathers and adolescents.* Routledge. London.

Siddique, C and D'Arcy, C (1984) Adolescence, stress and psychological well-being. *Journal of Youth and Adolescence.* 13. 459–474.

Siegler, R (1988) Individual differences in strategy choices: good students, not-so-good students, and perfectionists. *Child Development.* 59. 833–851.

Sigel, R and Hoskin, M (1981) *The political involvement of adolescents.* Rutgers University Press. New Brunswick, NJ.

Silbereisen, R and Kracke, B (1993) Variation in maturational timing and adjustment in adolescescence. In Jackson, S and Rodriguez-Tome, H (Eds) *The social worlds of adolescence.* Erlbaum. Hove.

Silbereisen, R and Kracke, B (1997) Self-reported maturational timing and adaptation in adolescence. In Schulenberg, J, Maggs, J and Hurrelmann, K (Eds) *Health risks and developmental transitions during adolescence.* Cambridge University Press. Cambridge.

Silbereisen, R, Boenkhe, K and Reykowski, J (1986) Prosocial motives from 12 to 18: a comparison of adolescents from Berlin and Warsaw. In Silbereisen, R, Eyferth, K and Rudinger, G (Eds) *Development as action in context.* Springer-Verlag. Berlin.

Silbereisen, R, Noack, P and von Eye, A (1992) Adolescents' development of romantic friendship and change in favourite leisure contexts. *Journal of Adolescent Research.* 7. 80–93.

Silbereisen, R, Lamsfuss, S, Boehnke, K and Eisenberg, N (1991) Developmental patterns and correlates of prosocial motives in adolescence. In Montada, C and Bierhoff, H (Eds) *Altruism in social systems.* Hogrefe & Huber. New York.

Silverberg, S and Steinberg, L (1990) Psychological well-being with early adolescent children. *Developmental Psychology.* 26. 658–666.

Simmons, R and Blyth, D (1987) *Moving into adolescence: the impact of pubertal change and school context.* Aldine De Gruyter. New York.

Simmons, R and Rosenberg, M (1975) Sex, sex-roles and self-image. *Journal of Youth and Adolescence.* 4. 229–256.

Simms, M and Smith, C (1986) *Teenage mothers and their children.* DHSS Research Report No. 15. HMSO. London.

Simpson, B, McCarthy, P and Walker, J (1995) *Being there: fathers after divorce.* Relate Centre for Family Studies. Newcastle University. Newcastle.

Skellington, R and Morris, P (1992) *Race in Britain today.* Sage. London.

Small, S and Eastman, G (1991) Rearing adolescents in contemporary society. *Family Relations.* 40. 455–462.

Smetana, J (1988) Adolescents' and parents' conceptions of parental authority. *Child Development.* 59. 321–335.

Smetana, J (1989) Adolescents' and parents' reasoning about actual family conflicts. *Child Development.* 60. 1052–1067.

Smetana, J and Asquith, P (1994) Adolescents' and parents' conceptions of parental authority and personal autonomy. *Child Development.* 65. 1147–1162.

Smith, C (1996) *Developing parenting programmes.* National Children's Bureau. London.

Smith, D (1995) Towards explaining patterns and trends in youth crime. In Rutter, M (Ed.) *Psychosocial disturbances in young people: challenges for prevention.* Cambridge University Press. Cambridge.

Smith, R (1985) Occupationless health: I feel really ashamed: how does unemployment lead to poorer mental health? *British Medical Journal.* 291. 1409–1413.

Smith, T (1997) Adolescent gender differences in time alone and time devoted to conversation. *Adolescence.* 32. 483–496.

Smithers, A and Robinson, P (1995) *Post 18 education: growth, change and prospect.* Council for Industry and Higher Education. London.

Speak, S (1997) *Young single fathers: participation in fatherhood.* Joseph Rowntree Foundation. York.

Spencer, M and Dornbusch, S (1990) Challenges in studying minority youth. In Feldman, S and Elliott, G (Eds) *At the threshold: the developing adolescent.* Harvard University Press. London.

Spoth, R, Redmond, C, Hockaday, C and Shin, C (1996) Barriers to participation in family skills preventive interventions and their evaluations. *Family Relations.* 45. 247–254.

Statens offentliga utrednigar (SOU) (1994) *Ungdomars valfard och varderingar.* Rapport No. 73. Civildepartementet. Stockholm.

Stattin, H and Kerr, M (1999) Parental monitoring: how much do we really know? *Child Development.* In press.

Stattin, H and Magnusson, D (1990) *Pubertal maturation in female development.* Erlbaum. Hillsdale, NJ.

Stattin, H and Magnusson, D (1996) Anti-social development: a holistic approach. *Development and Psychopathology.* 8. 617–645.

Stein, J and Reiser, L (1994) A study of white middle-class adolescent boys' responses to 'semenarche' (the first ejaculation). *Journal of Youth and Adolescence.* 23. 373–384.

Stein, M (1997) *Transition from care.* Barnardos. Barkingside, Essex.

Steinberg, D (1987) *Basic adolescent psychiatry.* Blackwell Scientific Publications. Oxford.

Steinberg, L (1987) Impact of puberty on family relations: effects of pubertal status and pubertal timing. *Developmental Psychology.* 23. 451–460.

Steinberg, L (1988) Reciprocal relations between parent–child distance and pubertal maturation. *Developmental Psychology.* 24. 122–128.

Steinberg, L (1990) Autonomy, conflict and harmony in the family relationship. In Feldman, S and Elliott, G (Eds) *At the threshold: the developing adolescent.* Harvard University Press. London.

Steinberg, L (1996) *Adolescence: 4th Edn.* McGraw-Hill. New York.

Steinberg, L and Silverberg, S (1986) The vicissitudes of autonomy in early adolescence. *Child Development.* 57. 841–851.

Steinberg, L, Dornbusch, S and Brown, B (1992) Ethnic differences in adolescent achievement: an ecological perspective. *American Psychologist.* 47. 723–729.

Steinberg, L, Lamborn, S, Darling, N and Dornbusch, S (1994) Over-time changes in adjustment and competence among adolescents from authoritative, authoritarian, indulgent and neglectful families. *Child Development.* 65. 754–770.

Steinberg, L, Mounts, N, Lamborn, S and Dornbusch, S (1991) Authoritative parenting and adolescent adjustment across various ecological niches. *Journal of Research on Adolescence.* 1. 19–36.

Sternberg, R (1988) *The triarchic mind.* Viking Penguin. New York.

Stewart, F (1992) The adolescent as consumer. In Coleman, J and Warren-Adamson, C (Eds) *Youth policy in the 1990s.* Routledge. London.

Stoller, C, Offer, D, Howard, K and Koenig, L (1996) Psychiatrist's concept of the adolescent self-image. *Journal of Youth and Adolescence.* 25. 273–283.

Strasburger, V (1995) *Adolescents and the media: medical and psychological impact.* Sage. London.

Sullivan, T and Thompson, K (1994) *Introduction to social problems: 3rd Edn.* Macmillan. London.

Surridge, P and Raffe, D (1995) The participation of 16–19 year-olds in education and training: recent trends. Centre for Educational Studies Briefing Paper No.1. University of Edinburgh. Edinburgh.

Sutherland, P (1992) *Cognitive development today: Piaget and his critics.* Chapman. London.

Tanner, J (1962) *Growth at adolescence.* Blackwell Scientific Publications. Oxford.

Tanner, J (1973) *Scientific American.* 229.

REFERENCES

Tanner, J (1978) *Foetus into man.* Open Books. London.

Tanner, J, Whitehouse, R and Takaishi, M (1966) *Archives of Disease in Childhood.* 41.

Taris, T and Semin, G (1997) Parent–child interaction during adolescence and the adolescent's sexual experience: control, closeness and conflict. *Journal of Youth and Adolescence.* 26. 373–398.

Thomson, R and Holland, J (1998) Sexual relationships, negotiation and decision-making. In Coleman, J and Roker, D (Eds) *Teenage sexuality: health, risk and education.* Harwood Academic Press. London.

Thornberry, T and Christenson, R (1984) Unemployment and criminal involvement: an investigation of reciprocal causal structures. *American Sociological Review.* 49. 398–411.

Thornton, A and Camburn, D (1987) The influence of the family on premarital attitudes and behaviour. *Demography.* 24. 323–340.

Thornton, D and Reid, R (1982) Moral reasoning and type of criminal offence. *British Journal of Social Psychology.* 21. 231–238.

Thornton, M, Chatters, L, Taylor, R and Allen, W (1990) Sociodemographic and environmental correlates of racial socialization by black parents. *Child Development.* 61. 401–409.

Thornton, S (1997) The social logic of subcultural capital. In Thornton, S and Gelder, K (Eds) *The subcultures reader.* Routledge. London.

Tiggemann, M and Winefield, A (1984) The effects of unemployment on the mood, self-esteem, locus of control, and depressive affect of school leavers. *Journal of Occupational Psychology.* 57. 33–42.

Tizard, B and Phoenix, A (1993) *Black, white or mixed race?* Routledge. London.

Tobin-Richards, M, Boxer, A and Petersen, A (1983) The psychological significance of pubertal change: sex differences in perceptions of self during early adolescence. In Brooks-Gunn, J and Petersen, A (Eds) *Girls at puberty: biological and psychological perspectives.* Plenum Press. New York.

Tobler, N (1986) Meta-analysis of 143 drug treatment programmes: quantitative outcome results of programme participants compared to a control group. *Journal of Drug Issues.* 16. 537–567.

Torney-Purta, J (1990) Youth in relation to social institutions. In Feldman, S and Elliott, G (Eds) *At the threshold: the developing adolescent.* Harvard University Press. Cambridge, MA.

Townsend, J, Roderick, P and Cooper, J (1994) Cigarette smoking by socio-economic group, sex and age: effects of price, income and health publicity. *British Medical Journal.* 309. 923–927.

Townsend, J, Wilkes, H, Haines, A and Jarvis, M (1991) Adolescent smokers seen in general practice: health lifestyle, physical measurements, and response to antismoking advice. *British Medical Journal.* 303. 947–950.

Treboux, D and Busch-Rossnagel, N (1995) Age differences in parent and peer influences on female sexual behaviour. *Journal of Research on Adolescence.* 5. 469–488.

Tremblay, R and Craig, W (1995) Developmental crime prevention. In Tonry, M and Farrington, D (Eds) *Building a safer society: strategic approaches to crime prevention.* University of Chicago Press. Chicago.

Tremblay, R, Vitaro, F, Bertrand, L, LeBlanc, M, Boileau, H and David, H (1992) Parent and child training to prevent early onset of delinquency: the Montreal longitudinal study. In McCord, J and Tremblay, R (Eds) *Parenting anti-social behaviour: interventions from birth to adolescence.* Guilford. New York.

Trew, K (1997) Time for sport? Activity diaries of young people. In Kremer, J, Trew, K and Ogle, S (Eds) *Young people's involvement in sport.* Routledge. London.

Tromsdorff, G and Kornadt, H-J (1995) Prosocial and antisocial motivation in adolescents in East and West Germany. In Youniss, J (Ed.) *After the wall: family adaptations in East and West Germany.* New Directions for Child Development, No. 70. Winter. Jossey-Bass. San Francisco, CA.

Turiel, E (1978) The development of concepts of social structure. In Glick, J and Clarke-Stewart, K (Eds) *The development of social understanding*. Gardner. New York.

Turtle, J, Jones, A and Hickman, M (1997) *Young people and health: the health behaviour of school aged children*. Health Education Authority. London.

Udry, J (1990) Hormonal and social determinants of adolescent sexual initiation. In Bancroft, J and Reinisch, J (Eds) *Adolescence and puberty*. Oxford University Press. Oxford.

Udry, J and Billy, J (1987) Initiation of coitus in early adolescence. *American Sociological Review*. 52. 841–855.

Ullah, P and Brotherton, C (1989) Sex, social class and ethnic differences in the expectations of unemployment and psychological well-being of secondary school pupils in England. *British Journal of Educational Psychology*. 59. 49–58.

Urberg, K, Degirmencioglu, S, Tolson, J and Halliday-Scher, K (1995) The structure of adolescent peer networks. *Developmental Psychology*. 31. 540–547.

Van Acker, J (1997) The family project approach. *Journal of Adolescence*. 20. 419–430.

Van Roosmalen, E and Krahn, H (1996) Boundaries of youth. *Youth and Society*. 28. 3–39.

Verkuyten, M (1993) Self-esteem among ethnic minorities and three principles of self-esteem formation. *International Journal of Psychology*. 28. 307–321.

Verkuyten, M (1995) Self-esteem, self-concept stability, and aspects of ethnic identity among minority and majority youth in the Netherlands. *Journal of Youth and Adolescence*. 24. 155–176.

Vernberg, M (1990) Psychological adjustment and experiences with peers during early adolescence: reciprocal, incidental, or unidirectional relationships? *Journal of Abnormal Child Psychology*. 18. 187–198.

Vogel, J, Andersson, L, Davidsson, U and Hall, L (1987) *Ojamlikheten I Sverige*. Rapport No. 51. Statistiska Centralbyran. Stockholm.

Voran, M (1991) Grandmother social support to adolescent mothers: correlates of support and satisfaction. Unpublished Masters dissertation. University of Virginia.

Wadsworth, M (1979) *Roots of delinquency: infancy, adolescence and crime*. Martin Robertson. Oxford.

Wakschlag, L, Chase-Lansdale, L and Brooks-Gunn, J (1996) Not just 'Ghosts in the Nursery': contemporaneous intergenerational relationships and parenting in young African-American families. *Child Development*. 67. 2131–2147.

Walker, L (1989) A longitudinal study of moral reasoning. *Child Development*. 60. 157–166.

Wallerstein, J and Blakeslee, S (1989) *Second chances: men, women and children a decade after divorce*. Ticknor & Fields. New York.

Ward, S and Overton, W (1990) Semantic familiarity, relevance, and the development of deductive reasoning. *Developmental Psychology*. 26. 488–493.

Waterman, A (1982) Identity development from adolescence to adulthood: an extension of theory and review of research. *Developmental Psychology*. 18. 341–358.

Waterman, A (1992) Identity as an aspect of optimal psychological functioning. In Adams, G, Gullotta, T and Monteymayor, R (Eds) *Adolescent identity formation*. Sage. London.

Waterman, A and Goldman, J (1976) A longitudinal study of ego identity development at a liberal arts college. *Journal of Youth and Adolescence*. 5. 361–369.

Waterman, A and Waterman, M (1971) A longitudinal study of changes in ego identity status during the freshman years at college. *Developmental Psychology*. 7. 167–173.

Waterman, A, Geary, P and Waterman, M (1974) A longitudinal study of changes in ego identity status from the freshman to the senior year at college. *Developmental Psychology*. 10. 387–392.

Webster-Stratton, C (1996) Early intervention with video-tape modelling: programmes for children with oppositional defiant disorder or conduct disorder. In Gibbs, E and Jensen, P (Eds) *Psychosocial treatments for child and adolescent disorders*. American Psychological Association. Washington, DC.

Webster-Stratton, C and Herbert, M (1994) *Troubled families – problem children*. Wiley. New York.

REFERENCES

Wellings, K, Field, J, Johnson, A and Wadsworth, J (1994) *Sexual behaviour in Britain*. Penguin. London.

Wentzel, K and Erdley, C (1993) Strategies for making friends: relations to social behaviour and peer acceptance in early adolescence. *Developmental Psychology*. 29. 819–826.

Werner, E (1989) High risk children in young adulthood: a longitudinal study from birth to 32 years. *American Journal of Orthopsychiatry*. 59. 72–81.

Werner, E and Smith, R (1982) *Vulnerable but invincible*. McGraw-Hill. New York.

West, D (1982) *Delinquency: its roots, careers and prospects*. Heinemann. London.

West, D and Farrington, D (1977) *The delinquent way of life*. Heinemann. London.

West, P and Sweeting, H (1996) Nae job, nae future: young people and health in a context of unemployment. *Health and Social Care in the Community*. 4. 50–62.

Wilkinson, H (1996) But will they vote? The political attitudes of young people. *Children and Society*. 10. 242–244.

Wilkinson, R (1990) Income distribution and mortality: a natural experiment. *Sociology of Health and Illness*. 12. 391–412.

Williams, H (1996) *Health and illness in adolescents: a national overview*. Health of the young nation. Department of Health. London.

Williams, R and Ponton, L (1992) HIV and adolescents: an international perspective. Special Edition of the *Journal of Adolescence*. 15(4).

Williamson, H (1997) Status Zer0 and the 'underclass'. In MacDonald, R (Ed.) *Youth, the 'underclass' and social exclusion*. Routledge. London.

Williamson, H and Butler, I (1995) Children speak: perspectives on their social worlds. In Brannen, J and O'Brien, M (Eds) *Childhood and parenthood*. Proceedings of the International Sociological Association Committee for Family Research Conference, 1994. Institute of Education. London.

Willis, P (1990) *Common culture*. Open University Press. Milton Keynes.

Wilson, P (1995) Working space: a mentally healthy young nation. *Youth and Policy*. 51. 60–63.

Winefield, A (1997) The psychological effects of youth unemployment: international perspectives. Special Issue of the *Journal of Adolescence*. 20. 237–352.

Winefield, A, Tiggemann, M, Winefield, H and Goldney, R (1993) *Growing up with unemployment: a longitudinal study of its impact*. Routledge. London.

Winn, S, Roker, D and Coleman, J (1995) Knowledge about puberty and sexual development in 11–16 year olds: implications for health and sex education in schools. *Educational Studies*. 21. 187–201.

Wold, B and Hendry, L (1998) Social and environmental factors associated with physical activity in young people. In Biddle, S, Sallis, J and Cavill, N (Eds) *Young and active?* Health Education Authority. London.

Woodroffe, C, Glickman, M, Barker, M and Power, C (1993) *Children, teenagers and health: key data*. Open University Press. Milton Keynes.

Wyman, P, Cowen, E, Work, W and Parker, G (1991) Developmental and family milieu correlates of resilience in urban children who have experienced major life stress. *American Journal of Community Psychology*. 19. 405–426.

Wyshak, G and Frisch, R (1982) Evidence for a secular trend in the age of menarche. *New England Journal of Medicine*. 306. 1033–1035.

Yates, M (1995) Community service and identity development in adolescence. Unpublished PhD dissertation. Catholic University of America. Washington, DC.

Yates, M (1999) Community service and political-moral discussions among adolescents: a study of a mandatory school-based program in the United States. In Yates, M and Youniss, J (Eds) *Roots of civic identity: international perspectives on community service and activism in youth*. Cambridge University Press. Cambridge.

Yates, M and Youniss, J (Eds) (1999) *Roots of civic identity: international perspectives on community service and activism in youth*. Cambridge University Press. Cambridge.

Youniss, J and Smollar, J (1985) *Adolescent relations with mothers, fathers and friends*. University of Chicago Press. Chicago.

Youniss, J, McLellan, J, and Strouse, D (1994) 'We're popular, but we're not snobs': adolescents describe their crowds. In Montemayor, R, Adams, G and Gullotta, T (Eds) *Personal relationships during adolescence*. Sage. London.

Zakin, D, Blyth, D and Simmons, R (1984) Physical attractiveness as a mediator of the impact of early pubertal changes in girls. *Journal of Youth and Adolescence*. 13. 439–450.

Zani, B (1993) Dating and interpersonal relationships in adolescence. In Jackson, S and Rodriguez-Tome, H (Eds) *Adolescence and its social worlds*. Lawrence Erlbaum. Hove.

Zaslow, M (1989) Sex differences in children's responses to parental divorce: samples, variables, ages and sources. *Americal Journal of Orthopsychiatry*. 59. 118–141.

Zick, C and Allen, C (1996) The impact of parents' marital status on the time adolescents spend in productive activities. *Family Relations*. 45. 65–71.

Ziehe, T (1994) *Kulturanalyser*. Brutus. Stockholm.

Zimmerman, M, Copeland, L, Shope, J and Dielman, T (1997) A longitudinal study of self-esteem: implications for adolescent development. *Journal of Youth and Adolescence*. 26. 117–142.

Zinneker, J (1990) What does the future hold? Youth and socio-cultural change in the FRG. In Chisholm, L, Buchner, P, Kruger, H-H and Brown, P (Eds) *Childhood, youth and social change: a comparative perspective*. Falmer. London.

Author index

Subject index